Contents

Introduction

This book has been written to assist students, teachers and lecturers studying and delivering the BTEC First Diploma in Business. This book is designed to provide students and teachers with the foundations of the learning and assessment of the course, using real-life business case studies and examples wherever possible.

There are nine units detailed in this book. As a student, you will only have to complete the first **three** compulsory units and **three** of the specialist units. Units one, two and three are the compulsory units, the first being the only unit which is assessed by means of an externally set and marked assignment (by examiners appointed by Edexcel). The remaining two compulsory units and the six specialist units are assessed internally (by your teacher or lecturer).

The scope of this course covers all of the necessary basics in business within the compulsory units and the specialist units allow you to concentrate on areas such as starting your own business, online businesses, or sales and customer service.

The book is structured so that each of the headings follows the exact wording of the course outlines and content. You will find various activities in the book, either individual work or group work, graded with stars to show their difficulty. They are designed to help you carry out tasks or research to reinforce your understanding of the topics. Many will help you build up the necessary research and information to complete your assignment for the unit. New business words are highlighted with a *Key Word* definition and there is a full *Glossary* at the end of the book.

The *Want to Find Out More?* features in the book direct you to websites and other sources of information to investigate the topic or idea further. At the end of each unit, there are a series of questions, 20 in the compulsory units and 10 in the others, to help you revise the unit.

A specially designed *Teacher Support CD-ROM* is also available which provides lesson plans, advice to students, answers and guidance to all of the activities in this book and a series of stimulus and research materials to aid students in the completion of their evidence required for each of the units.

All weblinks featured in this textbook and also on the teacher support CD-ROM are listed on the teacher support CD-ROM. These are monitored by Nelson Thornes to ensure they are up-to-date. If you do discover any broken links, please contact Nelson Thornes so that they can be updated.

Jon Sutherland and Diane Canwell
June 2005

INDIVIDUAL WORK
★

GROUP WORK
★ ★

Keyword

WANT TO FIND OUT MORE?

BTEC FIRST Business

Diane Canwell
Jon Sutherland

Published in 2005 by:
Nelson Thornes Ltd
Delta Place
27 Bath Road
CHELTENHAM
GL53 7TH
United Kingdom

05 06 07 08 09 / 10 9 8 7 6 5 4 3 2 1

A catalogue record for this book is available from the British Library

ISBN 0 7487 9431 X

Page make-up by Pantek Arts Ltd, Maidstone, Kent

Printed in Great Britain by Scotprint

Photograph credits:
Corel 461 (NT) pp.9, 74; Corel 671 (NT) p.11; Corel 677 (NT) p.142; Corel 790 (NT) p.33; Digital Vision 1 (NT) pp.27, 40, 97; Image Club OG2 p.105; Ingram ILG V2 CD6 (NT) p.50; Ingram/Image Library V1 CD3 (NT) p.183; Ingram/Image Library V2 CD4 (NT) p.246; Instant Art (NT) pp.219, 222, 225; James Lauritz/Digital Vision C (NT) p.211; Martin Sookias/Nelson Thornes (NT) p.34; Photodisc 5B (NT) p.261; Photodisc 28 (NT) p.79; Photodisc 37 (NT) p.75; Photodisc 40 (NT) p.168; Photodisc 44B (NT) pp.77, 301; Photodisc 55 (NT) p.160; Photodisc 61 (NT) p.46; Photodisc 68 (NT) pp.110, 118, 140, 202; Photodisc 69 (NT) p.25, 64, 137, 148; Photodisc 70 (NT) p.47; Photodisc 73 (NT) p.37; Photodisc 75 (NT) p.162, 202; Photodisc 79 (NT) p.83; Rubberball (NT) pp.119, 242; Stockbyte 9 (NT) pp.43, 45.

UNIT 1

Introduction to Business Activity

In this unit, you will discover the wide range of different business activities that are taking place locally, nationally, in Europe and internationally. You will also begin to appreciate that different sorts of business organisation have a number of alternative aims and objectives. Some businesses are primarily concerned with making profits, whilst others are in the voluntary or not-for-profit sectors.

The unit also looks at the key decisions that are made by the management of these business organisations and how they attempt to reach targets. All of their targets need to be planned and monitored and action taken if the organisation is off-course.

This unit is externally assessed by an Integrated Vocational Assignment (IVA), which is set by the examining board. The IVA will cover all of the assessment criteria covered in this unit. To prepare yourself fully for this IVA, you must:

- Explore business activities undertaken to achieve key goals
- Investigate the classification of business activities in contemporary Britain
- Consider ways in which businesses use resources to achieve their aims and objectives
- Examine management processes that facilitate the achievement of business aims and objectives.

BUSINESS ACTIVITIES

profit – a business's ability to sell its products and services for more than it costs them to acquire or provide those products and services

Keyword

Organisations are not just businesses. They are not all concerned with making a **profit**.

One of the best ways to think about organisations is to focus on the fact that they are all concerned with success. An organisation wants to be able to supply its products or services to its customers in the most efficient way. This goal of success can be applied equally to organisations that supply services at no cost to the customer and to businesses that supply products or services at a cost to their customers.

Success is measured in many different ways and the way it is measured very much depends on the goals of the organisation. Every organisation has key aims and objectives that it wants to achieve. Understanding what these aims and objectives mean can help you appreciate what the organisation is all about.

Here are some examples of the aims and objectives well-known organisations:

- Federal Express is an international courier delivery service. Its aims and objectives are as follows: 'FedEx is committed to our People-Service-Profit Philosophy. We will produce outstanding financial returns by providing totally reliable, competitively superior, global, air–ground transportation of high-priority goods and documents that require rapid, time-certain delivery.'

- Dell Computers are manufacturers and suppliers of computer hardware. Their aims and objectives are as follows: 'Dell's mission is to be the most successful computer company in the world at delivering the best customer experience in markets we serve.'

- Coca-Cola produces a world-famous range of soft drinks and refreshments. Its aims and objectives are even simpler: 'To put a can of coke within arms-reach of everyone on the planet.'

CASE STUDY   Bertram's Cycles

Bertram's Cycles have three shops in the east of England. They provide an unrivalled selection of cycles and cycling equipment. All stores have highly experienced staff. They offer some of the best discounts on top brands in the country. Bertram's have been in the cycling business for 20 years. The founder, Charles Bertram, was an Olympic cycling medallist. There has not been a question or query about cycling from one of their customers that Bertram's have not been able to answer.

> **GROUP WORK (1.1)**
>
> In groups of two or three, write a short statement of Bertram's main aims and objectives. Compare your statement with those from other groups in the class.

> *Keyword*
>
> **mission statement** – an organisation's vision of what it wants to achieve in the future. A good mission statement needs to be easy to understand, relevant to the organisation, ambitious and useful in motivating staff

As we will see later, organisations often call their aims and objectives **mission statements**. These mission statements describe, as clearly and briefly as possible, what the organisation intends to do, how it will attempt to go about it and state its long-term aims.

Activities

As you may now realise, organisations have very different objectives. Their objectives very much depend on what kind of activities the organisation is involved with and how they receive the bulk of their **income**.

We will now investigate the types of common business activities that are determined by how the organisation is funded. As we will see, this affects all of the aims and objectives of the organisation.

> *Keyword*
>
> **income** – cash or funding received by an organisation as either payment from customers for goods and services or as a grant of money from another organisation, such as central or local government, to provide those goods and services

Supply of goods and services free

You might ask yourself how an organisation can offer goods and services at no cost to the customer. The simple answer is that the organisation receives the funding it needs to provide those goods and services for free from another source other than the customer.

There are a large number of organisations that receive funding, either from central or local government, to provide services that the customer does not have to pay the organisation for. Other organisations, known as **charities**, also provide a range of services at no cost to customers.

> *Keyword*
>
> **charities** – organisations that exist to provide a service or to support a particular cause, e.g. Help the Aged and Oxfam. All of a charity's income, either from donations or other fundraising, is used to support new activities

Supply of goods and services for sale at below cost

There are other organisations that offer goods and services at a reduced cost. Rather than supplying goods and services for free, they charge customers a small amount, which does not cover the cost of supplying those products or services. These organisations are able to supply at below the cost to themselves because they receive funding from another source to help them do this. This is known as a *subsidised service*, which means that the shortfall in the costs is made up from another source.

An example of this is local councils offering recycling bins at substantially reduced prices in order to encourage households to recycle their waste. By using their funds from central government to encourage recycling, they can offer households recycling bins at affordable prices. The purpose of this part of the organisation is not to make a

---

> **GROUP WORK (1.2)**
> ★ ★
>
> 1 Here are some examples of products and services that you do not have to pay for every time you receive them. Are they being provided for free, or are they being funded in some other way?
>
>   a) Refuse collection
>   b) Parks
>   c) Street lighting
>   d) Road mending
>   e) Supermarket carrier bags
>
> 2 If you think that any of the above is free, where do you think the money comes from to pay for it?

profit but to encourage recycling, as this will reduce costs to households and the council in the future, as well as helping with the environment.

Supply of goods and services at cost

Some organisations offer products and services to their customers without making a profit from the sale. It may often be the case that these organisations are able to obtain goods and services that they can then pass on to their customers, as they are difficult to obtain elsewhere. Typical examples include equipment for disabled or older people. It may be difficult for these customers to choose and order particular items they need for their homes. So local and central government act as buyers for these people and sell on what they have purchased, without adding to the cost.

Supply of goods and services at a profit

This is perhaps the most common activity undertaken by organisations. Businesses will either produce or buy products and services and then sell them on to customers at a higher price in order to cover their own costs and to make a profit. Many of the products that you can buy in your local high street have passed through the hands of several businesses.

wholesaler – an organisation that takes delivery of large quantities of goods and then sells them on in smaller quantities to other businesses

Even things as simple as a bag of chips from a takeaway would have passed through the hands of several different businesses. Firstly the farmer would have to buy seed potatoes. He would then plant these and look after the crop until the potatoes have grown. He would then harvest the potatoes and probably sell them to a **wholesaler**. The wholesaler would then sell sacks of potatoes to your local takeaway, at a small profit. Alternatively, the wholesaler may sell the potatoes to an organisation that peels the potatoes and cuts them into chips, which they then sell to takeaways at a profit. The takeaway would then cook the chips and sell them to their customers, again at a profit.

GROUP WORK (1.3)
★ ★

Choose one of the following products and try to work out how many times it would be sold on by organisations before it reaches the high street and is ready to be purchased by a customer:

a) Hamburger
b) Music CD
c) Book or magazine
d) PlayStation game.

Key business goals and sectors

As we have seen, many businesses begin by setting out their aims, purposes and objectives as a statement of their goals, or what they wish to achieve. Organisations do not exist in isolation and there are many factors that can affect an organisation, so organisations need to be flexible.

Many organisations have a vision of what they wish to achieve in the short term (usually within the next year), the medium term (up to about three years into the future) or in the long term (where they expect to be in 10 years). As we have seen, businesses exist for many different reasons. Perhaps the most common is profit, but this is not the only reason and it is often only really relevant to organisations in what is known as the private sector.

Private sector

Business organisations in the private sector obviously differ enormously, but they do have some common features:

- They often use resources that are in limited supply, such as staff, money and materials.
- They provide something, either a product or a service.
- They have to compete with other organisations for sales and customers.

In order to achieve these three common features, they have to get involved in a number of different areas. These areas have to work well together and will include:

- *Managing employees*, usually through a personnel or human resource department.

- *Selling products or services*, usually with trained sales staff and customer service employees.

- *Distributing products or services*, to make sure that the maximum number of customers can obtain their products or services.

- *Purchasing products and services*, ordering stock to sell on or services to help them carry out their tasks.

- *Marketing products and services*, finding out what customers need and making sure that customers know that the organisation has these products or services available.

- *Keeping financial records*, to ensure that the organisation knows where it is financially and whether it is successful, as well as knowing how much it owes other businesses and how much other businesses owe it.

Generally the private sector is made up of organisations that are independent. Within the law they can sell products and services freely to customers.

There are several different types of private sector organisation which, as we will see later, often helps us to understand how large they are and how important they are in the market.

The smallest of the private sector organisations is the *sole trader*. Usually these are owned and run, or operated, by a single person, such as a small shop.

The second type of private sector organisation is the *partnership*, which is owned by between two and 20 people. They share the responsibility of running the business together.

There are two different types of private sector organisations known as *limited companies*. The first is known as a *private limited company* and you can recognise one of these organisations as the business has 'Ltd' at the end of its name. These organisations have **shareholders** and in the past they tended to be larger, family businesses. The most important thing about limited companies is that they are a separate, legal business. The shareholders have all invested money in order to own a part of the business. If the business fails they only stand to lose what they have invested, unlike sole traders and partnerships, which stand to lose everything if the business is forced to close.

The other type of limited company is known as the *public limited company*. You can recognise these types of business as they have 'plc' written after their name. Unlike a limited company, a plc offers its shares to anyone that wishes to purchase them. Their shares are bought and sold on a daily basis. These tend to be slightly larger limited companies with literally thousands of different shareholders.

There are two other different types of organisation in the private sector. The first is known as a *franchise*. Although you may not have noticed, there are franchises in every high street in the country, such as KFC, McDonald's, Burger King and Forbuoys newsagents. These are organisations that have been set up by an individual, or a group of individuals, who have bought the name and the expertise of an established organisation. They run the franchise as their own business, but pay a proportion of their profits to the owner of the name.

There are also *cooperatives* in the high street. Perhaps the most common is the supermarket that is often simply called the Cooperative Stores or Coop. They share out the profit amongst all organisations and individuals who are part of the group. They have joined together to become more efficient and effective and share part of their profits with their customers.

As we have already mentioned, the main goal of organisations in the private sector is to make sales at a profit. But what is a profit and how can a business make it?

The first point to remember is that in order for any organisation to make a profit, it needs to know what its costs are and it needs to keep a careful eye on its finances. The simplest way of describing a profit uses the following formula:

Keyword

shareholder – an individual who has purchased a part, or a share, of a limited company and has power over that business in relation to how many shares they own

INDIVIDUAL WORK (1.4) ★

Try to identify at least five examples of each of sole traders, partnerships, private limited companies and public limited companies. Does the type of business give you any clue as to their size?

INDIVIDUAL WORK (1.5) ★

Try to identify at least five examples of franchises in your local area. Try to find at least two that have retail stores and two that provide services.

Profit = Revenue from sales – Cost of production and supply

This means that in order for a business to make a profit, it needs to charge more for its products and services than it costs the organisation to produce and supply them.

Making these calculations can be complicated. An organisation not only needs to think about how much the products cost them to buy, but also a large number of other costs that it has to cover. Take a supermarket, for example, which buys food from farmers or wholesalers. The cost of that food is only a part of the calculation. The supermarket has to be able to cover the cost of transporting the food, the cost of the storage, the rent, rates, electricity and employees. Even the cost of carrier bags and till receipts is all part of calculating whether or not the supermarket has made a profit. Organisations use many different ways of working out how much they should charge for products and services in order to ensure that they cover all of their costs.

The simplest way is to add a certain percentage to each product and service in order to make sure that all costs are covered and that a small profit is made. Unfortunately life is never as simple as that and a business will always need to continue to adjust the prices it charges for a number of very good reasons, for example:

- A supermarket down the road may cut its prices and, if the supermarket does not follow suit, it will not make any sales.
- The cost of buying food at a particular time of year may be higher.
- Transport costs may have increased.
- Employee wages may have increased.
- The supermarket itself may need to be refitted.

The business needs to make sure that with these ever-changing problems it achieves at least a small profit, otherwise there would be little point in the business continuing to trade.

Public sector

The public sector consists of organisations that are either owned or controlled by the government. The most common forms of public sector organisations are:

- *Government departments and the Civil Service*, which are responsible for running government activities in a particular area, such as the Department of Trade and Industry that assists businesses, or the Inland Revenue that collects taxes.
- *Local government*, which are either county, metropolitan, district or borough councils. They provide services, assist businesses and promote the area.
- *Public corporations and enterprises* – although there are very few of these left, the Bank of England is a good example. They provide services or produce products and services and are directly owned by the government.
- *QUANGOs*, which stands for Quasi Autonomous Non-Governmental Organisations. These are organisations that are funded by the government to provide services, such as the Arts Council that provides grants to artists, theatres and film-makers.

Voluntary and not-for-profit sectors

As we have seen, it is not the purpose of voluntary and not-for-profit organisations to make a profit from their customers. Literally thousands of people offer their services for free to voluntary organisations. People provide their time at youth clubs, charity shops and animal sanctuaries, on helplines and as hospital or prison visitors. These people, directed by the voluntary organisations, provide essential services for many people who would otherwise not be able to afford to pay for these services.

Many of the charities attempt to raise funds in order to provide money for research into diseases and other health problems, and provide food for poor overseas countries and other disadvantaged people.

GROUP WORK (1.6)
★ ★

Think of any local businesses that have closed down in recent months. Why do you think that was? Do you think that they could not adapt to more competition? Were they not making enough profit?

GROUP WORK (1.7)
★ ★ ★

1 Your local council provides a wide range of different services for the community. It receives its funding to provide these services in two ways. What are they?

2 What kind of services does your local council provide?

3 Do you think there are any services it does provide that could be better provided by a private sector organisation?

CASE STUDY New album released to raise money for Sudan Crisis

Music industry stars including David Gray, R.E.M., Badly Drawn Boy, Ash and Faithless released a new album in 2004, 'Songs for Sudan', to raise money to help the people of Darfur, western Sudan.

Releasing 'Songs for Sudan', Badly Drawn Boy (Damon Gough), who contributed a track for the album said, 'Men, women and children are still dying every day in Sudan. People like us might not have the power to stop the violence but at least we can try and help the people who are affected by it. Oxfam is already saving lives, the least we can do is help them to save more.'

The album contains 14 tracks and features exclusive tracks from David Gray, Jet, Ash, and R.E.M. Other artists on the album include Badly Drawn Boy, Futureheads, Faithless and many more.

All artists and record labels donating tracks to this album have foregone their royalties.

The purchase price is £7.99 and £5.00 goes directly to the Oxfam Sudan appeal which could provide 15 people with clean drinking water.

The crisis in Darfur led to over a million people fleeing their homes in the face of fighting and insecurity. Over two million people were affected, with hundreds of thousands of refugees moving into neighbouring Chad.

At the time of writing, Oxfam is working to help over a quarter of a million people in Darfur and Chad, focusing on providing clean water, sanitation facilities and hygiene training. The situation in many places continues to get worse. In Chad conditions are rapidly deteriorating with more people still arriving and with a real threat of a cholera outbreak.

Source: www.oxfam.org.uk/press/releases/ sudan_album_release_030804.htm

> **INDIVIDUAL** WORK (1.8)
> ★ ★ ★
> Read the Oxfam case study and answer the following questions.
> 1 What do you think is meant by 'have foregone their royalties'?
> 2 Who do you think receives the other £2.99 for each album sold?
> 3 After visiting the Oxfam website, see if you can find another three major appeals that Oxfam is currently making.
> 4 What does 'Oxfam' mean and when did they begin working as a charity?

> **GROUP** WORK (1.9)
> ★ ★
> In groups of two or three, choose one of the following and find out which organisations provide the relevant assistance:
> a) For someone who wishes to start a new business
> b) For a disabled person who wishes to have their home adapted to help them get around more easily
> c) For someone who has recently moved to the area and wishes to find out about schools and local transport.

Business performance

As we will see later when we look at resources, aims and objectives in this unit, the ways in which a business can measure its performance very much depends on its initial business goals. Generally speaking, a business will measure its performance by comparing what it had hoped to achieve with what it has actually achieved. A business will give itself sufficient time to try to achieve its objectives or goals and will try to monitor how it is performing in the run-up to a particular date. Examples of how it might measure its performance are outlined in Table 1.1.

Size of business

The size of a business can be measured in a number of different ways: in terms of the number of people it employs, the number of stores, offices or branches it has, the amount of sales it makes or the amount of profit it makes. It would be wrong to assume that organisations that appear to be tiny, as they do not employ very many people, are not large businesses, as they may make large profits from what they do.

As we will see, organisations tend to be described as small, small to medium, medium or large. It is important to make sure that you do not assume that just because an organisation is classed as being large, it is necessarily more important than a smaller organisation. Many of the larger organisations rely on smaller businesses in order to survive, as indeed many of the smaller businesses rely on larger organisations.

Small organisations

In January 2004, the UK government changed the description of what they considered to be a small or a medium-sized business. Tables 1.2 and 1.3 show how the size of businesses is measured.

> **INDIVIDUAL** WORK (1.10)
> ★ ★
> Look at Tables 1.2 and 1.3. Which of the following businesses are either small or medium sized?
> a) Frank's Trading Company Limited: 27 employees, a turnover of £30.7 million and a balance sheet value of £19 million.
> b) Sarah & George Salons: 52 employees, a turnover of £5.5 million and a balance sheet value of £2.2 million.
> c) Percy Pringle & Sons: 203 employees, a turnover of £6.3 million and a balance sheet value of £2.79 million.

Table 1.1
Measurement of business performance

Measurement of business performance	Explanation
Maximise profits	The business wants to achieve the largest possible difference between how much something has cost to produce and supply, and how much they are able to sell it for.
Maximise sales	Not all products and services have a high individual profit. So in order to make a large profit, the business needs to sell a large number of products. A small profit on thousands of products may end up being more than a large profit on just a few sales.
Get bigger	The organisation may wish to grow in size, either by opening new stores or buying out the competition. It invests all of its profits in growing so that it can produce or supply products and services on a huge scale.
Provide a steady income	The organisation wants to grow steadily and is quite cautious as it wants to avoid growing too quickly and not being able to control all of its operations.
Break even	This means that the organisation simply wants to cover its costs. This is usually a measure of business performance adopted by a local council, government department, a charity or a not-for-profit organisation.
Provide funds for shareholders or owners	To provide a steady income for those who own the organisation. This needs to be sufficient to keep the owners or shareholders happy, but not too much to make the business less competitive.
Become the leader	To sell more products and services than its rivals so that its competitors are left behind and have to copy the successful business.
Beat the competition	Making more profit and achieving higher sales than any of its competitors.
Be efficient and responsive	To ensure that all of its dealings with customers are of the highest quality, that any problems are dealt with immediately and that products are always in stock.
Good sales service	To have well-trained, efficient and effective sales staff who can ensure that the customers are satisfied.
After-sales service	To have perfect systems in place to deal with complaints, queries and returns of damaged or faulty goods.
Easy access to benefits and grants	Measures of business performance for a public sector organisation, to make sure that these vital services are available with the least problems to customers.
Provide advice and guidance	Another public sector measure of business performance, to have accessible advice and guidance services for businesses and individuals, no matter where they are in the country.

Table 1.2
How small businesses are measured

	Now (from 30/1/04)	Before (before 30/1/04)
Turnover (no more than)	£5.6 million	£2.8 million
Balance sheet (no more than)	£2.8 million	£1.4 million
Employees (no more than)	50	50

Source: The Department of Trade and Industry

Table 1.3
How medium-sized businesses are measured

	Now (from 30/1/04)	Before (before 30/1/04)
Turnover (no more than)	£22.8 million	£11.2 million
Balance sheet (no more than)	£11.4 million	£5.6 million
Employees (no more than)	250	250

Source: The Department of Trade and Industry

Note: A business must satisfy at least two of the given criteria to be considered a small or medium-sized business.

WANT TO FIND OUT MORE?

The Foundation for Small and Medium Enterprise Development: www.fsmed.org
or
The Centre for Small and Medium Sized Enterprises: http://users.wbs. warwick.ac.uk/csme.

Small to medium-sized organisations

The European Union (EU) defines an SME, or 'small or medium-sized enterprise', as an organisation that employs fewer than 250 staff and has a turnover of less than €40 million (approximately £26 million). SMEs make up 99.8 per cent of all EU enterprises and employ more than 74 million people throughout Europe. The EU sees SMEs as a 'source of employment, innovation, entrepreneurship and growth'.

Medium-sized organisations

A medium-sized organisation is defined as being one that employs more than 250 people and has a turnover of more than €40 million (approximately £26 million).

Many medium-sized organisations operate on a national basis and include travel agents, betting shops and newsagent chains. They are major employers in the UK and are involved in businesses as varied as agriculture, production, construction, retailing, catering, business services and wholesaling.

Large organisations

Keyword

multinational – a business that runs operations in at least two different countries

There are a great number of different forms of large organisation operating in the UK. Some are UK businesses, whilst others are known as **multinationals**.

Typical large organisations include the following:

- Retail organisations, such as Marks & Spencer plc, Tesco plc and PC World.
- Computer manufacturers, such as IBM, Apple and Dell.
- Oil companies, such as Shell, Esso and BP.
- Franchise organisations, such as The Body Shop, McDonald's and Pizza Hut.
- Manufacturing organisations, such as General Motors (Vauxhall), Nissan and Ford.

GROUP WORK (1.11)
★ ★ ★

In groups of two or three, find out the answers to the following questions.

1 PC World is part of a larger group. Name the other two high street chains that are part of the same organisation.

2 Which supermarket chain owns Safeway?

3 Name five overseas countries in which The Body Shop has a franchise.

Scale of business

Whether you live in a city, a town or in the countryside, there is a network of business organisations to cater for all of your immediate needs and wants. Some of the businesses will be part of the public sector, such as refuse collection or healthcare. Others will be provided by the private sector, such as supermarkets, chemists or newsagents.

Different sizes of businesses provide the mix of local, regional, national, European or even global businesses to offer a wide range of products and services to customers.

GROUP WORK (1.12)
★ ★

Identify the 10 nearest businesses to either your school or college. Are they local businesses or do they belong to larger organisations?

Local businesses

Many local businesses are small, or small to medium-sized organisations. They may be the only office, workshop or store belonging to that organisation. Other local businesses may in fact be part of much larger groups and, as we have seen, they may be franchises, cooperatives or even directly owned by much larger organisations. Local businesses aim to cater for the immediate needs of the local community. They therefore include convenience stores, takeaways, launderettes, public houses and restaurants. Local councils also provide a range of services for particular communities and these would include swimming pools, parks, public toilets and a range of services, including refuse collection.

Regional businesses

Particularly in the countryside, where the population is far more spread out, it is not practical for businesses to establish themselves in every small community. So many

GROUP WORK (1.13)

★ ★

Where is your local council based? Find a map of the area that it serves. Why do you think its headquarters is based in this particular location?

organisations try to identify an ideal location in a particular area that could serve a large community, spread out in surrounding towns and villages. Many supermarkets have adopted this means of serving widespread communities.

You will also find that many county councils establish themselves in one of the larger towns or cities in a region. From here they organise and direct the council's operations throughout the region.

Some private sector organisations tend to establish their businesses in areas of the country that they know best. Some chains of retail stores can only be found in certain parts of the country and these can also be classed as regional businesses.

National businesses

There are a large number of private sector organisations that have stores or offices in virtually all the major towns and cities in the country. This is particularly true of supermarket chains, such as Sainsbury's, Tesco and Asda. Other retailers, such as Dixons, Game, Next and B&Q, have gradually established stores throughout the country.

There are also a number of government departments that are nationally based in order to provide services, such as benefits, assistance with jobs and help for businesses, even in the most remote locations.

Banks and building societies are also examples of national organisations that have set themselves up in all of the main population centres in order to serve their customers.

CASE STUDY Chain store massacre emptying UK high streets

The spread of large multiplexes and chain stores is slowly killing off small retailers, leading to 'ghost towns' across the UK, a worrying report has claimed.

The study, undertaken by the New Economics Foundation (NEF), found that the decline of independent shops, pubs and post offices in Britain was destroying local economies and jobs. The NEF said that closures of local businesses has created 'ghost towns' across the country, as wider economic forces and a lack of government support for enterprises empty the UK's high streets. According to the report, government regeneration strategies have done more harm than good by driving out local shops in favour of large multiple retailers.

Key findings in the study include:

- Wholesalers, vital to small retailers, have closed at a rate of six per week.
- Small food manufacturers declined by 12 per cent in 2002.
- Traditional pubs are closing at a rate of 20 per month.
- In the five years to 2002, 50 specialised stores such as butchers, bakers and fishmongers closed every week.

The report said that the decline of local firms, along with widespread closure of banks, has badly harmed local communities and has resulted in repeated job cuts, causing the slow death of small and independent retailers in our local communities.

INDIVIDUAL WORK (1.14) ★ ★ ★

Read the case study and then answer the following questions.

1 What is a regeneration strategy?

2 Why might national, European or global businesses be a threat to local businesses?

European businesses

The UK is one of the many countries in Europe that is part of the EU. Since joining the EU, it has become increasingly easier for British businesses to operate in the rest of Europe. It has also meant that European businesses have begun to establish themselves in the UK. In many major towns and cities in the UK, retail stores such as Lidl and Aldi, which are owned by European organisations, compete with UK chains such as Sainsbury's or Tesco. In turn, British businesses, such as The Body Shop, Marks & Spencer and Lush, have found ready markets in Europe for British products and services.

One of the major advantages of being part of the EU is that there are no longer any barriers to transporting and selling products and services across Europe. This has meant that British businesses have begun to think about the wider European market and now consider customers in France, Germany, Greece and Poland to be equally as important as their traditional customers in London, Norwich or Newcastle.

Global businesses

When we think about global businesses, we tend to think about huge organisations, such as Coca-Cola, Disney, Esso and Ford. All of these businesses are based in the US and there is barely a town or city in the UK, if not the world, where you cannot purchase some of their products or services.

Global businesses account for a huge amount of sales, profit and employment around the world. Increasingly these global businesses do not simply supply a country with their products and services, but they set up their own factories, offices and even retail stores in markets around the world.

Some of the global businesses are not instantly recognisable, as they have bought existing businesses in particular countries and kept that business's old name.

CASE STUDY Wal-Mart Stores

Wal-Mart Stores are based in Walton/Bentonville, Arkansas, USA. They are a discount retail chain and were founded in 1962. Their revenue is $244.5 billion per year and they employ 1.4 million people worldwide.

Wal-Mart began with a single store in Arkansas in 1962, and was founded by Sam Walton and his younger brother James. They built Wal-Mart into the world's largest retailer, with around 4,700 stores today. Sam's descendants own about 38 per cent. Sam's son Robson, 59, is now chairman.

Source: www.walmartstores.com

INDIVIDUAL WORK (1.15)
★ ★ ★

Read the case study 'Wal-Mart Stores' and then visit the website and answer the following questions.

1 What businesses do Wal-Mart own in the UK?
2 How many employees does Wal-Mart have in the UK?
3 How many stores does Wal-Mart have in the UK?

CLASSIFICATION OF BUSINESS ACTIVITIES

There are four different types of business activity:

- *Primary* business activities involve getting raw materials from the natural environment, e.g. mining, farming and fishing.
- *Secondary* business activities involve making things (manufacturing), e.g. making cars and steel.
- *Tertiary* business activities involve providing a service, e.g. teaching and nursing.
- *Quaternary* business activities involve research and development, e.g. IT.

The pie chart in Figure 1.1 on page 11 shows the *employment structure* in the UK – how the workforce is divided up between the three main employment sectors: primary, secondary and tertiary.

The employment structure of a country changes over time. Some countries are in the early stage of development. This tends to mean that they have a high percentage of the population working in the primary sector. This also means that most of the population are involved in agriculture.

When countries develop, they begin to create an industrial base, which means that more people are starting to work in the secondary sector. As machines replace employees in agriculture, fewer people are needed to work on the farms and in the fields. In addition to this, thousands of people leave the countryside and move to urban areas in search of work in the secondary sector.

Once a country has developed its secondary sector, the need for services increases. This means that the population want better education and health along with a host of other services including tourism. The tertiary, or service, sector grows even faster when more employees are replaced in the secondary sector by machinery, computers and robots. This tends to mean that the secondary sector declines and far fewer people are employed in industry.

CASE STUDY   The employment structures of the UK, Brazil and Ghana

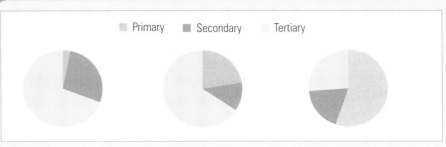
■ Primary   ■ Secondary   ■ Tertiary

Figure 1.1
Employment structure in the UK

Figure 1.2
Employment structure in Brazil

Figure 1.3
Employment structure in Ghana

The UK has a small proportion of people working in primary industry. Machinery has taken over many of the jobs in the primary sector and many of the primary resources (such as coal) have almost been exhausted. The UK has a shrinking secondary sector as machinery, computers and robots have taken more jobs. The tertiary sector is still growing with many people working in local and central government, the health service, education, financial services and other service-based jobs including the leisure industry.

Brazil is still developing its secondary sector, which means that a lot of people are still working in the primary sector. There are also many people working in the tertiary sector, the main reason for this is the popularity of Brazil as a tourist destination. In recent years there have also been major improvements in healthcare, education and transport.

In Ghana the majority of people work in the primary sector. Lack of investment in machinery still means that most people work in farming, forestry and mining. Very few people work in the secondary sector due to the lack of factories in Ghana.

INDIVIDUAL WORK (1.16)
★ ★

Read the case study. Brazil has a larger population than the UK, and Ghana has the smallest population. Answer the following questions.

1 If the UK has so many people working in the tertiary sector, where do the products come from for these people if the UK does not produce them?

2 Why might Brazil gradually move towards the mix of sectors shown in the UK pie chart?

3 In time, will Ghana be like the UK or Brazil? Why?

Primary sector

The primary sector of industry generally involves the conversion of natural resources into primary products. Most products from this sector are raw materials for other industries. Major businesses in this sector include agriculture, fishing, forestry and all mining and quarrying industries.

Farming

Agriculture (or farming) is the process of producing food, feed, fibres and other products by cultivation of certain plants and the raising of domesticated animals. Annually, the world produces the following:

- 624 million metric tons of maize
- 570 million metric tons of wheat
- 381 million metric tons of rice
- 96.5 million metric tons of cotton.

Certain rural areas in the UK have traditionally concentrated on particular types of farming and broadly speaking these are:

- Scotland – sheep, cattle, potatoes and arable (crops)
- South-east of England – vegetables, potatoes and arable
- East of England – pigs, poultry, vegetables and arable
- Midlands – mainly arable
- Wales – sheep and cattle
- South-west of England – sheep, cattle and arable
- North Midlands – pigs, poultry and arable
- Borders – sheep, cattle and vegetables
- Northern Ireland – sheep, cattle and potatoes.

WANT TO FIND OUT MORE?

Department for the Environment, Food and Rural Affairs (Defra)
Information Resource Centre
Lower Ground Floor
Ergon House
c/o Nobel House
17 Smith Square
London
SW1P 3JR
Tel: 0207 238 6951
www.defra.gov.uk

CASE STUDY Farming in the UK

Intensive production systems, the increased use of machinery and the increasing use of pesticides and chemical fertilisers have resulted in huge drops in employment in the sector. Between 1945 and 1992, the number of regular full-time and part-time hired and family workers on English farms fell from 478,000 to 135,000. The current figure stands at around 110,000. There has also been a knock-on effect on employment in other rural services.

At the same time, the environment has suffered. Since 1945 the UK has lost 95 per cent of its wildflower meadows, 30–50 per cent of ancient woodlands, 50–60 per cent of lowland heath land, 140,000 miles of hedgerows and 50 per cent of lowland fens, valleys and basin mires.

Changes in agricultural practice are the main cause of these losses. In addition, contamination of rivers, groundwater and drinking water from the use of artificial fertilisers and pesticides and continued soil erosion have become major issues.

GROUP WORK (1.17)
★ ★ ★

In groups of two or three, read the case study and answer the following questions.

1 What do you understand by 'a knock-on effect on employment in other rural services'?

2 What could be done to turn around the destruction of the natural landscape?

3 Why might the contamination of rivers be a problem?

Forestry

Forestry is the art, science and practice of studying and managing forests and related natural resources. Much research and development has been invested in learning about managing forest ecosystems, improving varieties of trees, and in better methods of planting, pest control, thinning, felling and extraction, and of processing timber into usable products.

The production of wood has become an increasingly profitable industry in recent years. The Forestry Commission, which is a government department, controls nearly half of all wood production in the UK.

Fishing

In 2003, some 631,000 tons of sea fish were landed into the UK and abroad by the UK fleet, with a total value of £521 million. In addition, the UK **imported** some £1,437 million worth of fish. The UK also **exported** fish and fish products to the value of £891 million.

The UK has a substantial fish processing industry of around 563 businesses, which employ some 18,480 people. At the retail level, there are approximately 1,400 fishmongers.

Approximately 87 per cent of fish is sold through supermarkets. Fish is also consumed in restaurants and in takeaway form from fish and chip shops, and a small proportion is used to make fish oils and animal feeds.

Extraction and mining

There are around 40 opencast sites and 20 underground coal-mining sites in the UK. The majority of them are located in the Midlands, the north-east of England, south Wales and southern Scotland.

As well as coal mining, many businesses are involved in the extraction of chalk, limestone, clay, salt, sand, gravel and shale. These materials are vital for road building, construction and house building.

Several organisations are responsible for providing a healthy and plentiful water supply and for the treatment of sewerage. These organisations are involved in the management of rivers, canals, streams, lakes, reservoirs, wells, springs and underground waterways. They provide water and waste facilities for homes and for industry. In agricultural areas in the UK the demand for water is very dependent upon the rainfall, whilst other industries need to use vast amounts of water on a daily basis.

WANT TO FIND OUT MORE?

Forestry Commission GB and Scotland
Silvan House
231 Corstorphine Road
Edinburgh
Scotland
EH12 7AT
Tel: 0131 334 0303
www.forestry.gov.uk

Keyword

imported – goods or services that are produced or provided by an overseas country and brought into the UK

exported – goods or services that are produced or provided by a UK organisation and sold to an overseas country

WANT TO FIND OUT MORE?

The Coal Authority
200 Lichfield Lane
Mansfield
Nottinghamshire
NG18 4RG
Tel: 01623 427162
www.coal.gov.uk

GROUP WORK (1.18)
★ ★

1 In pairs, find out the name of the organisation that provides fresh water supplies to your area.

2 Who deals with the sewerage?

3 Where is the nearest sewage farm and where is the nearest reservoir?

The UK was fortunate for many years to have significant amounts of gas reserves, particularly in the North Sea. As the gas under the seabed begins to run out, the UK is increasingly importing gas for its energy needs.

CASE STUDY   New gas pipeline

By 2010 the UK will be importing around 50 per cent of its gas requirements. This is likely to rise to around 70 per cent in 2020. Gas prices are likely to rise significantly over this period, mainly due to an expected doubling in demand for gas from continental European countries during the next 15 years. It is likely that in the future at least 20 per cent of the gas used by the UK will be imported from Norway. The gas will reach the UK via a 1,200 km pipeline, which is being rolled out along the seabed across the North Sea from Norway to the UK. The pipeline is part of a Norwegian energy project that is due to be finished in 2007.

INDIVIDUAL WORK (1.19) ★ ★ ★
Read the case study and answer the following questions.

1 Using the internet, find out where the pipeline will enter the UK.

2 Do you think the pipeline terminal will create many jobs in the UK?

3 What affect will this have on the local area?

WANT TO FIND OUT MORE?

Department of Trade and Industry
www.og.dti.gov.uk

Twenty years ago it was predicted that North Sea oil would run out by the year 2000. But UK oil production continues to increase; UK reserves of oil are now at around 2 billion tons, and 2 billion tons has been produced in the last 25 years. Some oil fields, particularly those to the west of the Shetland Islands, have been discovered only recently and are at an early stage of their productive life. Recent and future fields are expected to remain productive at least until 2020. Many of the world's unexplored oil fields lie under very deep water. The UK expertise in the oil extracting industry is therefore likely to grow in importance and make British technology an increasingly valuable export.

Secondary sector

Keyword

domestic consumers – household buyers rather than businesses

The secondary sector of industry is also known as the manufacturing sector. This sector of industry generally takes the output of the primary sector and manufactures finished goods or products to a point where they are suitable for use by other businesses, for export, or for sale to **domestic consumers**. This sector is often divided into light industry and heavy industry. Many of these industries consume large quantities of energy and require factories and machinery to convert the raw materials into goods and products. They also produce waste materials and waste heat that may pose environmental problems or cause pollution.

Manufacturing

Keyword

exports – sales by UK businesses to overseas businesses or countries, earning income for the UK

Manufacturing is the transformation of raw materials into finished goods for sale, or intermediate processes involving the production or finishing of goods. It is a large branch of industry and of secondary production. The UK relies on its manufacturing industry for the following reasons:

- Manufacturing accounts for a sixth of the economy.
- It provides two-thirds of all **exports**.
- It provides around 3.5 million jobs and millions more through related services.
- Seventy-five per cent of the UK's research and development is carried out by manufacturing organisations.
- Thousands of new products and processes are constantly being designed by manufacturing organisations.

Engineering

In 2000, the UK engineering industry had a turnover of almost £100 billion of which was exported. Machinery and equipment had a turnover of £ over 30 per cent being exported.

The engineering industry has a small number of large, successful businesses and a large number of small to medium-sized businesses, operating in areas as varied as **aerospace** and **telecommunications**. Many of the businesses produce highly profitable products and services that are at the forefront of engineering design and highly sought after by the rest of the world.

Construction

The UK construction industry produces around 8 per cent of the country's wealth and employs two million people. The UK construction industry is the third largest in Europe and the fifth largest in the world.

The industry exports £10 billion per year and is vital in providing the UK with much-needed housing, hospitals and road and rail networks. The majority of the organisations in the industry are small to medium-size businesses, although there are a small number of very large organisations operating in the UK. UK construction consultants operate in almost every country throughout the world.

Tertiary sector

The tertiary sector is involved in providing services, either at a personal or a commercial level. Personal services would include professions such as doctors, solicitors, teachers and fire-fighters. Commercial services aim to assist businesses and include banking, accountancy, training and marketing services.

Private services

Private, or commercial, services are provided to individuals or businesses by specialist organisations. They provide their expertise in a wide range of different areas. Many of these services have grown in size in recent years and collectively they provide an enormous amount of employment and income to the UK.

aerospace – manufacturing industry that produces parts and products for the aircraft industry, including rockets, engines and other equipment
telecommunications – the manufacturing and service industries that produce or provide communications equipment

WANT TO FIND OUT MORE?

To discover more about the **secondary sector in the UK**, visit: www.uktradeinvest.gov.uk

Table 1.4
Tertiary private services

Tertiary private service	Description of service
Accountancy	Accountancy covers all forms of financial services, including investment and the provision of financial expertise to businesses. The UK is the world's leading international financial services centre employing over 1 million people and with overseas earnings of £31.2 billion in 2000. The City of London is one of world's three leading financial centres and the largest centre for many international financial markets.
Administration	Many businesses choose to use a separate business to assist them with their administrative work. This can often take the form of a separate organisation dealing with their general office duties, personnel or legal and financial matters. This leaves the organisation free to concentrate on its own areas of expertise and to avoid having to take additional staff on to carry out these duties.
Banking	The UK has probably the most efficient banking systems in the world. There are more foreign banks based in the UK than in any other country in the world – 481 in 2000 – when London banks accounted for 19.1 per cent of global bank lending. The total wealth of the UK banks in August 2001 was £3,441 billion, of which 55 per cent belonged to foreign banks.
Communications	In 2002, the UK communications sector still managed to grow by 1 per cent and was worth £30 billion in 2002. The sector increased by 4.6 per cent in 2003 to reach a value of £31 billion.
Consultancy	There are estimated to be between 30,000 and 35,000 management consultants in the UK, with a total worth of around £5.5 billion, of which exports account for £1 billion. The majority of international work carried out by UK firms is in Europe.
Design	The UK is considered to be the design workshop of the world. UK designers have an international reputation, particularly in the areas of retail interior/exterior, branding, advertising, corporate identity, product design and multimedia. UK design consultancies generated £1 billion in export earnings in 2000.
tribution	Around 1.5 million people are either directly or indirectly employed by the distribution sector. This includes road haulage, warehousing and other forms of transportation.

Table 1.4 *continued*

Energy supply	The UK electricity industry supplies electricity to over 26 million customers. Energy supply also includes oil and gas and, more recently, wind farms are being constructed on the coasts around the UK to provide an all-year-round, clean energy source.
Entertainment	The UK entertainment industry includes musicians, actors and actresses, film, theatre, dance and a host of other entertainers. The UK entertainment industry is considered to be one of the best in the world and the West End theatres in London attract many thousands of overseas visitors each year.
Healthcare	Last year the UK exported over £14 billion worth of healthcare goods and services in addition to providing services such as the diagnosis of illness and laboratory technology.
Hospitality and medical	The hospitality industry contributes some £21.5 billion annually. The industry employs over 1.8 million people in the UK, working in around 300,000 establishments. By the end of 2005 a further 170,000 jobs will have been created. The private medical sector is also a major employer of medical staff. Health spending is due to rise considerably over the next five years.
Publishing	There are approximately 50,000 publishers in the UK and Ireland, although only around 2,500 of them are of any size. Over 130,000 new books are published each year, in addition to the many thousands of magazines and newspapers. UK book publishers export around £1.5 billion worth of books each year.
Repair and maintenance	The repair and maintenance industry includes garages that deal with vehicles and the innumerable repair services for domestic machines, such as dishwashers, televisions and CD players.
Research	The term 'research' covers an enormous range of different activities, including the development of new products, ideas and processes, as well as investigations into particular markets. Research also includes scientific and medical development of drugs and equipment for other sectors such as healthcare, retailing, security and energy supply.
Retailing	Retailing is the UK's top service sector industry, employing around 2.4 million people in the UK. Its turnover has risen from just over £80 billion in 1984 to in excess of £175 billion.
Security	UK security companies and their services are world leaders, achieving success with equipment and services in overseas markets, particularly in America, Europe, the Middle East and the Far East. The UK security industry was worth £4.37 billion in 2002, divided into electronic security £1.4 billion, physical security £331 million, police and public services £63 million and manned security £1.79 billion.
Tourism	Tourism is worth about £300 billion in the UK. It is one of the world's biggest industries and is growing fast, catering for both family holidays and business travellers. Tourism provides income for conservation and national heritage.
Transport	The UK exports a quarter of everything it makes each year. UK businesses have been involved in building much of the world's infrastructure (airports, railways, roads, bridges, ports, waterworks, power stations and electricity transmission lines).
Water supply and purification	The UK water industry (including the water utilities, contractors, consultants, equipment manufacturers, lawyers and financiers) is much in demand around the world. With the global water business worth up to $300 billion, the UK water supply and purification sector is the market leader in the world.

CASE STUDY UK entertainment

Videos, DVDs, CDs and games are an important part of the UK entertainment industry. With the exception of recorded music, all of these parts of the sector have grown and continue to grow year-on-year.

Table 1.5
Retail values in the UK entertainment industry (£m)

	2000	2001	2002	2003	% Change 2002/03
Recorded music	2,047	2,111	2,027	2,007*	−7%
Video (excl. rental)	1,200	1,539	2,050	2,421	+18%
Games (excl. rental)	934	1,057	1,173	1,259	+7%
Total	4,181	4,707	5,250	5,687	+8%

Source : Recorded Music: BPI figures for 2000–02. *Trade estimates for 2003. Video: BVA. Games: Chart Track/ELSPA.

INDIVIDUAL WORK (1.20)
★ ★
Using the data in Table 1.5, create a bar chart using computer software. Your bar chart should include the three different sets of data, as well as the total figures for each year.

Local and national public services

The public sector employs approximately a quarter of the UK workforce and includes:

- Central civil government departments and agencies.
- The National Health Service (NHS) and its local trusts.
- The Ministry of Defence.
- The Northern Ireland Assembly, National Assembly for Wales and Scottish Executive.
- Local authorities.
- Universities and colleges.
- Public non-financial corporations (e.g. the BBC), which also include nationalised industries such as the Royal Mail Group and the Civil Aviation Authority.
- The Bank of England.

The government's plans to improve public services has led to an expansion in the public sector workforce in recent years. Investment in the public sector increased by over 80 per cent between 2000–01 and 2001–02 and is set to more than double by 2004–05.

The proportion of the UK workforce employed in the public sector has been falling in the last two decades, from nearly 30 per cent in 1981 to under 20 per cent in 2001. The majority (almost 80 per cent) work in education, local government and the NHS.

A recent study from the Office for National Statistics revealed that around 86,000 new jobs were created in the public sector in the year to June 2002.

Public expenditure includes spending by central government, local government, and nationalised industries. For each pound of public expenditure:

- Central government spends 74p
- Local authorities spend 25p
- Public corporations spend 1p.

The main responsibilities of the government departments are given in Table 1.6.

Table 1.6
Main responsibilities of government departments

Department	Responsibility
Social Security	Pensions and welfare benefits
Health	National Health Service
Defence	Navy, army and air force
Education and Science	Schools, universities, the arts
Home Office	Courts, police, prisons, fire service
Employment	Training schemes, job centres
Environment, Food and Rural Affairs	Agricultural policy, food, roads, housing, local authorities
Trade and Industry	Regional and industrial policy
Foreign Office	Embassies
Energy	Electricity, gas, oil, atomic energy

Education

Although the majority of teaching jobs are in state-funded secondary schools (more than 180,000 teachers work in secondary schools), there are a variety of other forms of employment in the sector – from university lecturers to nursery school and playgroup assistants.

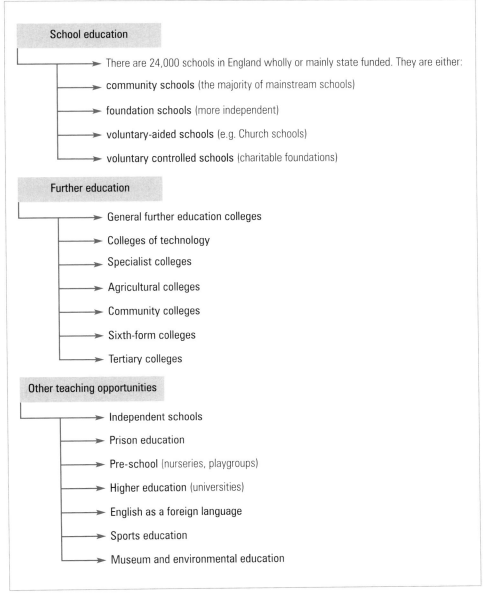

Figure 1.4
The education sector

Emergency services

There are 31 NHS ambulance service trusts in England (and three in Northern Ireland). They are the first and often the most important contact for around five million 999 callers every year. In 2002–03, the ambulance services received nearly 5.4 million 999 calls and provided over 4.8 million emergency responses.

There are 3,481 emergency ambulance vehicles, 628 rapid response vehicles and 78 motorbikes. The ambulance service employs 8,589 paramedics and 9,672 technicians and a total of 38,377 staff are employed by the service trusts. Some 61.3 per cent of the employees are male and 38.7 per cent are female.

The role of the *fire service* is to protect life and property and to provide a quality fire and rescue service. This involves identifying hazards and taking action to reduce risks, promoting awareness and being an effective emergency response and planning service.

The main responsibilities of the fire service include:

- Carrying out Fire Safety Inspections at all places of work
- Issuing Fire Certificates
- Informing, educating and promoting fire safety in the community
- Inspecting and monitoring petrol stores
- Issuing Petroleum Licences
- Planning and training for emergencies
- Providing a 24-hour response to emergency incidents.

The London Fire Brigade is the third largest fire-fighting organisation in the world, protecting people and property from fire within the 1,587 square kilometres of Greater London which has a population of seven million, increased by another 500,000 during working hours.

INDIVIDUAL WORK
(1.22)
★ ★

Look at Figure 1.5, which shows the pay received by fire-fighters in the UK, and then answer the following questions.

1 Which are the two most common yearly salaries for fire-fighters?

2 How many fire-fighters receive less than £18,000 per year?

3 How many fire-fighters receive more than £23,000 per year?

4 What is the total cost of the fire-fighters receiving £24,006 per year?

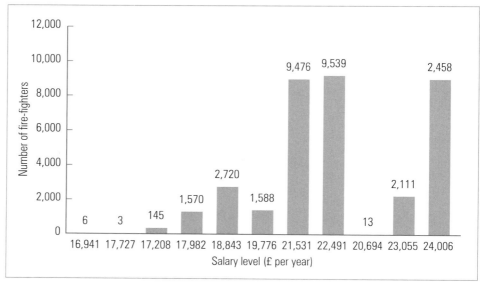

Figure 1.5
The number of fire-fighters at each salary level

Source: Employers' Organisation for Local Government, based on Fire Authorities returns survey 2002 (2001 figures for five authorities)

Healthcare

The NHS treats one million people every 36 hours. Approximately 1.3 million people were employed in the NHS in September 2003. This represented an increase of 60,000 since 2002 and an average increase of over 37,000 per year since 1997.

There were 633,375 professionally qualified clinical staff in the NHS, including 108,993 doctors, 386,359 qualified nursing, midwifery and health-visiting staff (including practice nurses), 122,066 qualified scientific, therapeutic and technical (ST&T) staff and 15,957 qualified ambulance staff.

There were a further 360,666 staff in support to clinical staff. These were in three key areas – 298,752 supporting doctors and nursing staff, 52,230 scientific, therapeutic and technical support staff and 9,684 ambulance support staff. There was also 199,808 staff involved in NHS infrastructure support. This includes 92,257 staff in central functions, 72,230 staff in hotel, property and estates and 35,321 managers and senior managers. There was 88,424 GP practice staff, excluding practice nurses.

Housing

Public sector housing refers to council flats or council houses in England and Wales still provided by local authorities (district councils, unitary authorities and London

WANT TO FIND OUT MORE?

Visit the **Department of Health** website www.dh.gov.uk/Home/fs/en.

INDIVIDUAL WORK
(1.23)
★ ★
After reading the
information on the
NHS, answer the
following questions.

1 How many people
work for the NHS
according to the
latest figures?

2 Why do you think
that the NHS is still
growing in size?

3 Convert the pie chart
into a graph using
Excel® software, or
similar.

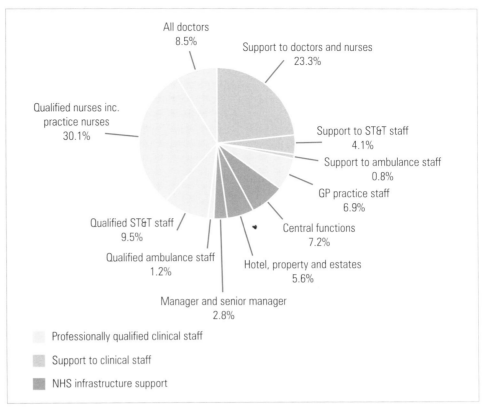

Figure 1.6
The number of staff in the NHS

borough councils). In recent years, local authorities in England and Wales have
handed over control of their housing to other organisations.

Some local authorities have passed the housing over to Registered Social Landlords
(RSLs). The RSLs are usually Housing Associations (HAs) though there are also trusts,
cooperatives and companies.

There are around 2,500 housing associations in England managing 1.45 million
homes. Boards of volunteers – including tenants, representatives from local
authorities and community groups, business people and politicians – manage the
housing associations.

Since 2001, 34 authorities in England have shared £3.3 billion in government funds
earmarked for public housing.

Law and order

The UK now has the highest ever number of police officers patrolling the streets. As of
December 2003 there were:

◊ 138,155 police officers (a rise of more than 14,000 in $3\frac{1}{2}$ years)

◊ 3,243 Community Support Officers.

Military activity

The Ministry of Defence is responsible for the armed forces of the UK and for the
defence of the country. Four government ministers and five Chiefs of Staff (the Chief of
the Defence Staff, the Vice Chief of the Defence Staff, the First Sea Lord – for the Royal
Navy, the Chief of the General Staff – for the British army and the Chief of the Air Staff –
for the Royal Air Force) head the Ministry of Defence.

In addition to the uniformed staff in each of the branches of the armed forces, the
Ministry of Defence employs around 100,000 civilian staff. The Ministry itself was
brought into existence in 1971.

CASE STUDY Record number of police officers

Police numbers have reached a record high of 136,386 [in 2003], Home Secretary David Blunkett announced.

Police recruitment figures up to the end of August show a record number of police officers – an increase of 4,118 since December 2002 – and that the wider police family has now reached 201,092 officers and staff. This includes a growing number of Community Support Officers (CSOs) and police staff introduced through the radical police reform programme.

Mr Blunkett said: 'Police numbers are at an all time high. At the end of August 2003, there were 136,386 police officers in England and Wales, the highest number since records began in 1921, 9,000 more than in 1997 and way ahead of our 2004 target.

'With more officers and staff than ever before and following very substantial growth in police funding, we are redoubling our efforts to ensure that more officer time is spent on front-line policing.

'It is vital that we make the best use of today's record number of police officers by continuing to take them out of the station and increase visibility, availability and accessibility.

'By cutting bureaucracy in the police service as part of the police reform programme, the Government is already freeing up officer time and bringing about a real difference to the everyday lives of officers on the front line.'

The Home Secretary set targets of 130,000 police officers by March 2003 and 132,500 in 2004. The 2004 target has been exceeded well ahead of the target date.

Source: www.homeoffice.gov.uk

INDIVIDUAL WORK (1.24)
★ ★
After reading the case study about the police, answer the following questions.

1 What does David Blunkett mean by 'cutting bureaucracy'?

2 Why might it be important to 'increase visibility, availability and accessibility'?

3 What do you think he means by 'The wider police family has now reached 201,092 officers and staff'?

Table 1.7
Numbers of defence personnel, 1 July 2001 (thousands)

Total UK-based personnel	**304.0**
Service	**205.7**
Civilian	**98.4**
Naval service	42.4
Officers	7.8
Other ranks	34.7
Army	109.5
Officers	13.9
Other ranks	95.6
Royal Air Force	53.7
Officers	11.0
Other ranks	42.7
UK-based civilians	98.4
Non-industrial	73.8
Industrial	24.5

Source: DASA (Civilian) and DASA (Tri-Service)

INDIVIDUAL WORK (1.25) ★ ★
After reading Table 1.7, convert the figures into a graph using Excel.

Only four countries in the world spend more on defence than the UK. These are the United States, France, Germany and Japan.

Planning

Both local and central government prepare development plans which affect virtually every area of our lives, including building, use of land, industry, use of natural resources, technology, the military and the police, and numerous other concerns. Planning helps the government to control development, matching the country's needs with a desire to protect and improve the environment, create employment and fit in with other plans already underway.

Table 1.8
UK expenditure on defence 2000-01 (estimates £billion)

	Expenditure	Percentage of total
Total expenditure	**23.6**	**100**
Split by:		
Expenditure on personnel:	8.8	37
of the armed forces	6.5	28
of civilian staff	2.3	10
Expenditure on equipment	9.8	41
Other expenditure:	5.0	21
Works, buildings and land		
Miscellaneous, stores and services		

Source: MOD Financial Controller (Corporate Financial Management)

WANT TO FIND OUT MORE?

The website of the **Office of the Deputy Prime Minister's Planning Directorate** can be found by following the 'Planning' link at: www.odpm.gov.uk.

The Planning Directorate is part of the Office of the Deputy Prime Minister. Its role is to support communities that 'are economically prosperous; have decent homes at affordable prices; safeguard the countryside; enjoy a well designed, accessible and pleasant living and working environment; and are effectively and fairly governed with a strong sense of community'.

Recreation

Local government is closely involved in the development and provision of recreational facilities across the country. The range of recreational facilities covers swimming pools, parks, museums, sports centres, libraries and the countryside.

Both the public and the private sector provide these recreational facilities. The first and most important role for any recreational service is to provide facilities for the local population. In many areas of the UK tourism is also a vital concern and larger, or additional, recreational facilities are provided for visitors to the area. This means that some areas of the UK have considerably more recreational facilities than others and usually these additional recreational facilities are provided by the private sector.

Within any area of the UK there is often a considerable amount of employment in the broad range of recreational services. The local government, charities or trusts that run the various facilities directly employ some employees. In popular tourist destinations the additional recreational facilities may be **seasonal** and only open at times when the area is popular with visitors.

Keyword

seasonal – describes a part of the year when either products or services are particularly popular, such as fir trees at Christmas or water sports during the summer

WANT TO FIND OUT MORE?

Visit the **Department for Culture, Media and Sport** and find out about all of the schemes and plans for the future, including sports and recreation: www.culture.gov.uk.

Social services

Spending in England on social services is around £9 billion per year, and the average local social services authority spends £60 million to provide services for local people.

Social services departments meet a wide variety of different social care needs, such as:

- Supporting older people who are no longer able to care for themselves without help.
- Supporting people with physical or learning disabilities, and those with sensory impairment, to allow them to live as full a life as possible.
- Delivering a full range of care needed by mentally ill people.
- Providing essential services to children who would otherwise be at risk of neglect or abuse.
- Bringing together the wider range of services, such as health and housing, on which their users also depend.
- Providing protection to the most vulnerable in their community.

CASE STUDY Family spending

The cost of public and private transport was the biggest single item in the £406 weekly budget for 2002–03, according to the Office for National Statistics, accounting for £59 in the average UK weekly budget. Its annual survey of expenditure puts recreation spending second, with food and housing in the next two slots.

The survey, carried out annually for nearly half a century, asks almost 7,000 households to track where their money goes on a daily basis. More than six in 10 of the households surveyed had just one or two people in them, and about a third included children.

The average for household spending each week ranges from £136 for the lowest income groups to £883 for the highest.

The breakdown in spending varies widely between poor and rich. The least well-off tenth of the population spent 16 per cent of their budget on food and non-alcoholic drinks, compared to 8 per cent for the most wealthy. Tobacco spending, on the other hand, peaks in the middle of the income spread.

Age also plays a part, with newspapers most important to the oldest participants and least important for the under-30s. And unsurprisingly geography dictates total spending, the survey showed. London's average weekly household budget

was £487 a week, with Wales footing the list at £335. Urban areas outside London showed low spending averaging £336 with a smaller proportion going on transport. Rural areas, in contrast, spent £458 on average.

The organisation has stocked a house in Surrey with items priced to show what burden they place on the average household.

The full figures per week were as follows:
- Transport £59.20
- Recreation and culture £56.40
- Food £42.70
- Housing and energy £36.90
- Restaurants and hotels £35.40
- Miscellaneous goods and services £33.10
- Household goods £30.20
- Clothes and shoes £22.30
- Alcohol and tobacco £11.40
- Communication £10.60
- Education £5.20
- Health £4.80
- Other £57.90

Total £406.20

INDIVIDUAL WORK
(1.26) ★ ★

Read the case study, then answer the following questions.

1 Using the figures at the end of the case study, create a bar chart showing these figures using Excel software.

2 If the lowest income was £136 and the highest £883, how might the Office of National Statistics have worked out the average spending?

3 Which group of people find newspapers more important?

4 Why might London be more expensive than Wales?

Volunteer agencies and individuals complement the work of social services. Often they will support individuals or groups who have a strong link with social services.

From 1 April 2004, the Commission for Social Care Inspection (CSCI) took responsibility for the registration of social services and the Commission for Healthcare Audit and Inspection (CHAI) become responsible for the improvement in quality and effectiveness of care, the carrying out of investigations and a series of reviews of healthcare.

> **WANT TO FIND OUT MORE?**
> Visit the **CSCI** website at:
> www.csci.org.uk and the **CHAI** at:
> www.chai.org.uk.

Voluntary/not-for-profit services

Even with the enormous range of private and public sector organisations, there is still a need for organisations to provide services, either by using volunteers or at a zero or reduced cost to users. Within the voluntary and not-for-profit sector, we can include a large number of different organisations, ranging from trusts, charities and groups that seek to promote particular interests. This last group includes organisations that are known as *pressure groups*. Pressure groups attempt to influence government in order to convince them to change their policies.

The Community Health Councils (CHCs) were established by Parliament in 1974 as independent bodies 'to represent the interests of the public in the health service in their district'. In other words, they represent local people in their local NHS and the services it provides. CHCs are legal bodies created under government legislation, but they are independent within the NHS. The main functions of a CHC are to:

- Monitor local NHS services.
- Comment on annual plans and consultation papers produced by organisations concerned with health.
- Visit hospitals, health centres, clinics, GP surgeries and ambulance stations to monitor healthcare and talk to patients and staff.
- Raise matters of local public concern with health organisations.

- Advise the public about local services and help them with complaints, problems and general enquiries.
- Hold public meetings of the full council at least four times a year and produce an annual report.

These are community facilities provided for the care of people with special needs, including those who suffer from problems arising from old age, mental health, learning and physical disabilities. The National Health Service and Community Care Act 1990 introduced changes in the provision of social care facilities for adults. As a result there has been a greater involvement by the private and voluntary sectors, and adults in need of care have been cared for in the community in a range of accommodation with varying levels of care.

Community care facilities are currently provided by social services departments and numerous voluntary organisations. Under the 1990 Act, county councils were charged with the responsibility of producing community care plans for their administrative areas and with coordinating the allocation of resources.

Relative growth and decline of business sectors

As we have seen, countries in their earliest stages of development tend to rely far more on the primary industries, which include agriculture, mining, fishing and the immediate use of raw materials. As they develop technology, or can afford to purchase technology and machinery, they gradually move into the secondary sector, where they become much more involved in manufacturing.

After a period of time there is a tendency for countries to reduce the amount of work involved in the primary and secondary sectors and concentrate on the tertiary sectors. This leaves the primary and secondary sectors open for other, less developed countries to become involved in. Either as a result of natural resources running out or being no longer profitable, countries tend to look for overseas sources of primary sector resources, which they can exchange for manufactured goods or for tertiary sector services.

In the UK until relatively recently most of the natural resources we needed came from our own country. But increasingly these are being imported. There has also been this trend in manufacturing, which has seen fewer businesses involved and far less people employed.

Growth of tertiary service industries

As countries become more developed there is an increasing need for tertiary sector services. The UK has always had a strong reputation throughout the world for banking, finance and insurance services. These have always employed large numbers of UK workers.

The UK also employs large numbers of people in the travel and tourism sector, **telesales** and marketing, the **media** and telecommunications. Many other businesses have taken on large numbers of workers to cope with the huge boom in retailing and in customer services. The UK has gradually transformed over the last 50 or 60 years from a country that had large numbers of people employed in the primary and secondary sectors to very few employed in the primary sector, falling numbers in the secondary sector and increasing numbers in the tertiary sector. Amongst the biggest areas of growth in the tertiary sector, apart from banking, insurance, retailing and customer services, have been the National Health Trusts, social services and government departments.

GROUP WORK (1.27)
★ ★
Try to find out whether any primary or secondary sector industries used to operate in your immediate area. A visit to the local library to find a local history book or a visit to a local museum may reveal the type of industries that used to be major employers in your area. Why do you think these industries are no longer running?

Keyword

telesales – also known as telephone sales, involves calling customers, either at home or at their workplace, and attempting to sell them products and services

media – the general term used to describe newspapers, television, radio, magazines and, increasingly, internet news and information services. The media also includes marketing, public and community relations

INDIVIDUAL WORK
(1.28) ★ ★

Look at Figure 1.7.

1 What was the overall percentage change in manufacturing between 1984 and 2000?

2 What was the overall percentage change in finance and business services between 1984 and 2000?

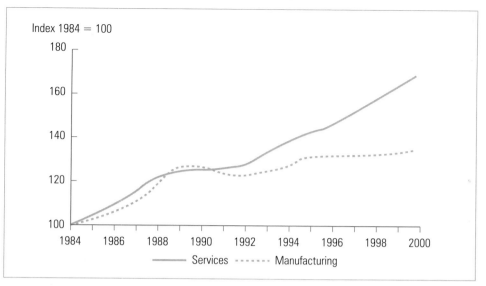

Figure 1.7
The rise of services
Source: The Henley Centre

Decline of primary and secondary industries

As we have seen, developed countries, such as the UK, have a tendency to reduce the importance of both the primary and secondary sectors as they develop the importance of the tertiary sector.

There are many reasons for the reduction in the number of people employed in the primary and secondary sectors. Perhaps the two most important are the fact that machinery has gradually taken over many jobs that used to be done by hand and the fact that it is actually cheaper to buy raw materials and manufactured goods from abroad.

Most of the manufacturing in the world now takes place in less-developed countries, where materials are cheaper and employees are paid a fraction of the wages that are paid to employees in more-developed countries. Many of these less-developed countries also have enormous reserves of raw materials, such as coal, oil, minerals and other resources that are processed by the secondary sector.

RESOURCES, AIMS AND OBJECTIVES

The aims and objectives of an organisation are closely linked to its available resources. A business may have very ambitious aims and objectives, but it must operate within the resources it has, or is likely to have in the near future. As we will see, the aims and objectives of organisations tend to change over a period of time, largely as a result of their experiences and relative success or failure. Being able to juggle available resources in order to achieve aims and objectives is a difficult and demanding job and, as we will also see later in this unit, businesses tend to organise themselves so that specialists can handle particular parts of their business in the most efficient manner.

Business resources

Business resources can be defined as being any input into the organisation, be it money, people, technology, education, experience or simply a great idea. All resources will cost the business money, even money costs a business money because they may have to borrow from a bank and pay interest on that loan. Every employee is an expense, as is every sheet of paper and every envelope.

CASE STUDY The labour market in 2002

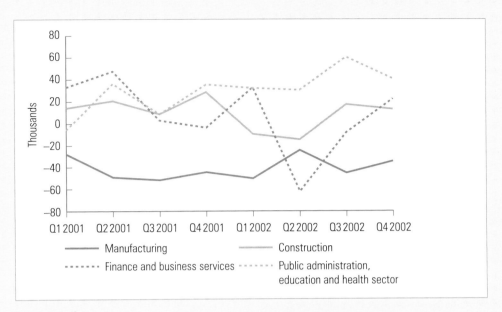

Figure 1.8
Quarterly changes in the number of people employed, UK, 2001-02

The number of jobs in public administration, education and health in the UK increased by 163,000 (2.4 per cent) during 2002. There was also a large increase in distribution, hotels and restaurants (105,000 or 1.5 per cent).

The largest decrease was in manufacturing where the number of jobs fell 154,000 (3.9 per cent) during the year, continuing the long-term decline in this sector.

Employment in agriculture and fishing fell by 49,000 (10.6 per cent) in 2002. The decline in this sector over recent decades has followed a series of food scares such as salmonella in eggs, BSE in cattle and most recently the outbreak of foot-and-mouth disease in 2001.

Employment in the finance and business services sector also fell slightly in 2002 (by 211,000 or 0.2 per cent), but showed signs of recovery towards the end of the year.

The total number of jobs filled by men is virtually the same as the number filled by women – 12.8 million compared with 12.7 million respectively in 2002.

As in previous years, men suffered more than women from the decline in manufacturing jobs. Male employment in this sector fell 105,000 (3.7 per cent) in 2002, compared with a fall of 48,000 (4.4 per cent) in female employment.

The growth in jobs in the public administration, education and health sector in 2002 benefited both sexes, but the growth was faster in female employment. In the finance and business services sector, while male employment declined in 2002, female employment increased.

Financial and business services accounted for about one in five jobs in the UK (almost 5.7 million) at the end 2002, compared with little more than one in 10 in 1981. This sector saw the largest increase in jobs between 1981 and 2002, part of the post-war growth of service industries and decline in manufacturing. Manufacturing jobs totalled 3.8 million at the end of 2002 compared with 6.2 million in 1981.

Men and women still follow very different career paths. About a quarter of female employees carry out administrative or secretarial work. Men are twice as likely as women to be managers and senior officials, and far more likely to be in skilled trades. Similar proportions of men and women work in associate professional and technical occupations, such as computer programmers, technicians and nurses.

INDIVIDUAL WORK
(1.29) ★★
Read the case study and then answer the following questions.

1 Which sector decreased the most in 2002?

2 Which sector increased the most in 2002?

3 Did males or females lose most in manufacturing?

4 In which sector did female jobs increase and male jobs decline?

5 Which jobs are men more likely to have?

6 Which sector accounts for one in five jobs in the UK?

Staff or human resources

Most businesses have now realised that their most valuable asset is their staff or employees. From the managing director to the cleaners, each and every person who works directly or indirectly for the business can have a positive impact on the organisation's success. Businesses try to find the most suitable individual to fill each post, but for smaller businesses this may be all the more important as these employees will have to carry out a wide variety of different tasks.

The larger the business, the more obvious each job role becomes. A retail outlet, for example, may have a manager, an assistant manager, cashiers, sales assistants, **merchandisers** and cleaners. All of these job roles will be clearly defined and each employee will know exactly what their duties are.

Businesses rely on the expertise of their employees in order to assist them in fulfilling their aims and objectives. Many businesses rely on their staff to help them save money, come up with good ideas, make sales, provide excellent customer service and, above all, to project the kind of image the business wishes its customers to see.

> *Keyword*
>
> **merchandisers** – individuals who are involved in organising shop displays, laying out the products on the shelves and making the shop as attractive as possible to customers

---

CASE STUDY The importance of staff

The Sole Bay Brewery was placed second in the 2004 National Complaints Culture Survey. The marketing director, Andrew Wood, said, 'It was not a case of paying staff more money but of telling them they had done a good job.'

The company carried out extensive training programmes, particularly for their customer service team. They used a number of tests to see how well their employees were performing. They ensured that customers who had a complaint were dealt with promptly and, above all, that the management of the business would support decisions made by the complaints team. As a result of all of their hard work, the staff had seen sales increase by 50 per cent over the previous four years.

INDIVIDUAL WORK (1.30) ★ ★

Read the case study and then answer the following questions.

1 The 2004 National Complaints Culture Survey saw that 54 per cent of customers were willing to complain, an increase of 15 per cent since 2001. Why might people be more willing to complain?

2 What do you think the role is of a customer service team that deals with complaints?

3 What kind of person do you think a business would look for to fulfil this role?

Finance and capital resources

All businesses need money, not only to invest in assets, such as buildings and equipment, but also to pay for their running costs and their staff wage bill. Businesses also need to purchase stock and to pay their bills. Once a business is established, much of their income will come from customers and profits made from these customers can be reinvested in the business.

Taking care of finance or capital resources is extremely important. A business needs to know how much money is coming in and how much money they must spend. Established businesses may have put aside some of their profits in order to help them through difficult patches, but most businesses will use **bank overdrafts** or **credit** from their suppliers to help them spread the costs. Other businesses may take out bank loans and, in the case of limited companies, they will be able to sell shares in order to bring in finance to the business for investment.

Not all businesses rely on profits or sales to customers in order to continue operations. Some organisations, as we have seen, do not seek to make a profit and indeed offer their products or services at cost, below cost or even free to their customers. These organisations manage their finances by making sure that they receive promised grants or funding from the government or other sources. Around 3 per cent of all new businesses are financed by grants and there are over 1,000 different grants available.

As we will see, financial resources are managed by both the senior management of the business and most importantly by the finance or accounts department of the business.

> *Keyword*
>
> **bank overdraft** – an agreed amount by which the business can spend more than it has in its account
>
> **credit** – the process by which a supplier provides products or services on the understanding that they will not be paid for immediately, but by an agreed date in the future

GROUP WORK (1.31)

GROUP WORK (1.31)

★ ★

In groups of two or three, think about the facilities, plant, equipment and type of building you would need as a clothes retailer. Draw up a list of the 'must have' items or facilities.

stock control – systems that keep track of products held by the business, which alert the business when levels have reached the stage at which they need to be reordered

payroll – usually a computerised system that informs accounts of the amount of money that needs to be paid to each employee, either weekly or monthly, as their wage or salary

Keyword

Facilities, plant, equipment and buildings

Spending on these items is known as capital expenditure. It includes assets, such as buildings, vehicles, machinery and other items that will assist the business by contributing to their profits. Plant and equipment refers to the machinery that a business needs in order to produce products, such as a print press for a newspaper, an assembly line for a car manufacturer or a furnace for a steel mill.

Not all businesses, of course, own their own plant, equipment and buildings. Some rent these and pay an agreed amount to the owner, whilst others lease this equipment. Leasing means borrowing for a longer period of time and often has the option to purchase the equipment or the buildings at the end of the lease period.

All businesses need to have suitable premises in which to operate. In the case of a telesales business, a suite of offices would be ideal, but in the case of a car repair business, a garage along with the necessary testing equipment would be needed.

Technology and problem-solving techniques

The term 'technology' refers to any advanced piece of equipment that could assist the business in carrying out its role. Technology therefore includes:

- Computer equipment, including printers and faxes.
- Telecommunications equipment, perhaps headsets and automatic dialling systems.
- Direct communications with suppliers and customers, either via computer or telephone links.
- Improved communications with banks and credit card companies.
- Mobile communications equipment, including mobile phones, intercoms, radio sets and tracking devices.
- Various new technologies to improve measurement, **stock control**, order processing, **payroll** and the production of accounts information.

Problem-solving may either be based on peoples' experiences of situations in the past, or on technology. With the possibility of being able to access information collected and stored on a computer, a business could solve potential problems before they actually happen.

Energy

All businesses need energy resources in order to operate. Primary sector organisations, such as farmers, would require diesel fuel for tractors and electricity to run other equipment. Manufacturing organisations may need coal, oil and electricity in order to run their complex machinery. Tertiary sector organisations tend to rely on electricity as their primary energy source.

All organisations, regardless of their size or the sector in which they operate, try to control the use of energy in order to keep costs down. Increasingly the government and the EU are demanding that businesses do not waste energy and that they put procedures in place to cut energy use. Typical examples that you may have seen include lights being placed on a timer, where a button is pressed and the light remains on only for two or three minutes before switching itself off. Computers can power themselves down if they have not been used for a period of time.

In addition to a business's desire to keep its energy costs low, there are also other concerns about energy. The generation of electricity, for example, has caused great concern as many of the older systems of producing electricity contribute to pollution and global warming. Increasingly alternative energy sources are being looked at, including wind and wave farms.

Location

The decision about location for a business can often be its most important. There are many factors that determine where a business chooses to locate, and these include:

- *Availability of staff* – the business needs to be able to find trained or semi-trained staff in a particular area, which could help them reduce their training budget.

- *Cost of staff* – in many cities, particularly in the south-east of England, the cost of living is very high, which means that wages and salaries have to be high in comparison to the rest of the country. Businesses may choose to locate in areas where the wages are lower in order to reduce the overall wage and salary bill.

- *Cost of premises* – the building or buildings in which the business operates can account for a large percentage of their costs. Buildings in city centres or near major shopping areas tend to be more expensive. Areas that have good travel links can also be expensive, but this has to be measured against the fact that cheaper areas for buildings may not have good transport links and may not have suitably trained staff.

- *Financial assistance* – certain areas of the country are designated either by the government or by the EU as in need of assistance. These areas are perhaps somewhat run down and have high unemployment. Businesses locating in these areas may receive grants or reduced rent in order to attract them.

- *Customers* – it may be important, particularly if the business is involved in retailing or manufacturing, to be close to their customers to help reduce transport costs.

CASE STUDY Arsenal's new stadium

'Following months of negotiation, Arsenal are today [23 February 2004] delighted to confirm that funding for their £357m stadium project has been secured and construction and regenerative work in and around the site has already resumed, thus ensuring the new 60,000 capacity stadium opens as planned for the start of the 2006–2007 season. To finance this highly complex project, Ashburton Properties have obtained a £260m senior loan facility from a stadium facilities banking group which comprises: the Royal Bank of Scotland PLC, Espirito Santo Investment, The Bank of Ireland, Allied Irish Banks PLC, CIT Group Structured Finance (UK) Limited and HSH Nordbank AG. Interest on the senior debt is set at a commercial fixed rate over the 14-year term. Arsenal are contributing the balance of the stadium project costs through funds from Granada, Nike and the sale of surplus land assets relating to the stadium site.'

Arsenal chairman Peter Hill-Wood added: 'This is excellent news for Arsenal. Over recent years we have established ourselves as one of the leading clubs in Europe and the stadium, which we can now positively look forward to, will provide us with the opportunity to sustain and build on this position. The financing of the group is now complex, but throughout the financing structure we have retained the twin objectives of continued investment in our outstanding playing squad and separate funding for the building of the stadium.'

Industry experience and market presence

Industry experience does not just mean the amount of time that the business has been operating. Indeed many new businesses have lots of industry experience. Industry experience really refers to the experience either of the managers or the employees of the business and how much they understand about the industry, the market and the customers that they serve.

Experience is a highly prized resource and experienced members of staff can expect to be paid well in order to ensure that they stay with the business. Their experience will assist the business in making decisions.

With so many businesses competing for customers, it is important that an organisation maintains some form of visibility to their customers. Market presence can be achieved by obvious measures, such as advertising or a large number of retail outlets. But it can also be achieved by reputation.

Reputation is often far more important than expensive television advertisements, but the key point is that to achieve market presence and to retain it, customers have to be constantly reminded that the business still exists. We may not necessarily need a plumber or an electrician every week, but when the point comes when we need one of these craftsmen, these businesses need to have reminded us that they should be the ones that we call.

Maintaining market presence is therefore more difficult for businesses that we do not use all the time but only need to use on particular occasions. This is also the case for businesses that provide seasonal products and services, such as travel companies, who need to constantly remind us throughout the year that we can book with them in advance.

Intangible assets and brand names

An intangible asset is a business term that is used to describe something that you cannot see, touch, sell or buy. An intangible asset may be the reputation of the business, the experience of its staff or the assumed quality of its products or services. The most important aspect of an intangible asset is increasingly the name of the product or service.

Coca-Cola or Pepsi-Cola are what are known as premium brand names. This means that they are very well known and that over a period of time customers have come to expect a certain level of quality and reliability from those products. The value of the Coca-Cola brand name has, in fact, nothing to do with how the drink tastes or what it looks like. The value comes simply from being so well known. This is regardless of the fact that if you were offered a cola drink without knowing which brand it was, you may not be able to tell whether it was Coca-Cola or not. But if you walk into a shop or are sitting in a restaurant you might well ask for Coca-Cola rather than a cola drink. This is the value of the intangible asset that is Coca-Cola's brand name.

The brand name of a business's products can, in fact, be sold at a price. When Nestlé purchased confectioner Rowntree, the purchase price was £2.25 billion. The fixed assets, such as plant and machinery, were worth only £250 million. The remainder was paid for the large portfolio of famous confectionery names, which could be used to generate huge revenue worldwide.

GROUP WORK (1.34)
★ ★

In pairs, write down at least 10 brand names that you think everyone else in your group will recognise. Now carry out some research by asking the other members of your group the following questions.

1 Do you use this particular brand name?

2 Why do you buy this particular brand name?

3 What makes you think it is better than other competing brands?

4 Do you know the name of the company that actually owns the brand name?

Aims

The larger the organisation, the more difficult it becomes to ensure that everyone in the organisation is moving in the same direction. The smaller the business, the more control the managers have over everything that is going on. As the business grows, the problems of coordinating all of the efforts of the business becomes increasingly more difficult.

Depending upon the nature of the organisation itself, we can identify a number of key aims or objectives that are common to many different types of organisation.

Survival

Survival may seem like an obvious aim and you are right in thinking that most organisations tend to think beyond this very basic goal. Unfortunately not all organisations have the luxury of being successful enough not to worry about how they are going to pay their staff and their bills.

Survival becomes important for organisations when they face difficult periods of trading. Perhaps customers do not want their products and services, or the types of customers they supply cannot afford to buy at present. Or, indeed, there may simply be too many competitors. Many organisations over their history face problem times when they have to seriously consider closing down and giving up. In times when survival is the only aim, the organisation may have to lose members of staff, cut costs and ride out the bad period.

CASE STUDY George Prior Engineering

The respected Great Yarmouth company, George Prior Engineering, was set to close on 1 October 2004, after 29 years in business. The company had already laid off 19 of its 48 staff due to lack of orders. In recent years the company had built a strong reputation for restoring historic ships, but major projects had dried up.

In a statement the company said that 'the deterioration of market conditions, both nationally and worldwide, have brought about this decision. Even locally, in Great Yarmouth, it is noticeable the number of vessels in the harbour and the volume of commercial shipping have decreased significantly. All sectors of the marine industry are under increasing financial constraints, which inevitably has a knock-on effect on us as ship repairers. Realistically, due to our size and resources, we are unable to compete with larger shipyards or overseas competitors whose overheads are substantially lower.'

The company statement went on to say that, 'Sadly, the common economic conditions have led to a lack of potential contracts in the immediate future. As a result, it is expected the entire workforce, including the administration team and the directors, will have to be made redundant.'

Guy Frankham, the Administration Director, said the company would honour its obligations to creditors, 'If we do go out, it will be with our heads held high.'

Source: http://business.edp24.co.uk

INDIVIDUAL WORK (1.35) ★ ★

Read the case study 'George Prior Engineering' and answer the following questions.

1 Identify three reasons given by the company for its decision to close down.

2 What will happen to the employees and why might it be difficult for them to find other employment?

3 What is meant by 'honour its obligations to creditors'?

Break-even

A business breaks even when its income is equal to its costs. In cases when its income exceeds its costs, the organisation has made a profit. But when its costs exceed its income, it is said to have made a loss.

In Unit 3 we will investigate how to calculate the break-even point. But for the purposes of this unit we only need concern ourselves with the fact that at the very least all organisations will attempt to ensure that their income covers their costs. Some costs are relatively easy to control. These are known as fixed costs. Typical fixed costs include rent, or perhaps the wage bill, particularly if the staff are being paid salaries. Fixed costs mean that the organisation will always have to find this money, regardless of how busy or how quiet trading may be at a particular time.

Added to the fixed costs are variable costs, which change according to how busy a business finds itself. A busier business may need to take on additional staff, or buy extra products. Generally speaking, the busier a business is the higher their variable costs. An organisation will then add its fixed costs and variable costs together in order to calculate their total costs. These total costs will then be compared to the organisation's income and if the income matches the total costs then the business has broken even.

Growth

Growth is often a natural development for an organisation, but it can sometimes be very risky. Businesses want to grow in order to keep pace with their competitors and, perhaps, to take advantage of their particular expertise or popularity. Growth can be measured in many different ways, from an increase in the overall income of the business, to employing more staff, offering a wider range of products or services or opening other branches or shops in new areas.

For many businesses, growth is a gradual process, financed by profits or loans that allow them to take advantage of the current situation of success. Businesses need to be careful about growing too fast. Whilst they do not want to be overwhelmed by customers that they cannot serve, they do not want to grow too fast and add huge costs

INDIVIDUAL WORK (1.36) ★ ★

1 Imagine that you run a small business. Your costs on rent, rates, electricity and telephone bill are approximately £1,000 per month. The goods you sell each month cost you around £1,000. How much money would you need to make each month to break even?

2 Assume then that your business became more popular and that you had to take on two members of staff that you paid £400 each per month. You also needed to purchase another £1,000 worth of stock each month. What does your income have to be now to break even?

to the running of the organisation without really knowing whether their income will increase. It is usually the case that the larger the organisation, the lower the costs become. Buying in bulk means lower prices and being able to produce more can also lead to cost cuts.

Again, as we will see in Unit 3, there is a strong link between the size of the business, its control of finances and its chances of success or failure.

Profit maximisation

Profit maximisation means selling a product or service with the largest possible difference between the cost of providing it and the price for which it is sold.

Profit maximisation relies on efficiency and making sure that time and money are not wasted on any single process in the production of a product or the providing of a service. It means making the best use of employees, premises and equipment. This is often referred to as producing products or services in the most economical way and then using the reputation of the business to convince the customer to pay the maximum price for the product or service.

Service provision

Many businesses pride themselves on their responsiveness to customers. Indeed, customer service is seen as being one of the most important aspects of a successful business. An organisation will seek to ensure that all contact with customers is of the highest possible quality and that in the event of a problem or complaint the issue is dealt with promptly, efficiently and courteously.

With so many businesses competing for the same customers and offering broadly the same products and services, excellent customer service is often the only reason why a customer will choose one business over another. Successful businesses will seek to understand their customers and what motivates them to buy, as well as making sure that customers find it easy and rewarding to have any form of dealing with the business.

Expansion of market share

Market share is the percentage of sales that are held by a particular organisation in the market. Market share can either be measured in terms of the income generated by sales, or the number of products or service packages sold. Generally speaking, a figure can be placed on a particular market. For example, the total number of a particular product sold throughout the whole of the UK might be 100,000. If a business sold 25,000 products each year it would have a 25 per cent market share. If, through advertising or special offers, it increased its sales to 30,000 a year it would have increased its market share to 30 per cent.

Businesses will obviously attempt to control as much of the market as possible and any increase in sales will mean that a competitor has suffered losses in sales.

Several businesses can increase their overall sales without losing any of their market shares. This is because the market may have grown in size and now, instead of 100,000 products being sold each year, 150,000 products may be sold. They have all increased the number of products sold, but their market share may not have changed.

Objectives

Objectives are meaningless if they cannot be measured or compared to actual progress or results. Aims can be seen as rather more vague targets, but objectives need to be very precise.

Organisations tend to identify the precise elements of their objectives by using what is known as the SMART technique.

SMART

The SMART technique is a way of setting, monitoring and measuring objectives so that it is clear to everyone that either progress has been made, action needs to be taken or the objective has been reached. Table 1.9 explains how a SMART technique could be used for a typical objective.

INDIVIDUAL WORK
(1.37) ★ ★

1 R.L. Anderson Ltd manufactures silk flowers. They sell £750,000 worth on average each year. They have calculated that their eight competitors sell between them £6.25 million worth per year. Calculate Anderson's market share.

2 Andersons decide to buy one of their smaller competitors. They sell £350,000 worth of silk flowers each year. Assuming that Andersons can continue this level of sales, what is their market share now, having bought the smaller company?

Table 1.9
How a SMART technique could be used for a typical objective

Meaning		Explanation	Example
S – Specific		Identifiable and measurable aspects of the objective	Increase sales by 20 per cent.
million– Measurable		Easy to calculate so the organisation knows if it has succeeded or failed	If sales were £1 million last year, they need to be £1.2 million this year.
A – Achievable		Can the organisation make the best use of its resources without setting the standards so high that it is impossible to reach them?	Last year the organisation increased sales from £800,000 to £1 million. Therefore it should be possible and achievable to make the same increase this year.
R – Recognisable		Can everyone in the organisation understand what is being measured?	Sales targets need to be shown in actual figures or percentages.
T – Time constrained (related)		Achieve target by a particular date and monitor the progress to that date	In order to be on target the business needs to achieve a 20 per cent sales increase in a year. They therefore know that to be on target they should have achieved a 10 per cent increase in the first six months.

CASE STUDY Adnams Books Ltd

Harry and Sylvia Adnam run a small book publishing company. They have 20 staff and produce around 50 books each year. The company has recently applied for a large bank loan of £1.2 million to expand. The bank has asked them, amongst other things, to prepare a SMART statement to show how they will expand over the next five years.

Adnams intends to increase the number of books they produce by 25 each year for the next five years. They expect profits to increase by 25 per cent each year. Their current profits are £200,000 each year. They expect to have to take on an extra five members of staff each year.

INDIVIDUAL WORK (1.38) ★★
Using the case study, state the SMART objectives of the business. Make sure that you make a comment against each of the five aspects of SMART related to their objectives.

Targets and milestones

Businesses may often set themselves very broad targets, or objectives. But they have very little hope in being able to achieve them if they do not plan carefully. In order to be on track to achieve a particular objective, a business may have to achieve the objective in carefully planned steps. In other words, it has to make gradual progress towards the objective.

The simplest way to achieve this is to establish when particular actions or events have to take place in the future, which will take them closer to achieving their objective. If the objective, for example, was to increase sales by 20 per cent by the end of the year, then if no progress had been made after six months it would be very unlikely that the objective would be achieved. This means that on particular dates in the run-up to the date when the objective needs to be met, the business will know that it has to have made sufficient progress in order to be successful. It may, for example, choose to review the situation at the end of every month and set targets at the end of each month as part of the overall objectives. Perhaps, in the case of a 20 per cent increase in sales, they may wish to have increased sales by 2 per cent at the end of each month, which should take them beyond their target of 20 per cent.

These smaller milestones, or targets, are far more achievable and much less daunting than the prospect of having to increase sales by 20 per cent overnight. In this way not only can the business monitor its progress, but it can also make adjustments as necessary and reward staff for their contribution each time they are successful.

MANAGEMENT PROCESSES

For organisations to ensure that they make the best use of their resources in order to achieve their aims and objectives, they need to set in place a management system. This management system needs first to organise the employees into logical groups to carry out particular tasks. The management also needs to ensure that these groups, or departments, which collectively contribute towards particular activities, are able to interact with one another and understand what other parts of the organisation are doing at any given time.

The management also needs to ensure that the performance of each of the parts of the organisation is acceptable and that any targets that have been set are being reached, or exceeded. In complicated organisations that have a number of different departments, failure in one of the departments could spell failure for the organisation as a whole. If the management recognises that there are problems then they will need to address the issue as quickly and as efficiently as possible, in order to ensure that overall performance is not affected.

Specialisation of labour into functional tasks and departments

Every organisation has its own way of structuring the functions, or tasks, that need to be carried out. Although the following section covers many common tasks or departments, not all organisations choose to divide their staff up into these particular areas. Some organisations may put their administration together with their finance operations; others may put marketing and research and development together, while, just as commonly, sales and the customer service function may be carried out by the same people.

Administration

Effective communication is the responsibility of all parts of the organisation. Each department has some degree of responsibility for communicating information to the rest of the organisation.

Many organisations have a central administration. The main function of an administration department is to control paperwork and to support all of the other departments, particularly by servicing their needs for secretarial work or administration duties, such as filing, mailing and data handling.

The role of administration departments has largely given way as a result of networked computer systems in businesses. It is probably more accurate to describe administration departments as being office services. They are involved in supplying equipment, stationery, training and, above all, organising effective communications within the organisation. This of course would include the distribution of documents and effective telephone and communication systems.

GROUP WORK (1.39)

★ ★

In groups of two or three, think of at least five routine tasks carried out by a member of an administration department.

Customer service

Employees become involved in customer service if they have any direct contact with the customer. Dealing with customers requires effective systems to handle enquiries and problems efficiently. Businesses wish to learn from any interaction they have with their customers and increasingly businesses keep records of dealings they have had with customers. Effective customer service means being able to negotiate and deal with even the most complicated problem or the most difficult customer.

You will be studying customer service in much more detail in Units 2 and 7 of this course.

Distribution

Distribution deals with the transferring of products from the supplier to the customer. There needs to be an accurate and efficient system in place to monitor the location and the status of all of these movements. Businesses try to keep their distribution costs down and constantly look for more efficient ways of moving products from warehouses to retail outlets or from retail outlets to their customers.

Larger organisations have very sophisticated distribution systems, including a network of warehouses that store the products before they are either sent out to the customer or distributed to retail outlets. Large warehouses use automated systems to move stock around the building and to keep an accurate tally of the stock levels of every product being stored.

Facilities management

Facilities management brings together a range of services, including buildings, office layout, air conditioning, furniture, telephones and computer networking. It aims to deal with the management of the facilities in order to make the working environment more efficient and to reduce costs.

Efficient facilities management can help with staff morale, **staff retention** and profitability. Typically, facilities management will attempt to create a working environment in which all staff can work to their maximum efficiency with the minimum amount of disruption and negative impact on their work.

Finance

Businesses need to keep records of all money coming into and leaving the business. These records allow the business to track their finances and assist them in controlling their spending and income levels and, ultimately, calculate whether they are breaking even, operating at a loss or making a profit.

Larger businesses have their own finance or accounts departments and these bigger organisations may have as many as three different types of accountants working for them.

- *Financial accountants* keep a record of spending and see how the spending has affected the profits.
- *Cost accountants* calculate the costs of the business and enable the business to identify which of their products and services are the most profitable.
- *Management accountants* handle the income and expenditure of the business's activities. They are able to set targets and allocate **budgets** to departments within the business.

IT

Many larger businesses need a dedicated information technology (IT) or computer service department. Their responsibility includes hardware, software, maintenance of databases, telecommunications and other computer-related equipment within the business. Most organisations use computers for a wide variety of different tasks and therefore the department that maintains these needs to be aware of new developments in technology. They provide support and guidance to regular users of computers.

We look in far more detail at the use of computers as a means of communication in Unit 4.

Marketing

The main function of the marketing department is to try to identify customer requirements. They also need to try to predict customer needs in the future. Usually marketing works very closely with the sales department. The marketing department may carry out extensive research on a particular market to try to find out exactly what customers want, where they want it, how much they want to pay for it and the best ways in which customers can be told about it.

The marketing department also works very closely with research and development, as well as production, as together they can produce attractive and saleable products and services. One of the most obvious responsibilities of the marketing department is to design and develop advertising ideas and marketing campaigns.

Personnel management

The personnel, or human resource, department is responsible for the well-being of the workforce so that they can contribute fully to the organisation. The department deals with the hiring and firing of employees, training, staff welfare, leave and pay.

Keyword

staff retention – an important aspect for a business, which involves trying to keep experienced and trained members of staff rather than giving them a reason to move to alternative employment

Keyword

budget – a business or a department's planned income and expenditure

The personnel department maintains records on all members of the workforce, both those working full time and part time. Increasingly these records are entered into specialised personnel computer software. The personnel department has links with all other departments within an organisation and they are closely involved in making sure that the workforce is working efficiently and effectively.

The full details of how personnel departments work are covered in Unit 5.

Production

The production department is involved in all of the functions related to producing goods or services for the customer. The production department monitors levels of waste to ensure the most efficient use of resources and checks the cost of raw materials and parts purchased to make sure the profit margins are maintained. The production department will also ensure that necessary machinery and equipment are purchased in order to produce products and, in close cooperation with the sales department, they will attempt to ensure that sufficient stocks of products are available to coincide with a sales campaign.

The production department will also be concerned with the amount of products being produced, their quality and their packaging.

Research and development

The research and development department works very closely with the marketing department, keeping a check on competitors' products and services. The main function of the department is not only to design new products and services, but to work out the most efficient method of producing or offering them. The department carries out a number of tests and checks designs, usually with the close assistance of the production department, who will have to make the products. The production department is closely involved at all stages, as they will have to produce the product according to strict standards and quality levels.

The department will also randomly test products being manufactured to make sure that they meet quality standards and they will also test competitors' products to see whether the organisation's products compare favourably to them. They will also keep a close eye on technological advances to see if design and production processes can be improved.

Sales

The sales department ultimately has the responsibility of convincing customers to buy the organisation's products and services. Assuming that the marketing department has correctly identified a product or service that is needed by customers and the research and development and production department have managed to create a product or service of sufficient quality, then in theory the sales department should have a relatively simple task. Unfortunately, however, no matter how superior a product or service may be, there is enormous competition in every market. The sales department employs experienced members of staff who have built up relationships with customers and can answer many of the questions and queries posed and deal with any doubts the customers may have.

The nature of a sales department differs from business to business. Some sales departments simply deal with other businesses, whilst others sell direct to the public. There is much more detail about sales in Unit 7.

Linking of functional activities and departments

It is important that we look at some of the different ways that an organisation will structure itself, as this has an impact on the way the owners can communicate with their employees. The structure of an organisation will vary depending on a number of factors, including:

- The size and nature of the market in which it operates (are there many customers and where are they?).
- The type of activity in which it is involved (what is made or sold?).

INDIVIDUAL WORK
(1.40) ★ ★
If you worked in the mailroom of an organisation, to which department would you send the following items of post?

a) A job application
b) An invoice requesting payment
c) An inventor's idea for a new product
d) A catalogue of office furniture
e) A box of keyboards
f) An office stationery catalogue

- The need to maintain good communications (how are communications carried out?).
- The size of the organisation (the number of employees).
- The number of branches or sites involved (locations).
- The type and number of customers (consumers or other businesses).
- How much it is affected by government legislation (laws relating to the business).
- The impact of new technology on the business (the use of machines and computers).
- How it was structured in the past (its history and the way in which the structure has developed).
- Its future plans (short, medium and long term).

Hierarchies

The best way to understand what a hierarchical structure looks like is to imagine a pyramid. At the top of the pyramid are the owners/directors, who make the decisions, but as you look further down, the pyramid widens. As it widens, more and more employees are involved, so the majority of the employees are at the base of the pyramid. The responsibility, power and authority are all much greater at the top of the pyramid and communication flows down from the top to the bottom. This type of structure would have the owners or the directors at the top, the departmental managers next, and the more junior employees at the bottom.

Flat structures reduce the number of layers involved in a hierarchical structure. The theory behind having fewer layers in the pyramid is that decisions can be made more quickly and efficiently. Each layer is able to communicate more easily with the other layers and this type of structure is often found in organisations that operate from a single site where all employees can meet with each other readily.

There are two further terms that we need to understand when considering the business structure and communication flows. These are:

- **Chain of command** – this is the structure of the organisation which shows how many levels of management there are and how information or instructions are passed up and down the organisation.
- **Span of control** – this relates to the number of individuals who report directly to a single manager.

> **Keyword**
>
> **chain of command –** the number of levels of management and how information is passed up and down the organisation
>
> **span of control** – the number of employees who are controlled by one manager or a supervisor

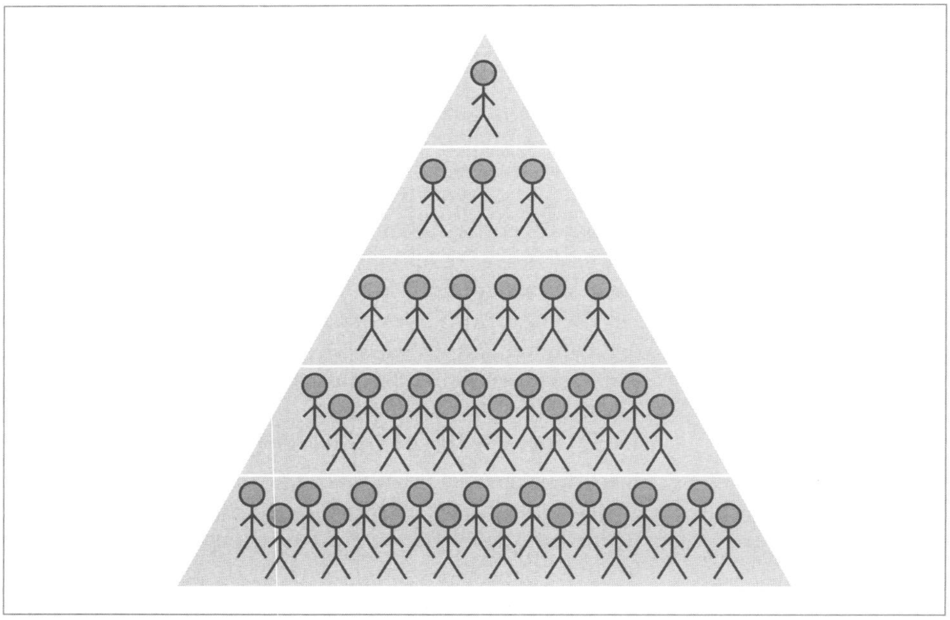

Figure 1.9
An example of a hierarchical structure

However large or small the business and whatever type of organisational structure is in place, it is important that the owners communicate their plans to those who will carry them through. A plan is most certainly more effective if it is written down, making it clear as to the nature of the actions, the timescales involved and the way in which the plan is likely to be implemented. It is not good practice for the owner of any business, however small, to pass on information only via word of mouth, as this can be an unreliable form of communication.

> **GROUP** WORK (1.41)
> ★ ★ ★
>
> Draw a pyramid like the one shown in Figure 1.9. Use the information below to draw the hierarchical structure of the business by placing the job roles in the correct section of the pyramid.
>
> Harry, Clive and Sheila – shop assistants
> Judith and Kevin – trainee shop assistants
> Luke and Rachel – assistant managers
> Tracy, Malcolm and Dave – part-time shop assistants
> Heather – shop manager
> Reggie – regional manager

Departments

A manager is someone who takes responsibility for running the business on a day-to-day basis. In a very small business, the managers may also be the owners and they will be responsible for every aspect of the business. However, in larger businesses the owner and/or the board of directors will communicate the plan to the individual managers who will help to implement it. It is worth mentioning at this stage that the managers of a large organisation are also usually employees of the business. There are likely to be a number of managers in charge of different aspects of the business activities, including:

- Human Resources Department – also known as the Personnel Department, deals with the recruitment, organisation and training of the employees of the business.
- Finance Department – in addition to paying the wages and salaries of the employees, monitors the income and expenditure of the business.
- Production Department – involved in all functions related to producing the products or services for the customer to buy.
- Purchasing Department – involved in buying all of the materials required for the business to function.
- Distribution Department – responsible for ensuring the safe storage of the business's products and the transportation of them to the customers.
- Sales and Marketing Department – sometimes these are two separate departments, but their main responsibilities lie in making sure that the customer is aware of the products that the business offers and then selling them to the customer.
- Administration Department – controls all of the paperwork and supports the other departments by servicing their needs for secretarial work, e.g. filing, mailing, handling information, etc.
- Research and Development Department – works closely with the marketing department by keeping a constant check on the products being offered for sale by competitors. It also develops new products for the business to sell.
- Quality Control Department – often part of the production department, it tries to maintain a consistently high-quality product.
- Computer (IT) Services Department – responsible for the hardware and software that the business uses, as well as the maintenance of telecommunications and other technological office development. It will ensure that the employees are using the most appropriate equipment and that they are trained in any new technology that the business acquires.

The manager's role in any of the above departments is to interpret and then communicate the plan to his or her employees. Without effective communication at this level, the individual employees will not have a clear understanding of their roles and responsibilities in carrying out the plan. The manager needs to make sure that the employees all understand the:

- Nature of the task they are expected to undertake.
- Timescales involved.
- Resources available, such as the right equipment and tools, the amount of time and finance, a place to work, etc.
- Expected outcome.

If the manager fails to communicate the plan and its associated tasks, the employees are unlikely to be able to complete the work successfully. Remember, if there are no goal posts it is unlikely that goals can be scored; if the rules are not clear then these may be broken or ignored; and if there is no clear deadline then it is difficult to work to an effective time plan. It is therefore the manager's role to:

- Communicate effectively the tasks that need to be undertaken.
- Give clear instructions as to the time the task should take.
- Provide the resources available to carry out the work.
- Give a clear indication as to what the end result should look like.
- Seek feedback from the employees that they understand the nature of the task and the associated issues relating to how it will be completed.

> **Keyword**
>
> **demotivated** – to lack an enjoyment of work and therefore carry out one's job less effectively

Another role of the manager is to ensure that those employees who are expected to meet the objectives are trained and instructed effectively. If an employee is unable to complete the task because of lack of training, then not only will the objectives not be met, but the employee may become what is known as **demotivated**.

Monitoring of performance

Performance management is the process of planning, implementing, monitoring and improving the efficiency and effectiveness of organisations and their staff. Performance management is a process which needs to be learned, documented and improved.

Usually, the process of performance management has four major stages:

1 Planning performance requirements
2 Implementing planned activities
3 Monitoring performance levels
4 Improving activities.

Performance monitoring has a number of advantages at various levels for the organisation. For the organisation itself, it allows the individual performance of an employee to be fitted into the overall needs of the organisation as well as allowing for planning, development and review.

At the employee level, it gives employees a sense of direction, provides an indication as to the training they need and allows the organisation to reward them for meeting particular targets. Performance monitoring is also useful for teams and departments as they can design their own work plans and know exactly what is expected of them and when it is expected.

Annual objectives and short-term targets

Objectives and targets begin at the top of the organisation, as the senior management will determine the overall objectives of the organisation. A plan can be written to measure overall performance and, from this general plan, individual plans for departments, teams and individuals can be written. The whole system needs to be integrated (so that it all fits together and everyone is moving in the same direction).

Table 1.10 is a typical integrated plan to monitor performance, objectives and short-term targets. Short-term targets are easily reached steps on the path to meeting the objectives themselves. The term 'strategic' used in the table refers to the overall plan of the organisation.

Table 1.10
A typical integrated plan to monitor performance, objectives and short-term targets

Month	Strategy	Team	Individual
1	Prepare information for strategic planning and allocate responsibility.		
2	Carry out a strategic analysis of current plan.		
3	Create a draft of the strategic plan. Then complete a second draft from the feedback from employees and managers.		
4	Talk to all people involved outside and inside the organisation, gather feedback from them and then write a third draft of the plan.	Prepare information for a business plan. Identify current year priorities from strategic plan. Use these as the foundation for the business plan.	
5	Finalise the strategic plan.	Create a draft of the business plan.	
6		Talk to all those involved outside and inside the organisation and using the feedback create a second draft of the plan.	Identify the improvements needed and any training needs to help ensure that the individual's contribution to the business plan can be successful.
7		Test draft two with all persons who contributed to draft one. Finalise the business plan for next year (July–June).	Prepare for development of next year's individual performance agreements. Inform staff and provide guidelines.
8	First quarterly review of strategic plan performance.	Finalise budget for next year, based on business plan.	Develop individual performance agreement, including learning and development action plan, for period 1 July–30 June.
9			Collect all individual performance agreements, including learning and development action plans.
10		First bi-monthly review of business plan performance.	
11	Second quarterly review of strategic plan performance.		
12		Second bi-monthly review of business plan performance.	First review for period 1 July–31 October.
13			
14		Third bi-monthly review of business plan performance.	
15			
16		Fourth bi-monthly review of business plan performance.	Second review for period 1 July–28 February.
17			
18		Fifth bi-monthly review of business plan performance.	Feed performance improvement requirements and learning and development needs into business planning process for following year.
19			
20	Fourth quarterly review of strategic plan performance.	Sixth bi-monthly review of business plan performance.	Annual performance review and overall assessment discussion.

Performance indicators

Key Performance Indicators (KPIs), or Key Success Indicators (KSIs), help an organisation define and measure progress towards their objectives.

Once an organisation has analysed its objectives, identified all its **stakeholders**, and defined its goals, it needs a way to measure the progress toward those goals. Key Performance Indicators are those measurements.

Key Performance Indicators are measurements, agreed beforehand, that identify the success factors of an organisation. They will differ depending on the organisation. For example, a business may have as one of its Key Performance Indicators the percentage of its income that comes from regular customers, or a school may see its Key Performance Indicators as the number of students obtaining high grades in examinations.

Whatever the Key Performance Indicators an organisation chooses, the most important thing is that they must be measurable. The goals for a particular Key Performance Indicator may change as the organisation's goals change, or as it gets closer to achieving a goal.

Corrective action

Performance monitoring should highlight, at the earliest possible point, any problems with reaching targets or objectives. Once a problem has been identified, the organisation will move as quickly as possible to deal with the situation. It will probably have already thought about what it can do in the event of a problem. These are often known as contingency plans. This means that an alternative plan has already been written, which aims to deal with problems that the organisation had considered might arise.

If the problem is sufficiently serious then a senior manager will probably be assigned to take immediate control and solve the situation. At departmental level, the manager in charge of the teams will be held responsible for sorting out the problem, perhaps assigning the job to some of the department's staff.

There are a number of problems that could arise, and we will deal with each of these under the following headings.

Matching performance to planned performance

As we have seen in Table 1.10, the systems put in place to monitor performance should pick up on problems almost as soon as they arise. The monthly and quarterly reviews that compare actual performance to planned performance will quickly identify how and where particular problems have cropped up and it will also identify who should now take corrective action to deal with the situation.

As all relevant stakeholders, both inside and outside the organisation, have been involved in setting the planned targets and objectives, they should all be aware of what is expected. They should know what steps to take if actual performance is different from planned performance. If organisations have missed something vital that is affecting their actual performance, they will adjust their objectives to suit. Usually, however, as the monitoring takes place at such regular intervals, problems that arise should not become too large to handle.

Dealing with over-production

Over-production takes place when the actual demand for products or services is considerably less than was expected. An organisation will usually set its production targets by looking at sales in the past and any changes in the market or customer demand that they can confidently predict. In many cases, production does not necessarily match what the organisation expected. If the organisation had predicted far higher sales than is actually the case, the business would have to take immediate steps to cut back production, otherwise they would be left with stock that they cannot sell.

Holding additional stock has a number of problems. Not only is there the problem of storing the products, but also there is considerable money tied up in the stock that they cannot sell. Businesses try to constantly adjust their production to match the actual demand. They will always have a small amount of stock in reserve and this is often called buffer stock. This buffer stock helps the business be prepared for a slight rise in demand that can be satisfied by their reserved stock.

Over-production can ruin an organisation, as they would have bought in raw materials and parts to make more products than they can sell. They would have set up their machinery and taken on employees to make a particular level of stock each month or each year. Organisations are therefore very careful in setting their production levels and whilst they do not want to disappoint the customer by not being able to supply them, equally they do not want to have enormous warehouses full of stock that they cannot sell. Production, therefore, is very much a balancing act and over-production is always a danger.

Dealing with over-spending

The organisation itself, the departments and teams will all have been allocated a budget. Each part of the organisation is known as a cost centre. This means that the wage and salary bill, the costs of housing the department and all other expenses have been calculated and the department is not meant to spend more than its budget.

Monitoring spending by constantly comparing spending to the budgets is the role of an accounts or finance department. Usually a cost accountant will keep a track of the spending and deduct this from the department's budget each time a bill is paid. If the cost accountant is doing their job correctly then over-spending will quickly be identified and the department involved can be told about the situation and be expected to cut back on spending.

Although the budgets are carefully worked out, it is not always possible to be accurate in assessing just how much a particular part of an organisation will need to spend. There may be unavoidable expenses, perhaps equipment has broken down and needs to be replaced or the department needs to take on additional staff. Before the department makes any decision about spending this extra money, not only will the cost accountant be informed but also the senior management will have to approve the additional spending.

Over-spending has severe implications for a business. Each extra pound spent is one less pound made in profit. Organisations try to keep a very tight control on spending and although it is not always possible to avoid unexpected expenses, all parts of the organisation are expected to stay within their budget unless they have a very good reason to do otherwise.

Dealing with under-selling

Under-selling occurs when, once again, the predicted amount of sales is actually less than was expected. There may be many reasons why this has happened. Many organisations base their predicted sales figures on what has happened in the past and a prediction of what might happen in the near future. Sales departments will also be given targets, either in terms of total sales value or number of products or services sold.

It is not always possible to predict accurately what might happen, even in the very near future. Many things can change that are outside of the control of the business. A rise in the cost of borrowing money could lead to a fall in sales. The closure of a local business that has put several hundred people out of work would result in them having less money to spend and therefore lead to a fall in sales.

Airlines and travel companies could not have predicted, when they set their sales targets, that people would be frightened to travel by air after the attacks on New York on 11 September 2001. This resulted in a fall in the number of people travelling across the Atlantic, a general drop in the number of people travelling by air and, therefore, a fall in sales for all airlines and travel companies.

CASE STUDY Trouble in the high street

Swan and Greaves estate agency had been enjoying an enormous increase in the number of house sales in the area. They had opened two new branches and taken on 10 new members of staff. Then there was a slump in house sales.

Their wage bill had increased by 200 per cent to £220,000 per month, yet even with the new staff on average they were only bringing in an extra £70,000 per month. They were still able to cover all their costs, but only just and they were finding it difficult to pay the local newspapers for the large advertisements. It was clear that the business was over-spending and something had to be done.

INDIVIDUAL WORK (1.42)

The estate agents in the case study had hoped that the increase in costs would be more than covered by an increase in income.

1 Why might the fortunes of a business such as Swan and Greaves be affected by a poor economy and an increase in interest rates?

2 If the estate agency had increased their wage bill by 200 per cent, would it be reasonable to expect the business's income to increase by a similar percentage?

Unit Revision Questions

1 Explain the word 'profit'.

2 What is a mission statement?

3 What is a wholesaler?

4 What is a shareholder?

5 What is a QUANGO?

6 What is an SME?

7 What is the primary sector?

8 What are domestic customers?

9 List five forms of seasonal work.

10 What is a merchandiser?

11 What is credit?

12 What is payroll?

13 What does it mean if a business manages to break even?

14 What is market share?

15 What is SMART?

16 In business terms, what is a milestone?

17 What is facilities management?

18 What is a span of control?

19 What is a stakeholder?

20 What is a contingency plan?

UNIT 2

Exploring Key Business Pressures

This unit aims to help you appreciate the fact that businesses operate in an environment that is constantly changing. Businesses face new and different pressures on almost a daily basis, either from their customers, competitors or other sources that threaten their chances of survival and hopes of growth. Understanding the market and customers is vital for businesses to perform successfully.

The unit looks at stakeholders, which includes any group or set of individuals that can have an impact on the business. The unit also looks at the external influences that can affect the business's chances of success and long-term achievement. In an increasingly global market, businesses face challenges at every turn that can affect their activities.

This unit is internally assessed and requires you to demonstrate that you understand all of the learning outcomes for the unit. You will need to understand how businesses adapt their activities in response to external and internal pressures. To achieve this, you must:

- Investigate the responses of businesses to customer expectations
- Explore the responses of businesses to competitive pressures
- Consider the impact on businesses of stakeholder expectations
- Examine the impact on businesses of key political, economic, social, technological and other external influences.

CUSTOMER EXPECTATIONS

Every business organisation now faces more effective competition than ever before. Competition no longer comes just from other businesses in the local area, but from national, European and even international organisations. This means that customers have an even greater choice. So whatever edge a business can obtain is vital to their success and survival.

Increasingly this means that businesses can no longer produce products or provide services and then simply hope to convince the public and other businesses to buy them. This 'make first then try to sell' technique rarely works any more and all businesses need to be aware of their customers' demands and match their expectations.

Customer expectations can be described as what the customer wants or demands in terms of quality, reliability, price and service from the organisation. These demands, or expectations, are high, because if a customer feels that an organisation cannot, or will not, offer what they expect then they buy from one of their competitors. Organisations are well aware of the choices offered to their potential customers and, according to how competitive the market is, they will have to make sure a competitor does not beat them on price, quality and service.

GROUP WORK (2.1)
★ ★

In pairs, make a list of at least five products that you both purchase regularly. For each product, you should decide what your expectations are from it. Do you both have the same expectations? Or do your expectations vary? If so, discuss why you think this is the case.

Markets

A business will try to identify the type of person or business that is most likely to buy its products and services. It does this by attempting to identify the common features, or characteristics, of these customers. Some businesses will focus on age or **gender**, whilst others will focus on the frequency of the customer's purchases of products or services from the organisation. As we will see, each customer, an individual or a business, has certain attributes that the organisation attempts to identify to help increase sales.

Sets of customers

For our purposes we need to identify three distinct sets of customers:

- Normally the term 'customer' can refer to an individual or a business. Usually a customer pays for the products and services they receive.

- 'Consumers' are usually individual customers, such as people who purchase products from a supermarket. You will often hear the term 'the consumer market' and this refers to individual members of the public as customers, rather than other businesses.

- The term 'client' is also used to describe customers. It has several different meanings. For example, a professional, such as an accountant or solicitor, would refer to their customers as clients whether they are other businesses or individuals. 'Client' is also often used by the public services. Dentists, doctors, social services and opticians often refer to their customers as clients rather than customers. Hairdressers, beauticians and cosmetic surgeons also prefer to use 'client' rather than 'customer' or 'consumer'.

In identifying the type of customer, the business seeks to match both its products and services to their expectations, as well as designing their advertising and publicity to suit their particular type of customer.

Internal and external markets

The terms 'customer', 'client' or 'consumer' are not just restricted to individuals or businesses outside the organisation. Indeed, any customer outside the organisation is referred to as an *external market*. In other words, they do not have any close association with the business itself; they are merely customers of the business.

Particularly in larger organisations, such as the National Health Service, there is what is known as an *internal market*. Parts of the organisation deal solely with customers within the organisation itself. An information technology department in a hospital, for example, would be responsible for installing and maintaining computer equipment for the rest of the hospital. They would not have external customers, as they do not deal with consumers.

In the same way, other large organisations have specialist departments that just service the needs of other parts of the organisation, for example administration would deal with routine and non-routine paperwork for the whole of the business. The personnel department would be responsible for recruitment and training of all members of staff within an organisation.

Customers

Retail buyers

For most high street stores, their primary customer is the retail buyer. As we have seen, they are known as consumers as they are the end users of the products and services sold by the high street shops.

There have been enormous changes in retail shopping over the past few decades. Not only has there been an increase in out-of-town shopping, which has led to the closure of many small retail shops in town and city centres, but there has also been an increase in the number of businesses setting up chains of stores around the country which broadly offer the same products and services, regardless of whether the store is in Glasgow or Guildford.

Retail customers are notoriously difficult to retain as loyal buyers. Supermarkets have been at the forefront of trying to ensure customer loyalty. They have developed customer loyalty programmes that offer their consumers an opportunity to benefit from continuing to buy from that particular store. Many other retail outlets, such as computer game sellers, electrical goods, clothing retailers and even petrol stations have developed customer loyalty cards to encourage their existing customers not to shop elsewhere.

As if the competition in the retail parks and high streets were not enough, retail outlets now have to deal with the increasing competition from online retailers. Many customers have discovered that it is far more convenient to shop online when it suits them, rather than visit a retail store during opening hours. To deal with this competition, some retail stores are opening for longer hours and often on a Sunday. Nonetheless, the shift from the traditional high street to the retail park and now to online shopping is continuing.

CASE STUDY Loyalty cards

Recent research has shown that some 67 per cent of UK adults have at least one store loyalty card. Around 40 per cent have Tesco Clubcards, 31 per cent Boots Advantage Cards and 27 per cent have Nectar Cards. Some 61 per cent of Tesco Clubcard holders always use their card when shopping in the store. Fifty-three per cent use their Boots Advantage Card and 58 per cent use their Nectar Card.

Despite many people using their cards, in recent research 86 per cent said they would trade their card for lower prices in the stores, whilst only 9 per cent said they would be happy to keep their loyalty card and not have lower prices.

GROUP WORK (2.2) ★ ★
Read the case study and answer the following questions.

1 How many people in your class or group have store loyalty cards?
2 Which stores or businesses offer the Nectar Card?
3 Why might people obtain store loyalty cards and then not use them?

Other businesses

intermediaries – businesses or individuals that are part of the distribution chain and handle products between the manufacturer and the consumer
public relations – using contacts in the media in order to ensure positive stories about the business are featured
consumables – items used by a business in the general course of their operations, which are not part of the products or services that they sell

Keyword

Many businesses do not have direct contact with members of the public as far as their buying and selling is concerned. Manufacturers, for example, tend to sell to other businesses that they refer to as **intermediaries**, which handle the distribution on to the public on their behalf. Many other manufacturers do not produce products that are suitable or designed for the public. Therefore, their primary customers are other businesses.

Typically, a food manufacturer, for example, would sell their products to wholesalers or supermarket chains, which would in turn sell the products on to members of the public, as consumers. Many other businesses, particularly in the service sector, deal solely with other businesses. They may provide financial support and advice, legal assistance, design, marketing and **public relations** support.

Central and local government departments

Both central and local government consume products and services just like any other business or organisation. Not only do they require office equipment, **consumables** (such as stationery), technical support, vehicles and vehicle maintenance and a host of other support services, they may also purchase products and services on behalf of others.

For example, local government is responsible for refuse collection. In some areas they provide each household with a bin or a series of refuse bins. These have to be purchased from the manufacturer. In other areas, they may still be using disposable sacks, which again have to be purchased from a manufacturer and then distributed to households.

In the majority of cases, when selling products or services to central or local government, a supplier will have to be approved and checked for their competitive prices and reliability.

In some cases, however, businesses that wish to sell products or services to government departments will have to bid for the opportunity to do so. This process is known as *competitive tendering*. Each business interested in providing the products or services is given a detailed description of what the department wishes to purchase. The business then decides the price at which they can afford to sell the products or services to the department and puts this amount in a letter, in a sealed envelope. This is then delivered by a specified date to the department and, after the date has passed, the department opens all of the bids and chooses the business that has offered to provide the products or services at the lowest possible cost.

CASE STUDY Best value

Since around 2000, local councils, the police and fire authorities, amongst others, have had a legal obligation to continually improve the standard and efficiency of their services. This has meant bringing in outside contractors when needed. The term 'best value' has effectively replaced compulsory competitive tendering, as this was considered to be more concerned with cost-cutting than quality of service. Local councils are now required to draw up an annual Best Value Performance Plan and their progress is measured against Best Value Performance Indicators, monitored by an independent body known as the Audit Commission.

GROUP WORK (2.3)

In pairs, visit the Audit Commission website at: www.audit-commission.gov.uk. On the home page click on Best Value Performance Indicators, then answer the following questions.

1 What was the name of the Act in 2000 that gave local authorities new powers?

2 What are ACPIs?

3 Where is the Audit Commission based?

4 Where can you find definitions of performance indicators that local authorities use?

discount – a reduction in the price of an order. It would be offered for a variety of reasons, including the payment of cash and if the customer orders regularly from the business

Voluntary sector organisations

Voluntary sector organisations are, in many respects, very similar to local and central government departments. They, too, are concerned with ensuring that the best value for money is obtained by the organisation for products and services.

Many businesses offer voluntary sector organisations significant **discounts** because the voluntary sector organisations are non-profit making bodies. Voluntary sector organisations have very tight financial controls, as most of the funding they receive, after having paid any necessary expenses such as wages, is used to provide the service that they have been set up to offer.

Customer attributes

An organisation cannot hope to satisfy the needs and wants of all consumers. Organisations segment, or break up, the market into sections, which display similar characteristics or behaviour. There are a number of segmentation characteristics that allow an organisation to divide their market into recognisable groups. We will look at market segmentation in much more detail later, but here are the main characteristics.

Age

Age is linked to an individual's purchasing power, that is, an individual's ability to independently make a choice and purchase a product or service.

Many products and services are specifically aimed at particular age groups. During children's television on independent networks (not the BBC, which does not carry advertising), the majority of the advertisements are for toys, games, music and food and drink.

The UK's birth rate has remained relatively stable over the past 20 years and women tend to live longer than men. Its population of around 60 million gives the UK an average age for men of 35 years and for women 38 years.

Buying patterns

Businesses can rate their customers in terms of the frequency of their purchases of products and services from the business. Regular customers could be described as

GROUP WORK (2.4)

★ ★ ★

In pairs, discuss the implications for the following types of business in these particular circumstances:

1 Assuming that people are living longer but are still encountering health problems, what might be the problems faced by a private health insurer?

2 If there were fewer teenagers in the country, what would be the implications for further and higher education and the music industry?

heavy users of products and services. Customers who purchase fairly regularly could be described as medium users. Customers who are less frequent are often described as light users.

Businesses are also interested in occasional customers and, of course, potential customers who used to buy from the business but no longer do so, or potential customers who have never purchased from the business.

A business will tend to concentrate initially on ensuring that its heavy, medium and light users are retained as loyal customers and, if possible, that the frequency of buying is increased. They will also make attempts to persuade occasional users, or lost customers, to start buying from the business once more.

INDIVIDUAL WORK
(2.5) ★

Think about TV advertising and why a business chooses to advertise their products and services at such a high cost. Are they advertising to:

a) Attract new customers?

b) Remind existing customers that the products and services they offer are still available?

Most TV advertising is aimed at the broadest possible range of existing or potential customers. As there is so much competition for customers, even loyal customers have to be continually reminded that they are better-off dealing with a business with which they already have a relationship.

Family status

Many organisations take the family status of their customers extremely seriously, particularly in the case of consumers as customers. Aside from the fact that around 30 per cent of all births are outside marriage, businesses use what is known as a *family life cycle* to describe the characteristics of their customers:

▹ The life cycle usually begins when we leave our parent's home and become independent for the first time. Businesses will specifically target these groups, which are interested in fashion, recreation and holidays.

▹ Once we are married or with a partner, possibly with two incomes but no children, setting up a home is the most important concern and these types of customers are interested in buying household items.

▹ Once children become part of the family, we tend to borrow more money on credit and purchase necessities rather than luxuries.

▹ As the children grow older, both parents tend to go back to work and, as there is more money in the household, holidays and luxuries become affordable.

▹ When the children have left the family home, the parents are interested in travel, recreation and home improvements.

▹ When one of the partners is left alone, hobbies become important, as do health matters.

Gender

Some businesses and organisations specifically target their products and services to appeal to a particular gender. Some products are specifically designed for a single gender, such as clothes, shoes and cosmetics. Other products could equally be used, and indeed are used, by both genders, but they have been advertised to appeal to one sex or the other. For example, some cars can be considered to be women's cars and their advertising is designed to reflect this.

GROUP WORK (2.6)
★ ★

1 Try to think of at least five products or services that could be used by either gender but are specifically aimed at appealing to just one gender.

2 Think of five products that are specifically aimed at females and five others that are specifically aimed at males.

Location

We can identify customers as either being local, regional, national or international. Many businesses are geared up to cater for one or more of these groups.

- A high street newsagent, for example, would primarily cater for local customers.

- A large, out-of-town shopping centre could well cater for both local and regional customers.

- Large businesses based near major transport links could cater for local, regional and national customers.

- Many businesses, via catalogues, mail-order systems and websites, can now cater for customers all around the world.

Customers tend to purchase regular items, such as food, from local or regional centres. They are more inclined to purchase items such as clothes and electrical goods either from regional, national or even international sources.

Being able to pay for products and services on the internet, using secure payment systems, has revolutionised the way we shop. Customers are no longer concerned with having a restricted choice in local or regional stores and, if they feel that they can find a better product or service at a better price, they are more inclined to purchase via the internet or from conventional catalogues and mail order.

Organisational size

An organisation's size, in terms of its characteristics as a customer, has two key features as far as a supplying business is concerned.

- The overall size of the organisation as a business customer will probably determine exactly how much that business purchases in products and services. A larger business customer will require a larger quantity of products and services over a year.

- Except possibly for the smallest business customers, these businesses will have their own purchasing department.

Usually the larger the business as a customer, the more sophisticated their purchasing requirements.

Needs and wants

Needs and wants are often referred to by sales and marketing specialists, as they often determine exactly how a potential customer sees a particular product or service. Certain products and services are absolute, basic needs, such as food, clothing and shelter. For a business customer needs will include vital products and services without which the business could not run.

In addition to these basic needs, customers often have wants. These are products and services that the customer desires to have, but does not need in order to survive, either as an individual or as a business.

As far as the general public as consumers are concerned, we are constantly exposed to advertising which tries to persuade us that we *need* the things that we want. Businesses are keen to change customers' views of products and services so that they become absolutely necessary, rather than just desirable.

Socio-economic group

Customers' attributes can be classified according to their socio-economic group. This has been done since 2001 using the National Statistics Socio-Economic Classification (NS-SEC), drawn up by the Office for National Statistics.

The NS-SEC is an occupation-based classification which has rules to provide coverage of the whole adult population. This classification is now used for most analyses and has eight classes, as shown in Table 2.1.

Table 2.1
The classes of the National Statistics Socio-Economic Classification

1		Higher managerial and professional occupations
	1.1	Large employers and higher managerial occupations
	1.2	Higher professional occupations
2		Lower managerial and professional occupations
3		Intermediate occupations
4		Small employers and own account workers
5		Lower supervisory and technical occupations
6		Semi-routine occupations
7		Routine occupations
8		Never worked and long-term unemployed

GROUP WORK (2.7)
★ ★

1 Using Table 2.1, what do you think is meant by the following terms?
   a) Professional occupations
   b) Semi-routine and routine occupations.

2 List five products or services provided by businesses or organisations aimed at Group 8 in the table.

Market segmentation

In all markets, different groups of customers have different needs. The market for any product can be split into individual *segments*, comprising clusters of users and customers who have similar requirements, characteristics and tastes. Market segmentation and positioning are critical activities in product design. They are crucial to ensure that the product features match the requirements of the target customers. The process can be considered in four stages:

1 Defining the total market
2 Segmenting the market
3 Targeting an opportunity
4 Positioning a potential solution.

It is difficult to segment a market unless it is first clearly defined. A market can be defined very tightly (for example, bicycle users) or much more generally (the personal transport market). How a market is defined affects the way it can be segmented. A segmentation of the personal transport market may include segments called 'car' and 'bicycle'. Whereas, a segmentation of the bicycle market may result in 'sporting male', 'office worker' and 'family shopping' segments.

There are a number of ways in which a market can be segmented. To be effective, the segmentation needs to identify the needs, purchasing motivations and desires of different clusters of customers. The choice of the segmentation method is of vital importance. It can include demographics, behavioural characteristics, purchase behaviour and many other factors.

The main purpose of market segmentation is to target interesting or attractive market segments. The organisation's products and services are then designed to match as closely as possibly the ideal requirements of the typical customers within that segment.

Matching products with market demand

Regardless of how efficient an organisation may be in producing or supplying products and services, it needs to be aware of trends in market demand. It does not want to offer products and services that do not match the demands of their customers. Many industries are continually developing and changing, making it a difficult task to match

the total range of products and services offered by the business to the day-to-day requirements of their customers.

Businesses will keep a very close watch on the development of a particular market and try to estimate not only the demand in the future, but also what features or benefits customers will be looking for in various products and services.

For example, the mobile phone manufacturer Nokia was, in the past, the leading seller of mobile phones in the world. It was already developing new mobile phone products that it believed would match the market demands. Unfortunately for Nokia, it missed the popularity of what became known as the clamshell mobile phone. Consequently other manufacturers, such as Sharp, were able to fill the market demand for these types of mobile phones whilst Nokia's sales fell. This example proves that even the most market-aware manufacturer can miss trends and changes in market demand and pay the price in terms of lost sales and revenue.

CASE STUDY — Nokia phone sales plunge

The Finnish company, Nokia, in the first quarter of 2004, although they sold 44.2 million mobile phones, saw their market share drop from 34.6 per cent to 28.9 per cent. They had been planning to increase their market share to 40 per cent by price-cutting. They had missed a change in the market in terms of design, allowing Motorola and Samsung, for example, to increase their market share by 2 per cent each. Worldwide some 600 million mobile phone handsets were likely to be sold by the end of 2004.

> **INDIVIDUAL** WORK (2.8)
> Using the internet, find out the names of 10 mobile phone manufacturers.

Exploiting market potential

Businesses constantly look for potential market demand for their existing or future products and services. This means that they need to be aware of the potential demand for their products and services. In some cases, a successful business will often show the way to other businesses, proving that there is a market for a particular product or service. Also this business, that has begun to develop the demand, may be overtaken by its competitors, which may have greater financial resources to take advantage of the situation.

Cut-price airline businesses, such as EasyJet, proved to conventional airlines that there was a demand for no-frills, cheap flights. The more traditional airlines attempted to copy the EasyJet model and take some of the market for themselves. British Airways, for example, established their own cut-price airline, Go. Unfortunately for British Airways they were not successful. EasyJet proved to be more efficient at providing this service and, as a result, British Airways was eventually forced to sell their cut-price airline service to EasyJet. The Go airline cost British Airways £25 million to set up in 1998 and when it was sold to EasyJet it was valued at £300 million.

Identifying potential future demand

For many businesses, the most difficult task is assessing potential future demand for their products and services. Businesses are constantly developing new products and services, many of which will not become available to their customers for months, or possibly years, ahead. This means that the business needs to look far into the future and try to make an assessment of what the market would want, perhaps in five or even 10 years' time. Businesses will look at similar products and services that are already selling and use this as the basis upon which to make forecasts of what the market may or may not want in the future.

Since many products and services take a long time to be developed, the business will also be constantly looking at any changes in the market that may affect the demand for the products and services when they are available. Not only will they look at buying trends, but they will also examine the products or services being offered, or being developed, by competitors.

INDIVIDUAL WORK
(2.9) ⭐ ⭐
Think of other products or services that have changed dramatically in the last few years. Why do you think the businesses involved have had to make these changes?

Adapting products to changing customer preferences

Very few products and services can remain virtually unchanged for a number of years. Businesses will continually adapt their products and services in line with changing customer demands.

When cars were first manufactured in the early part of the last century, there was an extremely limited choice of sizes and models, not to mention colours. Over the past 100 years or so, there have been tremendous changes, largely driven by customer preferences. Size, maximum speed, colour and a wide variety of other features have gradually been adapted or added to standard vehicles.

More recently the recording industry has become increasingly concerned about the number of people illegally downloading music via the internet. Whilst there have been some test cases in court to try to dissuade people from engaging in file sharing, the record industry has recognised that customer preferences are changing. Sales of CD singles have fallen dramatically and CD albums no longer sell in the huge numbers that they used to. Consequently, recognising that customers are well used to downloading music from the internet, many recording companies are switching over to selling music downloads as a back-up to their normal CD sales.

Customer attributes and demographics

As we have seen, businesses are very keen to understand as much as they can about their customers. They attempt to create a profile, including age, gender, buying habits, location and a multitude of other variables. In understanding as much as they can about their customers, businesses are better able to create or adapt products and services to suit their requirements. This process is a continuous one that requires the business to carry out **market research**, where they ask their existing customers, according to the profiles that they have created, about their feelings towards different products in order to gain a better insight into their customers' preferences.

market research – the gathering of data (information), usually about the buying habits of customers or on the activities of business competitors

Despite the fact that many businesses can sell their products and services via the internet or via conventional catalogues and mail order, they will always attempt to locate retail premises or branches in areas where the local population has a significant number of individuals that match their customer profiles. If, for example, a chain of baby-clothes retailers wished to look for a new location for a branch, they would probably not choose an area that has a higher than average number of retired people, as retired people do not match their customer profile.

Avoiding unsold or unsaleable stock

A vital part of a business's forward planning is to try to ensure that they have enough raw materials and components to make products or partly finished goods (known as work in progress) and finished goods ready for sale. These levels of stock are estimated on the basis of the business's projected calculations of future demand.

The problem with holding stock is that it is expensive, not only to store but also to purchase and to produce. Businesses need to hold enough stock to cope with changes in demand, or perhaps to ensure against suppliers not being able to deliver when required. Provided the business has sufficient products ready for immediate delivery to customers, they can respond to increased demand.

The accounts department of a business will always require low levels of stock, as stock ties up money that could be used elsewhere. If the business is manufacturing products, the production department will want high levels of raw materials and components, so that their production is not interrupted. The sales department, who deal directly with customers, will always want high levels of stock in order to meet any changes in demand.

If the business holds too much stock, they will be paying additional storage, insurance, lighting and **handling costs**. They will also be wasting a great deal of space in the factory or warehouse. Money will be tied up in this stock that cannot be spent elsewhere and, above all, a high stock level might mean that the business cannot sell the stock at all.

Businesses will then tend to try to hold just sufficient stock to cover present demand and any slight variation. If the business is left with unsold stock, or stock that is

GROUP WORK (2.10)
⭐ ⭐
Thinking about matching location with customer profiles, what kind of customers would best suit the following types of business?
a) A fitness centre
b) A multiplex cinema
c) An internet café
d) A horse-riding school
e) A public library.

handling costs – the costs associated with moving, protecting and storing products

no longer in demand, then they may be forced to drastically reduce the price in order to sell the stock. This, in turn, means that they would make less profit on the stock than they had otherwise hoped.

Monitoring market trends

To be successful and not to be caught unprepared for changes in demand, a business will try to ensure that they monitor trends in their area of operations. With so much available information, the business needs to assess continually whether or not the trends highlighted are relevant to them in the short, medium or long term.

It is usual for businesses to monitor the media and look for news of changes in market trends that may affect them. They can also, as we will see, search for possible changes in market trends by carrying out their own market research.

Trade press

There are many hundreds of magazines and newspapers specifically designed for particular industries. Small retailers, such as grocers, would be interested in *The Grocer* magazine or the *Independent Retail News*. Builders may refer to *Construction News*, farmers the *Farming News*, *Dairy Farmer* or *Arable Farming*.

These magazines and newspapers carry news stories, gossip, articles and information about the industry and are vital to businesses in order to keep abreast of new ideas and changes in the market.

How much information is available to you without having to subscribe to the magazine?

Local press

There are 28 local newspapers in London alone. Whilst many local newspapers carry little in the way of news and are mainly filled with advertisements, the local press can provide some useful information for businesses. At the very least, they will be able to look at news and advertisements from their major competitors in the area.

Regional press

The regional press covers specific areas of the UK, such as *The Northern Echo* which covers much of the north-east of England. The regional press usually carries significant amounts of information relevant to businesses, particularly success stories, regional buying trends and other useful updates.

National press

There are several UK national newspapers, such as the *Guardian*, *Express*, *Independent*, *Mail*, *Telegraph*, *The Times* and *Financial Times*, all of which carry a significant amount of business news and information. The *Telegraph*, for example, carries specific information for small businesses, technology and internet trading. As we will see, just like many of the local and regional newspapers, all of the national daily newspapers have large websites with a significant amount of free content available for research purposes.

European and global news sources

Not only are there a number of printed European and international newspapers, there are also a great many newspapers available on the internet in the English language. European newspapers include:

- Germany – *Frankfurter Allgemeine Zeitung* (English language edition)
- Ireland – *Irish Independent*
- Russia – *Moscow Times*, *St Petersburg Times* and *Pravda* (all in English).

As far as newspapers further afield are concerned, these include:

- USA – *Chicago Tribune*, *New York Times*, *Newsweek*, *USA Today* and *Washington Post*.
- Asia and Australasia – *The Australian*, *Peoples' Daily*, *Straits Times* and *Time Asia*.

WANT TO FIND OUT MORE?

Visit **The Grocer** website at: www.thegrocer.co.uk.

GROUP WORK **(2.11)**

★ ★

Visit www.wrx.zen.co.uk/britnews.htm and click on local newspaper links for the south of England.

1 How many local papers are listed here?

2 What area does the EDP-24 cover?

3 Click on the business link and find a recent article that would help a retailing business to assess current regional trends.

International business news stories are covered by:

- BBC News and World Service
- *International Herald Tribune*
- *Newsweek*
- *Time*.

Online sources

The internet provides a wealth of business news, although it is advisable to check both the date of the article and whether the information has come from a reputable source. Amongst the key business news sites are:

- Ananova at www.ananova.com.
- Abyz Newslinks at www.abyznewslinks.com.
- UK Newspaper Link at www.dailynewspaper.co.uk.
- Eldis News Service at www.eldis.org/news.
- The Google Directory of Newspapers, which includes over 60 business newspapers and nearly 4,000 others.
- News and newspapers online at the University of North Carolina at http://library.uncg.edu/news.
- Business news from around the world at www.totalnews.com.
- Up-to-date and archived business news from the BBC at www.bbc.co.uk.

Market research techniques

As well as tracking market trends from business news sources, organisations undertake their own forms of research. They do this in order to estimate customers' opinions of their products and services, and to gain an insight into the future needs of customers.

In offering any form of product or service, the business needs to establish a number of key points. These are some of the many questions that a business will ask regarding its products or services:

- Does the product or service satisfy or create a market need?
- Can we identify the type of customers for our products and services?
- Is the demand for the product just a passing trend or is the demand likely to continue in the long-term future?
- Do customers feel that the product or service is unique, distinctive or superior to those offered by competitors?
- What kind of competition does the product or service face locally, nationally and globally?
- Does it comply with all laws and regulations in the different countries in which it is sold?

In order to discover potential changes in demand, the business will undertake a number of different types of research. These include:

- Talking to industry contacts, including suppliers, wholesalers and retailers.
- Carrying out surveys with the public to see whether they would use the product or service.
- Finding out why their competitors' customers use their products or services.
- Carrying out tests to see how customers use the products and services.
- Continually monitoring what the competition is doing from news stories.
- Looking at economic and demographic information, which will, for example, reveal trends in employment, birth rates, location of businesses and a host of other basic information.

This website will show you the various market research methods and techniques used by businesses.

Action planning

Having identified their markets, their customer attributes, market demand and trends, a business will then set itself a series of objectives. These are often referred to as *action plans* as they identify a series of agreed objectives and, above all, how the objectives will be achieved. Each objective will have to have support and individuals assigned to make sure that the objectives are met. Target dates will be set for the objectives and progress will be reviewed on a regular basis and, if necessary, new objectives set.

Developing and maintaining customer awareness and responsiveness

Assuming that a business continues to remain aware of the demands of its customers, it should be in a position to respond to any change in demand or trend in the market. The purpose of continually considering customers' expectations, attributes and requirements is to alert the business at the earliest possible opportunity of any change that may affect the demand for its products and services.

Monitoring demand and trends must be a continual process and any indications of change should be promptly fed back to the decision-makers in the business. They can then make the necessary adjustments to the products and services in line with what has been discovered.

An unusual example of this occurred in France when the fast-food chain McDonald's started to run TV advertising to promote their products. As in all other countries, they used their character Ronald McDonald, but discovered that the French did not respond well to this character and they swiftly exchanged Ronald for Asterix the Gaul, a distinctly French character.

Responding to customer expectations

Businesses fail to respond to changes in customer expectations at their own peril. Because most businesses face enormous competition from other businesses, they try to be in a position where they can respond to a change in customer expectation, even before that expectation has changed. By continually monitoring demand and trends, and carrying out market research, the businesses are often in an advanced state of notice. Changes can be underway before they can have a negative impact on sales and profits.

With so much competition, businesses realise that customers are not loyal by nature. Therefore a business needs to ensure that they do not give customers any reason to look elsewhere for their products and services. Having spent considerable amounts of money and effort in attracting customers in the first place, it is often cheaper to respond to their expectations rather than risk losing them to a competitor.

Prompt adaptation of products and service arrangements

Until relatively recently British Telecom was the only provider of telephone services in the UK. Now many other businesses offer the same service, aiming to take customers away from British Telecom. There was a similar situation with gas and electricity, with only one provider offering these **utilities**.

Now that there are several suppliers to choose from for telephone services and other utilities, each business needs to be able to adapt instantly and either match prices, the level of service or offer improved products.

Businesses such as British Telecom need to be able to respond immediately to the competition in order to retain their customers. Indeed, in the last few years, after having lost many thousands of customers to its competitors, it is British Telecom that is now forcing its competitors to promptly adapt as their range of services has begun to be more reliable and cheaper.

Adapting under pressure

Adapting to change under pressure is not something that most businesses relish. Sometimes there are circumstances that a business could not have foreseen and, despite carrying out market research and monitoring trends, they may have missed a vital switch in demand.

Some changes in demand cannot be predicted. Petrol stations faced severe difficulties when there were shortages due to strikes or disputes about the price. Airline companies faced a massive drop in demand after the terrorist attack on the Twin Towers in New York in 2001. Many rural businesses suffered enormously during the foot-and-mouth crisis in 2001.

CASE STUDY   The Big Sheep

The Big Sheep is a tourist attraction in Devon that runs sheep races and duck herding. They were badly hit by the foot-and-mouth crisis in 2001 and at one stage they were losing up to £4,000 per day and were threatened with closure. The attraction adapted by setting up their own brewery and an internet café to attract tourists.

INDIVIDUAL WORK (2.14) ★ ★

Visit The Big Sheep website at www.thebigsheep.co.uk and find out what indoor attractions are available that can be visited despite bad weather.

Over the summer the attraction would normally employ up to 70 people, but they reduced this to five in 2001. When it reopened, there were few trained staff. What problems might have arisen as a result of this?

Disregarding customer expectations

A business can choose to disregard changes in market demand, hoping that they are only a passing phase. This is a dangerous step to take as a business may lose customers and find it very difficult to win them back.

Two very famous retail outlets have suffered by disregarding or failing to respond quickly enough to changes in customer demand:

- Marks & Spencer saw sales and profits fall dramatically when they failed to notice changing fashion trends and lost many customers to high street competitors, such as BhS and Debenhams.
- The supermarket chain Sainsbury's was, for many years, the leading food retailer in the UK. But it failed to invest in updated stores and was overtaken by Tesco and other food supermarkets and is now only just beginning to recover from its loss in sales and profits.

CASE STUDY   Squeezed out

In October 2004, Sainsbury's, the UK's favourite supermarket a decade ago, announced a £550 million restructuring and recovery programme. Sainsbury's had lost on price to chains such as Asda and had lost its core middle-class market to Tesco. Their recovery programme aims to create 3,000 jobs and increase sales by £2.5 billion in

the next three years. Tesco, which has 28 per cent of the market, dominates the supermarket sector. Asda who have 16.9 per cent follows them. Sainsbury's are third at 15.3 per cent. The programme will be known as 'Making Sainsbury's Great Again'. It will close 12 stores, refit 131 of its 461 and open petrol stations.

INDIVIDUAL WORK (2.15) ★ ★

Read the case study and answer the following questions.

1 What do you understand by the word 'restructuring'?
2 What do you understand by the term 'recovery programme'?
3 What do you think are Sainsbury's key objectives?

COMPETITIVE PRESSURES

In this section, we will look at the various competitive pressures that could affect a business. As we will see, a business needs to be aware of both its immediate and its distant competitors. It also needs to have a firm understanding of the market and how it is developing, and what impact trends are having on the market. A business will also constantly evaluate its own position, both in terms of what it is doing now and what it might do in the future. It will then compare these to its competitors. Ultimately, as we will see, a business will seek to strengthen its position, deal with threats before they emerge and take advantage of any opportunities that may arise, by planning for those opportunities in advance.

Competition

As far as customers, or consumers, are concerned, the higher the level of competition for products and services, the higher the level of quality and the lower the price paid. Increased competition drives down prices as more businesses are competing for sales.

But what exactly does a business consider to be competition? If a business bottles mineral water, does it consider Coca-Cola or a brewery to be their competition? The simple answer is probably yes, because they are all in the drinks market and a customer could purchase Coca-Cola or beer instead of the mineral water.

If we extend this to various food products available in a supermarket, is a frozen pizza in competition with a microwave ready meal? Again the answer is yes, as they both cater to the convenience-food market.

Therefore, when a business considers its competition, it needs to look at potential competitors in the broadest sense. Even a CD or a DVD is in competition with a book or a pen and pencil set if a customer is looking for a gift in a particular shop, such as WHSmith.

Looking at competition in this way makes the pressure on businesses even stronger and they must ensure that they not only offer the broadest possible range of products and services, but that they are competitively priced and of high quality. Added to this, they also need to be available in as many different outlets, or places where customers can purchase them, as possible.

GROUP WORK (2.16)
★ ★

Many standard products and services are available from a wide range of competing businesses, even in a relatively small area. Think about the following products. Write beside each one how many different stores, within walking distance of one another, sell the same product.

a) A bag of chips
b) A bottle of Coca-Cola
c) A local newspaper
d) A bottle of nail varnish
e) The details of a two-bedroom house for rent

f) A pair of football socks
g) A bag of 2-inch nails
h) A fountain pen
i) A pair of tights
j) A diary for next year.

Range of business organisations supplying comparable products and services to comparable markets

As we will see in the next section, most businesses are concerned with competitors that supply broadly similar products and services to broadly similar customers. 'Broadly similar' in terms of products and services means that an estate agent would be concerned with the activities of all other estate agents in the immediate area. A supermarket would be concerned with not only other supermarkets and grocery outlets in the immediate area, but also regional ones and certainly online supermarkets that deliver to their local area.

'Comparable markets' mean broadly similar types of customer. In a typical high street there may be a dozen or more clothes outlets. Whilst all of them sell clothing and accessories, they do not all have the same market. Some will be aimed at younger age groups and have fashionable clothing. Others may be catering for children or older people. This means that simply looking in the *Yellow Pages* under clothing might reveal a number of clothes shops in a particular area. But what it does not reveal is the nature of those clothes shops and which markets they are attempting to sell their products to.

Identifying the competitive market

In order to understand the difficulties businesses face in identifying their competitors, the following headings in this section ask you to look at a particular case. Initially you will discover that it is relatively easy to identify competitors. But the further afield you look for competitors, the more difficult it is to assess what impact they might have on a business.

GROUP WORK (2.17)
★ ★ ★

Before you read on, you need to imagine that you and your partner wish to set up a florist shop in your local area. You will offer cut flowers and plants to customers who pass your shop. You will also take telephone orders for weddings, funerals and special occasions and you will set up a website that allows customers to purchase plants and flower arrangements online. You will offer a full delivery service free of charge.

Think of a name for your shop and imagine the ideal location in your local area.

GROUP WORK (2.18)
★ ★

Using the *Yellow Pages* or your local *Phone Book*, identify the number of florists in your immediate area. For example, the city of Norwich has 23 florists. This is in addition to petrol stations and supermarkets, as well as market stalls and garden centres, which sell cut flowers or potted plants.

Local

The most obvious competitors are in a business's immediate local area. These competitors offer either exactly the same or very similar products and services and could easily attract customers who would otherwise purchase from the business. Normally businesses know a great deal about their local competitors.

Regional

In some parts of the UK particular areas are regional centres where you will find the majority of the businesses including retail outlets. These businesses cater for the whole of the area and draw customers in from the outlying towns and villages. In cities this is rather more difficult, but in London for example there are various centres, such as Croydon, Brent Cross, Oxford Street and Camden Town, all of which have several businesses offering similar products and catering to the same customers.

National

Gauging the number of competitors nationally is even more difficult. Many businesses although not located anywhere near their customers, can supply products and services and are direct competitors with local businesses. Insurance companies, online banks and travel agents all compete with local insurance brokers, bank branches and travel shops.

European and global

For florists, European or international competitors may not be a great threat, unless of course a customer wishes to have flowers delivered to an overseas location. They are competitors in the broadest sense, but the complications of payment, delivery charges and additional time concerns may well make them not as serious as local, regional or national competitors.

GROUP WORK (2.19)
★ ★

Using the *Yellow Pages* again, look at the florists in the region. If you live in a county, your *Yellow Pages* will cover the whole of that county. If you live in a city, you should include all the boroughs and the outlying towns.

How much more competition is there regionally compared to locally for your florist shop?

CASE STUDY Tesco's online rival

Tesco launched their online shopping service in 1998. It has around 1.5 million registered users. Its service provides delivery to over 95 per cent of the UK population. Iceland is the only company that covers more of the population with 97 per cent coverage. Asda's home delivery service only caters for around 10 million households. In 2002, Waitrose, part of the John Lewis Partnership, launched a new home delivery service. Initially it tested its systems just in Hertfordshire, but in June 2002 it expanded into London. It has a warehouse that can process the same amount of groceries as 20 large supermarkets. Unlike Tesco, Ocado, a new business, promises to deliver within a one-hour time slot and rewards customers with gifts if they are late.

INDIVIDUAL WORK (2.20)
Read the case study and answer the following question. For a home delivery service, why might the maximum population coverage be important?

GROUP WORK (2.21) ★ ★
It will not be easy to discover the extent of national competition for your florist shop. A simple search on the internet for 'flower delivery' revealed over 177,000 hits. Businesses such as Interflora, Flowergram, Next and a multitude of other UK-based businesses provide free or express delivery to anywhere in the country.

You can easily see how they might compare in price with your florist shop by checking their prices and their range of products and services online.

GROUP WORK (2.22)

★ ★

Summarise your findings from the previous group work activities.

1 What was the total number of local competitors?

2 What was the total number of regional competitors?

3 Which were the five major national competitors? Why do you think they were serious competitors to your florist business?

This is not necessarily the case for all businesses. It is sometimes considerably cheaper for customers to buy many products from overseas businesses. In the manufacturing industry, countries such as China can produce products at far lower cost than businesses in the UK due to their low wage rate.

Tanzania in Africa produces 322 million cut flowers per year. The flowers are transported to Europe, taking 10 hours, at a cost of $2 per kg of flowers. Some 90 per cent of the flowers produced are flown to Holland and the Tanzanian growers only receive between 15 and 20 per cent of the final price paid by customers.

Knowing the marketplace

As we will see in Unit 9, Starting Up a New Business, a detailed knowledge of the marketplace and the possible opportunities and threats to a business is an absolute basic essential. Knowledge of the marketplace allows a business to plan for likely issues that could affect the running of the business, its sales and its profitability.

In the next section, we will look specifically at how a market evaluates its market position. But in this section we turn our attention to the specific types of information that the business needs to be aware of and be in a position to react to at any time.

Approximate current market share

Market share is a notoriously difficult figure to calculate. Normally a business will attempt to assess the total value of a particular market and then work out their own share of that market. The problem arises with actually measuring that market in the first place.

A mobile phone manufacturer, for example, may calculate their market share by calculating the total number of mobile phones sold in a particular country in a specific year. They will then look at their own sales and compare this to the total sales. Unfortunately this does not show the whole picture. It is better to try to place a value, in terms of total sales figures for a particular market, and then to compare this figure with the total value of sales that the business has done in that market. In this way the actual value of the market, in income terms, can be calculated by the business.

As a simple example, if a particular market is worth £10 million and a specific business has £1 million of sales in that market then they have 10 per cent of the market.

Degree of competition

The more complex a business and the more markets in which it operates, the more complicated the situation regarding competition becomes. It would be fairly straightforward for a local toy shop to be able to assess the degree of competition it faces in the market. It would begin by looking at other toy shops in the immediate area, larger toy shops that may be based in the region, such as ToysRUs, and it will then look at online toy shops, toys sold through catalogue showrooms, such as Argos, and supermarkets and other outlets that have a limited toy selection.

Theoretically the small, local toy shop competes with all of these different businesses. But, on a Saturday afternoon, when children visit the high street, they will not have a huge amount of competition for pocket-money spending. The competition may only arise with major purchases, such as for birthdays and Christmas.

Many specialist stores, such as toy shops, those that sell CDs, computer games and chemists, all face competition from similar businesses. However, they also face competition from other businesses that do not specialise in their product or service ranges. A large supermarket, for example, would compete with all the specialist outlets mentioned above. Although the supermarket may not have the range offered by the specialist stores, it can take vital sales away from these outlets.

Supermarkets selling an organic food range have hit many health-food stores, which were once the only source of organic food, extremely hard. If customers can purchase organic food with their other shopping, then the likelihood is that they will not bother to visit the health-food store at all. This problem facing health-food stores has been mirrored by many of the other independent outlets such as toy shops and chemists.

GROUP WORK (2.23)

★

Thinking about organic food, list at least three reasons why a supermarket might choose to offer these types of products. What might selling them add to their attractiveness to customers?

Past market history and likely developments

One of the most common ways in which a business will attempt to predict future trends in the market is to look at the past history of the market in terms of sales and trends. A business that sells luxury goods could confidently expect that if the country's economy is strong, then their sales will be high. If the country's economy is weak and people are reluctant to spend money in an uncertain time, then their sales would fall. They would be able to see these trends having occurred in the past and, if there is the likelihood that these factors will repeat themselves, they can be prepared for that eventuality.

Most markets tend to follow a regular pattern. Sometimes they enjoy periods of growth, followed by a levelling off of demand and then, perhaps, a fall in demand. By recognising at what stage the market is at, at any given time, the business will not be caught unaware and either left with stock that cannot be sold or have insufficient stock to satisfy increased demand.

For many businesses, technology has a drastic impact on either their operations, their products and services or the customers that they serve. Banks, for example, have seen tremendous changes in technology that have seen **debit** and **credit cards** replacing cash and cheques in many transactions. Improved information communication technology has allowed online banking and telephone banking, neither of which were even thought of 10 years ago.

Other industries, such as the music trade, have seen a shift from vinyl records to CDs and then to downloadable MP3 music files. All of these developments have been driven by changes in technology.

Market concentration is the degree to which the top businesses in any particular industry control the lion's share of the market. In the UK food retail market in 1980 the top 14 retailers had a 23 per cent market share between them. By 2000 the top nine retailers had captured 63 per cent of the market. This gradual process resulted in smaller businesses being squeezed out of markets, as they could not compete with the sheer size and financial strength of the larger businesses. Although there are laws that prevent businesses from totally dominating a particular market, the gradual process of a handful of businesses controlling most of a market continues.

One of the ways in which larger businesses can gradually dominate the market share is to launch a takeover and acquire smaller businesses. In 2004 one of the biggest takeovers saw Morrisons supermarket chain buy the Safeway chain. The larger businesses use *market consolidation* (as this takeover process is known) to secure their market position, usually by acquiring smaller, successful retailers. In the supermarket business it has become increasingly difficult to develop large, out-of-town shopping sites as a result of the planning laws. An effective way around this problem is to purchase existing out-of-town stores and convert them into the larger business's own premises.

Evaluating market position

Having identified the key customers and their attributes, along with recognising market demand and trends, the business should have a clear idea of the market and its competitors. The next logical step is for the business to look at what they do and make a comparison between their efforts and those of their competitors. This section looks at the types of activity and concerns that the business would need to examine in order to evaluate its own market position.

SWOT analysis

SWOT (Strengths, Weaknesses, Opportunities and Threats) analysis is a means by which a business can describe the factors that may have an impact on operations.

- The strengths and weaknesses of the businesses are best described as its internal resources and capabilities, such as management skills or product or service quality.
- The opportunities and threats are the external factors that can affect the business. Competitors would be classed as a threat, and a new market an opportunity.

Keyword

debit card – a modern alternative to a cheque. The funds are immediately taken out of the account of the cardholder after having been checked by the issuing bank

credit card – a card that allows the user to make purchases on credit, up to a limit specified by the issuing bank, building society or finance provider

The purpose of SWOT analysis is to produce, in the easiest and most understandable way, a list of the key issues. Normally SWOT analysis is presented in the form of a straightforward grid, as can be seen in Figure 2.1.

Figure 2.1
SWOT analysis

The business will usually start a SWOT analysis by listing the internal factors, starting with its strengths and listing them in the Strengths box. It will ask itself a number of questions, including:

- What makes the business good at succeeding?
- What does the business do well?
- Why are customers pleased with the business's products and services?
- What advantages does the business offer customers and suppliers?

Above all, the business needs to be honest. If it is not objective, then the SWOT analysis will have no value.

Having looked at the strengths, the business now turns its attention to its weaknesses and lists them in the Weaknesses box. These are issues that affect performance and typically it will ask itself the following questions:

- What could be improved about the business?
- What problems does the business constantly encounter?
- What does the business do that could be improved?
- What must the business avoid?
- What does the competition do that is superior to what the business does?

Again the business needs to be honest. It needs to list its weaknesses as clearly and as honestly as possible.

Having looked at the internal factors, the business must now look at the external issues that impact on the business. It will begin by looking at opportunities, and list them in the Opportunities box. It will ask itself a number of questions, including:

- What market opportunities are available to the business?
- What customer needs are not being fulfilled by the business or its competitors?
- What important trends are taking place in the market?
- Are there any technological, legal or social changes happening that the business could take advantage of to improve its position?

The final issue is the threats facing the business, listed in the Threats box. Some of the threats will be more obvious than others and the business needs to consider both the actual threats and the possible threats in the future. Typical questions would include:

- Would a period of poor sales or a major customer going out of business seriously affect the business's future?
- What is the competition doing and is it taking away sales from the business?

    ♢ What would the competition do if the business tried to exploit an opportunity it has identified?

    ♢ Are there any trends or changes in the market that could have a negative impact on the business's products or services?

    ♢ Are there any technological changes that could have a negative impact on the business's products or services?

The main aim of SWOT analysis is not only to identify key issues, but also to organise them in such a way that the business can:

    ♢ Build on their strengths

    ♢ Minimise their weaknesses

    ♢ Take advantage of opportunities

    ♢ Deal with threats.

By looking at the four different factors together, the business is therefore able to answer the following questions:

    ♢ Can their strengths take advantage of the opportunities?

    ♢ Can their strengths deal with the threats?

    ♢ Can their weaknesses be cancelled out by taking advantage of opportunities?

    ♢ Can their weaknesses can be cancelled out by minimising threats?

GROUP WORK (2.24)
★ ★

In pairs, draw up your own SWOT analysis grid and try to identify the strengths, weaknesses, opportunities and threats for your school or college.

Product quality

Perhaps the most fundamental internal factor is an analysis of the business's products and services. A business will need to examine and make a judgement on whether their current products and services are of sufficient quality to remain attractive to potential customers. They will do this by comparing their products and services with not only the competitions' products and services, but also with the expectations of their customers. It may be the case that the majority of products and services offered by the business and its competitors do not meet its customers' expectations. Therefore, simply comparing the business's products and services to those of its competitors is not sufficient to be sure that they are of good quality.

Consistency

The term 'consistency' refers to the average quality of the products and services offered by the business, and it is also a measure of all of the services provided by the business. Consistency therefore means regular and guaranteed high-quality products and services, backed up by high-quality customer and after-sales service.

INDIVIDUAL WORK
(2.25) ★ ★

Are you a loyal customer? Do you have any store loyalty cards? Do you always shop in the same place for your clothes, CDs, takeaway food or other regular purchases? What is it about the business that you buy from that makes you loyal to them?

Customer service

Many businesses recognise that in the majority of markets, where products and services offered by a variety of different businesses are similar, the only real difference is the quality of the customer service. It is no longer the case that businesses can simply sell their products and services to a customer and then sit back and count their profits. Customers demand a far more extensive relationship with a business. They need to be able to contact the business should they have a problem and have that problem resolved quickly and efficiently. In ensuring that customers are dealt with in a prompt, efficient and more than satisfactory manner, businesses can establish a strong relationship with the customer, which means that next time they wish to purchase a similar product or service they will remain loyal to that business.

Image and branding

Businesses spend millions of pounds establishing an image for their products and services. The main purpose of developing an image, or a brand, for a particular product or service is to make it instantly recognisable to the customers. Having created an image and a brand name, the business will be keen to ensure that it retains its customers by constantly reminding them that the products and services connected with that brand are of a high quality.

Reputation

Once the business has established a brand name and an image for their products and services, they will seek to remind customers that their quality, reliability and usefulness are guaranteed. Over a period of time the product or service will achieve a reputation for its standard of quality, reliability and usefulness, which the business will ensure remains at a consistently high level.

Unique selling points

Unique selling points, or USPs, are characteristics of a particular product or service that sets them apart from any other product or service offered by a competitor. The business will use a product's USPs in its advertising or promotion of the product or service. They will use the USPs in order to compare the product or service with that of the competition, so that it is clear that the product or service is superior in some way.

It is the USP that will help customers to choose the business's products or services over those of the competition. In the majority of markets, there are tens or even thousands of businesses offering broadly similar products and services.

A good example of a USP is the pyramid-shaped PG Tips teabag. Although it does basically the same job as every other teabag, its unique shape makes it different from all the rest and, arguably, makes a better cup of tea.

Competitive pressures

The issues already covered in this section primarily deal with the strengths and weaknesses of a SWOT analysis. Competitive pressure is the first that addresses potential opportunities and threats. Competitive pressures relate not only to the amount of competition in the market, but also to the impact on the business of their activities. Each time a competitor launches an initiative to take advantage of an opportunity that they have identified, it becomes a threat for all of the other businesses in that market. Competitive pressure may come from a number of the largest businesses in the market, which, as we will see, may be more able to use their resources to gain market share. Competitive pressure may also come from smaller competitors, or indeed businesses that have just joined the market and have become new competitors.

Competitor resources and strengths

In many markets, the size of a business may determine the extent of their resources, which in turn could be their major strength. If a market is dominated by a handful of large businesses, they may be more concerned about fighting over market share with the larger competitors than with the smaller ones.

It is certainly the case that in the retail food markets the larger businesses, such as Tesco, Asda and Sainsbury's, are more concerned with countering one another's activities than trying to force a small corner shop out of business. Unfortunately their activities, such as longer opening hours, price cuts, home deliveries, a wider product range, whilst aimed at dealing with their larger competitors, have had a huge impact on their smaller competitors.

If a major business has more customers, higher sales and profits, better-trained staff and a more convenient location, then they have a huge advantage over their competitors. In reality, this is rarely the case and in most markets a competitor may have superior resources and strengths in certain areas, but a lack of resources and some weaknesses in others. This is not to say that they are balanced out, but it does give the smaller competitor a chance to compete even with the largest businesses. Many customers would actually prefer to buy from a smaller, more local business than a large impersonal business even if the local business is slightly more expensive.

GROUP WORK **(2.26)**
★ ★
Look at the following list of products and try to think of the USP of at least three of them.
a) A KFC meal
b) A pair of Nike trainers
c) Jamie Oliver's range of cookware
d) Your favourite football team's club shirt
e) Body Shop cosmetics.

INDIVIDUAL WORK **(2.27)** ★
Do you have a local store? If so, how often do your family use it? What do you buy there that you could obtain from a large supermarket? Why do you choose to use the corner shop rather than visit the supermarket for these products?

Action planning

As we have already seen, action planning requires a business to set its own targets and decide how it will achieve them. Often it involves making difficult decisions about plans for the future and a business needs to be focused about what it wants to do, as well as being realistic about what it will be able to do.

An action plan looks at where the business is now and where it wants to be in the future. Having established these basic facts, it must identify how it intends to get there. What steps will it have to take? How many smaller steps will this involve? There will often be several different routes that the business can, or in some cases is forced to, take before it reaches it goals. The next important consideration is the timescale. The business needs to establish a series of dates at which it could confidently expect progress to have been made. On these dates, the business will review the situation and see whether it has progressed as far as it anticipated towards its goals. The business may have to revise its plans at the review dates and, perhaps, add new goals or rewrite their plan to reflect any changes that have occurred. The main reasons why a business would action plan are as follows.

Consolidating and strengthening market position

Having achieved a particular market share, a business cannot rest on its successes as there will undoubtedly be a large number of competitors that are working to take away that market share for themselves. Having achieved a market share is, therefore, not the end of the business's work. It now has to protect that market share, which is known as **consolidation**. In other words, this means making sure that at least this level of market share can constantly be achieved. It can do this by ensuring that its current number of customers remain loyal to the business.

The second phase is to strengthen or increase the market share that has already been achieved. A business can do this by continuing to market their products and services and making more people aware that they are available. If the business can get itself into a strong position in the market, where the majority of potential customers have heard of the business, then it is less likely that new competitors will be able to take away the business's market share.

Addressing key competitive threats

Businesses need to continually analyse the strategies of their competitors. They need to be aware of what their competitors are planning and how this may impact on their business. The business therefore needs to be aware of:

- New competitors entering the market
- Changes in pricing by competitors
- New products or services offered by competitors
- Updated products or services offered by competitors.

All of these potential threats from the competition could affect the business in the short, medium or long term and it would need to react as quickly as possible in order to deal with these threats.

Identifying opportunities for expansion

Expansion can be achieved in a number of different ways. One of the most common ways is for a business to gradually increase its sales, which allows it to reinvest its profits into growing the business in terms of its range of products and services, as well as taking on more employees. A business needs to choose the correct time at which to expand and not choose a time when the market is experiencing difficulties. Having said that, if the market is strong and the competitors are doing well, they too will be seeking to expand at the same time.

An increasingly popular way of expanding is known as **acquisition**. This means that a business will seek to buy another business, either in its own market or in a market similar to that of the purchasing business. If two or more businesses choose to join together, then this is known as a **merger**. This means that the two businesses will

Keyword

takeover – when one business gains the total ownership of another business

now have a common management and structure and will be able to benefit from the expertise of both of the original businesses.

Another form of acquisition is known as a **takeover**. These are often referred to as hostile takeovers, as the business being acquired does not actually wish to be purchased by the other business. There are other forms of takeover, when the owners of the business being acquired are prepared to be bought by the other business.

CASE STUDY Morrisons and Safeway

In the spring of 2004 the Bradford-based Morrisons supermarket chain completed a £3 billion takeover of their rivals, Safeway. The other big three supermarket chains, Tesco, Asda and Sainsbury's, along with the owner of Bhs, Philip Green, had all made bids for Safeway. Morrisons will now have 550 stores throughout the UK and they will begin a process of converting 180 of the medium-sized Safeway stores into full Morrisons supermarkets.

The family-run Morrisons chain hopes to make annual savings of some £215 million from the takeover.

INDIVIDUAL WORK (2.28)

Read the case study and then answer the following questions.

1 How might the fact that four other businesses were trying to buy Safeway have affected the final price Morrisons paid for Safeway?

2 As far as customers are concerned, give two advantages and two disadvantages of there being one less independent supermarket chain in the UK.

STAKEHOLDER EXPECTATIONS

All organisations have what are known as *stakeholders*. These are individuals or groups, which have an influence on the organisation. The stakeholders range from employees, management, shareholders and investors which have a close relationship with the organisation to local and central government, customers and suppliers who have a less close relationship with the organisation.

Organisations realise the importance of making sure that stakeholders maintain their support for the organisation and incorporate these ideas into their overall strategies:

- *Stakeholder satisfaction* Which are the key stakeholders and what do they want and need?
- *Stakeholder contribution* What does the organisation want and need from their stakeholders, and what do the stakeholders want from the organisation in return?
- *Strategies* What strategies does the organisation need to put into place in order to satisfy these twin sets of wants and needs?
- *Processes* What processes does the organisation need to put in place to enable them to carry out their strategies?
- *Capabilities* What capabilities does the organisation need to put in place to allow them to operate and improve these processes?

We will now look in a little more detail at the different types of stakeholder and see what each of the stakeholders expect from an organisation and how the organisation handles the relationship.

Stakeholders

A business's key stakeholders are likely to be a combination of a number of different groups including: investors (principally shareholders and including other capital providers); customers and intermediaries (other businesses with whom the business deals); employees and unions; suppliers and partners; and regulators, pressure groups, and communities. Their relative importance will vary from organisation to organisation.

GROUP WORK (2.29)
★ ★
Before you learn any more about stakeholders, try to decide who your group thinks the stakeholders may be of your school or college.

GROUP WORK (2.30)
★
1 Who are the customers of your school or college?
2 Does your school or college have a means of discovering whether or not their customers are satisfied?

benefits – these include items such as assistance with moving expenses, season ticket loans, company cars or petrol allowances, and a work uniform

investment – the money they have put into the business

Stakeholder theory suggests that people who have legitimate interests in a business also ought to have a say in how it is run, even if they do not own the business. The most obvious non-owner stakeholders are the employees. Stakeholder theory also maintains that people outside of the business should have a say in how the business operates. Consumers, even community members who could be affected by what the business does, ought to have some control over the business.

Customers
In the early 1980s, organisations tended to measure customer satisfaction by tracking the number of customer complaints they received. Research showed that only around 10 per cent of dissatisfied customers ever complained. During the 1990s, research discovered that customers who were 'very satisfied' were six times more likely to repeat their purchase in the next 18 months than those who were just 'satisfied'. This was to lead to the development of customer loyalty programmes, which we see in many of the retail outlets. Latest research and programmes hope to track whether customers come back to buy more and recommend the organisation to others.

Customers usually need the desired goods and services, in the quantity required, at the time they choose and at a competitive price.

Suppliers
Many organisations see their suppliers as stakeholders, and are increasingly working in partnership with them. The organisation is keen to establish a close relationship with their suppliers in order to make their whole operation more efficient. This is achieved by learning from one another and exchanging skills with the confidence of a long-term relationship.

Employees
Generally, employees seek work that interests them and has some clear purpose. They also look for an employer that provides decent and safe working conditions and, of course, treats them fairly. Employees also want opportunities to grow and learn transferable skills and have a competitive wage, salary and **benefits** package. Organisations, on the other hand, generally need loyal employees, as constant replacement of trained employees is both expensive and disruptive. Organisations look to find employees who have high levels of productivity, flexibility and creativity. At the same time they are looking for employees that are good ambassadors in the outside world.

Employees usually need challenging work, reasonable hours and quantity of work, a good working environment, respect and a competitive wage or salary.

Owners
The owners of the business usually need the highest return on their investment, an increase in the value of their **investment** and a balanced risk in involving themselves with the business. In the case of sole traders, the sole trader is the owner of the business. In partnerships, it is the partners that are the owners of the business. In both of these cases, it is usual for the owners to have day-to-day involvement in the running of the business, so their efforts will be designed to provide them with the maximum return for their investment and their effort.

Shareholders own both private limited companies and public limited companies. However, this is where the similarity between the two businesses ends.

Private limited companies tend to have shareholders that actually run the business and are, therefore, in a similar position to owners of sole-trading businesses and partnerships. As the shares of private limited companies are not sold to the general public, it is usual for the shareholders of these businesses to actually be directly 'employed' as directors or managers of the business.

In the case of public limited companies, the general public can purchase shares and it is not usually the case that the majority of the shareholders have any close association with the business, other than being a shareholder. This means that their view and expectations of the business may be slightly different to those of all other types of owners. Being a shareholder means that they own a part of the business. They have made an investment to purchase the shares and therefore expect a reasonable return in terms of cash or more shares for that investment. Shareholders of public limited companies are, therefore, as concerned with the performance of the business as any other owner. But usually they do not have access to the management of the business, or understand why particular decisions are made, only that a decision may have affected the value of their investment.

Bankers

Every time a bank or financial institution becomes involved with a business, it knows that it is taking a risk, either in providing a loan or financial assistance. Banks charge businesses to manage their banking facilities and, when they loan money to a business, they expect the business to be in a position to pay the **interest** on a loan, but at an agreed point in the future to be able to pay back the whole of the loan. Loans, therefore, are part interest and part **capital**.

Banks are also businesses, with their own shareholders that, like any other owner, expect a reasonable return on their investment. Therefore banks are cautious in making their decision to make loans to other businesses. A bank would expect a business to which it has granted a loan to run its business in a cost-efficient and law-abiding manner.

Having provided a business with a loan, the bank has now become a stakeholder in that business. It is now interested in the performance of the business and will have a keen interest in decisions made by the business that could affect the business's ability to pay back the loan.

Trade unions

As we will see later in this section, staff associations and trade unions are primarily involved in the protection and advancement of the interests of their members. They are involved in negotiations with the employers, mainly regarding pay and conditions of work. Trade unions also provide legal and financial assistance, sickness benefit and education for their members.

Trade unions are stakeholders as they are often the legal representatives of the employees that, as we have seen, have a considerable interest in the running of the business and its future fortunes.

Employer associations

Perhaps the most well-known employer association is the Confederation of British Industry (CBI). There are, however, many hundreds of other employer associations, usually related to a particular type of business. Examples include the Bridge Building and Constructional Engineering Employers' Association, the Textile Employers' Association and the University and Colleges Employers' Association.

The CBI was established in 1965, and combined three former employer associations. It operates as a **pressure group** for businesses, aiming to promote their interests with the government, employees and to overseas countries. It is an independent organisation, with around 250,000 member companies.

Local and national communities

Businesses have become increasingly aware of the fact that the communities in which they operate can often be affected by their activities. A business, for example, that has large trucks coming and going from their premises at all times of the day and night would have an impact on homes in the local area. If possible the business would seek to reduce the impact of its activities on the local community, rather than have to deal with complaints and bad feeling towards them by the community.

Some business activities impact on the nation as a whole. The building of new motorways, airports and large shopping complexes can have an impact on a much wider area than the local community. The UK's roads are heavily used and whilst some pressure groups, such as the Road Hauliers' Association, are pressurising central and local government to improve the roads, other pressure groups from both the local and national communities, are opposed to any new motorways.

Keyword

interest – a charge made for borrowing the money. It is a percentage of the actual amount the bank has loaned the business
capital – the original amount of the loan before any interest charges were added

---

Keyword

pressure group – an organised group that seeks to influence government policy or legislation. They are often referred to as interest groups, lobby groups or protest groups. There are literally thousands of pressure groups in the UK

WANT TO FIND OUT MORE?

Visit the website of the **Confederation of British Industry** at: www.cbi.org.uk

Airport expansion has also been a problem. Again the UK's airports are over-used and, with more people wishing to fly abroad, there is increasing demand for more flights, but the current airports simply do not have the capacity to handle them. Airlines and the British Aviation Authority (who own and run the airports) wish new airports to be built and existing ones to be extended. But communities under the flight paths are opposed to them. The government always tries to tread the middle path and to allow businesses to expand, whilst trying to make sure that they do not have a negative impact on the community.

CASE STUDY Stansted expansion

In December 2003, the government announced a new 30-year plan for air travel in the UK. Stansted would have a second runway by 2011 and Heathrow a third runway by 2020. The announcement immediately angered both environmental pressure groups and home owners near to the airports. The major airlines had been complaining to the government for some years that unless additional runways were built, the airline industry would decline. Local residents and environmentalists are concerned with pollution and noise, not only from the aircraft but also from the increased numbers of passengers travelling to the airports.

INDIVIDUAL WORK
(2.31) ★ ★ ★
Find out the name of the nearest airport to you and see if there are plans to extend it in the near future.

1 What impact do you think this would have on the local community?

2 Are there national community considerations involved in the expansion of Stansted, Heathrow and your local airport?

Pressure groups

As we have already discussed, pressure groups are variously known as interest, lobby or protest groups. They seek to influence government and businesses. The CBI is a pressure group as it represents the interests of British businesses.

Some pressure groups are much smaller and may only have a few hundred members. The vast majority of pressure groups use legal means to get their points across. However, some pressure groups have been involved in illegal activities, such as planting bombs, as in the case of the Animal Liberation Front.

The primary role of a pressure group is to try to influence individuals that have the power to make decisions. As there are many thousands of different pressure groups, they are in competition with one another to get their points of view across. In 1998, for example, something in excess of 300,000 people attended the Countryside March in London. They were concerned about the government's policies for rural areas. As a result the government announced the appointment of a Ministry of Rural Affairs (which became Defra in 2001) and began to talk to the pressure groups about their concerns for the countryside.

Other examples of pressure groups include:

- The National Union of Students
- The National Farmers' Union
- The British Medical Association
- The British Union for the Abolition of Vivisection
- Liberty.

INDIVIDUAL WORK
(2.32) ★ ★

Using the internet, find the websites of the five pressure groups in the list above. Find out what their main aims are and what they hope to achieve.

Tax collection authorities

There are two major tax collection authorities in the UK. The Inland Revenue collects a percentage of all businesses' profits in the form of tax. HM Customs and Excise collects Value Added Tax (VAT) on the sale of certain products and services and this is collected at every stage of production and distribution.

Both of the tax-collecting authorities can be considered to be stakeholders as they have an interest in knowing precisely how much money a business has made and spent in a given period of time.

Stakeholder expectations

Whilst businesses wish to operate profitably, this does not mean that the business will make decisions that have a negative impact on their stakeholders. To ensure continuous business growth and success, the business will need to make sure that they operate in a stable environment and that they have the confidence of their stakeholders. These stakeholders, of course, include their customers, investors, employees and the wider community.

In terms of specific responsibilities towards stakeholders, Table 2.2 summarises these responsibilities and the stakeholder expectations, showing how they attempt to match one another.

Table 2.2
The responsibilities of businesses towards stakeholders

Stakeholders	Business's responsibilities
Shareholders	• Openness in all communications • A reasonable return to shareholders, whilst protecting their original investment
Employees	• Creating employment and development opportunities • Providing confidence to employees • Investment in employees as a vital resource
Customers	• The development and maintenance of long-term relationships with customers • Offering high-quality services and value for money • Openness and fairness towards customers, in terms of standards of behaviour, matching legal requirements and regulations
Suppliers	• Building mutually beneficial relationships with suppliers and other businesses • Ensuring value for money, increasing efficiency and eliminating waste
Community	• Contributing and participating in local communities where the business operates • Developing business, local recruitment and the retention of employees • Taking responsibility for the environment in terms of energy use (including costs of distribution), recycling and optimising disposable materials

CASE STUDY

Hampshire Fire and Rescue Services: Stakeholder expectations

It is not just commercial businesses that have stakeholders. Services, such as the Hampshire Fire and Rescue Service, also have a wide range of stakeholders with their own particular interests and expectations.

The first major stakeholder is the Hampshire Fire and Rescue Authority, which is looking for value for money in the provision of all the services, high-quality services, involvement in planning and decision-making and to be accountable to the general public.

The service operates within the areas of Hampshire, Portsmouth and Southampton County Councils; these too are stakeholders and have a number of expectations. They look for the costs of the service to be either at or below the allocated budget, and to have a close relationship in terms of policy and management practice.

The service also has responsibility towards the general public. They require a high-quality, fast-response service. They require information on fire safety, including education and training.

The suppliers to the service look for a continued relationship and involvement in research and development and cooperation. The employees' expectations are for job security, a reasonable financial package, job satisfaction, stability at work and involvement in decision-making. The trade unions seek job security for their members and an involvement in decision-making.

The final group of stakeholders includes central and local government, which are looking for the best value in fire cover at a consistently high standard. The other fire services in the area look for cooperation and the sharing of resources, as do the other emergency services, such as ambulance workers.

GROUP WORK (2.33)

After reading the case study on Hampshire Fire and Rescue Service, answer the following questions.

1 Which of the stakeholders are looking for value for money from the service?

2 Which of the stakeholders are looking to be involved in the decision-making of the service?

3 What do you think is meant by the term 'job security'?

Owners, shareholders and investors

Profits and returns on investment

These three stakeholders are effectively individuals or groups of people that have a financial stake in a business. As we have seen, owners can be the single owner of a business, as in the case of a sole trader, or a part-owner, as in the case of a partnership or a limited company. As we have also seen, owners tend to have a much closer relationship with the business than shareholders and investors as they usually work for, or on behalf of, the business.

Shareholders are often referred to as investors as they have made the decision to purchase some of the business's shares and are part-owners of the organisation. They will have paid the market rate for the shares and will expect two key returns on their investment. These are:

- The value of the shares will increase. In other words, if they had paid £1 for each of the shares they would expect that, over a period of time, the share will increase in value to over £1, rather than dropping below a £1. Businesses that are doing well attract investors, which drives up the price of the shares. If investors feel that the business is having difficulties, then people do not want to buy the shares and many will try to sell their shares before the price drops even further.

- Usually on an annual (yearly) basis, shareholders receive what is known as a *dividend*. This is a one-off payment made by the business to the shareholders as their share of the profits that the business has made. The dividend is made per share, so the more shares an investor has the higher the amount of money they will receive. If, for example, an investor had £1,000 shares and the business decided to pay 10p dividend per share, they would receive £100 as their dividend payment.

Taken together, the expectation of an increase in the value of the shares and regular dividend payments, shareholders and investors receive their share of the profits and the success of the business and is therefore their return on their investment.

In cases when the business does not have shares, such as a sole trader or a partnership, the owners or part-owners receive their share of the profits when they are made. This is the ongoing return on their investment in the business, assuming that the business is doing well. If the owners subsequently decide to sell the business, it should be worth far more than it cost them to set it up and run it, so this is another major return on their investment.

Banks and financial service providers

Service payments, debt management and debt and credit dependency

All businesses need the services provided by banks. The primary service is to provide a bank account and banking facilities for the business. Banks usually charge businesses a fee for running their accounts, because compared to an individual's bank account, the payments in and out of a business account are far more frequent and usually take up the time of specialist bank employees. They therefore charge a service payment to the business, in return for which the bank deals with all the banking requirements of the business.

Just like individuals, businesses also have **overdraft** facilities. This gives them a degree of flexibility with their money. It is often the case that a business will find itself in a position where it has to pay out money to suppliers, for example, before it has received payment from its customers. The bank and the business will agree a level of overdraft suitable for the business and its needs. The bank will be concerned to ensure that the business remains within its overdraft limits and will charge additional fees if they spend more than the agreed overdraft amount.

It is also the case that many businesses seek loans either from banks or other financial service providers. They obtain loans in order to fund current projects in the hope that future profits will be more than sufficient to pay back the loans. Many businesses have to rely very heavily on their banks or financial service providers in order to bridge the gap between their immediate needs for cash and their expected

Keyword

> **overdraft** – an agreed amount of money that the account holder can spend, even if there is a nil balance in their account

WANT TO FIND OUT MORE?

Visit the **Bank of Scotland** website, which is one of many banks or financial service providers in the UK that offers accounts and services to businesses. The website is at: www.bankofscotland.co.uk/business.

income in the future. Businesses have to be careful not to borrow too much money, which they cannot realistically expect to be able to pay back. Banks and financial service providers will look carefully at a business's need for this form of credit and make a judgement as to whether it is reasonable to assume that in the future they will be in a position to pay the credit back to them.

Staff and trade unions

As we have already seen, a trade union is an organisation of workers that seeks to protect and advance the interests of its members. It negotiates with employers on issues such as pay and conditions and also provides its members with legal and financial advice, as well as many other services. Above all, a trade union is an independent organisation separate from the employers that employ their members.

However, the employer, for the benefit of their employees, often sets up a staff association. This is not independent from the employer. The purpose of both types of organisation is to give the employees a single point of contact with their employers when negotiations, disputes or other problems arise.

Table 2.3 summarises the roles and expectations of staff associations and trade unions in their dealings with employers.

Table 2.3
Roles and expectations of staff associations and trade unions in dealings with employers

Role	Expectations
Wages	That employers offer their employees a competitive wage or salary, which matches the skills or expertise of the employees.
Benefits	That the employer offers their employees additional benefits, such as health cover, enhanced leave, company discounts, travel season-ticket loans or company vehicles.
Working conditions	In addition to making sure that the employer provides working conditions demanded by legislation, the expectation is for the employer to provide better working conditions, such as a cleaner and more attractive environment, staff canteen and access to decision-makers.
Job development and security	The expectation is for employers to provide opportunities for their employees to develop their careers, either by on-the-job training or the ability to attend courses outside the workplace. In addition, the employers are expected to provide their employees with job security, which means not fearing that they will lose their jobs and feeling that they are secure in their job position.
Equal opportunities and treatment of staff	There are a number of laws that the employer is expected to follow with regard to equal opportunities and the treatment of staff, such as religious and ethnic minorities. Equal opportunity means that the employers are expected to treat all staff, regardless of their circumstances, in exactly the same way, both in terms of how they are dealt with at work and their promotion prospects.
Observing health and safety	There are a number of laws that govern the health and safety of employees at work. Not only are the employers expected to adhere to these laws, but they are also expected to take all reasonable steps to ensure that their employees are not in danger, either in using equipment or machinery or are at risk from carrying out their daily tasks.

Staff turnover

As we have seen, skilled and experienced employees are one of the most valuable resources of the business. Staff turnover means the number of staff actually leaving the business to seek work elsewhere. High staff turnover can have a drastic effect on a business and many businesses are seeking ways in which they can ensure that their key members of staff remain with them. Businesses need to make sure that their staff feel that they belong and are valued. Businesses use a number of different methods to try to ensure that their staff remain with them. These include:

- **Motivating** their staff by being supportive and encouraging.
- Ensuring that from the very first day the employees are made welcome, know what they are supposed to do and how their job fits into the overall business.

Keyword

motivating – making employees more willing to work hard and take pride in the work they produce

contract of employment – a written, legal agreement between the employer and employee that states their rights, responsibilities and duties towards one another

Keyword

- Making sure that the **contract of employment** (the agreement between the employer and the employee) is fair and that the pay rates are competitive. In addition, staff benefits should be included as part of the package.
- Ensuring that the right person, according to their skills and experience, is placed in the right job. Also that staff training is available for employees that feel they need additional help to improve their work.
- Making sure that as often as possible employees can work together as a team. It has been seen over the years that teams not only work better but they also support one another.
- Ensuring that the employer offers flexible working because many employees have other commitments outside of work, such as children or elderly parents, and that they can balance their outside commitments with work.

CASE STUDY   Cost of staff turnover

The Chartered Institute of Personnel and Development has recently carried out some research that showed that the cost of replacing managers or professional staff is £6,000. The average cost of staff turnover per employee is around £4,000. The research discovered that employees in the public sector, such as teachers, are less likely to leave their jobs than those in the private sector. The public sector finds it difficult to recruit new staff. In the retail and leisure sector many businesses have a 50 per cent staff turnover each year. This is largely blamed on poor wages and a lack of opportunities to develop careers.

INDIVIDUAL WORK (2.34) ★ ★
Read the case study and answer the following questions.

1 Why might a business find it more expensive to replace a manager or a professional member of staff than an average employee?

2 Why do you think it might be the case that employees that work in the public sector are less likely to leave their jobs?

3 How might a business experiencing a 50 per cent turnover of their staff reduce this percentage?

Training and staff development

One of the most effective ways in which a business can ensure that its key members of staff remain with them is to offer them training and staff development. There is a bewildering range of different forms of training and staff development, but they can be best described in one of the following categories:

- *On-the-job training* The employee receives training, usually from an experienced member of staff or a specialist trainer, whilst they are doing their job in their place of work. This form of training allows the employee to understand how the training relates directly to their own work.
- *Off-the-job training* This type of training includes all types of education and staff development that takes place away from the workplace. The employee may attend a local college or training agency and receive instruction in areas that have a relevance to their work.

Sponsors: reputation and association, prospects and performance

Sponsorship is a business relationship between a provider of funds, resources or services and an individual, organisation or event. Businesses are often sponsors of local, national and regional events, sports, including football, and a host of other activities. The business will look at a number of different factors in deciding whether or not to become involved as a sponsor, these include whether:

- The event or sports organisation appeals to the type of customers the business serves or wants to attract.
- The event or sports organisation has the right kind of image for the business.
- The arrangement enhances the image of the business.
- There is an opportunity to communicate the nature of the products and services offered by the business.
- It will improve customer awareness and understanding.
- It will help with community, investor and trade relations.
- The business can obtain media coverage (such as a football match being televised or reported in a newspaper).
- It will help with customer loyalty.

The major businesses involved in sponsorship in the UK include those involved in insurance, alcohol, banks, motor vehicles, sports goods and clothing, food products, the media, power generation and non-alcoholic drinks.

The major growth areas in sponsorship are food, confectionery, cosmetics, travel, transportation, local authorities and government departments.

The key reasons why a sponsor may become involved are shown in Table 2.4.

Table 2.4
Key reasons for sponsor involvement

Type of product or service	Main objectives of the business	Additional objectives of the business
Beer	To attract younger customers	To encourage customers to take a responsible attitude towards drinking and driving
Soap powder	To reinforce the awareness and image of the product	To have a higher profile than the competitors
Motor cars	To convince the general public to test drive their vehicles	To increase the business for their dealers
Newspapers	To increase the number of younger readers	To put forward a younger and more trendy image
Banks	To attract students and younger investors	To forge links with different groups in the community
Soft drinks	To reinforce the awareness and image of the product	To convince parents and schools that the products are not bad for children

CASE STUDY   Barclaycard Premiership football deal

In 2001, Barclaycard agreed a three-year sponsorship deal with the FA Premiership Football League. Barclaycard would pay £48 million over the three years. Bob Potts, the chief executive of Barclaycard, said at the time, 'The Premiership will be the platform to take our business into a league of its own.' The chief executive of the FA Premier League, Richard Scudamore, said, 'It is a great opportunity for the league and Barclaycard to build on each other's strength and growing reputation throughout the world.'

GROUP WORK (2.35) ★ ★

Read the case study and then answer the following questions and carry out the additional activity.

1 What is Barclaycard's business?

2 Give three advantages to Barclaycard's association with the Premiership.

3 Using the internet, find out who is the kit sponsor of your favourite football team. What is the sponsor's type of business and in which sector do they operate?

Sponsors are careful in choosing the type of event or organisation they become involved with. They do not want a situation where the event or group that they sponsor has a negative effect on their business. Therefore they will look for a sponsorship arrangement that adds to their reputation and, above all, one that is a success.

Local communities and environmental concerns

Pollution, litter, noise, traffic, crime and environmental health

Wherever a business chooses to locate, it is the local, immediate community that may suffer as a result of the decision. Some businesses, aside from the construction of the premises that would involve building work and, perhaps the construction of roads, may have little long-term effect on a community. For the most part, however, all businesses, regardless of their location, do have some negative impact on the local community. At the very least, additional traffic, noise and pollution is brought to the area.

There are constant news stories that link pollution and environmental problems to health matters of communities. The use of chemicals, emissions from factories and vehicles, and a host of accidental leaks from factories have caused concerns. The soil may be polluted as well as the air and even the water.

It has been estimated that by 2025 there will be more than a billion cars on the road in the world. These cars put 900 million tonnes of carbon dioxide into the air. By 2025, it is expected that around two-thirds of the world's population will live in cities, making traffic jams and pollution even more of an important consideration.

Noise pollution from businesses, particularly those involved in manufacturing, transportation and distribution, are investigated by Environmental Health Officers. The number of complaints has doubled since 1994. Local governments are required to monitor the number and the source of noise complaints made in their area. Environmental Health Officers present their data by showing the number of noise complaints per million of the population. Surprisingly, the most common form of noise complaint is actually from domestic households, including parties and barking dogs. There were 1,273 complaints per million of the population regarding industrial or commercial premises, but there was an additional 372 from vehicles, machinery and equipment in the streets, a further 347 from road works, construction and the demolition of buildings and only 37 for road traffic. A growing number of complaints, which has in fact trebled since 1994, is noise pollution from aircraft, now at 101 complaints per million of the population.

Local councils are at the forefront of dealing with environmental health problems. A typical example is Burnley Borough Council. Their environmental health and cleansing services dealt with 40,000 requests for assistance in 2004. These included 17,000 cases when they had to remove waste that had been abandoned, 6,000 environmental health complaints, 1,800 pest control requests and 950 food safety and health safety inspections. In one year alone, they collected 30,000 tonnes of household waste, in addition to a vast amount collected from businesses.

WANT TO FIND OUT MORE?

To find out more about various forms of pollution and what the government intends to do about it, visit the **Department of Health** website at: www.dh.gov.uk and follow the link to 'Policy and guidance'. Click on the health and social care topics to see a full list of all of the concerns regarding issues such as noise pollution.

GROUP WORK (2.36)
★ ★

In groups of two or three, contact your local council and find out the full range of responsibilities of the local environmental health officers. What particular problems do they have with businesses in your area?

Pressure groups and ethical concerns over business practices

As we have seen, there are thousands of pressure groups that seek to influence both government and businesses. Generally it is in a business's best interests to ensure that they behave in a morally correct manner. This means that they should apply right and wrong to all of their business decisions. They can no longer simply be concerned with the most profitable way forward. They must take account of the fact that their actions and activities have an **ethical** consideration.

Businesses are made up of individuals that have their own values and principles. These individuals bring these values to work with them. Businesses are also concerned that they should develop their own 'corporate ethics', which means that the business itself has moral standards, values and principles. There are a number of advantages to running a business with ethical standards, including:

ethical – the way in which a business and its employees should respond to situations if they are to show integrity and social responsibility

Keyword

- The business's customers can be made aware of their ethical behaviour and, as a result, these customers and others may be more attracted to the business.

- The business may be able to forge relationships with other businesses or suppliers that share the same ethical standards and together they can be a force to be reckoned with in the marketplace.

- Employees will also benefit from an ethical standard as they will be more positive and motivated and proud to work for a business that has these standards.

Businesses also recognise the fact that having ethical standards may have disadvantages, including:

- The business may be less profitable as it may refuse to deal with other businesses that exploit their employees.
- Adopting ethics may cause problems with the way in which the business has traditionally carried out its operations and there may be a period of transition that could be a difficult time for the business.

Problems of sourcing from developing countries

Even some of the most well-known businesses in the world have been accused of exploiting child and female labour in developing countries. In 1997, the Hong Kong-based Asia Monitor Resource Centre discovered that the Walt Disney Co. was paying its Hong Kong workers 6p per hour and they were forced to work a 70-hour week. At the same time, in Haiti, the same company was paying its workers £1.50 per day. The cost of feeding a family each day in Haiti was £1.70. There were just three toilets for the 250 workers to use.

Nike is another major business that has been accused of exploiting employees from developing countries. The bulk of their trainers are made in Indonesia, China and Vietnam. In Indonesia, for example, an average family would need $75 per month to survive. Nike was paying less than half of this amount to their employees.

WANT TO FIND OUT MORE?

Visit the **Global Exchange** website at: www.globalexchange.org and follow the links to 'Sweatshops'.

Environmental damage

Shortly after midnight on 3 December 1984, poisonous gas leaked from a factory in Bhopal, India, owned by the US company Union Carbide. The gas swept across the nearby city and the result was 20,000 deaths and in excess of 120,000 people injured, including blindness and difficulties in breathing. Even today, tests indicate that the entire area is polluted. Some pollutants, such as mercury, are up to six million times higher than in normal conditions. Another chemical company purchased Union Carbide in 2001, but the problems still affect the inhabitants in the Bhopal area of India.

Although the Bhopal incident was an extreme example of how businesses can inflict environmental damage on developing countries, there are hundreds of examples of similar poisoning risks and contamination everywhere in the world. In September 2002, the United Nations Environment Programme announced a new drive for a healthier and cleaner world. It hopes to ensure that chemicals used by businesses are used in a far safer way by 2020 and that pollution in the seas is tackled by 2012. Klaus Toepher, the Executive Director of the United Nations Environment Programme said of the initiative, 'We now have an initiative to encourage industry to improve their social and environmental performance.' Only time will tell whether the United Nations' and other governments' efforts will make any progress.

Dangerous working conditions and payment of unacceptably low wages

There are many employees in the world who face both poor and dangerous working conditions, as well as low wages. It has been estimated that around 211 million children between the ages of five and 14 years work for a living around the world. Many of the child workers, as well as older workers, are forced to work in factories, making matches, fireworks, glassware and bricks, in extremely hazardous conditions. Unfortunately, at this time, many businesses and consumers in the more developed countries enjoy the benefits of cheap products produced by these workers in the lesser-developed world. Gradually, however, businesses and consumers are beginning to realise that these forms of exploitation would not be accepted in their own countries and they are putting pressure on businesses abroad that place their employees under these awful conditions.

WANT TO FIND OUT MORE?

Visit the **Ethical Trading Initiative** website at: www.ethicaltrade.org.

Tax avoidance and evasion

According to Oxfam, businesses operating in developing countries avoid up to $50 billion of tax every year. The businesses establish their legal headquarters in what is known as a tax haven. This is a country that does not levy tax on businesses that have established

WANT TO FIND OUT MORE?

If you want to find out more about **Oxfam**'s report on the hidden billions, visit: www.oxfam.org.uk and type 'hidden billions' in the search box.

themselves within their borders. These businesses do not pay tax in the developing countries, so there is more poverty than ever before as the governments of the developing countries cannot collect the taxes from the businesses. As a result, it has been estimated that 1.2 billion people worldwide do not have access to health facilities, 125 million primary school children do not have schools and 20 per cent of the world is living in poverty.

Supply of socially harmful products

In many countries in the world, governments have taken steps to try to prevent businesses from supplying socially harmful products. These include products such as tobacco, weapons, alcohol and milk substitutes for children. Harmful products are often targeted at vulnerable groups of consumers. Alcohol manufacturers often target poor countries or poor areas of the country, whilst in the developing world tobacco companies design advertisements to attract young people to smoking.

It is difficult for a government to control what a business does in another country, but increasingly governments have begun to pressurise businesses to stop exploiting developing countries by selling products that would not be legal in their own country.

CASE STUDY Milk substitute

According to the World Health Organisation and the United Nations Children's Fund, feeding babies with artificial milk substitutes causes 1.5 million child deaths every year, the equivalent of one death every 30 seconds. The worldwide market for breast milk substitutes is worth £20 billion per year. Only three governments, Brazil, Iran and Zambia, have brought in laws to prevent companies that sell breast milk substitutes from claiming that their product is superior to breast milk. In these developing countries free samples and gifts to mothers and health workers, along with misleading advertising and labelling on the products, have convinced millions of mothers not to breast-feed. At present these milk-substitute businesses are targeting China, where over 20 million babies are born every year.

INDIVIDUAL WORK (2.37) ★ ★

Read the case study and visit www.ibfan.org; click on 'English'.

1 Find out the names of the 16 companies involved in providing baby milk substitutes.

2 How many of them operate in the UK?

POLITICAL, ECONOMIC, SOCIAL, TECHNOLOGICAL, LEGAL AND OTHER EXTERNAL INFLUENCES

In considering political, economic, social, technological, legal and other external influences, a business is undertaking what is known as environmental analysis. It is variously known as PEST (Political, Economic, Social and Technological), STEP (Social, Technological, Economic and Political), STEEP (Social, Technological, Environmental, Economic and Political) or PESTLE (Political, Economic, Social, Technological, Legal and Environmental).

A business needs to look at all of these factors that can have an impact on their operations.

- *Political factors* include changes in legislation, such as data protection, environmental policies, employment law and legislation regarding products.

- *Technology* involves checking that new innovations or ways in which customers purchase products and services are not going to catch the business unaware.

- *Economic factors* include changes in the interest rate, the levels of employment and how well a country is trading with overseas nations.

- *Social or cultural changes* are also important, including the number of men and women, their ages, the number of children being born, the number of home-owning households and the amount of income a household has available to spend.

Legal changes are closely linked with political changes and businesses will ensure that they are aware of the intentions of various political parties before a general election and try to make a judgement as to how laws, which the political party wishes to bring into force, may affect their operations.

The business needs to be aware of its impact on the *environment*, how the community views its operations and whether or not the government is likely to bring in legislation that will force them to take on more environmental responsibilities.

CASE STUDY Ban on foxhunting

There are around 250,000 adult foxes in the UK. They produce around 400,000 cubs each year, the vast majority of which die in their first year of life. Foxhunting is said to account for some 20,000 foxes each year. The Countryside Alliance, which supports foxhunting, claims that nearly 16,000 people directly depend on foxhunting for their jobs. Defra, the government department responsible for agriculture, estimates this figure in fact to be no more than 1,000 people. It is said that over three-quarters of the population support a ban on foxhunting. As of November 2004 the government announced that it was their intention to make foxhunting illegal by November 2006.

INDIVIDUAL WORK (2.38) ★ ★
Read the case study regarding the ban on foxhunting.

1 Why do you think there is such a difference in the numbers of people quoted as being employed from the two different sources?

2 Assuming that the higher figure is correct, what impact might the ban on foxhunting have on rural communities?

3 What kind of businesses are threatened by this political move?

Impact of political issues

There is a wide range of political issues that could have an effect on businesses. The vast majority of these cause uncertainty and concern as businesses may be unsure as to the impact these political issues may have in the short, medium and long term.

Elections

In all democratic countries, such as the UK, elections take place every four or five years. In the months before an election date being decided, the political parties announce many new plans and initiatives, a large number of which will have an impact on businesses. Whilst businesses can do little to determine the outcome of an election (they can donate money to political parties to help them fight the election), they need to be aware of the implications of any of the major parties coming to power. The political parties release a summary of all of their policies, known as a manifesto, and businesses and employers' associations carefully read these manifestos to see how the plans might affect them. If a business is thinking about pushing through a particular project around the time that an election is called, they may have to rethink their strategies, as a new government may have policies that could affect their plans. Many businesses are cautious at these times and wait until the outcome of the election is known before making huge investments in terms of time and money.

Terrorist attacks

At the time of writing, it is over three years since the terrorist attacks on New York in September 2001. Around the world there has been an increased awareness of possible terrorist attacks. In March 2004 alone, British police arrested six alleged terrorists and seized 600 kg of bomb-making equipment. Currently there are 25 international terrorist organisations and a further 14 terrorist organisations based in Northern Ireland. As far as the government and many businesses are concerned, all of these groups represent a threat. Few people have ever heard of many of the organisations, yet governments, businesses and experts believe that all of them remain a credible terrorist threat.

WANT TO FIND OUT MORE?

If you want to find out more about the various groups and what the UK is doing to protect its people and businesses, visit the **Home Office** website, as they are responsible for countering terrorism in the UK. www.homeoffice.gov.uk; click on the link to 'Terrorism'.

Fear of war

With the exception of the war on terrorism, there has not been a major war involving the UK for a number of years. Nonetheless, threats of war, or conflict abroad that might involve the UK, can cause business a great deal of uncertainty. Wars inevitably mean deaths and destruction of property and these may either directly or indirectly affect UK businesses. The government advises British passport holders living or working abroad of any threats to their well-being from wars or potential conflicts. It is not always possible, of course, for these individuals to seek immediate safety and it is even more difficult for UK businesses to protect their property and operations in a war zone abroad.

Changing regimes in foreign countries

As we have seen, democratic elections can often mean a completely new government. This uncertainty regarding government changes is as important when it concerns an overseas country. Many overseas countries are democracies and they have elections. As a result the changes in government are relatively smooth.

In a large number of overseas countries, however, there is no democracy and individuals or groups that pay little attention to their own people, let alone overseas businesses. In the past, countries as close to the UK as France, Germany, Italy and Russia have all had these non-democratic forms of government. In a world where business is increasingly becoming global and British businesses are involved in hundreds of countries, it is inevitable that problems overlap from country to country.

CASE STUDY Zimbabwe

Since December 1987, President Robert Mugabe has ruled Zimbabwe. Many overseas countries were involved in mining, steel, cement, chemicals, clothing, food production and a variety of other industries, but over the years the president has seized their property and confiscated it. Other political parties have been forced into silence, thousands have starved and very few countries will now have anything to do with Zimbabwe. As a result of the difficult situation in the country, very few international businesses risk becoming involved with Zimbabwe. The population of Zimbabwe now faces the situation where shortages of food, clothing, petrol and other things have changed their lifestyles.

GROUP WORK (2.39) ★ ★

Read the case study and, using the internet, find out more about businesses in Zimbabwe.

1 What is the current political situation?

2 Would it give confidence to an international business to invest in the country at the moment?

3 Which countries did Zimbabwe trade with before their current problems emerged?

> **Keyword**
>
> **inflation** – a rise in the average price of goods and services in an economy
>
> **balance of payments** – the difference between a country's income and expenditure on overseas trade

Impact of macroeconomic variables

Macroeconomic variables are situations that affect the economy of the country or the world as a *whole*. The UK and the world go through changes in levels of business activity. It is generally the case that there are four major forms of variable that could have a direct impact upon business. These are the:

- Rate of general economic growth in the country
- Rate of **inflation**
- Level of unemployment
- **Balance of payments**.

Implications of major economic trends

The rate of overall *economic growth* of a country has a direct impact on the fortunes of its businesses. Economic growth or the lack of it refers to the general level of business activity in a country. This means that all business activity taken together can be seen as a vital indication of whether or not the country is experiencing economic growth. In other words, if the majority of businesses in a country are experiencing greater demand and probably making higher profits, then the country is experiencing economic growth.

The *rate of inflation* has a direct impact on prices. As we will see when we look at consumer spending and confidence, there are times when the increase in the prices of products and services outstrips household incomes. This means that households are less able to afford products and services. The problem with inflation is that there is a tendency when this happens for employees to demand higher wages so that they can still afford to purchase the products that they demand. As every increase in an employee's salary adds to the business's costs, this means that businesses have to charge more for their products and services. This, once again, pushes up prices and causes inflation. Governments are very concerned that the country does not get into this cycle and, in order to prevent unnecessary spending, they often increase the interest rates so that people do not borrow money to buy more and push inflation up.

If a country is experiencing a period of high *unemployment* then it has a dual impact on the country and on businesses. The first impact it has is that the unemployed cannot afford to purchase products and services at the same rate that they could when they were employed. This means that there is a lower demand for products and services. The second problem is that with so many people out of work they need to be supported by those in work. In order to pay for their benefits and housing, it is usual for governments to increase the tax on those in work and tax business profits more heavily.

A country's *balance of payments* may appear to be a very complicated issue. But in reality it is really quite simple. Imagine an employee as a country. The employee earns a certain amount of money each month. We can pretend that this is the money that the country earns from overseas by selling products and services. The employee also buys products and services each month and we can compare this to what the country buys from overseas. Ideally, the amount the country earns should be more than it spends on buying, otherwise, as with an employee who spends more than they earn, there will be a point when they cannot over-spend any more. This is how the balance of payments works. Countries literally try to balance what they buy with what they earn. Often this is not possible and many countries, including the USA, owe billions of pounds to overseas countries, where they have bought more (imported) than they have sold (exported). So, therefore, the balance of payments is equal to the difference between the imports of a country, what they have spent, and the exports of a country, what they have earned.

Some overseas countries do not have any option but to import more than they export, as either the products and services they produce are not wanted abroad or they have a relatively low value. They still need to buy technology, medicines, vehicles and a host of other products and services that they cannot produce themselves.

Booms, recessions and slumps

A *boom* is a period of rapid economic growth, when the economy is growing so fast it cannot continue growing at that rate for the foreseeable future. During booms, businesses experience an enormous increase in demand and are able to earn large profits.

A *recession* is a period when the economy begins to slow down and there is considerably less demand for products and services. Businesses find themselves in a position where it is difficult to sell their products and services. In many cases businesses are unable to predict that a recession is about to happen.

A *slump* usually occurs when businesses begin to react to a recession. In the knowledge that there is reduced demand for their products and services, they cut back on the production of products and on the delivery of services. This means that they need fewer employees. The employees become unemployed and as there are increased numbers of unemployed, there is less demand for products and services. And so the cycle continues until the economy is in a very poor state of health. It is for the government to step in and provide encouragement to businesses to increase production and take on more staff in order to break the cycle. This is usually done by making it easier and cheaper for businesses to borrow money and take the risk in investing when times are uncertain.

GROUP WORK (2.40)

★ ★

Look through some of the national newspapers available in your school/college or local library and see if you can find the answers to the following questions.

1 At the present time, what is the state of the UK's economy?

2 Is the UK considered to be in a state of economic growth?

3 Does the UK owe a huge amount of money to other countries?

Variation in spending and confidence

Businesses also need to be aware of changes in consumer spending and confidence. Generally, households respond to fears of higher unemployment and economic slowdowns by spending less, particularly on luxury items such as cars or home improvements. On the other hand, when the economy is doing well and people are confident about their job security, they will be willing to take the risk and borrow more in order to purchase luxury items.

It is not only businesses that are concerned with these changes in consumer confidence and spending. The Bank of England, which sets the interest rates, looks carefully at consumer confidence. From their assessment they can make estimates of future demand for products and services and adjust the interest rates, either to increase confidence (reduce interest rates) or curb confidence (increase interest rates).

Consumer confidence, therefore, is affected by:

- The interest rate and mortgage rates.
- Changes in general unemployment and individuals' job security.
- Inflation.
- Changes in direct and indirect taxation (income tax and VAT).
- The availability of lump sums (such as profits from shares).

The housing market

In theory at least, just like any other market, the number of houses available for sale compared to the number of people wishing to buy homes should affect the prices of those homes. In most markets, if there are more products available than are demanded by customers then prices fall in order to attract more customers. When there are few products available, but many customers who wish to buy them, then prices increase because customers are prepared to pay more for the product.

This has been the nature of the housing market over the past few years. There have been more potential house buyers than properties available. As we will see in the case study below, eventually there comes a point when, even if there is a limited supply of houses and the demand is still high, prices reach a point where they are no longer affordable.

Since houses are probably the single most expensive purchase a household will make, they are seen as a very useful indicator of how the economy in general is performing. High demand usually means consumer confidence and an expectation that their incomes will continue to rise for the foreseeable future. Therefore they seek to make the decision to buy either their first or a larger home. In situations when households feel that their jobs are not secure and they lack confidence in their long-term ability to be able to pay a mortgage, they either decide to stay in their current home or they choose to rent a property to live in.

CASE STUDY   The housing market

In 2004, there were enormous housing price rises across the UK. Wales saw a 38 per cent increase in just one year and even the already expensive London area saw an 8 per cent rise. In the previous 12 months there were five interest rate rises, but little seemed to hold back the enormous price increases. On average, compared to the previous year, house prices in September 2004 were 17.8 per cent higher.

What was of particular concern was the difference between mortgage borrowers' salaries and house prices. In London and the south-east, house prices were 6.75 times the average wage. In the north-west, they were 5.78 times more. There has been a recent slow down in the number of houses sold, as prices have continued to rise compared to rises in wages and salaries.

INDIVIDUAL WORK (2.41) ★ ★

Read the case study and answer the following questions.

1 Why do you think the huge difference between wages and salaries and house prices is so significant?

2 Why do you think that London house prices are more expensive than anywhere else in the country?

3 Why do you think Wales might have experienced such a huge increase in house prices?

Interest rate changes

The fortunes of many businesses can be affected by changes in interest rates. Generally speaking, rising interest rates mean that consumers cut back on spending, as they do not wish to borrow additional money. A prime example of this effect is the fortunes of Britain's largest consumer electronics retailer, Dixons. After the Bank of England had increased the interest rate on five occasions before October 2004, Dixons had recorded the slowest increase in their sales for the year. Their Chief Executive, John Clare, said, 'The rate of sales growth has slowed in recent weeks and we are cautious about the outlook for consumer expenditure.' Their relatively poor performance was despite the fact that new wide-screen televisions and iPod music players were selling well.

Taxation changes

Changes in taxation can affect a business in two radically different ways.

- If taxation is increased, as far as the tax collected on a business's profits is concerned, then the business will have less money to reinvest and to pay to its investors.

- If taxation is increased, as far as customers are concerned, this means that they will have less **disposable income** and, therefore, less money available to buy products and services.

There are two major forms of taxation:

- *Direct taxation* takes the form of tax collected on either profits, wages or salaries.

- *Indirect taxation*, such as Value Added Tax (VAT), is taken on the value of products and services each time they are sold.

> **Keyword**
>
> **disposable income** – the money available to an individual or a household after the payment of tax and other deductions and after the payment of all essential bills, such as mortgage, rent, council tax and utilities

Central and local government spending

Central and local government spending can be a strong influence on the fortunes of businesses, regions and the country as a whole. Government spending includes the construction of motorways, major developments, the setting up of departments, and the purchasing of vehicles and equipment. This is in addition to all the standard spending required to run government offices, including the wages and salaries bill.

There is a theory that suggests that every pound spent by the government has what is known as a *multiplier effect* in the economy. If, for example, a local government department takes on 10 new members of staff and pays them £12,000 a year each, then they have put £120,000 into the economy. Some of this will be collected as taxation, but the balance will be spent on housing and various businesses' products and services. This money in turn, which has been earned by these businesses, can be used to employ their own new staff, who will then spend money on housing and buy other products and services, and so on.

Impact of social issues

As we have seen, businesses cannot operate without coming to the attention of governments, consumers and the community. There have been significant concerns about the way in which some businesses run their operations and, in virtually every case, the businesses in question have suffered if they have refused to take account of the criticisms.

Table 2.5 summarises three recent social issues that have caused many businesses to rethink the way in which they actually do business.

Table 2.5
Three recent social issues affecting businesses

Social issue	Explanation and impact
Product quality	Perhaps the biggest debate regarding product quality relates to genetically modified (GM) foods. The first GM plants were created in 1983, with the idea of creating new versions of crop plants that would improve the amount that could be harvested, making them resistant to disease and insects and to modify the amount of fat, protein or vitamins in the plants. In the UK, GM tomatoes, soya and maize are legally available, but there are many other processed foods, including biscuits and sauces, which include GM ingredients. Of more significance, many of the products created to feed animals have GM ingredients. Within the EU, any product that contains GM ingredients must indicate this on the label. A full explanation of the labelling requirements in the EU is shown in Table 2.6. The government and the EU ensure that all GM products are carefully checked before they are given approval to be sold in Europe.
Environmental damage	In the UK the government has adopted what is known as a *polluter pays policy*. This means that businesses that have caused environmental damage are responsible for paying for any clear-up operations necessary. This means that businesses that pollute rivers, water supplies, soil, and air or leave other traces of their operations must pay to deal with the situation. One of the biggest problems is dealing with nuclear waste. It has been estimated that the costs of dealing with current nuclear waste will be at least £2 billion.
Social injustice	Many consumers and employees have reacted very strongly to directors of businesses receiving huge bonuses whilst the business itself reduces its number of employees and, perhaps, closes factories or offices. Many people consider that this is an unfair act and that it should be the shareholders that have the right to decide on the level of directors' pay and whether or not they should be entitled to any bonuses.

Table 2.6
Labelling rules for GM ingredients in the EU

Categories	Example	Current situation	New rules
1 Products made from GM crops, but no GM material present	Highly refined maize oil, soya bean oil, rapeseed oil, alcoholic beverages	Labelling not required	Labelling required
2 Products made from GM crops and GM material present	Maize, soya bean sprouts, tomato, maize flour	Labelling required	As current
3 Labelling of food made using genetic modification technology	Cheese produced with the help of chymosin from GM micro-organisms	Labelling not required	As current
4 Labelling of food made from animals fed on GM animal feed	Milk, meat and eggs	Labelling not required	As current
5 Threshold for approved GM varieties	Approved maize and soya	Threshold is set at 1 per cent	Threshold agreed at 0.9 per cent in December 2002, but may be subject to change pending discussions in the European Parliament. There will also be a threshold of 0.5 per cent for non-EU approved varieties.
6 Food sold in catering outlets	Restaurant menus and takeaways	Optional (compulsory in UK where GM material is present in final food, in line with current labelling rules)	Labelling required, although detailed rules yet to be developed

CASE STUDY Fat-cat bonuses

The insurer Standard Life, having slashed payouts to its 2.6 million policyholders five times over two years, paid its former chief executive, Iain Lumsden, a staggering £1.13 million in salary and performance-related bonuses. When Sandy Crombie replaced him, the new chief executive received a 16 per cent increase, including £135,000 annual bonus. All of the other major directors received huge bonuses in excess of £80,000 each.

A spokesperson for the business, in response to criticisms, said, 'We have no doubt that the overall remuneration [salary and bonuses] we pay our top people is not excessive and it offers members [customers] good value.'

INDIVIDUAL WORK (2.42) ★ ★

David Stonebanks, a policyholder with Standard Life and the spokesperson for the campaign against these payouts said, 'The only thing I would say is that this is what we have come to expect. Policyholders will obviously not be happy at all. People have lost a lot of money, and yet they see the gravy train apparently rolling on.'

1 What do you think Mr Stonebanks means by the 'gravy train'?

2 If Standard Life's policyholders, as stakeholders of the business, are losing out, how might the business justify these payouts to top directors?

Impact of changing technology

Design, production and communication developments

With new technology developing fast, many businesses, particularly smaller ones, are finding it is having an impact on the way that they run their activities. Businesses have realised that in order to take full advantage of technological developments, in addition to keeping up with their larger competitors, they have to change their way of working. The business's managers have to realise the potential of the technological changes, particularly in smaller organisations, where there may be fewer staff experienced in the use of IT.

Larger businesses, however, are finding that the role of their IT staff is changing. These individuals are required more and more to become involved in the other areas and the needs of the business as a whole, such as finance and general management. In addition, many businesses are no longer employing specialist IT staff, but are **outsourcing** these skills.

Without doubt, the changing nature of information technology has had the greatest impact on businesses. The following major technological trends are gradually affecting nearly every business:

> **Keyword**
>
> **outsourcing** – using individuals or other businesses to carry out the tasks previously undertaken by employees of the business

- *The growth of e-commerce*, which means that businesses have to learn the new technologies involved in selling and marketing on the internet.

- *The trend towards remote working*, which has seen ever increasing numbers of employees either working from home or in offices connected only to the main business by computer.

- *The trend towards using outsourcing*. This is particularly the case in IT and in customer services, where businesses have established these services abroad.

CASE STUDY IT skills shortage

Over the next 10 years [2004–2014], UK businesses will need almost 200,000 new IT professionals. Universities are only producing 8,300 IT graduates a year. The UK is already lagging behind other countries and even employees that are using IT on a daily basis radically need to upgrade their skills. Many traditional IT jobs are disappearing as those who are involved in IT need to have a much broader range of skills.

INDIVIDUAL WORK (2.43) ★ ★

Read the case study and then answer the following questions.

1 What do you think is meant by the term 'skills shortage'?

2 How might employers assist their employees to upgrade their skills?

3 What is the business term that is used to describe the need to have a broader range of skills?

These trends, and others, mean that businesses need to be fully aware of technological changes in order to remain competitive. Businesses need to appreciate the potential of technological change. Certainly the vast majority of employees now need to be IT-literate, in addition to being able to write and have good numeracy skills. Employees that lack these skills now find their career prospects more limited.

Impact of changing legislation

Government legislation affects almost every area of business activity, including employment, setting up a business, financial activities, production and marketing. In addition to UK legislation, EU laws also have a direct impact on UK businesses. Increasingly, European law has become more important and overrides UK law.

Businesses need to be aware of any new or planned laws that could affect the way in which they operate. Each new law could change at least one aspect of their activities.

In July 2002, a new Employment Act came into force. It was an extremely wide-ranging piece of law which covered work, parents, disputes, equal pay, the hours worked and the right to take time off work for a variety of reasons. The main points of the law were:

- Working mothers would now be entitled to 26 weeks paid and 26 weeks unpaid maternity leave.
- Working fathers would be entitled to two weeks paternity leave.
- Employers would have to be more flexible as far as the mothers and fathers of young children are concerned in terms of the hours worked.
- Disputes at work would need to have clear sets of procedures, understood by both employers and employees.
- Trade union representatives would be entitled to time off to carry out their trade union duties.

In November 2004, the government announced that it intended to ban smoking in offices, factories and other work environments. The ban would eventually mean that in three or four years, 90 per cent of pubs and restaurants would be smoke free. It was part of the government's attempts to reduce the number of smokers by two million by 2009. The government intended to gradually phase-in the smoking ban and that by 2006 there would be no smoking in NHS and government buildings. By the following year any other enclosed public place would be smoke free and by the end of 2008 all licensed premises (pubs and restaurants) would also have a smoking ban.

Clearly these government plans will have a drastic effect on a large number of UK businesses, particularly pubs and restaurants. The feelings of the businesses involved were mixed, but the majority of them believed that a smoking ban would have a negative impact on their businesses.

CASE STUDY Healthy lifestyles

Over the course of the summer of 2004, the government involved 150,000 people in their consultations regarding healthy lifestyles. The government was concerned with the number of obese people in the UK and planned to restrict junk-food advertising and introduce a traffic light system to show shoppers how healthy the food is that they buy.

Red-labelled food will be considered to be too fatty or full of salt and therefore should be avoided. Orange-labelled food will be acceptable in moderation and green-labelled food will be considered healthy and recommended.

INDIVIDUAL WORK (2.44) ★ ★ ★
Read the case study. At the time of writing, these proposals have not been brought into force by the government, but it is highly likely that something like this will be made law in the near future. Think about an average day and the food that you eat. Try to place the food in either the red, orange or green categories. Now answer the following questions.

1 If food were labelled, as is suggested, would it change your eating habits?

2 How might this labelling affect business, such as McDonald's or KFC? Would it mean that fewer customers buy their products?

3 Do you think the government has the right to interfere in what people eat?

Impact of stock market variations

The *stock market* allows investors to buy and sell the shares of public limited companies. As we have seen when we considered stakeholders, shareholders are individuals that own a part of the business by virtue of the fact that they own shares in that business. They will have purchased the shares at a particular price, in the hope that at some point in the future the value of those shares will increase and that should they wish to sell them they will make a profit from the deal. Whilst they own the shares, they will earn dividends, which is a payment made by the business on each share as the investors' portion of the profits the business has made.

There are numerous reasons why share prices vary over time. Sometimes the price changes as a reaction to statements and plans announced by a business. Some of the statements and plans will be seen to be positive and more people will want to buy shares in the business. At other times these announcements may be met with a negative reaction and people will try and sell their shares; therefore the share price will go down. In other cases, however, there are situations beyond the control of the business that has an impact on their share prices. It is usually the case that if a business is making a reasonable or a stable level of profit, then the share price will also stay stable. If they announce poor profits then the share price is likely to drop. If they announce high profits then the share price may leap. All of this, so far, is in the control of the business.

Factors or events may arise that have a negative impact on the share price. Insurance companies, for example, after a particularly poor spell of weather, may have to pay out increased amounts of insurance to their policyholders. This would have an impact on their business, reduce their profitability and probably push their share price down. In reality, however, this is what an insurance business does; it covers policyholders for losses, such as a car accident or a gale tearing the roof off a home. But what happens when events are entirely out of the control of the business?

One such event, as we have already seen, occurred in September 2001, when the terrorist attacks took place on New York and Washington. Not only did they kill a large number of individuals, destroy businesses and buildings, but they also had a drastic effect on investors' confidence. Investors began to sell shares, concerned that their money was not safe on the stock market. Millions of pounds were wiped off the value of businesses overnight and it was only in late 2004 that a degree of confidence returned.

When the value of shares drops, businesses do not have access to this funding and they are forced to plough their profits back into the business in order to continue to operate. This means that shareholders do not receive the same level of dividends that they received in the past. This could well mean that even more shareholders choose to sell their shares.

Impact of key business failures

Every week of the year around 300 UK businesses fail. Higher fuel taxes and the national minimum wage are the main reasons given for these failures, and a probable increase by 2006 to 16,600 failures a year is expected.

CASE STUDY The stock market

Investors' confidence is extremely important and sometimes investors are extremely confident. When this takes place, the stock market is referred to as a 'bull market'. When investors lack confidence and wish to sell their shares and not reinvest, this is often referred to as a 'bear market'. Many things can cause investors' confidence to increase or decrease, such as a high rise in oil prices, the collapse of a major business, terrorist attack, war and a multitude of other reasons.

INDIVIDUAL WORK (2.45) ★ ★

Read the information given in the case study, then research the following.

1 Find out the dates of the last three major stock market crashes.

2 When was the last time that there was a major boom in the stock market?

3 Suggest three things that could happen to a business if its shares drop to a fraction of what they were originally worth.

In the UK, the vast majority of business failures are in the leisure and wholesale sectors, but there are still over 2,000 manufacturing businesses failing each year. Other major reasons for the high level of failure are increases in the interest rate.

Although the closure of even the smallest business causes difficulties for the owners, employees, suppliers and other stakeholders, when this happens to vast businesses the effects can be enormous. Arthur Andersen was once the world's fifth-largest accounting business. In January 2001, Joseph Berardino became the head of the business. His period in power was marked by huge accounting scandals and when the massive energy business, Enron, collapsed in 2001, Andersens, who had been their **auditors**, came under suspicion.

Andersens had a turnover of $9 billion and had a reputation for having the highest ethical standards, but as it was discovered there were a string of major frauds taking place. In October 2002, Arthur Andersen was fined £322,000 and given five years' probation. By this time, of the 85,000 people that had worked for Andersens, only 3,000 still had a job.

Enron, a Texas-based energy business, had been the world's largest energy trading company. It had been involved in gas, electricity and water supply. In 2001, it was discovered that they had been committing fraud and no fewer than nine US banks were involved. Thousands of shareholders lost a total of £17.4 billion. The business collapsed. Enron's founder, Kenneth Lay, was charged with fraud and their stakeholders sued the top executives of the business for $25 billion. Michael Copper pleaded guilty to money laundering and Andrew Fastow received a 10-year prison sentence.

Bernie Ebbers established WorldCom in 1983. They were involved in telephone services and by 1997 they had taken over 50 other businesses. They set their sights on MCI, one of the largest telephone service businesses in the USA. WorldCom, because of their high share price, was able to secure a $37 billion merger with MCI in 1998. In 2000, they tried to buy another telephone service provider, Sprint, but because they would then have controlled too much of the market, the takeover was blocked and the US government began investigating WorldCom. Their share price began to fall and in April 2002 Ebbers resigned, just as a huge fraud at WorldCom had been uncovered.

Between them, Enron and WorldCom had cost investors $240 billion. Lay and Ebbers were behind two of the biggest financial scandals in history. The frauds had begun as early as 1980 and both men had lied about the profitability of their businesses in order to boost the share prices. Major banks were involved and they had funded the businesses throughout two decades. The businesses' debts were hidden and it appeared that both of them were making huge profits. In 2000, Enron claimed they had made $1 billion profit whereas in fact they had made a loss. When the stock market

CASE STUDY Golden Sun Holidays

In September 2004, Golden Sun Holidays, a major tour operator, was forced into bankruptcy. It had been in difficulties for some years and had failed to pay hotels and apartment owners abroad that they featured in their brochures and used as accommodation for their travellers. They had received enormous criticism over the years for placing their customers in accommodation inferior to the accommodation that they had booked. Many hundreds of hotel and apartment owners had not been paid for nearly two years and when the business collapsed over 10,500 holidaymakers were abroad on holidays with Golden Sun. The company was licensed to sell 200,000 holidays each year and some 20,000 people had already paid for their forthcoming holidays. Luckily for these people and those that could have been stranded abroad when the business collapsed, the Air Travel Organisers' Licensing (ATOL) organisation ensured that those who had booked would be refunded and those abroad would be flown home at the end of their stay.

INDIVIDUAL WORK (2.46) ★ ★
Read the case study. For additional information, visit the Civil Aviation Authority website at www.caa.co.uk and use the search facility to find the latest information about Golden Sun. Then answer the following questions.

1 What is an ATOL bond and what is its purpose?

2 What might be the impact of Golden Sun's collapse on hotel and apartment owners abroad?

3 What other travel-related businesses might be affected by the collapse of Golden Sun Holidays?

4 Golden Sun Holidays has what is known as a 'sister company'. What is this business called?

collapsed, in March 2000, WorldCom could no longer cover up their losses. Enron's auditors, Arthur Andersen, discovered a major accounting error and the company's share price collapsed. They were forced into bankruptcy.

Literally thousands of people lost billions of pounds/dollars. The banks that had funded many of the operations were fined tiny sums in comparison to their own profits. The Citigroup, which had been involved for many years, was fined $300 million, a sum that they could easily afford as in 2003 alone they made $16 billion profit.

Unit Revision Questions

1 List three customer expectations of their bank.
2 What is an internal market?
3 Give another name for the term 'end user'.
4 What is an intermediary?
5 What is NS-SEC?
6 What is market research?
7 What are handling costs?
8 Name three different utilities.
9 What is the difference between a debit card and a credit card?
10 What is a SWOT analysis?
11 What is a USP?
12 What is meant by 'consolidation'?
13 What is a merger?
14 What is capital?
15 What is a dividend?
16 What are corporate ethics?
17 What is PESTLE?
18 What is disposable income?
19 What is outsourcing?
20 What is the role of an auditor?

Investigating Financial Control

This unit looks at the vital business calculations that have to be made by all organisations. The unit aims to help you understand why it is important for an organisation to continually look at its costs and revenues to ensure that they are profitable or, at the very least, that they break even.

Organisations that fail to control their cash flow can suffer from grave difficulties and the inability to control cash flow is one of the key reasons why businesses fail. The unit looks at how budgets that are monitored can assist a business in planning its financial future. You will also investigate common types of fraud in financial transactions and how businesses seek to deal with these problems.

This unit is internally assessed. In order to pass this unit, you must:

- Investigate how businesses may make a profit and break even
- Explore cash flow management
- Examine the use of budgets for planning and monitoring expenditure
- Review the importance of recording transactions.

PROFIT AND BREAK-EVEN

Profit is the difference between the selling price and the production cost. Production costs include not only the cost of manufacturing a product, but also all the other costs incurred in the process of producing or delivering a product or a service.

As we will see, businesses often use the term 'net profit', as this is a better indication of the profit actually being made by the business. Net profit is the amount of money made by the business after all of the costs have been taken into account.

A business reaches the *break-even point* when their total **revenue** equals their total costs. Break-even graphs are used to illustrate the total costs and total revenue. At the point when the two lines cross, the business is said to have broken even. Businesses will use break-even analysis to calculate the level of sales that are needed to break even. A business can use this information to work out the impact of a change in price or the level of sales needed to cover a new bank loan.

As we will also see later in this unit, break-even graphs are also used to work out what is known as the *margin of safety*. This is the amount by which demand can fall before the business starts to make a loss instead of a profit.

> **Keyword**
>
> **revenue** – the income received by a business in exchange for selling its products and services

Calculation of profit

Profit, for commercial businesses, is the most important consideration. It is relatively simple to calculate as all that is needed is the total revenue (income) of the business and their total costs. The basic formula is:

$$Profit = Total\ revenue - Total\ costs$$

For example, if a business made £100,000 in sales this would be their total revenue. If the cost of running the business was £80,000, then this would be their total cost. Their profit would be calculated by subtracting the total costs from the total revenues, which would leave the business with a £20,000 profit.

Before we move on to look at revenue and costs in more detail, we need to understand that there are several different types of profit. It is worth remembering that whatever the type of profit, the actual profit is always used in one of two ways:

CASE STUDY Heritage sites fail to break even

In 2004, only nine of the 68 properties and historic buildings open to the public and staffed by the National Trust for Scotland were operating at a profit. In 2002, just six of the then 66 properties were performing in the same manner. The charity has only managed to increase the number of its attractions which produce enough revenue to cover their costs by three, a mere 4.4 per cent of their total.

In 2001, the Trust began reforms to contain a cash crisis and stem falling visitor numbers. In the five years leading up to the implementation of the reforms, tourism in Scotland had declined by 20 per cent and numbers of visitors to NTS properties had fallen by as much as 15 per cent. It all contributed to a deficit of some £2.5 million.

The reforms have already reduced the gap between its operating costs and income from the low of £2.5 million to just over £500,000, with expectations that it will be out of the red by 2005.

A spokesperson for the Trust said: 'Of course, we have to remember that the trust is a charity and not a commercial organisation – clearly it would be unrealistic to expect all our properties to run at a surplus or even to break even. However, even a charity must operate in a financially prudent way.'

INDIVIDUAL WORK
(3.1) ★ ★
Read the case study about heritage sites and answer the following questions.

1 What do you understand by the term 'deficit'?

2 What do you understand by the term 'operating costs'?

3 What do you understand by the term 'surplus'?

4 What do you understand by the phrase 'financially prudent'?

◆ To pay shareholders their dividends

◆ To reinvest in the business (by buying more property or machinery).

Gross profit is the revenue earned by the business minus the cost of making that revenue. The formula looks like this:

$$Gross\ profit = Sales\ revenue - Cost\ of\ sales$$

As we will see later when we look at costs and revenue in more detail, this figure is often calculated to see how much profit the business is making compared to the actual direct costs involved in making that amount of revenue. In other words, how much do the products, components, sales, employees and other directly related costs compare to the overall sales figures achieved by the business.

For example, Bircham's Building Supplies had sales revenue of £376,000 last year. All of the costs associated with those sales cost the business some £312,000 that year; therefore the gross profit is £376,000 – £312,000, which is £64,000.

INDIVIDUAL WORK **(3.2)** ★ ★
Percy's Unicycles have three stores. The first shop in Chichester has sales revenue of £66,000, the second shop in Bridport has sales revenue of £47,000 and the new shop in central London has sales revenue of £129,000.

Cost of sales for the first shop were £18,000, for the second it was £19,000 and for the London shop £47,000.

Calculate the gross profit for each of the shops individually and for the whole business.

Operating profit is another measure of profit and provides a better indication of the actual profit being made by the business. This time, the calculation takes into account all of the other overheads (costs) associated with doing business. The overheads include such necessary costs as rent and rates. The formula for calculating operating profit is:

$$Operating\ profit = Sales\ revenue - Cost\ of\ sales + Overheads$$

Operating profit provides a clearer indication of the profitability of a business as it takes into account all of the other necessary expenses of running the operation. Businesses cannot ignore the costs of rent, rates and other expenses and how this has an impact on the profitability.

Using the information about Bircham's Building Supplies above, this is how operating profits can be calculated. Bircham's had a sales revenue of £376,000 last year. All of the costs associated with those sales cost the business some £312,000 that year. Their overhead costs for the year amount to some £28,000. Therefore the calculation of operating profit is £376,000 less £312,000 (the cost of sales) and £28,000 (the overheads). This leaves the business with an operating profit of just £36,000.

Percy's Unicycles have three stores. The first shop in Chichester has a sales revenue of £66,000, the second shop in Bridport has a sales revenue of £47,000 and the new shop in central London has a sales revenue of £129,000.

Cost of sales for the first shop were £18,000 and their overheads were £16,000, for the second shop they were £19,000 and the overheads were £22,000, and for the London shop £47,000 and overheads of £40,000.

Calculate the operating profit for each of the shops individually and for the whole business.

Business must also take account of the fact that they need to pay tax on their profits. In order to arrive at this figure, the business first has to calculate its pre-tax profits. The business begins with its operating profits and then subtracts what is known as 'one-off' items. Typical one-off costs can include the costs of restructuring the business and paying out redundancy. The pre-tax profits are calculated using the following formula:

$$Pre\text{-}tax\ profits = Operating\ profit + One\text{-}off\ items$$

Once again, we can look at the same business and see the impact on pre-tax profits of a one-off item. Using the information about Bircham's Building Supplies again, this is how operating profits can be calculated. Remember that Bircham's had sales revenue of £376,000 last year. All of the costs associated with those sales cost the business some £312,000 that year. Their overhead costs for the year amounted to some £28,000. We know that the business had an operating profit of £36,000. In the same year, the business decided to make one of its delivery drivers redundant and subcontract the delivery service to another business. This redundancy cost the business £18,000. Therefore, the business had pre-tax profits of £36,000 plus £18,000. This means that their pre-tax profits were £54,000.

We have already mentioned the fact that a business must pay corporation tax. The current corporation tax main rate is 30 per cent. A small business will pay 19 per cent if they have taxable profits between £50,000 and £300,000. The starting rate is zero for companies with taxable profits of £10,000 or below.

The way in which a business calculates its *profit after tax* is to start with its pre-tax profits and then deduct the amount of corporation tax payable. Bircham's Building Supplies had a pre-tax profit of £54,000. They are classed as a small business; therefore they pay 19 per cent corporation tax on their profits. This means that Bircham's must pay the Inland Revenue 19 per cent of their £54,000 pre-tax profits. Bircham's must therefore pay £10,260 to the Inland Revenue leaving them £43,740. It is then their choice what they wish to do with this amount. It could be paid to the shareholders or reinvested in the business in the hope that the investment will improve the profits in the coming year.

We can now see in Table 3.1 how all of the calculations fit together and how this allows the business to make an accurate calculation of its expenses and its profits.

Table 3.1
Calculation of profit

Gross profit is the revenue minus the direct costs (cost of goods sold).

Sales revenue
– Cost of sales
= Gross profit

Operating (net) profit is the gross profit minus the indirect costs (overheads).

– Overheads
= Operating profit

Pre-tax profit is the operating profits plus any one-off items, e.g. redundancy payments.

+ One-off items
= Pre-tax profit

Profit after tax is the profit that is left after corporation tax has been paid.

– Tax
= Profit after tax

Calculating total revenue

The revenue of a business is, basically, its income from its operations. Obviously, the amount of revenue generated is important and as we have seen there is a close relationship between the revenue and the costs of the business. It is important for the business to make the gap between costs and revenue as wide as possible as the greater the difference, the greater the level of profit.

In the early stages of a new business or when a business launches a new product or service, they may not be able to obtain high revenues. There are a number of reasons for this:

- Perhaps the product or service is not well known by the potential customers and they are not buying it in high numbers.
- The business needs to gradually adjust to be able to produce or obtain large numbers of the new product or may not have the facilities to offer the service to a wide market.
- The prices of the new products and services may have to be low as a result of customers not being prepared to pay high prices for them as they are unproven.

Before we look at the way in which a business calculates its total revenue, we must turn our attention to how a business might begin by estimating what they might receive from sales during the course of the forthcoming year. In order to estimate the sales revenue (the income from products and services sold to customers), they will make an estimate as to the number of products and services they might sell in the coming year. They can then work out the average selling price of their products and services and then multiply the estimated number of sales by this figure. The total revenue estimate uses the following formula:

Sales revenue = Estimated number of products and services sold × Average selling price of the products and services

If a business estimates that it will sell 10,000 products in the coming year and that the average selling price is £19.99, then the calculation is:

Sales revenue = 10,000 × £19.99 = £199,990

Even when the business is working out the true sales revenue for a year, the two key figures remain the same. The complication comes when you consider the fact that a business may sell different amounts of each product or service and that those products and services are sold at different prices. For any business, the improvement in their sales revenue rests on these two factors. They can either sell more products and services or they can sell their products and services at a higher price. Both of these strategies are aimed to increase sales revenue, but in competitive markets, raising the sales price of products or services is a dangerous move, as it may well mean that sales actually fall as customers buy from the competitors who may have lower prices.

Probably the only major exception to this is the high-technology field where businesses spend huge sums of money researching and developing their products and want to protect them with **patents**.

As an alternative to either increasing prices or the number of products and services sold, a business may actually choose to drop their prices. The business does this in the knowledge that they will make less profit on each product or service sold, but in the hope that this will mean that they will be able to attract more customers and sell more.

INDIVIDUAL WORK
(3.6) ★ ★
Thould and Thornes Ltd sell high price perfumes and after-shave lotions. In an average year they sell around 10,000 products at an average price of £34.50. What is their estimated sales revenue for the next financial year?

Keyword

patent – a right granted by the government to an inventor to stop others from making, using, offering for sale, or selling the invention

---

INDIVIDUAL WORK
(3.7) ★ ★

Thould and Thornes Ltd, as we have seen, sell around 10,000 products per year at an average price of £34.50. In actual fact, they sell 5,000 products for £34 per year and 5,000 for £35.

1 If they were to increase the average price from £34 to £36 and from £35 to £38, what would be their new total revenue figure?

2 If they were to drop the prices from £34 to £32 and sell 6,000 products, and from £35 to £33 and sell 6,000 products, how would this affect their total revenue figure?

3 As an independent adviser, which of the two strategies would you recommend to the business?

Calculating total costs

There are two main ways of looking at costs, the most common being the accountants' view which considers the value of the resources used by a business in order to operate. The alternative is known as *opportunity cost*. This can be a confusing term as it refers to the impact on a business if they choose one alternative over another, meaning that they cannot afford to do both. If, for example, a business decides to invest in replacing all of its delivery vans at a cost of £175,000, it cannot go ahead with the opening of a new retail outlet that would have cost about the same amount. The business makes the decision to go ahead with the replacement vans and 'foregoes' the advantages of being able to open a new store.

For the most part, however, when we consider the total costs of a business, we use the accountants' view of costs. This set of calculations needs to begin with what is known as the costs of production. The first things that the business needs to know are:

- How much does it cost to supply customers with products or services at the current price being charged?
- Are the actual estimated costs the true cost figures?
- Does the business have sufficient funds to cover the costs of supplying the products and services being sold at the current price?

In order to work out the total costs to a business of supplying products and services, we need to investigate three key types of cost: fixed costs, variable costs and semi-variable costs. These different types of cost will be used later when we consider break-even.

Fixed costs are costs that do not change, regardless of how many products or services the business is either producing or supplying. Typical fixed costs include rent or rates, both of which may have to be paid either monthly or yearly. Regardless of how well the business is doing, the business will have to find enough money to pay these fixed costs.

Obviously, as the costs for these items are fixed, they do not increase or decrease. This means that if the business makes better use of their facilities and either produce more products or provide more services, then the importance of these fixed costs is reduced. The same is true if the business is not as busy; they still have to cover the fixed costs, even if the business is not selling many products or services, and even if it is a factory which closes down for annual holidays during the summer.

A business tends to apply a portion of their fixed costs to each product or service they sell. In other words, if a business has fixed costs of £100,000 and sells 100,000 products (also known as *units*), each year, then it will apply the fixed costs to each unit at the rate of £1 per unit. This is a vital part of the overall costs of each unit, which the business supplies to its customers. If the business increases the number of units it produces or supplies to 200,000 per year, the fixed costs are still £100,000, this means that 50p is added to the costs of each unit meaning that the business can either sell the units at a lower price and still make a higher profit, or they can keep the prices stable and make even more profit. This way of applying fixed costs to units works the other way too, if the business only produces 50,000 units instead of 100,000, then each unit has £2 added to its cost, reducing the profit on each and every unit sold.

Although we have said that fixed costs do not change, they do over a period of time. Rent and rates may increase year on year, but since the business is only interested in the costs in the year in question, they are classed as being fixed as far as calculations are concerned.

Variable costs change directly in response to the **output** of a business. These costs include labour, fuel and raw materials. The more the business is producing, the greater these costs will be. Any change that increases output would increase variable costs, whereas any decrease in output would reduce variable costs.

If a business estimated that the costs to produce a particular product were £8 per unit and they produced 100,000 units in a year, then the variable costs associated with that level of output would be £800,000. If they doubled production and the costs remained the same per unit, then their variable costs would also double to £1.6 million per year.

The variable costs are not like the fixed costs because they can also be described as being *direct costs*. Direct costs means that these are costs to the business which are closely associated with the production of a product itself. Therefore they include all of the materials, components, packaging, power and labour to produce that unit.

It is also usually the case that if a business is able to increase its output, its variable costs per unit reduce. They can make cost savings in a number of different areas, including:

- Installing more efficient machinery to produce the products faster.
- Using new machinery, which may mean they do not need as many employees to operate the equipment.
- Obtaining larger discounts on raw materials and components from their suppliers as they are buying more.

INDIVIDUAL WORK

(3.11) ★ ★

Thould and Thornes Ltd produce their own range of perfumes, which they sell at £34 each. Currently they produce around 2,000 bottles per year. They have been told by their supplier that if they were to produce 3,000 bottles per year the current price of £9 per unit, which they pay the supplier, would be reduced by 20 per cent.

Calculate the current variable cost paid to the supplier based on 2,000 bottles and the new variable cost based on the 20 per cent discount. What is the individual unit variable cost and what is the total variable cost in both cases?

For example, in the case of Thould and Thornes, if the business works out that at an output of 100,000 each unit costs them £8 to produce, they may discover that when they double their output those direct costs drop to £7 per unit. This would mean that instead of a total variable costs figure of £1.6 million they will have saved £200,000 in variable costs and that the new production figure of 200,000 units will only cost £1.4 million.

Before a business can work out its potential savings as a result of increasing output, it will usually assume that a 20 per cent increase in output would cost them, at least in the short term, a 20 per cent increase in their variable costs. Working things out on this basis is a far safer way to plan ahead than assuming that savings will be made.

Not all costs can be fitted into the fixed or variable categories. A business that offers home deliveries can class the cost of a van as a fixed cost. No matter how much the van is used, they will still have to insure it and pay for its road tax. However, if the van needs to be used more frequently due to increased demand then several costs will increase. More fuel will be used and the van will probably have to be serviced more regularly as there will be wear and tear on the tyres and engine. In this situation, the van can actually be classed as a *semi-variable cost* as its exact cost is dependent on how much it is used.

Now that we have considered the main types of cost, it is possible to calculate *total costs*. Remember that these total costs have enormous implications for the business in terms of its profits. Some businesses have very high fixed costs and they contribute to most of their total costs. Businesses such as these must ensure that they sell a large number of units so that these costs can be spread across all of the units that they sell. As mentioned, some businesses can receive enormous benefits from increasing their output as they may well see their variable costs drop as a proportion to each unit as output increases. It is therefore desirable for businesses such as these to increase output to the highest possible level.

INDIVIDUAL WORK **(3.12)**

★ ★

The table details the fixed and variable costs of a business producing springs at various levels of output. Make a copy of the table. In each case, work out the total cost and the cost per spring at different levels of output.

Fixed and variable costs of Bert Springer Springs Ltd at various levels of output

Level of output	Fixed costs (£)	Variable costs (£)	Total costs (£)	Costs per spring (£)
100,000	50,000	5,000		
150,000	50,000	7,000		
200,000	50,000	9,000		
250,000	50,000	11,000		
300,000	50,000	13,000		
350,000	50,000	15,000		
400,000	50,000	17,000		
450,000	50,000	19,000		
500,000	50,000	21,000		

Profitable operation

As we have seen, profit compares a business's revenues to its costs and that profit is equal to the total revenue of the business less its total costs. We have also seen that profits are used either to pay dividends to shareholders or are reinvested in the business.

The amount of profit that a business makes is a key indication of their success. In addition it shows several other things:

- That the business can produce funds that can be reinvested in the business in order to make them more efficient and more profitable in the future.

- That the business is a good risk as far as investors are concerned and that shareholders would want to buy shares in the business, with the expectation that the share price will increase and they will receive reasonable dividends.

- That in around 60 per cent of cases it is the profit made by the business itself that is used to help a business grow. Financial institutions, such as banks, would be looking for the business to make an investment of their own into future development, in addition to any loans made by the banks to assist them.

> **Keyword**
>
> **asset** – an item that has a cash value. In the case of machinery, the asset is used to produce products. Other assets could include land, buildings or patents

The fact that a business shows, in a given year, that it has made a profit does not actually reveal the whole picture. A business may have made a profit simply as a result of its normal trading operations. However, within the amount of profit being shown the business may have obtained funds from a different source. Perhaps they have sold one of their **assets**, such as a building, machinery, vehicles or even a patent.

Potential investors need to look very carefully at the source of the profits a business has made. If the business has genuinely made a profit from its trading operations, then investors will consider this to be a high-quality profit. If the profit has been made from the sale of assets, then the investors may take a dimmer view and they will wonder whether the sale of the assets will affect the profitability of the business in the future.

Although in the majority of cases businesses will pass on most of their profits to their shareholders, or will retain it for reinvestment, in some cases they keep some of the profit back. The profits that are paid to shareholders are known as *distributed profit* and the profits they retain are known as *undistributed profits*. The business may use the undistributed profits immediately to reinvest in the business, perhaps to finance a new business activity. In other cases they may place this money in a reserve. They can use this reserve if they think that they are facing the prospect of a less profitable year in the near future.

CASE STUDY Analysing costs, revenue and profit

A large number of businesses under-estimate their costs and over-estimate their potential revenues. If a business simply raises its prices, this does not mean that they will produce more revenue. They will inevitably lose customers, particularly if competitors do not raise their prices at the same time. Customers may choose to switch to cheaper products or services so, in order to counteract this, the business that has raised their prices must stress their quality and availability of their products.

Cotter & Co. is a long-established family-run estate agency. They have an excellent reputation for reliability and quality of service. For many years they were the only estate agency in the area, but they chose not to take advantage of the situation by charging higher prices to property sellers. For the past five years they have kept their charges at 1.5 per cent of the selling price of the house, but when a new estate agency opened in the area they found it necessary to match the 1 per cent that this new competitor was offering. The drop in revenue was seen almost immediately and now they feel they have only one option; to increase the charge back to 1.5 per cent.

INDIVIDUAL WORK (3.13) ★ ★
Cotter & Co.'s profits have obviously suffered by matching their new competitor's prices. What might be the implications to the business if they raise their price to 1.5 per cent?

Calculating break even

Break-even sales levels and the impact of changing costs and prices and illustrating break-even

Although it is not always possible for new businesses, or new businesses launching new products and services, to cover their costs with their sales revenue, ultimately this is their goal. Break-even takes place when the sales income from the products and services sold is equal to the total costs incurred by the business.

If a business had total monthly costs of £20,000, which incorporated all of their fixed and variable costs, they would need to achieve a sales income of £20,000 in order to break even.

A business will use break-even calculations for a number of reasons, including:

- To estimate the output needed to meet desired profit levels.
- To look at how price changes may affect profit and break-even.
- To look at how changes in fixed or variable costs may affect profits, level of output needed and break-even.
- To decide where to buy raw materials or components that contribute towards their variable costs.
- To assist them in making calculations that they can then show to finance providers in order to acquire loans.

To calculate the break-even point, three vital figures are required:

- The amount the product or service is sold for
- The total fixed cost of the business
- The variable costs per unit.

The simplest way to calculate the output level required to break even uses the following formula:

$$\frac{Fixed\ costs}{Selling\ price\ per\ unit - Variable\ costs\ per\ unit}$$

If a business's fixed costs per month are £20,000, the selling price per unit is £1,500 and the variable costs per unit are £500, then their calculations, applied to the formula, will look like this:

$$\frac{£20,000}{£1,500 - £500}$$

If the business subtracts their variable costs of £500 from the selling price of £1,500, this leaves them with £1,000. £20,000 divided by £1,000 means that they must sell 20 units per month in order to break even.

The break-even point is defined as being the point at which the level of sales is not great enough for the business to make a profit and yet not low enough for the business to make a loss. In other words, earnings from sales are just sufficient for the business to cover its total costs. This occurs when total revenue from sales exactly equals the total cost of production.

Break-even point occurs when total cost = Total revenue

From this, it can be assumed that if total revenue from sales is greater than total costs, then the organisation concerned makes a profit. If the opposite is true and the total revenue is less than total costs, then the organisation can make a loss. It is essential that organisations take this very important factor into account. The organisation will find that it is essential to determine how many units of output it must produce and sell before it can reach its break-even point. As we have seen, the total cost of a unit of production is made up of two factors, the fixed and variable costs, where:

Total cost = Fixed costs + Variable costs

and the total revenue is given by the number of products sold multiplied by the selling price:

INDIVIDUAL WORK
(3.14) ★ ★
Himalaya Tents Ltd sells high-cost, professional tents to mountaineering expeditions. Their total costs each month amount to £40,000. On average their tents are sold for £2,000 each.

1 How many tents would they have to sell each month in order to break even?

2 If their total costs increased by 50 per cent, how many additional tents would they have to sell in order to still break even?

INDIVIDUAL WORK
(3.15) ★ ★
A business has fixed costs of £30,000 per month. They have an average selling price of £600 per unit and variable costs per unit of £450. Calculate the number of units that must be sold in order to break even.

$$Total\ revenue = Price \times Quantity$$

If you sell five chocolate bars at 25p each, your total revenue is £1.25 (5 × 25p).
How does a business determine its break-even point? The easiest way to do this is by
the use of graphs. We have already examined the relationship between costs and
output and now know that within a certain range of output, specific costs remain fixed,
regardless of the quantity of units produced.

Figure 3.1 shows how these fixed costs (FC) can be shown on a graph.

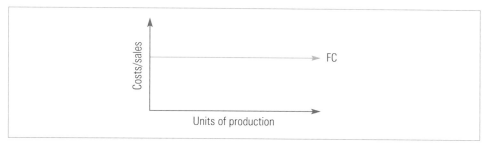

Figure 3.1
Fixed costs

As we have seen, variable costs change in relation to the level of output. In other
words, the higher the output, the higher the variable costs. Unlike the fixed costs, which
remain constant, the variable costs (VC) mean that we need to add an upward, left to
right sloping curve, known as the variable-cost curve, as can be seen in Figure 3.2.

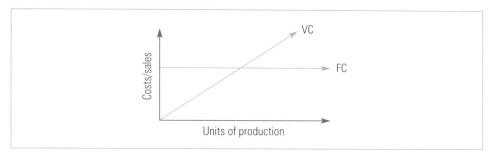

Figure 3.2
Variable cost curve

If we now add these two lines together we can put our total cost curve onto the
diagram. This is represented by shifting the variable cost curve upwards, at all points,
by the value of the fixed costs. In other words, we start where the fixed-cost line hits
the costs/sales and then draw a line parallel to the variable-cost line. This gives us the
total costs (TC), which is equal to the fixed costs plus the variable costs. This can be
seen in Figure 3.3.

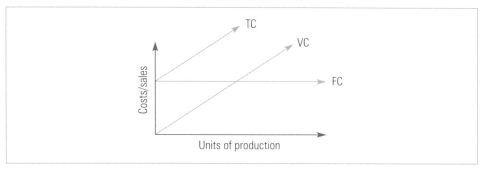

Figure 3.3
Total cost curve

The next step is to add the total revenue line to the diagram. This line will also be left to right, upward sloping, as it follows that the more the business sells the greater amount of revenue they receive. If, for example, the business were to sell five chocolate bars at 25p, then they would receive a total revenue of £1.25, whereas if they sold 10 chocolate bars they would receive a total revenue of £2.50. The total revenue line (TR) starts from the same point as the variable-costs line and it should be remembered that if a business makes no products, then they receive no revenue. Figure 3.4 illustrates the addition of the total revenue line.

INDIVIDUAL WORK
(3.16) ★ ★

1 Using the following figures, construct a break-even chart:
Selling price £30
Variable costs per unit £12
Fixed costs £18,000
Maximum capacity of the business 2,000 units.

2 From your graph, estimate the break-even points for the units of production and also estimate the level of profit or loss when the business produced 1,500 units.

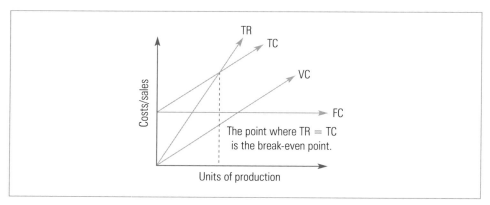

Figure 3.4
Total revenue line

As we have seen, when drawing a break-even chart it is vital that it is correctly labelled. Having created a fully labelled break-even chart, we can now consider what is known as the margin of safety.

Margin of safety

The margin of safety can be shown on a break-even chart. It is the amount by which demand can fall before the business starts to make a loss. Essentially it is the difference between sales and the break-even point (BE), as shown in Figure 3.5.

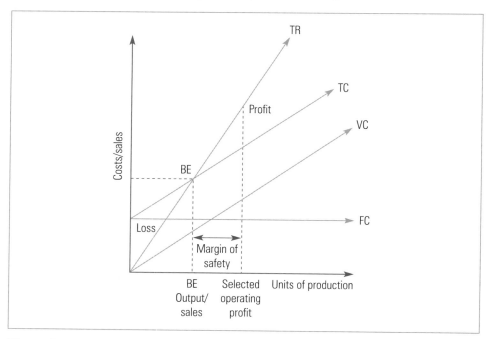

Figure 3.5
The margin of safety

Profit margin per unit

Assuming that the business has ready access to their fixed and variable costs, can calculate their total costs and they have clear figures of their total revenue, it should be straightforward to work out their break-even point. Many businesses will have what is known as a *selected operating profit*, as featured in Figure 3.5. This is in excess of their break-even point and provides them with a steady and reliable level of profit, capable of covering all of their costs.

The difference between the break-even point and the selected operating profit is, as we have seen, called the margin of safety. However, we now need to turn our attention to individual units of production.

The actual costs per unit are a total of the variable costs and the amount of the fixed costs that the business wishes to apply to each unit. As we have seen, if these two figures remain the same and the business increases the selling price of its products, then the profit margin per unit will increase. If, for example, it costs the business £2.50 in variable costs and it applies £1 to each product as their contribution towards fixed costs, then the total cost per unit will be £3.50. If they sell each unit for £5, then the profit margin per unit is £1.50. Normally if, for example, the variable costs increase by 10 per cent, the business may be tempted to increase their prices in order to offset this additional cost. Remember that this does not mean that the business should increase its prices by 10 per cent. An increase of 10 per cent in the variable cost is actually 25 pence, which means that their new total costs per unit are £3.75. If they were to increase their prices by 10 per cent, the new price would be £5.50, which means that instead of making £1.50 per unit they would now be making £1.75. This means that their profit per unit has increased by 25p and that they should have increased their price to £5.25 to cover the increase in variable cost and to maintain their existing profit margin.

INDIVIDUAL WORK
(3.17) ★ ★

A business sells on average 10,000 units at £34 per unit. They have fixed costs of £78,000 and based on the production of 10,000 units their variable costs are £89,000.

1 What is the profit margin per unit?

2 What would be the profit margin per unit if they increased prices by 10 per cent?

3 What would be the profit margin per unit if variable costs increased to £102,000, based on the original selling price of the unit?

Total profits and losses over a range of sale levels

Businesses will be concerned with establishing their exact break-even point. At the very least they will try to adjust their output and consequently their total revenue in order to cover their total costs. Beyond this, they will seek to establish a sales level that provides the business, and consequently its owners or shareholders, with an acceptable level of profit. Remember that when we constructed the full break-even chart, we could see that once the business's total revenues had exceeded their total costs, the business had begun to make a profit. The further the total revenue line moved away from the total cost line, the greater the profits that were being made.

On the other side of the break-even point, the further the total revenue line slipped away from the total cost line, the greater the losses being incurred by the business. If the business is able to construct an accurate break-even chart then they should be able to tell, at every level of output, the exact profit or loss that they will experience.

Management action

Various factors can have an effect on a break-even chart. They can broadly be broken down into internal factors and external factors. We will look at each of these in turn.

Internal factors, such as employing extra employees, will cause fixed costs to rise, therefore the total costs will rise and the business's break-even point will rise. If the business increases its prices then the total revenue figure should rise more steeply, meaning that the break-even point falls. If the business was to decide to replace employees with machinery then, whilst their fixed costs will rise as a result of the investment in the machinery, their variable costs on direct labour would fall. Therefore exactly what would happen to the break-even point depends on the total cost of the investment and the total amount of money saved by reducing the number of employees.

External factors may also have an impact on the break-even chart. If there is a reduction in demand for the business's products or services, then a business will usually reduce its margin of safety, although of course the break-even point will remain the same. If the business is forced to cut prices then the business will probably see their total revenue line rise less steeply, which means that the break-even point will also rise. If a business's variable costs increase then both the variable-costs line and the total costs line will rise, pulling up the break-even point.

INDIVIDUAL WORK
(3.18) ★★

McGregor Enterprises produce 200,000 units per year, with an average selling price of £50. Their raw materials per unit cost them £5.70. Their direct labour costs are split into two groups, £6 per unit for unskilled labour and £8 per unit for skilled labour. In addition to this, they pay their management a total of £64,000 per year. Administration costs £112,500 per year and their other salaries amount to £118,500 per year. Their other fixed costs amount to £98,000 per year.

Construct a break-even chart based on this information. State the amount of profit or loss made by the business at 100,000 units, 150,000 units and 200,000 units.

CASH FLOW MANAGEMENT

Cash flow management is the process of monitoring, analysing and adjusting a business's cash flows. But what are cash flows? Simply, they are the day-by-day incomes and expenditure (costs and expenses) that a business experiences in the running of its operations. Obviously, the most important thing is for a business to avoid having cash shortages. These are caused by there being too big a gap between the point when money comes into the business and when it goes out of the business.

As we will see, businesses will use a variety of different cash flow management techniques in order to keep a close eye on their cash flow situation.

Only by being aware of existing flows of cash into and out of the business can the business even begin to forecast what might happen in the near future. Businesses will monitor income and expenditure, probably noting their current position on a daily basis.

Using spreadsheets

In addition to monitoring payments and receipts (cash coming into the business), a cash flow can help a business to create a cash flow forecast of future income and expenditure. In order to do this, a business needs to be able to:

- ◊ Work out their income.
- ◊ Work out their expenditure.
- ◊ Work out their short-term cash flow problems.
- ◊ Identify any areas where additional income may be generated.
- ◊ Know at any point where money is owed, either to the business or to another business.

Cash inflow is money received and cash outflow is money that the business has spent. The main cash inflow headings include:

- ◊ *Start up capital* In the case of new businesses this includes all cash investments made by the owners. This investment will be used to pay any initial expenditure. In existing businesses this heading would be replaced by any balance of funds from the previous trading period.
- ◊ *Loan receipts* This details money that has come into the business in the form of a loan, possibly from a financial service provider, such as a bank.
- ◊ *Sales receipts* This is the income from any sales made by the business.
- ◊ *Interest receipts* This is money received by the business in the form of interest from any other investment, perhaps interest on money in a bank account.

    ◊ *VAT recoveries* If the business is of a sufficient size, it will be registered to pay Value Added Tax (VAT). VAT is levied at every stage, each time a product is bought or sold. The business may have paid out more VAT than it has received, in which case Customs and Excise will pay the business the balance. Of course, if the business has received more VAT than it has paid out then this item would be transferred to the cash outflow.

There are various cash outflow headings, which are essentially expenses. There are a number of headings that can be used under the cash outflow:

    ◊ *Payments for assets* These are the costs of all machinery, office equipment and other items the business may have bought. They do not include consumable materials, such as office materials like stationery.

    ◊ *Raw materials* These are all of the items that are used by the business to produce its products or provide its services.

    ◊ *Wages and salaries* These are the total amounts of wages paid, including overtime payments.

    ◊ *Rates and telephone bills* A business will have to pay water rates, sewerage rates and, of course, telephone bills. Many businesses will spread the cost of these by making equal monthly payments to the providers.

    ◊ *Other running costs* This category includes rent, rates and payment for power and other consumable items, such as office stationery.

    ◊ *Interest payments* These are payments made by the business as a result of having taken out hire purchase agreements or credit agreements to purchase assets.

    ◊ *Loan repayments* If a business has a loan, it will have to repay the capital amount plus interest over an agreed number of months.

    ◊ *VAT payments* If the business has collected more VAT than it has paid to other businesses, then it will owe Customs and Excise the balance.

INDIVIDUAL WORK
(3.19) ★ ★

A new business has start up capital of £20,000. At present it does not have any loans. In its first month, its total sales revenue was also £20,000. It received no interest payments and it is not registered for VAT. In the first month the business bought £10,000 worth of assets. Raw materials cost them £2,500. Wages and salaries cost £4,000. Their water rates and telephone bills amounted to £400 and they estimated that their other running costs amounted to another £400. There were no interest or loan repayments.

Create a cash flow showing their total cash inflows and total cash outflows for the month. What will be the balance that the business begins with at the start of next month? Use Excel software to create your cash flow.

The use of spreadsheet software, such as Excel, allows the business to enter and store data in a grid format. It allows the business to perform numerical and statistical calculations. Once an appropriate formula has been entered the program itself will make all the necessary calculations. Any entries on the spreadsheet can be changed, as can the formula. The effects of changes to the spreadsheet are automatic so there is no need to recalculate.

Text can also be entered onto the worksheet to provide entries with labels or titles. When figures are entered onto the spreadsheet they can form the basis of any calculations the business requires. The basic formulae used when constructing a cash flow spreadsheet are relatively straightforward. They will allow the business to multiply (*), divide (/), add (+) or subtract (–). There are also particular functions that the system will recognise, such as 'sum', which means to total the column or specified sections of the spreadsheet.

Monitoring actual cash flow

A business would usually have prepared their cash flow forecast in advance. They will have anticipated particular levels of income and expenditure and would hope that the actual figures closely match these forecast predictions. By ensuring that the business's revenues and expenditures are monitored, the business can compare the forecast against the actual figures. This should alert them to the fact that the actual figures are either better or worse than they had anticipated. This means that if the income is not as good as had been expected, then they are forewarned and can take action before the situation becomes serious. They might well approach their bank and ask for additional overdraft facilities, or they may ask for a short-term loan to cover the shortfall in their income.

If the actual figures are better than those forecast, then investment plans that had been earmarked for some time in the future could be brought forward, as could the purchase of a new piece of machinery, equipment or the employment of additional staff.

INDIVIDUAL WORK (3.20) ★ ★

1 Using the data from Activity 3.19, create a new Excel spreadsheet that predicts exactly the same income and expenditure over a 12-month period. Make sure that you amend the balance that is carried over from month to month.

  What would be the total balance in the business's bank account at the end of the 12-month period?

2 Now amend your spreadsheet as their raw materials have increased from £10,000 per month to £12,500 per month and their wage bill has now increased to £3,500 per month. You should assume that all other income and expenditure remains the same.

  How has this affected the business's bank balance at the end of the 12-month period?

Credit control

invoice – the document that gives full details of the products or services sold and the prices. This is given to the buyer of the product or service and provides the financial information that will be recorded in the sales daybook

Regardless of the efforts made in selling products or services, a business is only assured of continued success and survival if they actually receive the money. Many businesses, particularly those that deal with other businesses as their customers, work on a credit basis. This means that the business provides the products or services and then produces an **invoice** or bill for those products and services. Every business will have its own particular terms for business. It is normal practice for businesses to be given at least 30 days to pay their bills. This means that the business that has supplied the products or services has already incurred costs but has not yet received payment to cover those costs. This is where credit control comes into the equation.

Businesses will therefore need to be aware of revenue that may be due immediately and revenue that could be expected within the next few days, weeks or even months. They also need to keep track of whether the invoices that they have sent out have actually been paid on time.

Invoices are usually raised or created within 72 hours of a product or service being supplied. The business purchasing the product or service would then have 30 days in which to pay.

Credit control begins here, as one of the frequent reasons why invoices are not paid is that there was something wrong with the products or services. The business providing the products or service should check within 48 hours after the delivery that everything was in order.

If payment has not been received by the end of the agreed period, then the supplying business's credit control would begin a series of contacts with the customer to find out what the problem is. Sometimes, if the customer is having difficulty in paying, the supplying business may accept part-payment of the invoice, with the balance being paid in a few days time.

Bearing in mind that cash flow problems are responsible for causing around 70 per cent of new businesses to fail within their first year, good cash flow is essential for growth and survival. Poor cash flow has ruined even some very successful businesses and no business is safe from cash flow problems.

CASE STUDY Credit control Australian style

The Australian telecommunications business is no different from many other types of business around the world. Recent figures suggest that credit control problems account for over 10 per cent of all customer complaint issues. This has risen from just over 7 per cent. Australian telephone companies in nearly 40 per cent of cases prevent customers with payment problems from making long distance calls, thereby reducing their overall bills. Credit control problems are only fourth in ranking in terms of problems experienced by Australian telephone companies to billing queries, faults and lack of service in particular areas.

GROUP WORK (3.21) ★ ★

Assume you are a small business and two of your largest customers are actually the worst in terms of paying you for your products and services. The two customers, after negotiations, have 60 days to pay you, but on average they both take 120 days each.

1 Using the ideas in the case study, what do you think would be the implications to your business if you threatened to charge them interest after 60 days?

2 What do you think the implications would be if you suggested to them that the payment period be reduced to 30 days?

BUDGETS FOR PLANNING AND MONITORING EXPENDITURE

Budgets are used to set targets in order to control costs and revenues. Budgets are a vital part of a business's planning strategy, as the budgets detail the business's intended expenditure, as well as their income. Budgets allow a business to identify where costs and revenues will occur and also provide the basis upon which these can be monitored.

A business will usually begin their budgeting activities by trying to estimate the likely revenues for the coming year. Once this has been established the business can then allocate acceptable costs to their operations, leaving them with a reasonable amount of profit. For smaller businesses this is a relatively simple task, but for larger businesses costs and revenues are broken down into specific departments or functions of the business, which are also known as **cost centres**.

> **Keyword**
>
> **cost centre** – a particular part, perhaps a department, of a business that can have specific costs allocated to it

The purpose of breaking down the overall budget into smaller parts is to allow each manager of a department or an area of the business to monitor their own budget and contribute to the overall control of the budget.

There are various reasons why businesses choose to design a budget, including:

- To make each department or individual aware of the limits of their spending.

- To provide each area with a means by which they can compare their actual efficiency – remaining within budget or not spending the full budget would be seen as a success, and exceeding the budget as a failure.

- To allocate spending at departmental or cost centre level so that the manager that knows precisely what needs to be spent and when can make the spending decisions.

Actually setting the budget in the first place is often difficult; there are so many different things that could affect both the revenue and the costs. For the most part, a business will use the previous year's figures for the basis of the next year's budget.

Using a spreadsheet

Spreadsheets are a valuable tool not only in constructing a cash flow, but also in preparing and then monitoring a budget. The process is almost exactly the same as the individual preparing the budget will have to consider all of the expenditure and then attempt to adjust it to match a particular figure, which may have been allocated to them to spend during the year.

INDIVIDUAL WORK
(3.22) ★ ★

Hamish McDonald runs the IT department for a medium-sized business. He has been asked to prepare his budget for the coming year. His guidelines are that he may spend 10 per cent more than he spent last year. Hamish's wage and salary bills were £98,000. Equipment purchases were £110,000, but £50,000 of this will not need to be spent in the coming year as the new network is now in place. His parts and components cost £14,000, consumables, such as disks and CDs amounted to £4,000. His other various costs amounted to £1,200.

Initially Hamish has been asked to prepare a budget showing his proposed expenditure for the first six months of the coming year. He needs to break down the spending on a monthly basis and has been told to assume that he will spend the same amount of money each month.

Prepare Hamish's budget using an Excel spreadsheet.

Monitoring monthly expenditure

By cost centre, against budgets, and favourable and unfavourable variances

Budgets are used by a business to control and monitor its costs. The senior management of a business will approve each department's budget and then, to a large extent, allow that department to manage their own budget.

By bringing all of the departmental budgets together, the business can see exactly how operations are proceeding and, in most cases, each departmental budget's spreadsheet can simply be added to the business's master budget. As this is usually now carried out using computers, the information can be at the fingertips of senior management and departmental managers at any time.

The senior managers and the departmental managers can see precisely how spending is developing in each and every cost centre. They can make instant comparisons with the level of spending which was budgeted, and what it was like at the same point in the previous year. This means that adjustments can be made as soon as there is a difference between the anticipated spending and the actual spending.

Because budgeting is not an exact science, it is inevitable that at times either the spending or the revenue will be different from what had been predicted. Differences are known as *variances*. A variance is the amount by which the actual figures are different from the budgeted figures. Normally managers will check for variances on a monthly basis. Not all variances are necessarily bad. Over-spending causes what is known as a *negative* or *adverse variance*. This means that costs are higher than had been predicted and will, therefore, have an impact on the profits of a business. Sometimes, however, variances are positive and spending is actually less than had been budgeted. In these cases the difference is known as a *favourable variance*.

The purpose of regularly checking budgets for variances is to allow the business to react and take action before the situation gets out of hand. If, for example, sales revenue was not as high as had been predicted, then in order to maintain profits the business would cut back on its advertising and, perhaps, its production of goods.

INDIVIDUAL WORK
(3.23) ★ ★

Eurocartridge Ltd recycles and refills ink cartridges for printers. It had budgeted to sell £300,000 worth of Hewlett Packard cartridges. In actual fact by the end of the year they had already sold £360,000 worth of these cartridges. They also sell recycled Epson cartridges and had budgeted that they would also sell £300,000 worth during the year. Their actual figures were £260,000 worth. At the beginning of the year they found a new supplier of ink and they had originally budgeted £62,000 worth of spending to their ink suppliers. The new supplier so far had only invoiced them for £58,000. The business had also worked out its spending on employees, which amounted to £89,000. Extra work had meant that overtime had to be paid and that the wage bill for the year was in fact £95,000.

Look at the sales revenue for the two main products, the cost of the ink and the labour costs. Which of the spending items were favourable variances and which were adverse variances?

Budget variances

Reporting budget variances, adjusting actual to planned expenditure and revision of future budgets

A business, or a cost centre, will only be aware of a budget variance if the information is accurate. By breaking down spending to cost centres, businesses rely on the fact that the manager responsible for that cost centre will be in a position to keep a close eye on spending and revenues. A business that has broken down its budgeting into cost centres will be able to see which areas of the business are performing well and, of course, identify those that are not. Areas that are proving to be a problem can be given support before the situation gets out of control.

Budget holders should immediately report a budget variance and provide reasons why this has occurred and what impact it will have on their overall budget. Some additional costs are unavoidable, but the cost centre may have to cut back spending on other areas to compensate. Additional revenues do not necessarily mean that the cost centre can spend money in excess of its established budget. Sometimes this may be possible, but the additional difference between a higher level of sales revenue and the estimated sales revenue means that the business will be more profitable.

Once it has become clear that there are variances in the budget, the management of the business needs to move quickly to adjust the spending so that it falls back in line with the budget. It is not always possible to cut back on spending in some areas of the business and in some cases other budgets elsewhere in the business will be cut in order to offset the overall negative impact of additional spending elsewhere.

Whilst businesses will have established their next year's budget on the basis of the current year's actual figure, they will be aware of the fact that certain areas of the budget will not be the same as the current year. If, for example, a transport company was aware of the fact that diesel prices would increase in the coming year, they would automatically incorporate the higher prices into the budget for the coming year. If the business knew that certain parts of their operation would need more funding as a result of variances in the current year, again they would adjust the budget for the coming year to take this into account.

INDIVIDUAL WORK
(3.24) ★ ★

Smooth Air Systems install air conditioning units into retail outlets. They budgeted to install 700 units at an average cost of £4,800 each. Their total variable costs were £280,000 and their total fixed costs were £210,000. As it transpired, their actual sales figures were 650 units at an average price of £5,200. Their actual variable costs per unit were £450 and their total fixed costs had risen to £220,000.

1 Using a spreadsheet, complete all of the figures for the budget and the actual figures, including number of units sold, price per unit, total sales revenue, variable cost per unit, total variable cost, total fixed costs and profit.

2 Identify each variance from the budget and state whether it is favourable or adverse.

RECORDING TRANSACTIONS

Many businesses break down their operations so that each department or cost centre is responsible for recording and monitoring their financial activities. Businesses need to know far more, however, than their total sales and costs. They need to know which department or cost centre is the most profitable and which products or services are selling the best. As we will see, the vast majority of retail outlets and supermarkets use electronic tills and sophisticated computerised accounting systems to capture this information immediately the sale is made.

For businesses, whatever their type of activity, it is important to know which are their most popular products and services. This knowledge will allow them to concentrate on their best selling lines and, perhaps, phase out products or services that are no longer popular.

It is not necessary in this unit to look at the different types of documents involved in the recording of a business's financial transactions, as this is covered in Unit 6 Introduction to Business Administration. We will, however, look at the main types of transaction recording.

Manual sales recording

Not all businesses have sophisticated cash registers that record the date and time of the purchase and exactly what was sold at that time. Many smaller businesses rely on a simple cash register and use a book to note down what has been sold. The business would then use this log for a number of purposes, including:

- To total the number of particular products sold, so that they can be reordered from their supplier.
- To compare what has been sold with the remaining stock, so that they can keep a track of their stock levels.
- To provide them with a means to compare the total amount of money that they have put through the cash register with the value of the products in their log book.

Cash register recording

Some other businesses use a simple system that relies on a cash register to record the type of product sold. In a gift shop, for example, the cashier may enter in the price of the product and then hit a key to identify it as a type of product, such as a card, wedding gift or small teddy bear. This allows the business to see which particular types of products are selling best in their shops and they can then adjust where the products are placed in the shop and how much space is given to them. This system does not record the actual product itself, so it would be difficult to know whether a birthday card, an anniversary card or a wedding card had been sold. Obviously a business could use more buttons, if the cash register used had this facility.

Bernice has bought herself a new cash register and she can now record the sales in four categories: cards, artificial flowers, ornaments and vases, and pictures and mirrors. On her first day using the new cash register, she sells five plastic tulips at £1 each, a pottery dog for £5.50, an oval mirror for £15, a framed poster of Britney Spears for £12, a box of Christmas cards for £4.99, a glass jug for £6.50, three silk lilies for £1.50 each, a vase of plastic ferns for £10 and a pack of wedding invitation cards for £7.95.

1 Organise her sales for the day into the four categories and calculate the totals for each category.

2 Were there any problems in categorising any of the products she sold? If so, state which products gave problems.

Direct computer input via software products

Many retailers use what is known as Electronic Point of Sale (EPOS). This is a system that allows the barcode on each product to be scanned at the cash till. The barcode is a unique identifying code for each product sold in the retail outlet. The cash till relays the information straight to the store's computer and the computer in turn relays back the price of the product to the cash till.

The customer is then given an itemised receipt that describes each product purchased, including the size, colour, etc., the price paid and details of any discounts available on that product. Meanwhile the computer itself removes that item from the stock figures of the retail outlet.

EPOS has revolutionised the way in which businesses control their stock. It also provides vital information about the busiest times of the day, so that extra staff can be made available, the most profitable products sold and a host of other useful information.

INDIVIDUAL WORK (3.27) ★ ★

1 Visit the Sage Line 50 page on the Sage website and note five purposes of the software.

2 Identify the other Sage Line products and which type of businesses they are aimed at for providing similar features.

Petty cash recording

Regardless of the size of the business, they will all have a petty cash book. This is used to keep a record of small cash payments. It could be used for a number of small purchases, including stationery, postage stamps, travel and expenses and refreshments. The individual responsible for maintaining these records is often known as a petty cashier and, in the majority of cases, this will only be a part of that person's job.

Anyone who wishes to claim money from petty cash must complete a petty cash voucher. This describes what the money was spent on, how much was spent, and will have a signature from the person who is claiming the petty cash and an authorising signature from that person's budget controller. In the majority of cases, petty cash vouchers need to have a receipt attached to them.

The petty cashier has what is known as a *float*, which is a small amount of money from which petty cash claims can be paid. If, for example, a petty cashier had a float of £50 and paid out £35 during the week, according to the records and the amount left in the float he or she should be left with £15. The float is also known as the *Imprest*.

The petty cashier enters the details of each petty cash voucher into a petty cash book. Usually this book has a number of headings, under which each of the claims can be placed. This allows the petty cashier to keep a track of how much has been spent and for what purpose. At the end of each period, probably a week, the petty cashier makes sure that all of the vouchers have been collected and matched against each payment. The petty cashier needs to ensure that the totals of all the vouchers and the figures put into the petty cash book balance, in other words, that they amount to the same level of spending. The total can then be subtracted from the original float and if all have been recorded correctly this should equal the balance left in the float.

The petty cash vouchers and book, along with the remaining float is then usually taken to the accounts or finance department. They check the figures and then give the petty cashier sufficient money to restore the float to its original level before any payments had been made.

INDIVIDUAL WORK (3.28) ★ ★

Nollie is the petty cashier for a small business. She has £100 Imprest at the beginning of the month. The following petty cash transactions take place and she pays out:

£3.44 for stamps on 1st
£2.25 for envelopes on 2nd
Cleaner's materials of £14 on 6th
A ream of photocopy paper for £3.99 on 12th
£7.34 on stamps on 15th
£12 to the window cleaner on 19th
Taxi fare to a visitor for £8.50 on 23rd
A set of felt-tip pens for £3.99 on 28th
Self-adhesive labels for £4.99 on 28th

1 How might Nollie organise these payments in columns according to the type of purchase?

2 What is her total spending for the month?

3 How much should she have left in her float at the end of the month?

Daybooks

For our purposes we will look at two different kinds of daybook. One will cover sales and the other will cover purchases made by a business. Basically, a daybook is very similar to a petty cash book as it records each and every invoice or sale or purchase that has been made by the business.

If a business is making a credit sale, then they will have created an invoice. The business will keep a copy of each of the invoices and will enter the details into the sales daybook. Some businesses call their sales daybooks 'journals'. Sales daybooks do not tend to have cash sales included because they are entered into a cashbook. Normally a *sales daybook* is simply a list, in date order, of any sales that were made on credit. They will show: the date, the name of the customer, the invoice number and the final amount of the invoice.

The entries are collected, usually over a week or a month, before being transferred to the main accounts, and then a new series of entries are started.

Just as many businesses may sell products on credit, they also make numerous purchases on credit. The purpose of a *purchases daybook* is to keep track of everything they have purchased but not yet paid for. Before anything is written into the purchases daybook a number of checks need to be carried out. These are:

- When the products or services were ordered, because sometimes a business will receive products that have not been ordered.

- Whether the products were received in a fit state to use, or whether only part of an order has actually been delivered.

- Whether the prices are correct and the details on the invoice are what was agreed when the order was made.

- Whether all calculations on the invoice are correct – if several items were ordered, do they actually add up to the total given on the invoice?

Once again only credit purchases are entered into the purchases daybook. Cash purchases go straight into the cashbook. Again the purchases daybook is a list, in date order, this time including any purchases that have been made on credit by the business. It will show: the date, the name of the supplier, the invoice number and the final amount on the invoice.

The entries are kept usually for a period of a week or a month before being passed on to accounts. The total of the purchases made over the period is calculated before the entries are passed on.

Common sources of fraud in the handling of sales transactions, why fraud is a concern and simple fraud prevention measures

No one knows the exact extent of employee fraud in UK businesses. As just one example, the insurer Norwich Union uncovered a fraud by their employees that amounted to £1.5 million. Businesses look out for telltale signs of fraud taking place and, regardless of the type of work that someone does, a fraud could be taking place. According to CIFAS, an association dedicated to the prevention of financial crimes, there are a number of warning signs, which include:

- An employee who appears to be under stress but does not have a high workload.

- An employee who always wishes to work late and does not wish to take leave.

- Sudden changes of lifestyle.

- Customer complaints about missing statements or unrecorded transactions.

- Close relationships with suppliers and suppliers that insist on dealing with just one person.

- A key employee who has too much control over purchases without someone. checking.

In a recent survey, up to 70 per cent of the people questioned said that they would commit a fraud if they had the opportunity. Around 24 per cent, amounting to 900,000 small and medium-sized businesses, have suffered in recent years from employee fraud. Around 2 per cent of them said it is a frequent problem. Businesses with fewer than 15 employees have suffered from fraud in 19 per cent of cases and of those with over 36 staff, 48 per cent have suffered fraud. Businesses led by men have a 25 per cent chance of a fraud, compared to those led by women, that have an 18 per cent chance.

INDIVIDUAL WORK
(3.29) ★ ★
The following transactions have occurred at Burywood Removals Ltd:

- They have received an invoice for 100 cardboard boxes, but the boxes have not yet been delivered.
- A delivery of computer stationery has arrived, along with an invoice.
- An invoice has already been completed for a customer that is moving in five days time. The normal procedure is to send the invoice out five days after the removal date.

What would you do with each of these transactions? Are any of them ready to either be put into the sales or purchases daybooks? If so, which of the two daybooks are relevant in each case?

CASE STUDY Fraud research

In 2003, CIFAS carried out research to find out the types of employee fraud and how many businesses were affected. Nearly 130 businesses were involved in the survey and all but two had experienced employee fraud. Of the businesses surveyed, they had lost a total £1.3 million due to fraud and some of the larger businesses were dismissing over 100 staff a year for employee fraud. In 60 per cent of cases, the employees were involved with someone else from outside the company during their fraud activities.

INDIVIDUAL WORK
(3.30) ★ ★
Fraud seems to be widespread.

1 What kind of frauds could a cashier in a shop carry out?

2 How might the business prevent this from happening?

In 2002 alone, credit, debit, store and fuel card fraud cost UK businesses £424.6 million. All a fraudster would need is a pen and a stolen card. All they have to do is to sign their name on a receipt and many forged signatures do not have to be that good as sales assistants are very unlikely to check the customer signature. Card fraud is seen as a fairly low-risk and high-profit crime and it is growing at a rate of 30 per cent each year. It is hoped that the new chip and pin system, which requires transactions to be verified with the cardholder's four-digit pin number, will mean that transactions will no longer be verified just by the customer's signature. The benefits are enormous, as it is the machine and not the cashier that accepts or refuses the card. Pin security was introduced in France in 1993, particularly for fuel cards, and since then there has been an 80 per cent reduction in transaction frauds.

Many businesses are switching over to chip and pin and the deadline to adopt the new technology was 1 January 2005. A large number of businesses, however, are not ready and it seems that for a few months fraudsters will still be able to use the signature to obtain products.

Closed circuit television (CCTV) is often used to prevent what is known as *internal shrinkage*. This means watching point-of-sale areas in retail stores to see if cashiers are involved in fraud or theft. The monitoring systems can watch what cashiers do and provide the proof of what was sold, to whom, at what price and when. Given that crime as a whole cost the UK retail industry £1 billion in 2004, businesses are keen to develop any form of security that will protect them. CCTV is used in a large number of retail stores and in shopping centres.

CASE STUDY Retail CCTV

In 1999, UK retailers spent £612 million on crime prevention methods, including CCTV. At the Legal & General's St George's Shopping Centre in Preston, where there are around 200 shops, a large number of cameras cover all public areas, including escalators and the outside of shops. They can operate both in daylight and in very low light, they are waterproof and have motorised zoom lenses. The British Retail Consortium, in the same year, worked out that customer theft accounted for £740 million, which was up 23 per cent from the previous year.

GROUP WORK (3.31) ★ ★
Are you aware of the security measures in force at your local shopping centre? Are you even aware that you are being watched, both inside and outside shops? Try to find out how significant theft from retail stores is in your area. A visit to your local police force's website or, perhaps, a local Chamber of Commerce website will reveal this information.

Unit Revision Questions

1 What is the formula to calculate profits?

2 What does sales revenue less cost of sales and overheads equal?

3 Who pays corporation tax?

4 If costs exceed revenue has the business made a profit?

5 What does the estimated number of products/services sold multiplied by the average selling price equal?

6 What is a patent?

7 Give three examples of fixed costs

8 How do variable costs relate to output?

9 What is an asset?

10 When total costs equal total revenue what has a business achieved?

11 What is the margin of safety?

12 Why might the use of a spreadsheet aid cash flow management?

13 What is credit control?

14 What is a budget?

15 What is a cost centre?

16 What is the difference between a favourable and an adverse variance?

17 What is EPOS?

18 What is Imprest?

19 What is the purpose of a purchases daybook?

20 What is internal shrinkage?

UNIT 4

Business Communication

This unit looks at the importance of communication within the workplace. All employees need to be able to understand and carry out instructions that are given to them verbally by managers and colleagues. As well as coping with verbal instructions, it is also important to become competent in written communications. Many instructions are given to employees in a written format and, as job roles develop, written instructions and information needs to be passed on by all employees.

The unit also looks at interpersonal skills in dealing with different types of individuals in the workplace, and at the importance of effective preparation for business meetings and how this can improve the overall effectiveness of the organisation.

This specialist unit is internally assessed and to cover the requirements of the unit you must:

- 🖢 Explore the effective use of verbal instructions
- 🖢 Demonstrate effective business representation in personal dealings
- 🖢 Make effective use of written business communication
- 🖢 Investigate effective preparation for business meetings.

VERBAL INSTRUCTIONS

Effective communication in business is absolutely essential, as is communication within a team of people working together. Staff have to work hard, sometimes under pressure, but they also have to work accurately and try to make the right decision at all times. In order to do this there has to be effective communication.

Day after day information will flow in and out of the business. This all has to be checked, read, understood and communicated to someone else or another department within the business.

There are several advantages, but also some disadvantages to using verbal (spoken) communication as opposed to written communication. These are shown in Table 4.1.

Table 4.1
Advantages and disadvantages of verbal communication

Advantages	Disadvantages
Communication is quick.	Speech has to be clear.
Communication is cheap.	The person passing on the message has to be clear about what they are saying.
The voice can be used to emphasise points.	It is not ideal for long or complicated messages.
Immediate feedback can be obtained from the recipient (person being communicated with).	The recipient could be distracted by, for example, a telephone ringing or a noisy office.
Confirmation can be obtained that the recipient has understood the message.	A conflict of opinion could cause an argument or disagreement.
Body language and facial expressions can be used to help explain things.	There is no written confirmation that the conversation has taken place.

Face-to-face communication and telephone conversations are two of the most important ways in which we communicate verbally every day. In any organisation there may be many different forms of face-to-face communication, including:

- Conversations that take place in the office or at a person's desk.
- Brief chats in the corridors or at lunch breaks in the canteen.
- Informal meetings, when one or two members of staff meet to talk about something.
- Formal meetings, when a group of employees are called together to make decisions or sort out problems.
- When one member of staff is giving instructions to another employee.
- When talking to customers, either in person or on the telephone.

There are many points that need to be considered when carrying out any form of verbal communication. These include:

- Whether or not the message is being made clear.
- The pitch and tone of voice being used.
- Whether the recipient is listening and paying attention to what is being said.
- Whether the recipient feels free to ask questions.
- When not to speak or interrupt.
- The body language used – this is particularly important in the face-to-face form of verbal communication.

Body language can take several forms and includes:

- Facial expressions
- Gestures
- Posture
- How close we are prepared to get to another person
- Eye contact when speaking.

Listening is important in all verbal communication. We all listen to a number of different people during a single day, but not many of us could remember exactly what has been said to us in each one of those conversations. That is why it is a good idea, particularly at work, to make notes of any important conversations or particular instructions, so that what has been said can be remembered accurately.

Listening to task instructions

Throughout the course of any working day, most people could receive instructions from a number of different people. Being able to listen effectively is even more important if the person giving the instructions is not sure of a number of things, including:

- The exact details of what they need to tell the listener
- How interested or receptive the listener is
- How knowledgeable the listener is about the subject of the instructions.

In order for the listener to understand the instructions, they have to:

- Hear the instruction clearly
- Interpret the instruction
- Evaluate their response to the instruction
- Act upon the instruction and make use of the information they have heard.

If we are to make good use of our listening skills, it is important to:

- Concentrate on what is being said.
- Avoid becoming distracted, either by other people or by letting our attention drift elsewhere.

- Repeat the words or phrases used in the conversation in one's head if concentration lapses.
- Look at the person speaking and respond by nodding or smiling.
- Be ready for the other person to stop speaking – this is most noticeable if one is not concentrating; a sudden silence can be embarrassing for both people.
- Respond by commenting on what has just been said or by asking a question once the other person stops speaking.

GROUP WORK **(4.1)** ★

How good a listener are you?

1 In pairs, get your partner to tell you about a recent holiday or outing they have taken. Let them talk to you for three minutes about their visit, but do not interrupt them or ask any questions.

2 Now recount everything that you have remembered about their visit. Did you remember most of it or did they have to remind you about some things?

3 Now swop roles and repeat stages 1 and 2.

Interpreting task requirements, seeking clarification and confirming persons with whom liaison is required

Any task will have an objective, either for the individual, the team of people involved or the business as a whole. In order to carry out the task properly and to meet the objectives, the listener will have to be clear about:

- Why the instructions have been given
- For whom the work is being done
- The outcome of the task involved
- When the task has to be completed.

'Clarification' means making clear or dealing with any confusion that might arise out of the objectives. The clearer the objectives, the better chance the person instructed to carry out the task will have of achieving them.

The clarification of objectives can come from those who have set the objectives in the first place. This means that the senior manager, middle manager, supervisor or team leader who has set the objectives explains clearly what the objectives are. Based on this, the person given the instructions will then set in motion all of the steps needed to fulfil the objectives.

Figure 4.1 shows the process involved in receiving instructions through to reporting that the task has been completed.

If the instructions given or the explanation of the tasks and objectives are not clear, then the person receiving the instructions should always make sure that they fully

Figure 4.1
Task cycle

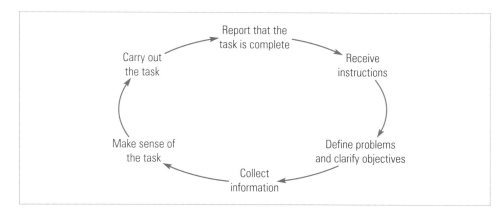

INDIVIDUAL WORK (4.2) ⭐

Turn the following closed questions into open questions by starting with the right words.

1 Did you enjoy school today?

2 Did you go out at lunchtime?

3 Was the bus on time?

4 Did you see many people that you knew at the cinema?

5 Have you eaten much today?

understand what is involved. Sometimes this involves asking a series of questions in order to obtain more information or to clarify the set of instructions.

Questions can be divided into two types:

- *Closed questions* are those where the person answering might only need to say 'yes' or 'no' in reply. For example:
  - Did you have a good time at the party?
  - Will you be home at the usual time?
  - Do you have enough money?

- *Open questions* are those where the other person might have to give a more detailed reply. They usually start with: How, Which, What, Why, When, Where or Who. For example:
  - Who else was at the party?
  - What time do you expect to be home?
  - How much money have you got?

Someone needing to clarify instructions or the objectives involved in carrying out a task would obviously need more than a 'yes' or 'no' reply to their questions. They would want full answers. However, it is not a good idea to ask question after question, but better to stick to one subject and not move on to another until full answers have been received.

Whatever type of question is required to obtain clarification, the following should be always be remembered:

- It should always be clear what is being asked.
- The question should not repeat something that has already been asked or said.
- The right tone of voice should be used. The way a question is asked can make a big difference – care should be taken not to sound sarcastic, or try to be funny.
- The question should be asked at the appropriate time and not when someone else is speaking.

Asking reasonable questions about what is expected is acceptable. Sometimes people are too busy to answer questions, but it is always better to get a question answered than continue a task with unclear instructions.

It is always sensible to ask for help and advice, as well as ensuring that the instructions and tasks involved are on the right track. Experienced colleagues are often the best people to approach for clarification as they may have faced the same problems in the past.

The word 'timescale' refers to both the amount of time that an employee has been given to complete a task and the deadline by which they must finish it. This means that any task needs to be prioritised in terms of its importance. Broadly speaking, tasks can be divided into the following categories as far as priorities are concerned:

INDIVIDUAL WORK (4.3) ⭐

Using the four categories in the above list, prioritise your workload at school or college at the moment.

1 Which category do most of your tasks fall into?

2 If many are urgent and important, how do you prioritise them?

- Urgent and important tasks
- Urgent, but not important tasks
- Important, but not urgent tasks
- Not urgent, nor important tasks.

Performance of responsible tasks on time

Within any job there will be a series of timescales and priorities. If, for example, you worked as an office administrator, you would find the following tasks are required of you:

- A series of routine tasks, such as filing, answering the telephone and photocopying.
- Larger tasks to complete, such as checking and ordering stationery.
- Tasks that do not occur very frequently, such as preparing for the end-of-year accounts, sending out a mail-shot to customers or clearing out the stock cupboard.

◊ Unexpected tasks, which tend to crop up when you least expect them, such as dealing with something because someone else is not available to do it.

As we have already discussed, these tasks can be regarded as either important or not important, urgent or non-urgent.

Only the person doing the job can actually decide whether a task is important or urgent enough to drop everything else and get on with it. Sometimes the following questions need to be answered before a decision can be made:

◊ What are the consequences if the deadline is not met?

◊ Where did the task come from?

◊ How long is the task going to take?

◊ Can the deadline be changed?

A deadline is the latest date by which a particular task must be achieved. When given a task with a deadline it is important at the earliest stage possible to begin to work towards the completion of the task at the required time.

Sometimes the decision regarding prioritising work does not fall to the person carrying out the work. The manager or supervisor may instruct particular tasks to be carried out immediately, to the exclusion of all other work. Equally there may be instances when colleagues need particular tasks to be carried out immediately in order to support their own schedule of tasks.

INDIVIDUAL WORK
(4.4) ★ ★

Managing your day and the workload applies to any job. People always have several tasks that may demand their time. Imagine that your business allows you to work flexi-time, which means that you have the option of either starting at 08.00 and finishing at 16.00 or starting at 09.00 and finishing at 17.00. The following list shows several deadlines and tasks that you have in a typical day at work. Put the work in the right order so that all the tasks are completed as close to their deadlines as possible.

• You have to make a 10-minute telephone call to Mr Flynn before 10.00.
• You have to call Mrs Petersen sometime today and it could take up to 15 minutes.
• You have to photocopy and collate 100 copies of the business's price lists before 12.00.
• A large document needs word processing and this will take you at least an hour. It has to be ready by midday.
• You have to be in a meeting at 14.00 that is likely to last at least an hour.
• It is going to take you at least 30 minutes to get the stationery order ready for the supplier. If you do not fax the order to them before 16.00 they do not guarantee the next day delivery that you need.
• You must call Mrs Scadding at 15.30. The call should take about 15 minutes.

Understanding of job role

Department, team and business structure

If tasks are to be carried out to deadlines and the objectives of a business met, it is important that all employees know what is expected of them.

Businesses want their activities to run efficiently and they try to help employees realise where they fit into an organisation by providing them with procedures and policies that have to be followed. These procedures and policies mean that all the employees of the business are working in a similar way towards their own sets of tasks and deadlines.

Knowing how one employee's job role links with other in their team, department, and ultimately with other departments within the organisation, will help the individual to realise their position within the business and the importance of the tasks they do.

On the face of it, an employee should know what is part of their job role (or duties) from their **job description**. But this is not always the case, as the job description is only a guide as to what is expected of an employee. Very often it is only after a little experience in the job role that it becomes clear exactly what the duties are. Perhaps

Keyword

job description – a document which explains what the job involves and is useful for matching the right person to that job more importantly, it also becomes clear how much one employee's job role affects the work of other people, teams or departments within the business.

We already know that businesses set up their operations by using a series of different functions, or departments, to carry out specific areas of their activities. Teamwork is also often vital to a business. Provided each individual employee knows what they are supposed to do, how to do it, what they need to do it and by when it has to be done, then the purpose of their job role is helping the business to meet its own set of objectives.

Absence and under-performance

Sometimes it becomes obvious that for a variety of reasons there will be a problem with meeting deadlines or achieving targets that have been set. This could be for any of the following reasons:

- There are not enough employees available to do the work.
- There are several key members of staff responsible for meeting the deadline that are off sick or on holiday leave.
- There are too many deadlines all around the same time and the work is piling up.
- There is not enough information available to complete the task.
- The other members of staff that could provide the required information are not available.

If any of the items on the above list become regular occurrences within a business, they will have a knock-on effect on an employee's ability to carry out their regular job role.

Understanding of team interdependence

In many businesses, employees are expected to work as part of a team and to contribute to the activities and success of that team. Teams are created for a variety of reasons, but they often have the following objectives:

- To help the business solve particular problems
- To help the business make particular improvements
- To help individual team members learn and develop
- To help encourage a feeling of team spirit within the business
- To encourage employees to be creative
- To encourage employees to exchange their ideas
- To encourage employees to work together in a constructive manner
- To develop the individual team members' skills
- To develop the skills of the team as a whole.

Teams can be created to carry out a variety of different tasks or for a specific series of short- or long-term jobs. A business's customer service provision is a good example of the way a business would use a team.

Sometimes teamwork can be frustrating, particularly if an individual's goals and talents have to be put to one side so that the team can meet its goals. Teamwork requires patience and understanding, but it can be enjoyable work, particularly if the team members work well together. It has been proven that businesses that create teams often produce far better results than several individual employees working alone.

Businesses try to get their teams working as well as possible, as quickly as possible and team leaders have a major role to play in making sure this happens for the business.

The business, through a manager, supervisor or team leader, may try to control the way in which the team operates in order to ensure that tasks or particular roles in the business are managed effectively and efficiently.

Research has proved that businesses are particularly keen on developing teams for the following reasons:

- Teams increased **productivity** by up to 80 per cent.
- Teams increased the quality of work in about 70 per cent of cases.

Keyword

productivity – the output or efficiency of a particular department or section, or indeed a whole business

INDIVIDUAL WORK
(4.5) ⭐

Would you make a good team member at work? To find out, answer the following questions with either Always, Sometimes, Occasionally or Never.

1   Are you able to work long hours?

2   Do you find problems a challenge?

3   Can you come up with good ideas to solve problems?

4   If you started an activity and were struggling, would you be prepared to keep going?

5   Are you able to keep going with an activity or problem until it is completed, regardless of how you feel about it?

6   Would you always put your own duties before anything else, including your leisure activities and your family?

7   Do you consider success to be measured in terms of how much praise you get?

8   Are you able to cope if you are unsure about how to carry out a particular task?

9   Do you consider yourself to be self-confident?

10   Are you able to take criticism?

11   Do you tend to ask for feedback on your performance so that you can do better next time?

12   Do you feel that your success or failure relies on others too much?

13   Do you tend to be a leader in certain situations?

14   Are you good at finding the right person or source of information to help you achieve what you want?

15   Do you have the ability to realise that in certain circumstances you may need help?

16   Do you set high standards for yourself?

17   Do you take risks rather than being cautious?

18   Are you healthy?

19   Do you have the ability to pass jobs on to others?

20   Are you able to identify which decisions are important and which are unimportant?

21   Do others think of you as a survivor?

22   Do you find coping with problems a real difficulty?

23   Do you respect other people's views and opinions?

24   When others express an opinion or offer advice or information, are you able to accept what they say?

If you have answered these questions mainly with Always or Sometimes, then you are probably a good team worker.

🍃 Teams reduced the amount of wasted time and materials that a business experienced by 50 per cent.

🍃 Individuals working in a team said their job satisfaction had increased by over 65 per cent.

🍃 Nearly 60 per cent of teams managed to improve their customer satisfaction levels for their business's products and services.

The different functions of any team can be broken down into three main areas:

🍃 *Tasks* – the time and effort the team puts into achieving its objectives.

🍃 *Interaction* – the contact between the individual team members, for example talking about how tasks will be achieved and asking for support to get things done.

🍃 *Self* – the individual team member making sure that he or she is doing what is needed in the best interests of the team.

A team needs to have a good mix of individual members, all with their own sets of skills, abilities and experience. They should support one another. Individuals can often be one of the following types, as shown in Table 4.2.

Table 4.2
Characteristics of individuals

Task-based characteristics (those that get the job done)		Function-based characteristics (those that enable the work to be done)	
Initiators	People that set goals and suggest ways in which things can be done and ways of dealing with team problems	Encouragers	People that accept others and are responsive and friendly towards them
Information or opinion givers	People that provide the team with figures, ideas and suggestions	Expressers	People that share their feelings with the team and help establish relationships
Information seekers	People that need facts and figures to get their work done	Compromisers	People that want the team to work and will give way on things if it helps the team to function
Elaborators	People that clear up confusion by giving examples and explanations	Harmonisers	People that try to deal with problems in the team and reduce tension
Summarisers	People that pull together various facts and ideas and keep the team informed of progress	Gatekeepers	People that encourage some of the team to get involved with a task but freeze out others that they do not want working on it
Agreement testers	People that check that everyone else in the team agrees with them and the way in which the task should be done	Standard-setters	People that try to set the minimum standards of work and try to get everyone in the team to stick by them

INDIVIDUAL WORK (4.6) ⭐

1 Do you recognise yourself in any of the categories listed in Table 4.2? Do you have more than one of the characteristics listed?

2 What about other members in your group, perhaps those you have worked with in a team? Pick five other people and discuss with them whether or not the characteristics you consider them to have are the same ones that they think they have.

Teams have to organise themselves in the most effective way possible if they are to achieve their targets, complete tasks and meet deadlines. The classic way to approach target setting is to remember the word SMART, an acronym that stands for: **S**pecific, **M**easurable, **A**chievable, **R**ealistic, **T**imely.

Team planning is vitally important. All the tasks set for the team should be broken down into manageable pieces, which are more manageable because they are under the direct control of the team members. The manageable pieces have to be prioritised and written down so that there is no confusion about them. By planning for the team as a whole, individual team members can also plan their own workload, which takes some of the pressures off individuals and the team leader. The plan is their map of how they will proceed and could include:

- The general objectives of the team
- The major objectives of the team
- What steps can be taken to meet the objectives
- How the team can achieve their objectives
- The role of each of the team members
- The deadlines involved.

Team planning usually takes place during meetings arranged to decide what the team has to do and how it will be achieved. A meeting may proceed in the following way:

- Team members evaluate their current position (where they are at the moment).
- Team members consider any forthcoming deadlines by which certain goals must be achieved.
- Team members decide how to prioritise the goals or deadlines.
- Once each team member has expressed their opinion about the first three items on this list they will try to reach a team agreement.
- Individual team members are allocated individual responsibilities arising out of the priorities and deadlines they have agreed.
- The individual team members identify the resources they require in order to help them fulfil the responsibilities they have been allocated.

GROUP WORK (4.7)
★ ★ ★

Your assignment is to submit a bid to an Egyptian Pharaoh, who wants you to build him one or more pyramids. Your bid will take the form of a five-minute presentation.

Three or four of you will work as the team to produce the bid and another one of the group will act as an observer. That person will note down how you have agreed certain things during the activity and tell you later which roles he or she thinks each of the team members have adopted.

You will need:

- Paper
- Card for building your model of the pyramid or pyramids
- Scissors, glue, rulers, pens, flip chart and a calculator.

Your team task is:

Your team is a business that builds pyramids. The Pharaoh, who is likely to live another 10 years, has approached you. He wants you to build him an impressive monument. He is not sure whether he wants one big pyramid or two smaller ones. It is your decision as to what to build. He is also not sure where he wants the pyramid(s) to be built. Again, he wants you to give him your recommendations.

The Pharaoh has put aside 10.5 million gold pieces. If you spend more than that, he will have you executed.

He also wants to see the completed pyramid(s), so you have 10 years to build. If you do not have the pyramid(s) finished within the 10 years, he will die and leave instructions that you are to join him in the pyramid(s) once they are completed.

For the presentation you will need to use a scale model, or models, and flip-chart paper. On the flip-chart paper, you will need to show your calculations and other information you feel is important. Your presentation needs to include:

- The proposed site
- The size of the pyramid or pyramids
- The time it will take to complete
- The total cost
- Scale model or models
- A sales slogan promoting your organisation.

The following information has been provided to help you work out your bid:

- The employees are slaves. They work seven days a week. They do not get paid, but it costs half a gold piece each day to feed each one of them. If you do not feed them they will die.
- You have a total of 1,000 slaves available to you.
- It takes 20 slaves to move one block of stone.
- There are four different sized pyramids available to make:

  Size 1 (Small)   – needs 80,000 blocks of stone
  Size 2 (Medium)   – needs 120,000 blocks of stone
  Size 3 (Large)   – needs 170,000 blocks of stone
  Size 4 (Massive)   – needs 240,000 blocks of stone.

- The cost of the blocks of stone are:

  From the Odan quarry   – 50 gold pieces each
  From the Mepash quarry – 30 gold pieces each.

- Transportation and erection takes the following times:

  Mepash quarry to site A   = 3 days
  Odan quarry to site A   = 1 day
  Mepash quarry to site B   = 2 days
  Odan quarry to site B   = 4 days.

Further instructions:

You should allow one hour to make all of the necessary calculations and prepare your bid. Your presentation should last no longer than five minutes.

REPRESENTATION IN PERSONAL DEALINGS

If it is important to a business to create the right image to its customers and the general public, then it should be equally important to the employees of that business. The way we dress, the image we present, the way we write to or speak to customers, what we say and how we say it all affect the impression they get of the business as a whole.

The organisation will also have set ways in which they want their employees to deal with the customers and with their fellow employees. These set ways are known as *procedures* and the employees should be made aware of these when they first start their job. Sometimes organisations issue booklets to all of the employees and these contain the procedures for dealing with customers. The procedures will be about all aspects of customer care.

The following headings identify the ways in which an employee could help to ensure that they are representing the business in the best possible way.

Appropriate and confident manner

There are a number of ways in which an employee's manner and degree of confidence can be important. There are three ways in which an employee could be described as being 'professional' in their behaviour at work, all of which are related to one another.

An individual's personality will often determine their attitude at work and their behaviour whilst at work. For many years researchers have been looking at personality and how this affects behaviour and attitude. Most seem to have come to the same conclusion: that there are five main factors that determine an individual's personality. These are:

- *Conscientiousness* Being conscientious means being happy to be busy and taking a pride in the quality of work that is done.

- *Neuroticism* Being neurotic means that the individual is very nervous of situations, particularly ones that might cause them problems or be difficult to deal with. It is quite common to be nervous the first time something new has to be done, perhaps talking to customers without help for the first time, or having to deal with a problem on one's own for the first time. This really is a measure of how a member of staff copes with these situations after they have had their training and have experience of such situations.

- *Extroversion* Being an extrovert can often mean that an individual is loud, outgoing, confident and never really bothered with what they are asked to do because they feel able to do most things. Many businesses like to employ extroverts as other people are often more comfortable with someone who is outwardly confident and enthusiastic.

- *Agreeableness* Being agreeable is a measure of a person's ability to get on with other people in a variety of situations. It is therefore a measure of someone's ability to work with others in a team, to share work or to get on with customers. It is not just being likeable; it is also about being adaptable and flexible.

- *Openness* Being open means being approachable, truthful and honest and having an ability to get along with others.

As virtually all jobs involve working alongside other people, or dealing with customers, on a daily basis, the business will want to employ individuals who have the right kind of personality, attitude, level of confidence and behaviour at work. We can all start the day feeling tired, irritable or unhappy, but it is a measure of an employee's ability to continue to do a professional job and not show any of these negative attitudes that makes them valuable to a business.

Dress sense and industry conventions

For organisations whose employees have direct contact with their customers, it is important that the staff look presentable. To represent a company in the best way, an employee would have to think about:

INDIVIDUAL WORK
(4.8) ★ ★

Do you have an appropriate and confident manner? Think about the qualities listed above and be honest in your answers. Are you:

- Conscientious?
- Neurotic?
- An extrovert?
- Agreeable?
- Open?

If you cannot decide for yourself, ask one of your fellow students or your tutor what they think.

- The way they dress for work.
- Their personal hygiene.
- The way they behave when they are at work.
- Their personality – whether or not they are often grumpy or sometimes a bit too loud.
- Their general attitude when they are at work – whether or not they look as if they are approachable and how they treat other people.

Some people are issued with a uniform that they have to wear for work. Uniforms are issued by some organisations for a number of reasons, including:

- They form part of the company image in that the uniforms may have the company logo printed on them.
- The employees will always be easy for the customer to find because they will all be wearing the same clothes.
- It avoids having to pay their employees an allowance for their work clothing.
- It means all their employees will turn up for work in the appropriate clothes and, hopefully, they will all look smart and well presented.

If an individual does not work for an organisation that issues a uniform, then they will be expected to dress in clothes appropriate to the job. This means as smartly and as tidily as possible. Very often organisations insist on certain *dress codes*. These are rules about what can or cannot be worn for work. Some of them are based on health and safety reasons, for example:

- Long hair needs to be tied back if the job involves working with food.
- No nail varnish can be worn when food is being handled or prepared.
- Dangling jewellery should not be worn in case it gets tangled in equipment or machinery.

As well as health and safety clothing, sometimes organisations insist that their employees wear name tags on their clothing or wear a pass. Name tags and passes are worn for security reasons, to make sure that only authorised people get into certain areas of the organisation.

What is chosen to wear for work very much depends on the job being done. For instance, some organisations insist that male employees wear a collar and tie to work and some do not allow their female employees to wear trousers.

Whatever clothes are worn for work, there is another consideration about what is being worn. It is how clean the clothes are. It would be useless for a business to give its employees a uniform to wear if they arrived for work with stains on their trousers or tops.

Very few people have money to spend on new clothes all the time, but if they are washed regularly and taken care of, it should not be necessary to keep buying new ones. Clean clothes, clean hair, clean shoes and a clean body all add up to being presentable. Personal hygiene does not just mean cleaning your teeth and having a wash, bath or shower in the morning. It includes your clothes.

GROUP WORK (4.9)
★ ★

In pairs, consider whether you know someone who is issued with a uniform for work. Or maybe you have to wear one for a part-time job you do. What do you think are the advantages and disadvantages of wearing a uniform for work?

- Clothes should always be clean and changed daily.
- Personal hygiene is important – shower or bath daily and use a good antiperspirant deodorant. If perfume or an aftershave is used, make sure it is not too strong smelling.
- Females should not apply make-up too heavily.
- Shoes should be clean and sensible.
- Hair should be clean and neat.
- Fingernails should be clean and neat.
- Oral hygiene (the mouth) is also important. Teeth should be cleaned every morning and a pack of mints should be kept handy to freshen the breath.

Degrees of formality

Another important part of the way people behave at work is the issue of formality. This means the way in which one is expected to behave at work, particularly when dealing with colleagues or customers. The degree of formality will very much depend on the type of business and the size of the business, as well as the activities of their operations.

For example, in your local garage, if the receptionist wishes to call one of the mechanics to the telephone, he or she may just call out their first name. The receptionist would probably do this even if there were a customer waiting at the desk.

However, some organisations expect their employees to behave in a much more formal way than this. Often the more senior members of staff, possibly the senior management, expect the junior employees to call them by their title and surname, for example, Mr Saunders, Miss Foster or Mrs/Ms Blythe. Sometimes this degree of formality is only required if there is a customer present and during their times alone the employees will call each other by their first names.

The basic rule to remember regarding formality at work is that a new employee should always call someone by their surname until they are told that it is acceptable to use first names. It will become obvious to the new employee what the degree of formality is within their working environment, as well as how other members of staff are required to be addressed in front of customers.

Tone is about the approach you may adopt in what you say or write. Tone means putting something across in the right kind of way to get the right kind of reaction from the person you are communicating with. This means that you will adopt a different tone in different cases to match the needs of the person you are communicating with, otherwise they may not understand or appreciate what it is you are saying or writing. Tone can depend on the type of individual you are addressing in speech or in writing. Tone will be different in the sets of circumstances shown in Table 4.3.

Table 4.3
Matching the appropriate tone to situations

Type of person		Tone to be used
Person working with you, not senior to you		Friendly, familiar tone, not too formal, can use jargon if you both understand it.
Person working with you, senior to you		Friendly, but not too familiar. You may need to be formal, you can use jargon.
Customer		Friendly, polite and respectful. There is a saying that 'the customer is always right', but sometimes they are not. You must be clear, forceful, but not rude.
Supplier		Friendly, polite, quite formal. Depends on how well you know the supplier. They will expect you to be rather formal, but need you to be clear.

GROUP WORK (4.10)
★★
Choose a partner in your group and try out different ways of using tone to say the same thing. Your partner will take the role of each of the following:
a) A person working with you
b) Your manager
c) A customer
d) A supplier.
Use the following information and the appropriate tone in each case:
'The business will be closed next Tuesday for stock-taking.'

Conduct in meetings

There is another formality that can apply to many businesses and it is the way in which members of a meeting conduct themselves. This is also known as meetings protocol. Although individual businesses will often have their own particular meetings protocols, the following are the general rules for how formal meetings should be conducted:

- The chairperson has to ensure that the meeting 'is in order' before it can start or continue.
- All those wishing to speak have to direct their comments via the chairperson. In large meetings it is sometimes necessary for the person wishing to speak to either raise his/her hand or to stand in order to gain the attention of the chairperson.

INDIVIDUAL WORK
(4.11) ★ ★
In a later task in this unit you will be holding a meeting with a group of your fellow students. To prepare for this meeting, write a list of conduct issues that you think your group should conform to during the meeting. What are your main protocols?

- When someone is speaking, whether it is the chairperson or another member of the meeting, it is good conduct for the rest of those at the meeting to listen attentively.
- Small conversations within groups at the meeting should be avoided. It is not possible to follow all the points being made if one is having a conversation of their own.
- If a vote has to be taken during the meeting, the chairperson asks for those in favour to raise their hands and be counted.

Informal meetings do not have this degree of formality, but it is expected that all those attending will concentrate and be polite. They will also be expected to direct their questions or suggestions through the chairperson, rather than just making comments to the group as a whole.

Greeting and leaving business contacts

The business contacts of a business may be calling for any one of a wide range of reasons, from attending a meeting to enquiring about products, delivering parcels or repairing faulty machinery. Some of these visits may be pre-arranged by appointment, such as a meeting with a specific member of staff, whereas others may involve people arriving unannounced, such as a delivery or salespeople.

The business's reception area is the first impression a visitor will receive of the organisation and it is important that this image is as good as possible. In order to achieve this, the area needs to be kept clean and tidy and the staff employed to cover reception duties should have a confident and friendly manner towards the visitors. The reception area should be manned at all times. Cover should be arranged for lunch and coffee breaks and for holiday and sickness periods. Some organisations employ gatekeepers who ensure any visitors are expected.

When business contacts are met, the employee should try to do the following:

- Greet the contact courteously and use their name in the greeting, for example, 'Good morning Mr Smith', or, 'Good morning Brian' if the contact is a regular visitor to the employee and they are on first name terms. In business situations it is usual for the two to shake hands.
- Smile when the contact is met so that they feel welcome.
- If the contact is well known to the employee, then some personal chat can take place, for example, 'How was your holiday?' or, 'Did you have a good weekend with your son last time we met?'
- Offer them refreshments (if appropriate) and let them get settled before starting to talk about the purpose of the visit.
- Concentrate while the meeting is taking place and make notes of important points, so that the contact can see the level of concentration and the intention to do a good job.
- Give the contact positive feedback and promise that the matter will be dealt with positively.

INDIVIDUAL WORK
(4.12) ★ ★
We have detailed for you the ways in which an employee can successfully deal with a visitor to the business's premises.

Write down how you think an employee should take a telephone call from one of the business's contacts. How should the employee greet the caller and reassure them that the employee is competent to take a message? How should the telephone call end?

When the contact leaves the employee, the employee should:

- Shake hands once more.
- Tell the contact it was nice to see them again.
- Promise them that the matter will receive the employee's full attention.
- Make sure they have full details of who they may need to contact or the employee's telephone number/email address.
- Give them details of the next step to be taken (either what the contact has to do or what the business will be doing).
- Wish them a safe journey (if appropriate).
- Leave them with confidence that the meeting was a success and that they would be welcome another time.

Awareness of appropriate discretion

Confidentiality and sensitivity, dealing with supervisors and senior staff

In many cases employees are required to deal with information that involves them having to respect confidentiality. Security of such sensitive information needs to be paramount.

Confidential information is difficult to define, but it largely covers information that, under normal circumstances, a customer or other person would not need to know. Some information circulating in a business will be marked as 'confidential' but this does not mean that other information that is not marked is not confidential.

Confidential or secure information is not suitable to leave lying around the desk. Neither is it appropriate to discuss it with others, even their opinion of it or what to do with it. Here are some examples of confidential information:

> **Keyword**
>
> **appraisal** – meetings between employees and their team leaders, line managers or supervisors. During appraisal meetings, targets are set and action plans for improvement drawn up

- Personal details about employees (their addresses, bank account details and telephone numbers).
- **Appraisal** information or confidential notes, letters or memos about employees.
- Payroll details (salaries and pay scales).
- Business information (such as product details, suppliers, costs and prices).
- Plans (ideas and plans to be undertaken by the business in the future).

Here are some basic precautions to take when dealing with confidential material:

- Be careful about photocopying – it is easy to leave a copy in the copier or someone could be looking over the employee's shoulder.
- Make sure documents are locked away and not left lying unattended on the desk.
- Envelopes containing confidential information should be sealed if they are to be distributed to other people.
- The shredder should be used to destroy unwanted documents or copies.
- An employee should always check with their team leader or supervisor to make sure that particular documents are confidential.
- If a confidential document is on the computer, switch off the screen or close the document before leaving the computer.

> **INDIVIDUAL WORK (4.13)** ★
>
> Make a list of at least three pieces of confidential information your school or college may have access to. What would be the implications if the wrong people saw them?

When giving out any form of information, you need to consider whether it is confidential, even if it is not marked as such. For example, if you were working for a computer manufacturer, you would not be able to tell someone the sources of the components used to build those computers. If you were working in a hospital you would not be able to give out any information about patients. If you were working in a bank you would not be able to tell anyone the details of another customer's bank account.

> **INDIVIDUAL WORK (4.14)** ★ ★
>
> You work as an administrative assistant on Ward 4 of your local hospital. During one morning you have received the following requests for information from relatives of some of the patients. How would you respond to each of these questions? Say whether or not you would be confident to give out this information, and if not, why not.
>
> 1 Can you tell me what my brother is allowed to eat please? He is hungry and wants us to bring him some extra food.
>
> 2 What time can I visit this afternoon please?
>
> 3 Can you give me Dr Patel's mobile number please? I have been trying to get him or his secretary for a week now and I really need to speak to him.
>
> 4 Can you tell me which staff nurse will be on duty on Thursday please?
>
> 5 I am not a relative; I am a reporter on the local newspaper. Can you confirm the name of the man that was brought in by the police last night and is now in intensive care? We want to come in and interview him.

CASE STUDY Devon Holiday Cottages

The following telephone conversation took place at Devon Holiday Cottages one morning.

'Good morning, Devon Holiday Cottages.'

'Hello, this is Clive, is that Sarah?'

'Yes it is.'

'I don't know if you remember me Sarah, but I work for Framlingham Stationery and I visited you with the sales rep last month.'

'Yes I do Clive, hello, what can I do for you?'

'I was wondering if you could sort me out a cottage for August to fit six people?'

'Yes, I don't think that will be a problem. Do you want me to send you a brochure?'

'Yes that would be useful, but I wanted to talk to you about prices. I talked to Simon, the sales rep, on the way back from your office and he told me that you had sorted him out a 20 per cent discount for a holiday next July.'

'Did he really?'

'Yes and I wondered if you could do me the same deal?'

'I'll have to check on that Clive.'

'Thanks. Oh and one other thing, you know Florrie in your office? She's not got a boyfriend has she? I want to send her a bunch of flowers. Could you give me her home address?'

'I can't really say and I can't give you the address. It's against company policy.'

'Go on, I only want to send her a bunch of flowers.'

'Alright then, she is single and she lives at 42 Nelson Drive, Taunton. But don't tell her it was me that told you.'

'Thanks, that's lovely. I'll look forward to getting the brochure and hearing from you about the discount.'

INDIVIDUAL WORK
(4.15) ★ ★

Read the case study and answer the following questions.

1 What information should Sarah have had to hand to tell Clive?

2 What information should she not have told Clive?

3 How could she have withheld the information about Florrie without offending Clive?

4 What might be the likely result of Sarah having given Clive confidential information?

Conveying business information to a reliable degree of accuracy

Deferring or avoiding comment or judgement, referring to a supervisor or responding at a later date

All information passed on to either a colleague or a customer should be as accurate and as complete as possible. It is not always possible for an employee to give a customer all the information they require, as the information may not be to hand, or they may not be confident enough to convey it. In such cases, it is a good idea to check with another person to ensure the facts are right. The employee, in such cases, should assure the customer that they will call back with the information, or ask them to wait while they find out the answer to their query.

Some information can be obtained easily, but the more complex the customer's query, the more difficult it may be for the employee to find the correct information immediately, and to be confident that it is correct.

If a customer is asking a specific question there is little point in telling them about other things that they might be interested in, or giving them more information than they really need. It is often a case of deciding what to say and what not to say, what to put in and what to leave out. The more complex the information is, the more chance there is they will not fully understand it or will be confused by it.

It is vital that business information is accurate. This may sound an obvious statement, but one incorrect figure or a decimal point in the wrong place could cause enormous problems, not only for the business itself, but also for the customer. The same would apply to the address on an envelope. It can cause unnecessary delay and inconvenience if a document goes astray in the post because of an inaccurate address. Some businesses design their documents in duplicate or triplicate so that such inaccuracies can be spotted easily.

All documents and information given by the business should be checked thoroughly before being passed on or issued. The person completing the documents should do this, although this is not always as easy as it sounds. Sometimes one simply cannot see one's own mistakes and it is more efficient to either get someone else to check it or to read it to them and they check the figures and data.

GROUP WORK (4.16)

★ ★

Paula has recently started work in an engineering business. One of her responsibilities involves taking the phone calls and passing on messages to her boss. Over the last three days, Paula has made a number of mistakes because she has not been accurate enough:

- While her boss was at lunch on Tuesday, a visitor called to see him. Paula took the visitor's name, but spelled it incorrectly.

- That same day, her boss gave her a telephone number to dial in order to speak to a customer. Paula copied it down wrong and when she dialled the number she got the wrong person.

- Today Paula's boss has a meeting 100 miles away and he had decided to take the train. Yesterday Paula gave him the train times, but she copied the wrong time for his departure. Paula's boss has just phoned to say that he had to wait an hour and is now late for his meeting.

What are the consequences of the mistakes Paula has been making? Discuss this as a group and come up with your most important consequences. Compare them to the consequences the rest of your class have come up with.

Recording

Discussions, key comments, agreed actions, making legible and coherent notes

Note-taking is important. It is not always possible to remember what people have said and what decisions have been made; notes provide the user with their own record to use when required. Business notes are taken in a variety of situations at work, for example when telephone conversations are taking place, during meetings and when being given instructions.

There is no right or wrong way to take notes, but to be efficient and make sure they are understood, there are a number of skills that could be developed:

- Think before you write – remember that the words you write down may not be referred to for several days and you need to know what the sentences actually mean.

- Raise any questions at the time if there is something you do not understand.

- Try to develop your own way of standard note-taking – you may prefer to use plenty of sub-headings, or you may choose to underline particularly important parts of your notes.

- Try to keep your notes in a notebook, so that you will always know that the notes are there and they cannot be lost on separate scraps of paper.

- Leave gaps between the main sections of your notes so you can add additional information later if it crops up again in the conversation or meeting, and it will also make the notes easier to read.

- Concentrate on the main points and do not get lost in the detail, as some of the detail may not be related to the main point and not everything is of equal importance.

- Remember you need to take good notes and helpful notes and not to save paper.

- Make sure that you can actually read what you have written – the faster you write, the less chance you have of being able to read your own writing later. If you abbreviate (shorten) words or put in initials for people, you will need to remember what these mean.

- If you are in a meeting, try to find a seat which gives you an uninterrupted view of those who are speaking – they may also show you diagrams or visual aids which you will need to look at, but may not have to write down in your notes as these may be given to you as a hard copy later.

INDIVIDUAL WORK
(4.17) ★
In a future task in this unit you will be required to take notes at a meeting of other members of your group. You should practise your note-taking skills, using the checklist above, so that you are prepared for this piece of work. Try taking notes from the TV news, from discussions in your group or from what your tutor's instructions are.

In a meeting, an average person will speak at a rate of between 125 and 140 words a minute, but the average note-taker can only write around 25 words a minute. This means that you cannot possibly write down every word, so you will need to listen carefully and translate what is being said into your own notes. As long as you are writing legibly, in a clear and logical way, you need not worry about spelling, grammar or punctuation. The notes are for your benefit and not for anyone else.

Reporting

Accuracy and conciseness, action points, deadlines and timescales

Reporting back to those who have set work can be either formal or informal. Normally teams and departments have regular meetings at which the progress of work is discussed. However, reporting back also happens informally and an employee may be asked at any time by their team leader or supervisor to tell them how far they have proceeded with a task and whether they have had any difficulties.

Reporting back means giving a clear, concise and honest update on progress and is also an opportunity to alert others that help or assistance may be needed, or that a task may not be completed to the deadline given.

INDIVIDUAL WORK
(4.18) ★ ★

Design a questionnaire containing at least 10 questions about how at least five of your fellow students are progressing on their BTEC First course. Your questionnaire should obtain information about:

- Any outstanding work they have and the deadline for completion
- Any points that they know require immediate action
- Any points they would like to improve on, but not necessarily immediately
- What they intend to do about their outstanding work
- Their timescale for the completion of their action points.

Take notes whilst they are talking if you need more information than can be contained on the questionnaire.

Report back in written form to each of those interviewed, stating accurately and concisely what you have learned from their responses to your questionnaire.

WRITTEN BUSINESS COMMUNICATION

The use of written communication, as opposed to verbal communication, is also common in all businesses. The advantages and disadvantages of the written method of communication are given in Table 4.4.

Table 4.4
Advantages and disadvantages of written communication

Advantages	Disadvantages
Written communications are more formal.	It can take a long time to get the communication right.
A record of the communication is created (which can be kept and filed).	It needs to be accurate and error free.
The communication can be re-read and referred to later.	It must not have spelling mistakes and look messy because this gives a bad impression of the business.
The communication can be copied for others to read.	It needs to legible (the receiver must be able to read what the sender has written).
It is ideal for difficult communications as there is a distance between the sender and the receiver.	
Written communication can use diagrams and instructions to back up the words.	

Before we look at the ways in which organisations contact those outside the business, for example their customers, we should first consider the various ways that those inside the organisation have for presenting written communications to each other, including: memos, reports, newsletters, notices, agendas, minutes of meetings, company newspapers, notes and messages, and email messages.

INDIVIDUAL WORK
(4.19) ★ ★

What method of written internal communication do you think the managers of a business would use to inform their employees about the following issues:

a) To invite a manager from another branch of the business to join them for lunch after a meeting

b) To provide the results of some research to all the managers of the business

c) To inform all employees about a change to the car parking arrangements

d) To tell someone they have a pay rise

e) To tell all employees the details of the forthcoming Christmas party.

Businesses communicate with their customers, or suppliers, using the written form of communication, including:

- *Business letters*, to the customer or a number of different customers (we look at business letters a little later in this section).

- *Compliment slips*, which could be included instead of a letter, for example, with a copy of the organisation's brochure.

- *Brochures or catalogues*, which would be glossy and expensive to produce, for example those you find in travel agencies. These detail the products, services and other information about the business for the customers to browse through.

- *Business cards*, which would be left by one of the representatives of the business. These are normally used to remind the customer of the name of the representative and the representative's telephone number or email address.

- *Leaflets* about the business.

- *Advertisements* about the business, including any special offers or discounts they may be using at the present time.

- *Maps* that might be included in brochures or sent out with leaflets, showing customers how to reach the organisation.

Professional, appropriate expression

Whatever kind of written communication is used, whether it is to the employees of the business or to its customers or suppliers, it is important that a professional approach is maintained. Businesses will have what is known as a *house style*, using their company headed paper on all written communications. They will also use their company logo, to remind customers about who they are and what they sell or stand for.

Think about all of the different ways in which you talk or write to different people in your life. Do you speak the same way to your friends as you do to your parents or teachers? Would you use the same language to your employer as you would to your closest friend? Probably not, and there are also ways in which you are expected to use your tone and style of speaking and writing in different situations at work.

The way you talk to someone you work with will differ enormously from the way you might talk to customers. This is what is meant by a professional manner and using the appropriate expression.

Vocabulary is your use of words, the way in which your choice of words has to change in different circumstances. You cannot always expect people to understand what you are saying if you use jargon or complicated words that they are not familiar with. You would not be expected to understand what others are saying if they bombard you with words that were difficult to grasp. Use of vocabulary is not about intelligence, showing off by using complicated words, or even trying to impress someone. The most important thing about your use of vocabulary is that whoever you are talking to or writing to understands what you mean. After all, talking and writing is about communication, and to make it a two-way communication both sides need to understand what the other is saying or writing.

Style is often a personal way of passing on that information to others, but in some cases, businesses will have preferred ways of doing this. Style can actually mean several different things:

- It may mean that the business has a preferred way of formatting documents, such as letters, and may well have preferred ways of opening (i.e. starting)/or closing (i.e. ending) letters.

- Style may also mean that the business has preferred spellings, such as using 'z' instead of 's' in words such as 'organisation' (organization).

- Style can also be set out in the use of particular forms which the business expects everyone to use.

- Style may be conversational (write like you speak), or technical (which assumes the reader will understand technical jargon), or formal (which will require you to be polite, tactful and clear about what you say or write).

Style, in most cases, means that you have to know how to speak or write in particular circumstances.

Normally, style differs in the following situations:

- You will have a particular style when dealing with colleagues at work who are on the same level as you are (and probably know you quite well).

- You will adopt a different style if dealing with someone who is senior to you.

- You will adopt a different style if dealing with customers or suppliers.

- You will use another style for writing, depending on the type of business document or format.

- You will have yet another style if you are preparing a document which will be read by others who you do not normally work with.

INDIVIDUAL WORK
(4.20) ★ ★

Look at the following types of communication style. One could be used in email, another in a formal business letter to a customer and the other in a telephone message for your manager. Identify which one is suitable in each case.

a) 'I regret, therefore, that under current company policies, we cannot refund your payment at this time.'

b) 'Toni, get me the figures for last month when you've got a chance, cheers, Mike.'

c) 'When you were at lunch, Mr Sinclair called. He is keen to talk to you about an order, but wouldn't confirm his order until you have spoken to him. Can you call him back please between 3 and 4 this afternoon? His number is 07924443333.'

Spelling, punctuation and grammar

We have discussed throughout this unit the importance of using the correct format for business communications and making sure that they are well-presented. However, none of these considerations will make any difference to the impression given in a business document unless the use of the English language is good.

Although our reliance on computers includes the use of word processors, which have a spell-check facility built in for checking the spelling, it is very important that all documents are proofread to make sure there are no errors. A word processor cannot be relied upon to identify words that are spelt correctly but are the wrong word, for example 'weather' and 'whether'. All types of documents, from memos and business letters to reports, articles and job descriptions need careful checking. Mistakes can creep in, particularly in the use of punctuation, grammar, spelling and the general use of English, which can end up making the sentence or paragraph both confusing and hard to understand. The careful checking of all finished work is therefore essential.

INDIVIDUAL WORK
(4.21) ⭐ ⭐
Proofread this text and identify the spelling mistakes and errors in the use of English that appear:

A verb is a word what describes a action. It is sometimes known therefore as a doing' word. For e.g. 'The manager open the door'. A sentence is not compleat withough a verb. For example 'The new ofice layout a big success'. This does not make a compleat sentence without the missing varb – is. The doing or action words in a sentence is usually the verbs.

Poor or inaccurate spelling in a business document can be very annoying for the person receiving the document. This would be the last thing a business would want – to upset its customers or suppliers because of a simple thing like spelling a word wrong. But, nevertheless, these errors do occur and unfortunately the only way that an individual can improve their spelling and use of the English language is to keep on thinking about it.

If you are not very good at spelling, then you need to make sure that you:

- Pay attention to the spell-check facility on your computer – if the machine identifies a spelling error it will underline the word in red. If it identifies a grammatical error it will identify the words or phrase in green.

- Get used to using a dictionary – it is all very well saying, 'How can I use a dictionary if I don't know how to spell the word?', but if you get into the habit of having a dictionary on your desk and double-checking each time you are not sure, then you will find you will eventually be able to spell several of the words you were unsure of.

- Get used to asking someone else – most people prefer to see a correctly spelled word because the individual writing it has asked for help, rather than constantly having to tell them to go away and do the typing again. If you are unsure how to spell a word and cannot find it in the dictionary, then ask for assistance from a colleague.

Lots of people have problems with the plurals of words. A plural of a word means 'more than one' and is usually formed simply by adding an 's'. For example, the plural of 'dog' is 'dogs'. However, some words can be both singular (one) and plural, such as 'sheep'. Other words need more than just 's' to transform them into a plural. For example, words ending in 'y', such as 'library' or 'facility', require the 'y' to be removed and 'ies' added to the end to make the plural – 'libraries' and 'facilities'. Words ending in 'ss', for example 'mass', usually require an 'es' to be added to give the plural, i.e. 'masses'.

Some nouns ending in 'f' or 'fe' need to drop the 'f' and replace it with 'ves' to make a plural. For example, the plural of 'calf' is 'calves' and 'knife' is 'knives'.

INDIVIDUAL WORK
(4.22) ⭐ ⭐

Write the plurals of these nouns:

a) donkey · b) family · c) ability · d) gateau · e) architecture · f) leaf · g) record · h) jacket · i) paper · j) activity · k) knife · l) life

If you know that you have a problem with spelling, then every time you come across a word you need help with, write it down correctly in a small notebook. This may sound a bit like getting ready for a spelling test at school, but it is the only way you will get to grips with the problem. The more times you practise spelling it, the better you will become.

INDIVIDUAL WORK
(4.23) ⭐ ⭐

People often have problems spelling the following words correctly. Use these to start off your list of words, to make sure you can spell correctly.

acceptable · accommodation · assessment · behaviour · budgeted · colleague · committee · convenient · criteria · definite · environment · hygienic · initial · initiative · liaise · necessary · receipt · receive · recommended · separate · transferred · undoubtedly

Another confusing area of spelling to some people is the words 'their', 'there' and 'they're'. They sound the same but have different meanings. They are likely to occur when writing any form of business communication or document and it is easy to confuse them and use the wrong word, but this can make nonsense of a sentence. Try to remember:

- 'Their' means 'belonging to them' and could be used to describe 'their work', or 'their children' or 'their home'. 'Their' is the plural of 'his', 'her' and 'its'.
- 'They're' means 'they are' and is like 'I'm' or 'We're' in that a letter is missed out.
- 'There' is used to show a place or to indicate something, for example 'There is' or 'Go over there' or 'I'll meet you there'.

Punctuation refers to full stops (.), commas (,), question marks (?), semi-colons (;), colons (:), apostrophes (') and capital letters (at the start of a sentence).

Here are some golden rules to help you remember how to use punctuation:

- A full stop should be used at the end of a sentence. (Remember that a sentence should also contain a verb.)
- A capital letter should be used at the beginning of a sentence and when using the names of people and places (proper nouns).
- A question mark is used to replace a full stop at the end of a sentence when a question has been asked in the sentence.
- Commas help the reader to understand the meaning of a sentence and also indicate where the reader may pause briefly in their reading. Commas are mainly used:
  - to separate items in a list:

    My brother collects stamps, foreign coins, comics and old photos.
  - to separate phrases and clauses in a sentence:

    Peter, the captain of our team, is the tallest and oldest player.

    The man, who had been to work, came home on the train.
  - after 'Yes', 'No' and linking words like 'However' at the start of a sentence:

    Yes, you can go to Anne's house now.

    However, there are some golden rules: …

    Or within a sentence:

    There are, however, some golden rules: …
- A semi-colon is used to join two sentences which are closely related in meaning:

  We were thinking of going on holiday again in September; June seems such a long way off now.

  Semi-colons can also replace commas in separating items in a list.
- A colon is used to introduce a list:

  We will have to take lots of items with us: the beach ball, the umbrella and something to wear if it turns cold.
- The apostrophe is commonly used in written communication and often causes confusion to many people who use it incorrectly. There are two different uses of the apostrophe:
  - to show that a letter or letters have been missed out of a word, for example, 'I'm' for 'I am' or 'won't' for 'will not'
  - to show that something belongs to someone or something, for example, 'the manager's car' or 'the dog's tail'. This is known as the possessive apostrophe.

There is only one exception to the use of the possessive apostrophe and that is the word 'it'. When you see the word 'it's' it always means 'it is' because you do not put a possessive apostrophe into 'its', for example:

It's a good car but its paintwork is in a poor state of repair.

If you were unsure where to put the apostrophe in Activity 4.25, turn the words around to show who owns the items, for example:

The desk of Claire

The office of the director

The dog of Jon

The coat of the girl

When there are several owners of something, the apostrophe goes after the 's', for example 'the companies' shareholders' or 'the bees' hive'.

INDIVIDUAL WORK
(4.26) ★ ★

The following sentences contain no punctuation at all. Rewrite or retype them, inserting the correct punctuation marks and spelling throughout:

1 the naughty boy was told therefore to report to the headmistresss office the next morning bringing with him his latest school report his outstanding homework and his packed lunch

2 maurices car was always giving him problems so he decided he would sell it soon and buy himself something brighter quieter and more reliable

3 when we all go to greece this year we have made a decision that we will travel by boat it is so much more relaxing than the airport

4 she expects to depart the station at 4 oclock and to arrive at birmingham just before it gets dark

5 if there late then we will have to find somewhere to sit and wait for them to arrive that should not be to difficult

---

Observance of appropriate discretion

As with confidentiality of information, it is also important for any employee to observe what is known as discretion. This sections explains why an employee would have to be discreet about the business's activities.

Confidentiality and sensitivity in business dealing, dealing with competitors, new product development

Confidential information is also known as *sensitive information*. As we already know, any employee that has to deal with confidential information will ensure that only those that are authorised are able to see it.

Much confidential information is kept on computer. Customer records, for example, would be held on computer by many businesses and they would not want to let their competitors know any of their customer details. Another reason for confidentiality of customer information is the Data Protection Act 1998. This is the legislation (law) governing how organisations keep information about customers on computer.

If sensitive information is kept on computer, businesses can make sure it remains confidential in a number of ways, including:

- Ensuring its employees have to use a password to use the computer system.
- Ensuring their staff have **screen-savers** so that they do not leave confidential material on their computers when they are away from their desks.
- Ensuring that computers are not situated in public areas of the business, for example the reception area, where the general public can see the screen.

Potential internal problems and negative publicity

A business would want their employees to keep sensitive information safe and use discretion if the business is experiencing difficulties.

Confidentiality regarding the work carried out by an employee's business, their plans or their customers is essential at all times. If there is ever any doubt that information could prove to be embarrassing, even in the most innocent of

---

WANT TO FIND OUT MORE?

Have a look on the internet and see if you can find out some information about the Data Protection Act 1998. How does it protect customers?

screen-saver – a moving imagine on the computer screen that appears if the computer is not used for a few minutes

conversations, it should not be mentioned. Employers expect a degree of confidentiality with regard to information leaking out, but this is equally as important in dealing with issues when discussing them inside the organisation. Discussing matters that could affect other departments or employees can cause unnecessary friction and problems and perhaps even **disciplinary procedures**.

Commercially-sensitive information, such as a business's plans to take over, or merge with, another business can be of high financial value to a business's competitors. Bad news about a business's performance or failures can equally be of great interest to their competitors and could, in extreme cases, cause difficulties for the business, such as their shares dropping in value and investors becoming concerned about the situation.

Appropriate use of occupationally relevant technical language

Technical style refers to written work where you need to use numbers, units, equations or technical jargon. There are a number of things to bear in mind regarding your technical style:

- *Clarity* You need to be clear so that there is no room for confusion. A reader or listener should not have to stop to work out what you mean.
- *Clear purpose* There should be no misunderstanding about what you are saying or writing. Remember that readers in particular are busy people and will not have the patience to work their way through muddled or confused documents.
- *Say it briefly* Clearly state your ideas. Your important ideas should have sub-headings and provide the structure of your document.
- *Use appropriate words* You should always use the most appropriate words and back up what you are saying with charts, tables, graphs, icons, illustrations or drawings.
- *Be concise* A skilled writer will replace key common phrases with much shorter words or descriptions (e.g. 'along the lines of' becomes 'like' and 'for the purpose of' becomes 'for').
- *Jargon* Use only words that everyone will understand (if you are writing for readers who will understand the jargon then this is acceptable). In many cases, documents may be read by people who do not understand jargon, so it is best to either avoid this or to provide a glossary of terms if jargon is absolutely necessary.

You probably know by now exactly what is involved in this unit. Have another look at the unit content for Unit 4. It is quite jargon-based. Translate the first assessment objectives into common language so that someone who does not know about the course would understand what is involved.

Awareness of professionally appropriate standards

Most organisations have a preferred method in which they like their written communication to appear. This is known as the business's house style and it can incorporate all of its communications. But for the purpose of this qualification, the following headings describe the standards needed for telephone messages, letters, reports and email messages.

Telephone messages

Telephone message pads are often printed on brightly coloured paper and vary in the way in which they are laid out. But they have spaces to note down the most important details of the messages. Remember that accuracy and efficiency are essential.

When outside callers or other people in the business wish to talk to someone, that person may not be available. One of the common tasks in business is to write messages from other people accurately. You can leave the message on the relevant person's desk for them to look at when they return. In many cases, you will need to summarise in the message the important information that needs to be passed on, which may include telephone numbers, names, dates or details about orders. Unlike a summary of written material, you do not have the benefit of being able to look back at the information and make a judgement as to what is important and what is not. You will have to summarise as you listen to the message. You can always ask the person to repeat certain things, such as telephone numbers.

INDIVIDUAL WORK
(4.29) ★ ★

Imagine you have just picked up the telephone and the caller wants to speak to Katie Walsh, but she is at lunch. Note down, as a message, the most important parts of the following conversation:

'Hello, my name is Suzannah Burman. I'd like to leave a message for Katie Walsh please. I should have phoned earlier, but I've been a bit busy doing my shopping and when I got to the car to drive home I found I had a flat tyre, so it took me longer than expected. Would you tell Katie that Alex has called me and his cold is a lot better now. He phoned to say that he will be back in work tomorrow. He can't remember what shift he is on tomorrow, perhaps she would be good enough to find that out for me. He tells me that he must visit the doctor tomorrow at 9.15 so in any case he won't be able to get into work until at least 10.30 and he hopes that is alright. Thanks very much and will you tell Katie that Alex would like to thank her for sending the get well card, bye for now.'

It is important to pass on messages quickly and accurately. It would be very frustrating to try to pass on a message word-for-word, so when taking a message for another individual the following points should be remembered:

- 💧 Listen very carefully to the message.
- 💧 Make notes as you listen.
- 💧 Your notes should contain key words and important information, including the date and time of the call and the name and details of the caller.
- 💧 Once you have taken the message, and before you pass it on, write it out in a form that can be easily understood.
- 💧 Do not include any unnecessary information.
- 💧 Make sure you mention names, addresses, telephone and fax numbers, order numbers and any deadlines which need to be met.
- 💧 You can then pass on the message by telephone, or write it on paper or a telephone message pad, or pass the message on face-to-face.
- 💧 You should ensure that your tone and style is correct when both receiving and passing on the message.

Letters

Even the simplest letter must follow a particular format and set of conventions. These are rules that say how the document will look. Each different type of business communication, or document, has a different set of formats and conventions. By following these, the person or people who receive or see the communication will have a much better chance of understanding the information contained in it.

Normally a business letter is sent to an individual outside the organisation itself. Letters may be written for a number of different purposes, including:

- 💧 Contacting potential customers – people who are either buying or may buy the organisation's products or services.
- 💧 Communicating with suppliers – who are other businesses that may provide items such as products, photocopy paper or office equipment to the organisation.

INDIVIDUAL WORK
(4.30) ⭐
We have given you five reasons why a business might write a business letter. Can you think of any others? Write down your other reasons for an organisation writing a business letter. Remember that a business letter goes to someone outside the organisation.

- In answer to a customer complaint.
- To tell existing customers about a new product the business might be about to make available.
- Contacting a future employee who has applied for a job with the organisation.

Business letters need to be neat, accurate and well-presented as businesses see their letters as being a reflection of their professionalism in all things that they do. They will tend to use headed paper (see Figure 4.2), which means that many of the details in the following list are printed on the paper and appear on every letter that leaves the organisation. This also means that the person preparing the letter does not have to type these details every time a letter is sent out. The headed paper will usually contain the following information:

- Name and address of the business.
- Telephone and fax numbers of the business.
- Email address of the business.
- Website address of the business.
- Registered address of the business (this could be a different address to the normal postal address of the business).
- The business's registration number (a number given to the business by Companies House where most businesses have to register that they have been created).
- The business's owners or directors.
- The names of other businesses associated with the business, such as professional organisations.

A business letter will be ordered in a certain way to make sure it contains all the necessary information. As well as the name and address of the business on the headed paper, it will contain:

- The name and address of the recipient (the person the letter is being sent to).
- The date the letter is being prepared or sent.
- Sometimes a reference – which can be the initials of the writer or a set of numbers. This will help the writer of the letter to know where to file it and also to keep all the paperwork together if there are lots of letters relating to the same subject.
- The word(s) 'URGENT' or 'CONFIDENTIAL' which also helps the recipient to recognise how important the letter is.
- A *salutation* – this is the start of the letter and could be 'Dear Mr Smith' or 'Dear Sir'. If the name of the recipient is known, then it is usual to use it and start with their name. If the name of the recipient is not known, then it is more appropriate to use 'Dear Sir' or 'Dear Madam'.
- A subject heading – which will help the recipient to see immediately what the letter is about.
- The paragraphs contained in the letter.
- The *complimentary* close – this is the way the letter ends. If 'Dear Sir or Madam' has been used in the salutation, then the letter is ended with 'Yours faithfully'. If the name has been used, for example 'Dear Mr Smith', then 'Yours sincerely' is used in the complimentary close.

nelson thornes	Delta Place 27 Bath Road Cheltenham GL53 7TH United Kingdom	+44 (0) 1242 267100 +44 (0) 1242 221914 mail@nelsonthornes.com www.nelsonthornes.com

Figure 4.2
An example of a business's headed paper

💧 The name of the person sending the letter (and their job title), placed after the complimentary close, leaving enough room for their signature.

💧 If the letter includes any additional items (called *enclosures*), this is indicated at the end of the letter by 'Enc', or 'Encs' for more than one enclosure.

Businesses will have different rules about how their business letters are displayed. The most common way of displaying a business letter is the fully blocked method of display. This means that each part of the letter starts at the left-hand margin (see Figure 4.3). Fully blocked letters use 'open' punctuation – no commas at the ends of lines in the address, salutation and complimentary close.

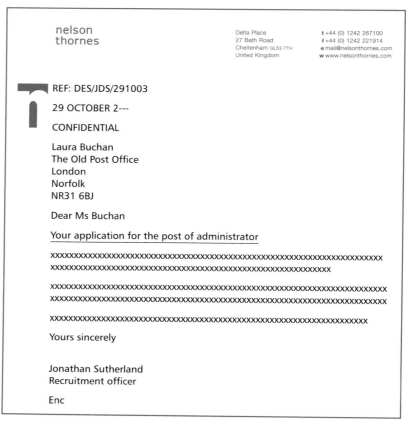

Figure 4.3
An example of a business letter using the fully blocked style

Some businesses may prefer to use the indented style where each paragraph is indented from the left-hand margin and the subject line and complimentary close are centred, as shown in Figure 4.4. This is the older, more traditional style of laying out a letter and used to use more formal punctuation (as shown in Figure 4.4), though open punctuation is now acceptable.

Reports

Report writing is not only vital to a business, but is also carried out in order to achieve goals or objectives. Businesses can commission reports for many different reasons, including:

💧 To identify problems and find solutions to these problems

💧 To provide progress reports on particular projects

💧 To investigate particular areas of the business's activities

💧 To identify the need to change policies.

Although reports can be written as memos (a memo is an internal document) for fast responses to problems, a more formal and longer form of report can also be used.

Figure 4.4
An example of a business letter using the indented style

There are many different ways in which these reports can be written, but generally they have the following sections:

- *Title page* – the subject of the report.
- *Terms of reference* – what you have been asked to do or research.
- *Procedure* – how you have gone about gathering the information which you have included in the report.
- *Findings* – what you have found out.
- *Conclusion* – here you conclude and sum up your findings.
- *Recommendations* – on the basis of your findings and conclusions, you make your recommendations.
- *Appendices* – documents, charts, diagrams, tables and other information which is referred to in the rest of the report. This is where the more extensive information is placed in the report.

You should also sign and date your report.
Sub-sections can also be used in a formal report, for example:

1. *Title page*
2. *Terms of reference*
3. *Procedures*
4. *Findings*
   4.1 …
   4.2 …
   4.3 …
5. *Conclusions*
6. *Recommendations*
7. *Appendices*

INDIVIDUAL WORK
(4.31) ★ ★

You recently bought a toy for your little nephew's birthday present. On the box it stated that batteries were included. On the day of his birthday, your nephew was in tears because he could not play with his toy because there were no batteries in the box. You now want to write a letter of complaint to the toyshop.

Write your letter using the correct layout for a fully blocked letter. Use today's date. The address of the toyshop is:

Children's Toys
The Precinct
Swinfield
Surrey
SW1 5BF

You should sign the letter yourself. Be careful about your spelling and punctuation and use an appropriate style and tone for your letter.

Email

Many businesses now use emails as a supplement to more tradition forms of business communication, such as the letter. The simplest way of making sure that email is suitable to be sent is to ask yourself how you would feel and react if the email was sent to you.

As with letters, all of the communication comes from the words and it is essential that they are read correctly and understood. There are 10 commonly made mistakes regarding emails, listed in Table 4.5.

Table 4.5
Common mistakes in emails

Email problem	Description and solution
Unclear subject lines	This is the title given to the email. It should be clear, concise and neutral. Negative words or expressions are best avoided.
Poor greeting or no greeting	Emails should always begin with a friendly salutation. It is not good practice to launch straight into the message.
Abbreviations which are not commonly understood	Abbreviations can cause difficulties in terms of misunderstanding and misinterpretation. Full versions of words should be used as even ASAP or FYI can be misinterpreted.
Unnecessary CC of the posting	Only make courtesy copies to those parties that are directly related to the situation or email message.
Sloppy grammar, spelling and punctuation	By not taking the time to spell or grammar check messages, the sender runs the risk of creating a negative impression to the receiver. Emails containing misspellings and poor grammar lower the credibility of the message.
Using all capital letters to make a point	Using all capital letters in a message could be misunderstood and the receiver may conceive it as anger, rather than emphasising a particular point.
No closing or sign off	Writing a friendly closing is as important as a friendly greeting. Try to end emails on a positive note, regardless of the content of the message.
Difficult to read	Care should be taken not to allow sentences to run on. Points should not be repeated and paragraphs should be identified and formatted.
Unfriendly tone	Even if the content of the message is sensitive, the email should never give the impression that the sender is being hostile.
Unclear request	Any requests should be expressed accurately and appropriately in a clear and direct manner so that there is no confusion.

PREPARATION FOR BUSINESS MEETINGS

> **constitution** – the rules made when the business was first started up that state the procedures and policies of the organisation
>
> **minutes** – a written record of what took place, what was discussed and agreed, including actions to be taken before the next meeting and by whom
>
> *Keyword*

Meetings are held in all organisations. They can be informal or formal, requiring a range of communication methods and administrative support. Formal meetings are often governed by the **constitution** of the business. This means that when the rules of the organisation were written, they included those relating to the procedure for formal meetings. Organisers of formal meetings must ensure they have a good knowledge of the procedures involved.

Types of formal meeting include:

- *Annual General Meeting (AGM)* These meetings are held once a year and are used to assess the trading or affairs of the business over the previous year. Officers, for example the chairperson, secretary and **minutes'** secretary, are elected at the AGM for the coming year. AGMs are open to all shareholders of the business and 21 days' notice must be given prior to the meeting. If this notice is not given, it is not considered constitutionally correct to hold the meeting, therefore making it invalid.

- *Board meetings* The directors of an organisation attend board meetings, which are chaired by (headed by) the chairperson of the board of directors or that person's deputy. Any type of business can be discussed at these meetings, and they do not always have to be run in a formal manner. Depending on the size of the organisation, they can sometimes be regarded as informal in smaller organisations.

- *Statutory meetings* After a report has been circulated to all members, a statutory meeting is called so that the directors of the business and its shareholders can communicate. It is a requirement of the law that these meetings take place and, particularly in the case of local government committees, businesses are required by an Act of Parliament to hold them.

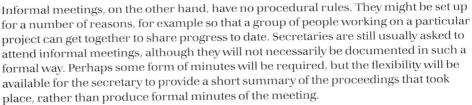

Informal meetings, on the other hand, have no procedural rules. They might be set up for a number of reasons, for example so that a group of people working on a particular project can get together to share progress to date. Secretaries are still usually asked to attend informal meetings, although they will not necessarily be documented in such a formal way. Perhaps some form of minutes will be required, but the flexibility will be available for the secretary to provide a short summary of the proceedings that took place, rather than produce formal minutes of the meeting.

Types of informal meeting include:

- *Departmental or section meetings* These may be called by the head of department or section in order to pass on information to the rest of the staff. Alternatively they may be called in order to receive reports from certain members of the section who have been working on a particular project.

- *Management meetings* These take a similar form to a departmental or sector meeting in that the head of the section may be informing or receiving information. A group of managers, for example the production, sales and research and development managers, may need to meet in order to discuss a particular new promotion or a new range of products.

- *Working parties* A working party is a team of people that all have a similar aim or objective. They may need to meet to give or receive progress reports or to pass on information obtained. A working party is set up so that a group of individuals, each with a different responsibility or expertise, can work together on one particular problem or issue.

Meetings can be either internal or external to the business. An internal meeting is attended by employees of the business, and held within the business's premises. An external meeting is held at alternative premises and may be attended by individuals who are not employed by the organisation, such as shareholders. External meetings tend to be more formal, whilst internal ones are more often of an informal nature.

Meetings are held in order to allow verbal communication to take place. They can be held for a variety of reasons and in order to discuss a range of topics. However, usually meetings are held for one or more of the following reasons:

- To share information.
- To share new ideas or proposals. New proposals can be discussed and are often voted on.
- So that employees feel involved in the day-to-day running of the business and their interest is maintained.
- So that assistance in certain areas can be sought by more than one individual.
- To report back on an activity that has been taking place.
- So that the activities of the organisation can be coordinated.
- So that any problems can be discussed and any rumours or anxieties quashed.

In a busy working week, it is not always possible for individual employees to meet on a face-to-face basis to talk about their ideas or problems. A meeting allows for several individuals to meet at an arranged time to discuss particular topics. Depending on the type and size of the business, a secretary or administrative assistant may be involved in a number of different types of meeting. These will vary in their formality and the number of individuals involved.

Ability to carry out appropriate preparatory organisation

The term 'tabling documents' means getting all the paperwork ready that is required for a meeting. Members attending the meeting will all need their own individual copies of any relevant documents and the person arranging the meeting would lay these papers at each place around the table.

As we have already seen, meetings take place for a variety of different reasons, and are attended by various different individuals or small teams of people. Such meetings have to be formally documented, either because of the business's procedures or because a record needs to be kept for future reference and action.

Preparatory documents and circulating documents

The first document we need to consider when thinking about preparing for a meeting and circulating any appropriate documents is the *Notice of Meeting*. The notice of meeting is a form of communication that calls everyone who is entitled to attend the meeting. It is possible to use any method in an informal meeting, but with a formal meeting the rules and regulations laid down in the business's procedures would be followed. If people from outside the business are to attend the meeting, the notice will be sent with a covering letter. If the meeting only involves those internal to the business, a memorandum will be attached. Possible methods of preparing a notice of meeting may include:

- Written or typed advance notice
- Verbal notice
- Notice-board posting.

Whatever form of notice is used, the following basic information must be included:

- The venue (where the meeting is to be held)
- The day, date and time of the meeting
- Details of any special business to be discussed at the meeting
- The type of meeting (where appropriate)
- The name of the person calling the meeting (usually the chairperson)
- The date of the notice.

The document that is used to inform those people who are to attend a meeting about the nature of that meeting is known as an agenda. An agenda gives the date, time and venue of the meeting. It also sets out the programme of business that the chairperson wishes to discuss.

25 November 2---

NOTICE OF MEETING

There will be an Acquisitions Meeting for all editors involved in the Health and Social Care department of the publishing house on Friday, 3 December 2--- at 09.30. Current projects will be discussed as well as amendments to publishing deadlines.

Helen Scott

Figure 4.5
An example of a notice of a meeting

Specifically, the agenda will contain the following information:

◊ The date, time and venue of the meeting.

◊ The title 'Agenda' will confirm the purpose of the document.

◊ Item 1 is always the apologies received from members not able to attend. Apologies are sent to the meeting via the chairperson. A record is kept for the minutes of the meeting so that all concerned will know that those unable to attend had been invited and that they had 'sent their apologies'.

◊ Item 2 is always the checking for accuracy of the minutes of the previous meeting. Once this task has been accomplished, the minutes will be signed by the chairman of the meeting.

ABC Ltd
Meeting of all First-Aid Qualified Staff

A meeting of all staff holding a current first-aid qualification will be held in the training centre on Friday, 25 January 2--- at 11.15

AGENDA

1. Apologies for absence
2. Minutes of the last meeting
3. Matters arising from the minutes
4. Report from Brian Phillips on recent government legislation regarding first-aid requirements
5. Details of forthcoming training courses for qualified staff
6. Implications of cover required for staff absence
7. Any other business
8. Date of next meeting

Helen Scott

Figure 4.6
An example of an agenda

INDIVIDUAL WORK
(4.32) ★ ★

Your boss has to chair a number of meetings and it is part of your job role to prepare and circulate (send out to the relevant people) the appropriate documents.

Your first task is to prepare a notice of meeting. You should include the following information:

Tuesday, 4 February 2---
At 10.00
Your boss is Simon Brett and he is the Sales Manager
He wants to call the meeting in his office of all sales representatives to discuss whether or not current sales targets are being reached.

INDIVIDUAL WORK
(4.33) ★ ★

Using the information from the previous task where you produced a notice of meeting, add the further information given below to produce an agenda for that meeting. You can use the example of an agenda shown in Figure 4.6 for the layout. The items to be discussed at the meeting are:

• Individual reports from regional sales representatives

• Implications on overall sales figures

• Initiatives for new sales representatives

• Current sales figures.

⬙ Item 3 always deals with any matters that have arisen from the minutes of the previous meeting.

⬙ The remaining items to be dealt with during the meeting are then listed, each with a separate number.

⬙ 'Any other business' (AOB) gives members the opportunity to introduce any matters they wish to dis cuss that have not been included in the agenda.

During the course of the meeting, either the chairperson or the minutes secretary will distribute a series of documents that need to be completed by the members of the meeting. Those attending the meeting will sign the attendance sheet so that their names can be listed on the minutes of the meeting. Some businesses do not use an attendance sheet and the secretary merely writes down the names of those attending. Any other papers that the chairperson has said are necessary would be distributed to each of the members of the meeting.

Advance organisation

Meeting facilities, refreshment, accommodation

Arranging a meeting can be time-consuming, particularly if some of those attending are involved in travel and overnight stays. Any arrangements should be made wherever possible in advance of the date of the meeting. Being organised well in advance will often mean that the meeting will run smoothly. Very often the staff that work most closely with the chairperson of the meeting will be responsible for arranging the travel and accommodation arrangements for those travelling some distance to attend a meeting.

Matters that should be arranged ahead of time include:

⬙ Finding out the travel and overnight accommodation requirements of anyone external to the business, or those attending the meeting from another branch of the business.

⬙ Booking the meeting room – this may be the chairperson's office, or it could be a board room or a business's meeting room.

⬙ Ordering any refreshments that may be required during the meeting – this may just be tea/coffee and biscuits, or it may involve lunch for a number of people.

⬙ Booking any car parking spaces required for visitors to the meeting.

The day before the meeting is scheduled to take place, the following activities need to be carried out:

⬙ Collect together spare copies of the agenda for distribution at the meeting.

⬙ Get the minutes of the previous meeting from the file as this will be required for the meeting.

⬙ Gather together any relevant papers and information documents concerning items that are to be discussed from the agenda.

⬙ Make a list of any people that have sent their apologies because they are unable to attend the meeting.

⬙ Make sure adequate stationery is available for the meeting table (this could include writing paper, pens, etc.) plus an attendance sheet for signing (if used).

On the day of the meeting, the following need to be arranged:

- Confirm the parking arrangements.
- Contact reception and notify staff of the names of the visitors expected.
- Arrange with the switchboard to re-route any calls (unless emergency calls) while the meeting is in progress.
- Make sure that the meeting room is ready before the allocated time for the meeting to start. Check the heating, lighting and ventilation, and ensure sufficient seating is available.
- Place the writing paper, pens, copies of the agenda and other documentation at each seat around the table.
- Provide jugs or bottles of water around the table.
- Place a 'Meeting in Progress' notice on the meeting room door.
- Place the list of apologies next to the chairperson's seat, as this will be the first item on the agenda.
- Provide the chairperson with the minutes of the previous meeting as these will be read at the start of the meeting.

INDIVIDUAL WORK
(4.34) ★ ★

In preparation for the forthcoming meeting of sales representatives that Simon Brett is holding, you should now write yourself a checklist of what has to be done. In this case nobody has to stay overnight, but all of the reps will be travelling from their own region to attend the meeting. Draw up your checklist under the headings 'One week before', 'The day before' and 'On the day'. Your checklist should start with your instruction to send out a notice of meeting and end with the time the meeting starts.

Assisting in the effective running of appropriate meetings

Once the meeting gets underway it is the role of the chairperson to take control. But obviously he or she will require some assistance and this is often the role of the minutes secretary. Usually the minutes secretary will sit beside the chairperson and sometimes, if the minutes of the last meeting were not circulated, the secretary will be asked to read them out to the meeting members.

A successful meeting relies on organisation and the following are guidelines for such a success:

- The minutes of the previous meeting must be signed by the chairperson to allow them to be regarded as a 'true and accurate record' of what had taken place.
- The minutes of the current meeting must be taken (we deal with how this should be done later in this section).
- Safety and security procedures should be followed at all times during the meeting.
- Confidentiality of information is vital to businesses. For this reason all paperwork should be returned to their files as soon as the meeting has finished.

Deputising in the event of emergencies

Named individuals in a business will be invited to attend particular meetings, but due to pressure of work, sickness and holidays, sometimes these individuals cannot attend. In these circumstances someone has to go to the meeting on their behalf and this is known as *deputising*.

This can cause problems for the person expected to deputise, particularly if they have not been given very much notice. They may not be aware of what was discussed at the last meeting or what kind of decisions have to be made or which topics are to be discussed. This means that it is important for those attending meetings to keep records, such as the minutes, which can be read by the person deputising to bring them up to date on the current discussions.

Appropriate advance clarification of meeting purposes

Agendas will list topics, issues and other matters that need decisions. If those attending the meeting need additional information, then it is usual for any other useful documents to be attached to the agenda when it is circulated. Those that attended the previous meeting will know the purpose of the next meeting, as together they will have decided the agenda items and may have, in the meantime, come up with other issues that need to be discussed.

Sometimes the items on the agenda require an individual to explain a particular situation or report back on progress since the last meeting. Other items on the agenda may need immediate decisions and those attending will have been given all of the background information to help them make their minds up as to the best course of action.

Knowing what will be discussed or decided upon at the next meeting gives those attending a chance to research particular areas, discuss the matter with colleagues and to decide what they think is the best course of action.

Time allocation and focused guidance of discussion

It the chairperson's responsibility to make sure that not only the decisions that need to be made are actually made, and information that needs to be passed on is passed on, but also that the meeting does not overrun.

Time will be allocated to a meeting and the chairperson will have the responsibility of making sure that all of the agenda items are covered in the time given. This means that it is the chairperson's responsibility to cut discussions or arguments short if there is a danger that no decision will be made and that items further down the agenda will not get a chance to be discussed.

To do this, the chairperson must make sure that discussions or arguments do not stray away from the topic being discussed. If other matters arise from discussions, then these can be added to a future agenda. The chairperson must always remind those at the meeting that particular decisions will need to be made and that the meeting cannot finish until they have been decided. All points and conversations must take place through the chairperson, who will choose individuals to state their case or make their argument before passing on to someone else. The chairperson should not allow conversations to take place between those attending without allowing the rest of the group to contribute.

GROUP WORK (4.35)
★ ★ ★

In groups of six, you are going to hold a meeting. You must elect a chairperson and a minutes secretary and prepare an agenda. You can choose the items on the agenda, but you could use this opportunity to evaluate some work you have done or discuss a proposed event or issue related to your course. Each member of the group should have an input into the meeting. You should each contribute to the discussions that take place and each propose a motion on which you all vote.

Appropriate consultation of meeting delegates

Individuals that have been invited to attend a meeting are those that have a stake, or opinion, regarding particular issues. In any business there will be differing views and it is the purpose of a meeting to bring all those views together so that all of the participants are aware of the different ideas or viewpoints.

It is the chairperson's responsibility to give everyone an opportunity to say what he or she needs to say about an issue, so that the rest of the group can hear their opinion. Only when everyone has had an opportunity to speak will the chairperson move on to encourage those attending the meeting to make a decision about what was being discussed.

Appropriate clarification of agreed conclusions

A *motion* is a proposal at a meeting. In other words, it is an issue that needs to be discussed and then decided upon by those at the meeting. Motions that are voted upon are called *resolutions*. It is a good idea that all business should be introduced to the meeting in the form of either a motion or a resolution, as this will allow everyone to give their views about the issue in question.

Usually, motions will have to be written and signed by the proposer and supported by a seconder. If someone intends to support or propose a motion, they should ensure that they are well prepared for the meeting by ensuring that they:

- Have read all the minutes, reports, briefings and other documents relating to the issue.

- know all the people at the meeting and are aware of any particular interest or objection to certain proposals or points of view. It may be necessary to gain the support of several people at the meeting in order for a motion to be carried forward.

Compilation of accurate notes and meeting records, preparation and circulation of meeting minute, checking key details

During the meeting a series of notes have to be taken. These notes will later become the minutes of the meeting. These minutes are then distributed to all those who attended the meeting and a copy is filed. It is essential that an accurate written record of the meeting is provided for all those who attended and also for those who were unable to attend. At the next meeting, these minutes will be read under item 2 of the agenda and anything that needs reporting on as a result of the minutes will be dealt with under item 3.

Minutes will be presented in the same order as the agenda and would include:

- A list of those present at the meeting.
- A list of those not present, but who sent their apologies.
- A statement that confirms the minutes of the previous meeting had been read and signed as being a true record.
- An account of discussions that took place during the meeting.
- A note of tasks that were allocated to individuals.
- Reports that were received from individuals.
- Actions to be taken in the future as a result of the meeting.
- An account of any decisions that were made as a result of discussions.
- Details of individuals to whom decisions taken may refer.

Minutes should be concise and precise, but they should not lose any accuracy in this process. The style of writing should be brief and to the point. Often a form of

---

4. **Report from the Chief Safety Officer**

   Mr Mills reported that the recent government legislation concerning health and safety at work procedures would require careful consideration. The new procedures would be copied and distributed to all concerned. Mr Mills stated that he would like a sub-committee to be formed to study the legislation and report back at the next meeting.

   Mr Taylor, Mr Brenner and Ms Oliver volunteered to form the sub-committee and agreed to meet on Tuesday, 27 June 2-.

5. **Implications of possible new extension to the office block**

   Ms Oliver reported that she had seen the plans for the new office block and was concerned that not enough space had been allocated to each member of staff using that block. After some discussion it was decided that Mr Mills would speak to the architects and report his findings to the next meeting.

Figure 4.7
An extract from a set of minutes

numbered listing is used against each minuted item, which helps remind those present at the meeting about any decisions made or actions needed that they have to undertake before the next meeting. Figure 4.7 shows an example from a set of minutes.

Certain organisations, particularly local authorities, must have their minutes available for public inspection. The details of any motions voted upon or amendments made to these motions must be clearly detailed in the minutes.

INDIVIDUAL WORK (4.36)
★ ★ ★

1 You now have to prepare your own set of minutes of the meeting you have recently held. Make sure that your minutes follow the same order as the items on the agenda. Did you arrange another meeting in the future? If so, put the date of the next meeting in the appropriate place. Use numbered listing against each agenda item in the minutes if this is appropriate.

2 Was your note-taking sufficiently efficient for the preparation of the minutes to be quite straightforward?

3 Compare the content of your set of minutes with those of members of your group in attendance at the meeting.

Unit Revision Questions

1 Name five ways that you could ensure you have understood a set of instructions.

2 What does the word 'clarification' mean?

3 Give one example of a closed question.

4 Give one example of an open question.

5 What do you understand by the word 'procedure'?

6 What do you understand by the term 'dress code'?

7 What do you understand is meant by the term 'confidential material'?

8 What would you do if you did not understand a task that had been set you?

9 Name five things to remember when note-taking.

10 What is a business's house style?

UNIT 5

Employee Contribution to Working Conditions

This unit looks at how you can make an effective contribution in the workplace. Acquiring the necessary skills and knowledge to do this will be extremely useful in your first career steps.

This unit covers many aspects of work, including:

- Employment contracts and employment law
- Recruitment, appraisal and staff development
- Conflict and how it is resolved
- Change and development and how to adapt to it
- Acquiring new skills and improving your employability.

This unit is internally assessed. To cover the various aspects of the unit you must:

- Explore terms of employment contracts
- Consider the processes of recruitment and staff development
- Investigate key features of industrial relations
- Explore adaptability to change.

TERMS OF EMPLOYMENT CONTRACTS

There is always a contract between an employee and employer. An employee may not necessarily have a contract in writing, but a contract still exists. How can this be the case? This is because an employee agrees to work for an employer and the employer agrees to pay the employee. This relationship forms the basis of the contract.

The contract is intended to give the employee and the employer certain rights and obligations. The basic rights and obligations, as we will see, are known as *contractual terms*.

The most basic of these is that the employer undertakes to pay the employee for the work. The employer also has to give the employee reasonable instructions and the employee has to carry out these duties. The employee also has rights under the contract of employment, such as the right to a national minimum wage and the right to paid holidays.

A contract of employment is usually made up of two types of contractual terms, known as *express terms* and *implied terms*. The express terms are those that are agreed between you and your employer and include:

- The amount of wages, including any overtime or bonus pay.
- The hours of work, including overtime hours.
- The holiday pay, including how much time off the employee is entitled to.
- Sick pay entitlements.
- Redundancy pay.
- The length of warning (notice) the employer must give the employee if they are dismissed.

Implied terms are those which are not specifically agreed between the employer and employee. They include:

- General terms which are implied in most contracts of employment.
- Terms implied by custom and practice.
- Terms from agreements made with the employer by a trade union or staff association.

As we will see, there are a number of duties and obligations between the employer and the employee. These include:

- A duty of trust to each other (e.g. not to talk about sensitive matters outside the organisation).
- A duty of care towards each other and other employees (e.g. a safe working environment and the safe use of machinery).
- The employee having a duty to obey any reasonable request by the employer (e.g. as long as the request is legal).

Custom and practice often determine the relationship, duties and obligations between an employer and an employee. In many cases, the contract of employment does not cover all of the eventualities and both employers and employees look at what has happened in the past as a guide to dealing with situations.

CASE STUDY Ringing the alarm bells

At around 11.15 every morning of the week, the fire alarm went off at Garsides Insurance Co. Everyone knew what it was and did not move from their desks. It was not a drill; it was Enid popping out of the fire door for a cigarette with her coffee at break time. Enid was the only one left in the office that still smoked, all the others were happy with their decaffeinated coffee and muesli bars.

The new personnel manager hated it. It reminded her that the morning was only half way through and she thought it disrupted the office. She had

banned smoking outside the front door, closed the smoking room and it was clear from the many No Smoking signs dotted around the building that Enid could not smoke inside.

As she imagined Enid smoking her cigarette and sipping her coffee, the personnel manager wrote her a memo telling her that she was not to open the fire door ever again unless there was an emergency.

The next day, Enid made an appointment to see her along with the trade union representative. There was going to be trouble.

INDIVIDUAL WORK (5.1)
Enid and the trade union representative told the personnel manager that Enid and some of the other employees had been doing this for the past three years since the closing of the smoking room. They claimed that it was custom and practice and that she had no right to ban Enid from doing it. The personnel manager claimed she had a duty of care towards all the staff.

1 What did Enid and the trade union representative mean by 'custom and practice'?

2 What did the personnel manager mean by 'duty of care'?

Clarification of full terms of written contract of employment

Many employees work without written employment contracts and there are many reasons for this, amongst which are the nature of the work itself (part-time or casual work), jobs with odd hours, flexible working and, of course, self-employment.

If an employee does not have a written contract, this does not mean that the employee and the employer do not have responsibilities and duties towards one another. In many cases, the organisation's company handbook lists the terms and conditions of work.

Many employees who do not have a written contract will have to rely on a verbal agreement between them and the employer. Verbal agreements are no less valid than written ones, but they are difficult to pin down if there are difficulties.

Contract of Employment

1. Company

Name

Address

Chief executive

2. Employee

Name

Address

3. Place of work

Address

4. Job description

5. Collective pay agreement, safety representative

The following collective pay agreement(s) apply

Parties to collective wage agreements

Safety representative

Check that all of the following points comply with the collective pay agreement.

6. Duration of employment, working hours

First day of employment	Last day of employment (if applicable)
Weekly working hours	Daily working hours (from/to)
Breaks	Notice period

Holidays are to be decided according to the provisions of the Act relating to holidays.

7. Probationary period (if applicable)

Duration of probationary period	Notice during probationary period

8. Pay

Hourly/monthly pay	Overtime supplement (minimum 40%)	Public holiday allowance, night

Other supplements

Allowances/expenses

Salary is paid

Holiday pay is additional to pay

9. Other information

10. Signatures

Date	Employer's signature	Employee's signature

Figure 5.1
An example of a standard contract of employment

Look at the example contract in Figure 5.1 and answer the following questions.

1 What do you think is meant by a 'collective pay agreement'?

2 What is meant by 'Duration of employment, working hours'?

3 What is meant by a 'probationary period'?

Responsibilities and accountability

The employee's job title and description should be clearly outlined in the contract. It is not necessary to write a long description. However, enough detail should be given so that it is clear to both parties, for example:

> *The Employee's job title is: Production Controller.*
> *The Employee's main task is to assist the Production Manager in maintaining a consistent flow of production.*

In this example, it is clear to whom the employee will be accountable, in this case, the Production Manager.

In the following examples, to whom is the employee accountable?

1 George works with Peter, Helen and Aleisha in the accounts department. Freddie supervises them and Freddie gets instructions from Kevin, his boss.

2 Nigel is a sales assistant. On Mondays, Wednesdays and Saturdays he does what Sharon tells him. On the other days, apart from his day off, he works for Clive who is Sharon's boss.

BACS – the abbreviation for Bankers Automated Clearing Service – the employees' wages are paid straight into the bank and they can have access to the money immediately

Payment terms

The contract should clearly state the employee's salary or hourly rate and detail when their wages will be paid (monthly, weekly, etc.). In addition, the contract will need to state how their wages will be paid (**BACS**, cheque, etc.) and give details of any requirements from the employee to make payment possible (for example, a personal bank account), for example:

> *The employee's salary is £17,000 per annum. Payments are monthly by BACS directly into your bank account. If you do not have a bank account, you will need to open one.*

Perry's contract of employment states that he will be paid in 12 equal payments per year. His yearly pay is £12,000.

1 How often does he get paid?

2 What amount is he paid each time?

Procedures for grievance

From 1 October 2004, new statutory discipline and dismissal and grievance procedures were introduced. The purpose of a grievance procedure is to enable individual employees to raise grievances (problems) with management about their employment, either by themselves or with a representative.

Normally, the first step is for the employee to set out in writing the grievance which they have with the employer. The second step is for the employer to arrange a meeting to discuss the grievance. The employee has the right to the accompanied to this meeting by a colleague or perhaps representative from the trade union. At the end of the meeting, the employer has to tell the employee about the decisions made and that the employee has a right to appeal if they feel that the decision is unfair. Step three of the process allows the employee to make an appeal, which means that a second meeting is arranged, probably with a more senior member of the management. Again, the employee has a right to be accompanied to the meeting and the management must tell the employee of their decision at the end of the meeting.

The contract of employment should include the name and position of a person to whom an employee can present a grievance.

The purpose of grievance procedures is to attempt to settle the problem as soon as possible. The vast majority of problems are settled informally with an employee's immediate manager and do not have to go through the grievance procedure. Ideally, the procedure should be simple to follow, quickly resolved and followed up in writing. Organisations tend to have their own ways of dealing with grievances; it will depend on the size of the organisation and the way in which it is structured. The majority of the procedures will include:

- How and with whom to raise the issue
- To whom to apply next, if not satisfied
- Time limits to each stage
- The right to be represented.

An example of a grievance procedure as set out by ACAS (the Advisory, Conciliation and Arbitration Service) is given in Table 5.1.

Table 5.1
An example of a grievance procedure

	Guidance notes
1 Introduction It is the Company's policy to ensure that employees with a grievance relating to their employment can use a procedure which can help to resolve grievances as quickly and as fairly as possible.	*1 It is a good idea to set out company policy; it reminds managers of their role in dealing with grievances.*
2 Informal discussions If you have a grievance about your employment, you should discuss it informally with your immediate supervisor. We hope that the majority of concerns will be resolved at this stage.	*2 Informal discussions should resolve the vast majority of grievances.*
3 Stage 1 If you feel that the matter has not been resolved through informal discussions, you should put your grievance in writing to your immediate supervisor. The supervisor must give a response within five working days in an endeavour to resolve the matter.	*3 The first stage should allow supervisors to resolve the grievance without the involvement of any employee representative. The aim should be to resolve the grievance at the lowest relevant level.*
4 Stage 2 If the matter is not resolved, you may raise the matter, in writing, with the manager, who must give a response within five working days. You may be represented or accompanied at this meeting by a fellow worker of your choice or by a union official.	*4 The stages should reflect the levels of management in the organisation.*
5 Stage 3 If the matter is not resolved to your satisfaction, you should put your grievance in writing to the managing director or an authorised deputy. You will be entitled to have a meeting with the managing director or his/her authorised deputy to discuss the matter. The managing director or authorised deputy will give his/her decision within seven working days of the grievance being received. The managing director's decision is final.	*5 Time limits prevent issues running on and on, and encourage managers to deal with them promptly.*

Source: www.acas.org.uk

CASE STUDY **Trouble for Trudi**

This was the second time that Trudi had walked into the office 10 minutes late this week. She was tired and angry about oversleeping, but her boss Frank had made her work until nearly 7 p.m. every day this week.

He had called her into his office and told her off and said that this was her first verbal warning and that next time she was late he would send her home and not pay her for the day. The time after that she had better start looking for another job.

Trudi had burst into tears. After all she had done for the department to catch up on the backlog of work, she thought he would understand that she was tired, was working late and not getting paid for it and that she had not deliberately been late.

After she had calmed down, she thought long and hard about it all and decided that Frank should not get away with treating her like that.

> **INDIVIDUAL** WORK (5.5) ★★
> What should Trudi do? What should her first step be in beginning a grievance procedure about the way Frank has treated her?

Disciplinary action

Disciplinary action occurs when employees, in the view of the employer, fail to maintain the level of standards demanded of them. Disciplinary procedures are there to ensure that the employer deals fairly with the employee.

The vast majority of disciplinary problems can be sorted out by informal discussions between the employee and their direct manager or the human resources department. The purpose of a disciplinary procedure is to ensure that:

- Employees are encouraged both to achieve and to maintain standards of behaviour.
- There is a fair and consistent method of dealing with alleged failures by employees.
- Managers and supervisors are clear about disciplinary matters and how they should be handled.
- The number of disagreements about disciplinary matters are reduced.
- Only in extreme situations does an employee need to be dismissed.

Each organisation will have standard procedures for dealing with disciplinary matters. The following points tend to be common in most disciplinary procedures:

- They tend to be in writing.
- They aim not to discriminate on the grounds of race, sex, disability, sexual orientation or religion.
- They describe the penalties.
- They aim to deal with the situation as quickly as possible.
- They allow the employee to be accompanied in the meetings.
- They identify who is responsible for disciplinary action.
- They ensure that careful investigations are carried out before action is taken.
- They provide the employee with the right to appeal.

Table 5.2
An example of a disciplinary procedure

	Guidance notes
1 Purpose of the procedure The Company's aim is to encourage improvement in individual conduct and performance. This procedure sets out the action that will be taken when Company rules are breached.	*1 The purpose should remind people that the procedure is designed not as a dismissal procedure but as a means of encouraging employees to conform to acceptable standards.*
2 Principles If you are subject to disciplinary action: • the procedure is designed to establish the facts quickly and to deal consistently with disciplinary issues. No disciplinary action will be taken until the matter has been fully investigated;	*2 Employers often lose at Employment Tribunals because they did not comply with the procedure – so always follow the procedure.*

▶

Table 5.2
Continued

	Guidance notes

- at every stage you will be advised of the nature of the complaint, be given the opportunity to state your case, and be represented or accompanied by a fellow employee of your choice;
- you will not be dismissed for a first breach of discipline except in the case of gross misconduct, when the penalty will normally be dismissal without notice and without pay in lieu of notice;
- you have a right to appeal against any disciplinary action taken against you;
- the procedure may be implemented at any stage if your alleged misconduct warrants such action.

If you request, you have the right to be accompanied at a disciplinary hearing by a fellow worker or trade union official.

3 Informal discussions
Before taking formal disciplinary action, your supervisor will make every effort to resolve the matter by informal discussions with you. Only where this fails to bring about the desired improvement should the formal disciplinary procedure be implemented.

3 Make sure that employees and managers understand the difference between routine admonishments and action taken under the procedure.

4 First warning
If conduct or performance is unsatisfactory, the employee will be given a written warning or performance note. Such warnings will be recorded, but disregarded after ___ months of satisfactory service. The employee will also be informed that a final written warning may be considered if there is no sustained satisfactory improvement or change. (Where the first offence is sufficiently serious, for example because it is having, or is likely to have, a serious harmful effect on the organisation, it may be justifiable to move directly to a final written warning.)

4 It can be unfair to keep details of warnings on an employee's file indefinitely. Unless a warning is for a very serious matter, it should be disregarded after, say, six months to a year. The written warning should accurately record the warning given at the disciplinary interview. Do not write the warning before the interview.

5 Final written warning
If the offence is serious, or there is no improvement in standards, or if a further offence of a similar kind occurs, a final written warning will be given which will include the reason for the warning and a note that if no improvement results within ___ months, action at Stage 6 will be taken.

5 The warning should state clearly that dismissal would result from a failure to comply.

Dismissal or action short of dismissal
If the conduct or performance has failed to improve, the employee may suffer demotion, disciplinary transfer, loss or seniority (as allowed in the contract) or dismissal.

Except in cases of gross misconduct, employees should receive notice or payment in lieu.

6 Statutory discipline and dismissal procedure
If an employee faces dismissal – or action short of dismissal such as loss of pay or demotion – the minimum statutory procedure will be followed. This involves:
- Step 1: a written note to the employee setting out the allegation and the basis for it
- Step 2: a meeting to consider and discuss the allegation
- Step 3: a right of appeal including an appeal meeting.

The employee will be reminded of their right to be accompanied.

7 Gross misconduct
If, after investigation, it is confirmed that an employee has committed an offence of the following nature (the list is not exhaustive), the normal consequence will be dismissal without notice or payment in lieu of notice: theft, damage to property, fraud, incapacity for work due to being under the influence of alcohol or illegal drugs, physical violence, bullying and gross insubordination.

While the alleged gross misconduct is being investigated, the employee may be suspended, during which time he or she will be paid their normal pay rate. Any decision to dismiss will be taken by the employer only after full investigation.

8 Appeals
If you wish to appeal against any disciplinary decision, you must appeal, in writing within five working days of the decision being communicated to you to _____ (name or job title). If possible a senior manager who was not involved in the original disciplinary action will hear the appeal and decide the case as impartially as possible.

Source: www.acas.org.uk

CASE STUDY Larking about

Norman had been in trouble before, but that was 13 months ago when Norman and Stan were playing about near the delivery area. Norman had pushed Stan and a reversing truck nearly crushed him.

Norman had been marched in to see the Personnel Manager who was terrified that Stan could have been killed and ranted on about insurance claims and how bad a death would be for the business. Norman had smiled (he regretted that later) and the Personnel Manager went mad. He scribbled out a written warning to Norman and sent him home for the day. His last words had been: 'Come back tomorrow young man and if your attitude is no better, don't even bother!'

Norman had come in the next day and had kept his head down. He had been a model employee ever since – that was until this morning, when he accidentally dropped a box on Stan's head and knocked him out. First there was the ambulance, then the safety officer and the police, and then the dreaded Personnel Manager.

'Right,' he had said. 'I've had to talk to you about messing around before, haven't I?'

'Yes, but ...' Norman had replied.

'Yes but nothing. This is your final warning. Collect it in writing from my office in an hour. The next time, you're out of here.'

GROUP WORK (5.6) ★ ★
As a group, read the case study. Decide whether the Personnel Manager was fair to Norman. What should Norman have said and what should the Personnel Manager have done in the situation?

Once an organisation has written its disciplinary procedure, it is vital that all employees are either familiar with it or have access to a copy.

It is not always necessary to begin disciplinary procedures, but before this happens, it is usual for the following to take place:

- The organisation decides whether the matter can be resolved by informal discussions.
- The situation which has brought about the disciplinary matter has to be investigated fully.
- The employee involved in the disciplinary matter has to be told that they can be represented or accompanied by a person of their choice at all the meetings.

The disciplinary interview should ensure that the employee:

- Is made aware of any allegations against them
- Is given the opportunity to put forward their side of the story
- Is made aware of disciplinary action which can be taken against them if the allegations are proved to be true.

In many cases, this first disciplinary meeting will attempt to solve the situation. If it does, the employee will be given a warning and told:

- What improvements are expected
- When these improvements must be achieved

CASE STUDY Allegations

Geraldine knew this was serious. The shop manager had called in the police and they were threatening to arrest her.

'You realise you can be sacked for this?' said the shop manager when she had told Geraldine to close down her till and follow her to the office.

'Sacked for what?' she had asked.

'You know full well. I've got all the evidence I need,' she had told her.

Apparently a well-known shoplifter had been caught with three pairs of jeans from the shop in one of the shop's bags. She was asked

where she had got the bag and she had told the store detective that her friend Geraldine had given it to her. Geraldine remembered the girl; she had caught her last month when she tried to steal a coat from the shop.

The police were sat in the office taking notes and asking the shop manager whether she wanted them to arrest Geraldine. No one was listening to her. All the shop manager said was, 'No, I'll sack her and have done with it.'

With that she was given the balance of her pay in cash and told to leave.

GROUP WORK (5.7) ★ ★
Did the shop manager deal with the situation in the correct manner? What should have happened?

- What will happen if the improvements have not been made
- That they have an opportunity to appeal against the warning.

Notice and termination of contract

A typical contract of employment should refer to the following points with regard to notice and termination of contract:

- The amount of notice the employee has to give to the employer, usually expressed in weeks or months.
- Whether the employee will continue to be paid during their notice period and how much.
- Whether the employer can ask the employee to leave before the end of their notice period and whether they will pay the employee if this happens.

Normally, the employee is expected to work through the notice before leaving the company. However, in many cases, either the employee or their employer will want to cut short the notice period so that the employee can leave more quickly.

From the employee's point of view, once they have given notice they may be so excited that they want to join their new company as quickly as possible. Or they may detect some resentment toward them and feel that it is better to complete the handover process immediately so that they can go.

Once the employee has handed in their notice, their employer may not see them as a team player any longer or, in certain situations, feel that it may affect the morale of the remaining staff if the employee stays. In this situation, the employer may prefer that the employee leave the organisation as soon as possible.

The normal course of events is that if the employee asks to leave before the period of notice is finished, then he or she does not get paid for the period of notice not worked. On the other hand, if the employer wants the employee to leave before the notice period is up, then they generally pay the full salary or wage to the employee as if they had worked the full period of notice. Contracts of employment usually contain details about this situation.

One potential confusion regarding periods of notice is the entitlement to holidays. Employees may be owed holidays and, typically, employers may force the employee to take the holiday in the notice period. If the organisation does not force the employee to take the holiday then there are two real options:

- The first is to take the holiday (if allowed) as part of the notice period. A lot of people who are resigning book their holiday for the last few days of their notice

CASE STUDY   Statutory notice period is too short

Human resources professionals believe that statutory notice periods are too short, according to a new survey.

Current statutory requirements call for employers to give an employee at least one week's notice if the employer has employed them continuously for one month, rising to at least two weeks' notice if the employee has given two years' service.

The survey, carried out by Croner Consulting, found 38 per cent of respondents thought four to eight weeks would be more appropriate, and 36 per cent believed two to four weeks was the right length of notice to serve.

Only 12 per cent of those surveyed via Croner's web centre felt that notice

periods should be less than two weeks, while a further 12 per cent said eight to 12 weeks was the right amount of time.

A period of more than three months was favoured by the remaining 2 per cent.

Peter Etherington, employment law expert at Croner, advised that after notice is given, both parties should sit down and agree how the departure is to be handled with colleagues and customers, and then stick to what has been agreed.

'Failure to do this could lead to an awkward and swiftly deteriorating workplace situation, or even leave either party facing serious employment law problems,' he said.

INDIVIDUAL WORK (5.8)

Using the case study, answer the following questions.

1 What do you understand by the phrase 'current statutory requirements'?

2 What was the most popular period of notice suggested by organisations taking part in the survey?

3 What was the maximum period of notice suggested by some of the organisations in the survey?

period especially if they are planning to start their new job as soon as they have served their notice. The remaining holidays provide an effective break between their old and new employment.

💧 Alternatively, if the employee does not want to take their holidays (or are not allowed to), they may receive a monetary payment in lieu of holiday.

The employment contract should confirm exactly what the procedure is. If in doubt, the employee should ask their immediate superior or the human resources department for clarification.

More details about notice periods can be found on page 159.

Payment and leave in accordance with contract

Every employee, whether part time or full time, is covered by the Working Time Regulations and is entitled to four weeks' paid annual leave. A week's leave should allow an employee to be away from work for a week. It should be the same amount of time as the working week: if a worker does a five-day week, he or she is entitled to 20 days' leave; if he or she does a three-day week, the entitlement is 12 days' leave.

The leave entitlement under the regulations is not additional to bank holidays. There is no statutory right to take bank holidays off. An employee who is not otherwise paid for bank holidays may take bank holidays as part of his or her annual leave entitlement in order to receive payment for these holidays.

Employees must give the employer notice that they intend to take leave and the employer can set the times that employees take their leave, for example for a Christmas shutdown. If an employee's employment ends, he or she has a right to be paid for the leave time due and not taken.

> **GROUP WORK (5.9)** ⭐
> What types of business might have a Christmas or summer shutdown? What does this mean?

Maternity and paternity leave

Employees who are working parents have several key rights:

💧 They should receive paid and unpaid maternity leave.
💧 They should receive paid paternity leave.
💧 They are entitled to paid and unpaid adoption leave.
💧 They can request flexible working hours.
💧 They can ask for unpaid parental leave if they are parents of children under five.
💧 They can ask to be granted unpaid time off to care for dependants.

Most female employees are entitled to 26 weeks' maternity leave, regardless of how long the employee has worked for the employer, or the number of hours worked each week. Employees are either entitled to Statutory Maternity Pay or Contractual Maternity Pay. Some female employees, who have worked for their employer for 26 weeks by the beginning of the fifteenth week before the baby is due, may be entitled to a longer period of maternity leave (known as *additional maternity leave*).

To receive maternity leave, the employee must inform the employer by the end of the fifteenth week before the baby is due to be born, of the following:

💧 That she is pregnant
💧 The date that the child is due to be born
💧 The date that the employee wishes the maternity leave to begin.

Once the employer has received this information, they must write to the employee within 28 days and inform the employee of the date that they expect them to return to work from maternity leave. This return to work date is the twenty-sixth week after the employee went on maternity leave.

The employee does not have to give the employer any notification of their intention to return to work, but if the employer refuses to take the employee back after maternity leave, then the employee can claim unfair dismissal and sex discrimination.

During the maternity leave, the employee is entitled to all of their rights under the contract of employment. In other words, if there is a pay increase, the employee is entitled to receive it and they are also entitled to receive holiday pay.

Additional maternity leave may be available to certain employees. This is usually available to an employee if she has worked for the same employer for at least 26 weeks by the beginning of the fifteenth week before the baby is due to be born. The employee may be entitled to an extra 26 weeks' additional leave, which means that the employee is entitled to 52 weeks' statutory maternity leave.

Statutory Maternity Pay (SMP) can be claimed provided that the employee:

- Has worked for the same employer for 26 weeks continuously into the fifteenth week before the baby is due, regardless of the number of hours worked each week.
- Was pregnant at, or has had the baby by, the eleventh week before the week the baby is due.
- Had average weekly earnings of at least the National Insurance lower earnings limit.

Employees who are not entitled to Statutory Maternity Pay may be entitled to maternity allowance paid by the Department for Work and Pensions (DWP). The SMP is paid for up to 26 weeks, which is known as the Maternity Pay Period (MMP).

During the first six weeks of maternity leave, the SMP is paid at 90 per cent of the average gross weekly earnings. For the remainder of the maternity leave, SMP is 90 per cent of the gross weekly earning or £100, which ever is the lower amount. To claim SMP, the employee must tell their employer 28 days before the start of the maternity leave. The employer pays the SMP in the same way as the employee would have received their wages or salary, then claims the money back from the government.

The right to receive SMP does not depend on the employee actually ever going back to work. The employee will still receive the SMP and does not have to pay the money back if they do not return to work after the maternity leave.

Many female employees have a right to what is known as Contractual Maternity Pay, if the contract of employment states the employee's rights with regard to maternity leave and pay. In most cases, the contractual rights and pay are often better than the statutory rights and pay.

All female employees have the right to return to their old job after they have had 26 weeks of ordinary maternity leave. If the employer refuses the employee the right to return to work, then they can claim unfair dismissal as the reason is to do with the pregnancy and the maternity leave. Employees can also claim sex discrimination. Both of these claims can be made regardless of how long the employee has worked for the employer or how many hours a week they have worked.

Similarly, employees have the right to return to work if they have qualified for more than the standard 26 weeks' maternity leave. When the employee returns to work, they should be offered their old job back (unless this is not reasonably practical). In any case, the employee should be offered a job that is suitable for them, under the same terms and conditions of the old job. The pay must be at least the same as the old job.

Once again, if the employer fails to offer the employee their old job (or a reasonable alternative to that job), then there are grounds to claim unfair dismissal and sex discrimination.

Employees also have the right to return to work on a part-time basis after maternity leave. They also have the right to ask for more flexible hours.

Right to trade union membership

All employees have the right to join a trade union. They should not be dismissed, refused employment, harassed or made redundant on the basis that they are a member of a trade union.

Just as employees have the right to be a member of a trade union, they also have the right not be a member. They should not suffer from harassment, dismissal or other unfair treatment on account of the fact that they have not joined a trade union.

Once an employee is a member of a trade union, they have the right to take part in normal trade union activities. These include recruiting other members, collecting trade union subscriptions and attending trade union meetings.

The trade union activities must take place outside the employee's normal working hours (or in some cases during time agreed with the employer). An employee engaged in trade union activities cannot be expected to be paid for time taken off work when they are involved in trade union activities, unless this has been agreed with the employer beforehand.

Types of employment

As we have seen in other units, some people are self-employed, but the focus of this part of the unit looks at people in different forms of work with employers.

Before we look at the main types of employment, it is worth considering the fact that many jobs are thought of as being skilled or unskilled. Usually, there are three ways of looking at the skills aspect of work:

- *Core skills* These are very general skills applicable to almost every kind of job. They, of course, include basic literacy and numeracy, the ability to work with others and some understanding of information technology.

- *Vocational skills* These are specific skills that are needed for a particular occupation, but are often less useful outside that occupation. There is some transferability in these skills, for example an employee knowing how to operate a specific computer package. A person with this skill would be more likely to be able to use a similar one than a person without this experience.

- *Specific job skills* The usefulness of this type of skill is often limited to a fairly narrow range of occupations. It would perhaps be more appropriate to call these specific job skills 'knowledge'.

Think about the following types of skills. Which of the three categories above might they apply to?

a) The ability to work as a member of a team

b) The ability to be able to remember the organisation's policy on dealing with complaints

c) The ability to remember your company's product codes

d) The ability to use Excel

e) The ability to add up figures in your head.

Full-time employment

Full-time employment, as it suggests, means that the employee is working a full week (often as many as 60 or more hours, but usually about 40) and does this every week apart from the time they have for holidays.

Typical full-time jobs include teachers, local government officers and office workers. Usually, full-time employees are paid on a monthly basis, but others such as factory workers might be paid on a weekly basis.

The contract of employment for full-time workers will state the number of hours that they are expected to work, the availability and pay (or time off) for working overtime, and their holiday entitlements. Around 60 per cent of those in work have full-time jobs, but not all of them work standard 9 a.m. to 5 p.m. and may work **shifts**, at home, at night, or even three or four 12-hour days each week.

An increasing trend has been to allow employees to work flexi-time. This means that employees have the opportunity to work around their other commitments, perhaps to drop children off at school or to look after older family members. Instead of starting work at 9 a.m., they can start at 9.30 a.m. or 10 a.m. and perhaps finish work later in the day. Employers are also encouraged to allow employees, as long as they do their full weekly hours, to organise their time to best match their commitments. This has been especially useful for those with young children or older parents.

shift – a period of non-standard working hours, such as starting at lunchtime and working through into the evening or beginning earlier in the day and finishing after lunch

Keyword

Part-time employment

Part-time employment is common in the UK and it very much tied in with employees' needs to have flexible working arrangements. Traditionally part-time work has allowed employees with outside commitments, such as childcare, to balance their working life and their domestic life.

Normally part-time work is no longer than 25 hours per week. The majority of part-time workers are women, well over 50 per cent of the total number of employees in part-time work. Part-time workers have the same rights as full-time employees. They tend to work either part days, such as mornings, afternoons or the middle section of the working day, or may work evenings and weekends.

Temporary and permanent employment

When an employee begins work for an employer, the contract of employment will state whether the job is a temporary or permanent one. If the job is temporary, the contract will state that the employee has been taken on to work for a specified period of time, such as six months or a year. At the end of the period, the contract has been completed and the employee leaves the job. Temporary contracts are given to employees to cover long-term sickness, maternity leave or short-term needs of the employer to take on more staff. Both the employer and the employee enter into a temporary contract knowing that the relationship is for a limited period of time, although in many cases temporary contracts can lead to a permanent post.

The majority of jobs are classed as permanent as there is no definite period of time that the employee is expected to work for the employer. As we have seen, the contract only ends when the employee chooses to leave the job or, for disciplinary reasons, the employer terminates the contract. This is not to say, however, that permanent work is necessarily safe. An employer may wish to terminate the contract because the skills or job of the employee is no longer needed, or perhaps the business is about to close.

Typical temporary jobs include secretarial work, catering and, of course, seasonal work when employers take on extra staff perhaps in a shop to assist them in the busy period in the run-up to Christmas.

> **WANT TO FIND OUT MORE?**
>
> Visit the **National Statistics Online** at: www.statistics.gov.uk/instantfigures.asp. Find the section labelled 'Labour market' and click on 'More'.

INDIVIDUAL WORK (5.13) ★ ★

Visit the labour market page on the National Statistics website, then answer the following questions.

1 What is the total number of people employed in the UK?

2 What is the total number of hours worked by employees per week?

3 What is the average number of hours worked per week?

Observance of written job description and contract

The employee has a responsibility to the employer to work in a loyal, conscientious and honest manner. The employee is also expected to accept any reasonable and legal directions from the employer. This means that both parties must follow the terms of the contract of employment. As we have seen, the contract of employment can be a very detailed document but, above all, it is legally binding once both parties have signed it.

The employer is expected to exercise what is known as a *duty of care*. This means that the employer must not expect the employee to do anything that would lead to their being injured or hurt in any way during the course of their work. An employer must also provide sufficient work, pay the employee when agreed and maintain records on their behalf, including:

- Tax deductions
- National Insurance deductions
- Payments to pension schemes.

The employer must take care when advertising a job as this is considered to be the beginning of the contract of employment. A potential employee would accept the job on the basis of the details in the advertisement. Once the employer accepts the candidate, as we will see later, they take up references and then both parties will sign the contract. The contract lays out a number of key points, including:

- The employer will pay the employee wages or salary.
- The employer will provide work.

- If the employee incurs any expenses during the course of their work, the employer will refund them.
- The employer will provide the employee with a reference if they wish to leave.
- The employer will provide safe working conditions and working practices.
- The employer will provide information regarding work, pay, conditions and opportunities.
- The employer will act in good faith towards the employee.

In return the employee undertakes to:

- Obey any reasonable orders or instructions
- Serve the employer faithfully
- Keep any trade secrets confidential.

Line of reporting and key employee responsibilities

The contract of employment will usually be supported by a job description. This is a much more detailed document, which we will look at in the second section of this unit. It contains a list of the responsibilities and duties for a particular job and it also will state which part of the business the employee is working for and to whom they report.

All employees, regardless of their position in the business, will have a manager or supervisor. This is the individual that is responsible for directing their work and the individual from whom they receive their orders and instructions.

All organisations have various levels of supervision and management. Key orders and instructions come from the owners or directors of the business and are passed on to the next level down in the business. These managers have to then interpret the instructions and pass them on to people that work for them. The process continues all the way down the organisation and eventually broad policies or orders from the senior management become instructions about an individual's tasks. Normally an employee will have a single individual to whom they must report. That supervisor or manager will give them a series of orders and instructions and a series of tasks to carry out. Any issues that arise during the working day are handled by the supervisor or manager and individual employees can be given new tasks and duties to perform as and when required.

Completing tasks to a required standard

All businesses will have a series of procedures that detail the ways in which work should be carried out. Some organisations actually have manuals that describe very precisely the steps that need to be taken in carrying out any particular task. An employee will be expected to follow these procedures, make any checks required and fulfil the task to the standard the business requires.

Once employees have been trained to understand how a business wishes to carry out tasks, they will be given much more freedom to complete the work in the order they think is the best. It is the responsibility of supervisors and managers to always ensure that the tasks have been carried out to the required standard and that action is taken if steps have been missed or not completed satisfactorily. An employee may be asked to carry out the work again and, if there are still difficulties, the supervisor will show the employee how things should be done again.

Working hours

The contract should also give details of the employee's work hours and the days that they are required to work. It should also state what break periods the employee is given. If the employee may be required to work outside of the contracted hours, the contract should bring this to their attention and indicate the rate of pay (if this is the same as the current rate or different). For example:

The employee's working week will consist of 40 hours, from Monday to Friday and from 9 a.m. to 6 p.m. There is a one-hour lunch break: timing to be agreed with immediate supervisor. From time to time, the employee may be asked to work outside of the contracted hours. An hourly rate of 1.5 times the normal hourly rate will be paid.

Annual and sickness leave

Full-time employees are entitled to a minimum of four weeks' holiday each year (excluding bank holidays, which an employer can choose to give the employee time off for). Part-time employees will be given holiday entitlement on a pro-rata basis. The contract of employment should clearly state how much holiday entitlement the employee is entitled to for each year of employment. For example:

> *The employee is entitled to four weeks' (20 days') paid holiday per annum. At the end of five years' service an extra days' holiday entitlement is given – followed by a further one day of holiday entitlement for each of the next four years' service: bringing maximum holiday entitlement to five weeks (25 days).*

Period of notice

A notice period is required as employees and employers can often decide to terminate their relationship, and this should be stated in the contract of employment, for example:

> *The minimum notice periods are as follows:*
> *Time in employment – Minimum notice*
> *Under 1 month – No notice*
> *Over 1 month – 1 week*
> *2 years' service – 2 weeks*
> *3 to 12 years' service – 1 week for each year to a maximum of 12 weeks.*
> *In the case of the employee being dismissed for gross misconduct, the employer will decide if any notice period will be applied and/or worked.*

The notice period gives the organisation time to look for a suitable replacement for the employee.

If the employer wishes to terminate the contract of employment, it may well be due to a disciplinary problem with the employee. If, for example, an employee is caught stealing money from the business (gross misconduct), the employer has rights to immediately dismiss the employee with no notice or payment. Another example of when a period of notice may not apply is if an employee repeatedly turns up late (minor misconduct) and has been given their written and verbal warnings. The employer may give the employee notice of their contract termination. If the employee has been working for three years, the employer may decide to give three weeks' notice or dismiss the employee immediately with three weeks' advanced pay.

It is usual for the employer to inform the employee of the notice period required in writing and for the employee to inform the employer in writing that they wish the notice period to begin.

Table 5.3 gives a guide to normal notice periods.

Table 5.3
Notice periods

Length of time worked by the employee for the employer	Usual period of necessary notice
1 month	No notice required
Over 1 month	1 week
2 years	2 weeks
3 years	3 weeks
4 years	4 weeks
This continues until:	
12 years or more	12 weeks (maximum notice period)

Professional dress and relationships

Employers can insist that their employees dress in a particular way in order to reflect the overall image of the organisation. Usually, the following issues are considered when an organisation establishes its dress code:

- Employers can demand a dress code that is appropriate for the work involved, for example for safety and hygiene reasons.
- Employers can require employees who come into contact with the public or other organisations to conform to a dress code which will enhance the public image of the employer and assist its business.
- Employers usually act reasonably and balance the needs of the business with the rights of employees. The dress code has to reflect the business need, and be neither unnecessary nor, of course, discriminatory.
- The dress code needs to be spelt out in a policy which is clear and understood by all.
- The dress code must also be enforced in a consistent and even-handed way. If it is overlooked in any instances, then problems are likely to occur.

CASE STUDY Man wins tie case

A civil servant who complained about being made to wear a collar and tie to work has won a sex discrimination case.

Matthew Thompson, 32, said it was unfair he had to dress formally to work at the Jobcentre Plus in Stockport, Greater Manchester, when women did not.

He had told the Manchester tribunal that women were allowed to wear T-shirts — and even football shirts — without facing disciplinary action from managers.

The Public and Commercial Services (PCS) union, which backed the case, said it planned a further 39 cases if a 'sensible solution' was not now agreed with managers. The administrative assistant said he was delighted and relieved with the tribunal's decision. He added: 'The ruling vindicates what we have been arguing for some time, that the draconian application of the dress code in Jobcentre Plus is discriminatory.'

INDIVIDUAL WORK (5.14) ★ ★
Read the case study and then answer the following questions.

1 What do you think is meant by 'the draconian application of the dress code'?

2 Why do you think it is important for an employer to equally apply any rules or regulations to women and to men?

In our everyday lives we need to build effective relationships for a number of reasons. Organisations only function with the cooperation of their members. We all know that ineffective organisations are very frustrating and that effective organisations can demand much from their employees.

Confidentiality

Another employee responsibility is to maintain confidentiality about their work and their employer's business. There are many different types of sensitive information that an employee may come across which the employer does not wish to be made public. Even in a retail shop, an employee may be aware of the sales figures or how much profit is being made on a particular product. They may also know particular parts of the shop that are vulnerable to shoplifting. The employee must ensure that they do not talk about confidential matters with anyone outside the business. If, for example, an employee worked in a human resource department, they would know a great deal of sensitive information about employees, such as their bank account details, reasons for sickness or absence and any disciplinary problems they may have had in the past. Not only must employees not discuss these matters with individuals outside the business, but also they should not discuss them with fellow employees.

Use of IT facilities

Many employees use computers on a daily basis. The employer may have installed a number of software applications onto their system to allow the employee to carry out their work. Obviously employees are expected to follow health and safety guidelines for the use of computers.

There have been considerable problems in recent years with the use of computers at work. One of the most serious problems has been the use of the internet at work. Many employees will need access to the internet in order to carry out their work, but they are not supposed to use the internet for their own research whilst they are at work. Many businesses install programs that prevent employees from visiting certain sites or using particular searches, in an attempt to stop them from making personal purchases online at work, visiting chat rooms, downloading music or images or other activities that are not work related.

Observance of Data Protection requirements

The Data Protection Act 1998 sets out the rules and regulations about processing personal information. It applies to most paper records as well as information held on computer. The Act gives individuals certain rights and it requires any business or organisation that records and uses personal information to be open about how the information is used. There are eight key principles:

- The data must be processed fairly and lawfully.
- It must be obtained for specific and lawful purposes.
- It must be adequate, relevant and not excessive.
- It must be accurate and, where necessary, kept up to date.
- It should not be kept any longer than necessary.
- It should be processed in accordance with the individual's rights.
- It must be kept secure.
- It must not be transferred abroad unless protected.

> **WANT TO FIND OUT MORE?**
>
> The full **Data Protection Act 1998** can be found at: www.hmso.gov.uk; click on 'Data Protection Act 1998'.

Awareness of key elements of employment legislation

Both the employer and the employee should be aware of the main elements of employment legislation. These are laws that control and police the relationships between employers and employees. Some have been in existence for 30 years, whilst others are newer. Some have been added to or amended over the years and it is the responsibility of the employer to ensure that they are following the instructions and requirements of each of the laws in their day-to-day business activities.

Employment Act 2002

Many of the new arrangements related to paternity and maternity leave mentioned above were part of this new law. Under the terms of the new Act, an employee can request a formally request a change to their working arrangements, particularly if they have parental responsibilities. An employee must have worked for the business or organisation for at least 26 weeks and have responsibility for a child under six years old. This is part of the gradual change towards employees being able to have flexible working hours.

   The Act also included a new system that helps to resolve disputes between employers and employees, as the number of cases going to court had increased enormously. Finally the Act helped employees on what is known as fixed-term contracts. Essentially these are temporary contracts and many employees were not receiving the same rights and advantages as those who had permanent contracts.

Sex Discrimination Act 1975

In terms of employment, the Sex Discrimination Act 1975 prohibits discrimination against men, women or children at work. The Act covers four main types of sex discrimination:

- *Direct sex discrimination*, when a person is treated less favourably than a person of the opposite sex, for example a woman being discriminated against because she is pregnant.
- *Indirect sex discrimination*, when an employer places a condition on work that could lead to discrimination against one gender, for example the requirement to be under 1.77 m would discriminate against men.

- *Discrimination on the grounds of gender reassignment* – although not mentioned directly, employers must not discriminate against those that have chosen to change their gender.

- *Discrimination on the grounds of sexual orientation* – coupled with laws that came into effect in 2003, discrimination on the grounds of sexual orientation are now unlawful.

The Sex Discrimination Act 1975 therefore covers recruitment, treatment at work and dismissal. Employees have rights under the Act, regardless of how long they have worked for their employer or how many hours they work each week.

Race Relations Act 1976

The Race Relations Act 1976, as amended by the Race Relations (Amendment) Act 2000, makes it unlawful to discriminate against anyone on grounds of race, colour, nationality (including citizenship), or ethnic or national origin. The amended Act also requires public authorities to promote racial equality. The Act applies to jobs, training, housing, education and the sale of goods, facilities and services.

The Act makes it unlawful for public organisations to discriminate whilst carrying out any of their functions and requires them to promote equality of opportunity and fair race relations.

Equal Pay Act 1970

The Equal Pay Act 1970 (EPA) gives an individual a right to the same pay and benefits as a person of the opposite sex in the same employment, where the man and the woman are doing:

- Like work, or

- Work rated as equivalent under a job evaluation study, or

- Work that is proved to be of equal value.

The employer will not be required to provide the same pay and benefits if it can prove that the difference in pay or benefits is genuinely due to a reason other than one related to sex.

The EPA covers indirect sex discrimination as well as direct discrimination – where the pay difference is due to a condition or practice which applies to men and women but which affects a larger proportion of one sex than the other and it is not justifiable, irrespective of sex, to apply that condition or practice. A good example of this is when a woman might be paid a lower hourly rate because she is employed part time compared to a man who is employed full time, but effectively doing the same job.

Disabled Persons Employment Act 1995

Until 1995 the only law that dealt with the employment of disabled people was the Disabled Persons (Employment) Act 1944. The new Act makes it unlawful for an employer to discriminate against a disabled job applicant in the following ways:

- The selection for jobs

- The terms and conditions of employment

- Promotion or transfer to another area of work

- Training

- Employment benefits

- Dismissal.

Health and Safety at Work Act 1974

The Health and Safety at Work Act 1974 (HASAWA) requires an employer to provide a number of levels of protection for their employees, including:

- They must protect the health, safety and welfare of all their employees.

- They must do this 'so far as is reasonably practicable', which means that employers can claim that the costs are too high to cover a particular risk.

It allows the government to issue regulations, guidance and codes of practice that set out detailed responsibilities of the employer on health and safety matters, including working with computers, stress and hazardous chemicals.

The Act set up the Health and Safety Commission and an inspecting authority known as the Health and Safety Executive.

It brought in new powers and penalties to enforce the law.

The key points are:

To provide a working environment that is safe and without risks to health

To make arrangements for ensuring that safety and risks are reduced

To provide information, instruction and training, as well as supervision, on health and safety

To maintain the working environment so that new risks do not emerge

That employees can get into and out of their working environment without risk, even in an emergency

That facilities are provided for the welfare of the employees

That the employer prepares a safety policy.

Key employer responsibilities

The vast majority of employees have rights given by law. These are known as *statutory rights*. These are in addition to the rights which are part of the contract of employment. Typical statutory rights include the right:

To have a written statement of the terms of employment

To have an itemised pay statement

To be granted maternity leave

To receive pay in compensation for being made redundant

Not to be unfairly dismissed.

The employer has a wide range of responsibilities and many of these are legally based and must be carried out. Other responsibilities may relate to things that the employer does in order to make the organisation run smoothly, such as keeping employees informed about what is going on and the direction in which the organisation is going. As we have seen, many of the responsibilities of the employer are related to making sure that procedures are followed and that fair treatment is given throughout the organisation to all employees. We have also seen that employment legislation relates to working conditions, equality and health and safety. The following set of headings show specific employer responsibilities.

Prompt provision of written contract of employment

Every employee, regardless of the hours worked each week, is entitled to a written statement from their employer within two months of starting work. This written statement should cover the basic terms of the contract of employment. Employees are entitled to this statement even if the job finishes before the two months are up, provided that the job was supposed to last for more than a month.

The employee is entitled to ask (either verbally or in writing) for a written statement if the employer has not given one of these before the end of the second month.

Clarification of working conditions and key employee rights

The job advertisement may not necessarily reveal very much about the working conditions and employee rights. A job applicant will begin to learn about these issues when they attend their interview and, perhaps, are shown around the business. It is only when the new employee begins work that they understand the true nature of the working conditions and will have a job description that will outline their key working responsibilities. The contract of employment will also outline the employer's commitments to ensuring that employee rights are protected. Many businesses have employee manuals that outline many of the key rights in accordance with the law. Usually the written statement must include the following by law:

- The names of the employee and the employer.
- The date that the employee started work.
- The amount of pay and the frequency of the payments (weekly, monthly, etc.).
- The employee's hours of work.
- The employee's holiday entitlement.
- The length of notice to be worked in the case of the employee wishing to leave, or the employer wishing the employee to leave.
- The job title given to the employee.
- The location of the job.
- The disciplinary, grievance and dismissal arrangements.
- The employee's entitlement to sick pay.
- Whether there is an occupational pension scheme and whether the employee is entitled to join it.

Healthy and safe working environment

The Health and Safety at Work Act 1974 requires the employer to provide a healthy and risk-free work environment (as far as is practicable) for their employees. This means that the employer must assess any potential risks or hazards that could have an impact on their employees.

Most employers will have a health and safety representative, who will have been given training and will have a working knowledge of the Health and Safety at Work Act 1974. This representative will regularly inspect the working environment and report to the employer any particular hazards or problems that may have been uncovered. The employer then has a responsibility to deal with these issues. From time to time, a representative of the Health and Safety Executive, a local government employee, will inspect the working environment and carry out similar inspections to those carried out by the health and safety representative. If the employer has not responded to potential hazards, then they could run the risk of the business being closed down until the situation has been dealt with. Normally the inspector will give the employer a limited period of time to deal with the situation before further action is taken.

It is therefore in the interests of both the employer and the employee that health and safety issues are raised and then dealt with as promptly as possible.

Protection from discrimination and harassment

Again as mentioned earlier, it is the responsibility of the employer to ensure that discrimination and harassment of employees does not take place in the working environment. Laws cover various forms of discrimination, whether they relate to gender, ethnicity, disabilities, sexual orientation, age or religion.

The Equal Opportunities Commission periodically reviews the progress and implementation of discrimination policies. They recommend a number of issues that an employer needs to take account of when framing their equal opportunities policies. These are that:

- It is a desirable thing for an employer to have an equal opportunities policy.
- Any policy should be strictly adhered to.
- The employer should clearly state the different forms of direct and indirect discrimination.
- Any organisation should have a commitment to equal opportunities, as it is in the best interests of the organisation and its employees.
- All employees should be made aware of the policy.
- Employees should be trained to maintain the policy.
- Recruitment and promotion should be equal.

- Employment contracts should not discriminate.
- All of the organisation's facilities are open to everyone.
- A named person should monitor the policy.
- The policy should be reviewed and updated as necessary.
- Any grievances related to discrimination are dealt with in a prompt and fair manner.
- No individual should suffer victimisation.

GROUP WORK (5.16)
★ ★

ACAS (the Advisory, Conciliation and Arbitration Service) is an organisation that helps deal with disputes and problems between employers and employees. Visit their website at: www.acas.org.uk.

Find their advice leaflet on bullying and harassment at work. What examples do they give of unacceptable behaviour in organisations that amount to bullying and harassment?

RECRUITMENT AND STAFF DEVELOPMENT

Recruitment and staff development duties are the responsibility of the personnel or human resource department of a business. As we will see, they are responsible for ensuring that the correct recruitment procedures are followed, that employees undergo periodic appraisals and that opportunities are made available for training and personal development.

The human resource department needs to follow a series of procedures that are not only outlined in employment law, but also incorporate the policies and procedures of the organisation itself. Each organisation will have a particular way in which it prefers to advertise, select and recruit new employees. It will also have a series of procedures related to its appraisal systems and related documents, as well as providing opportunities for training and personal development.

Explanation of professional recruitment procedures

In this section we will look at the ideal way in which a business should carry out its recruitment procedures. Not all businesses have the opportunity or the willingness to follow through all of these steps – the business may be too small or they may have different forms of recruitment, such as recommendation instead of formally advertising a post and following a definite series of steps in their recruitment.

Equality of opportunity

Obviously an employer would seek to find the very best potential candidates for any available position. Potential candidates need to be attracted to making an application without any fear that they will be discriminated against because of their personal circumstances. This means that, in deciding that a job post needs to be filled, a business must ensure that it does not require the potential employee to have particular qualities or circumstances that might eliminate an otherwise ideal applicant.

There are very few jobs that can be advertised that can exclude certain people. Most jobs are available to either gender, and indeed to any race or religion. There are only a handful of examples that can be advertised that can exclude certain groups.

GROUP WORK (5.17)
★ ★
As a group, think about which particular jobs could lawfully ask for only men or women to apply.

Public advertisements

To attract the widest selection of potential candidates for a job, an organisation needs to launch a recruitment campaign, including advertisements in: job centres; local, regional and even national newspapers and magazines; and specialist publications relating to the type of business they are in. The advertisements need to reach the broadest possible audience.

Normally a job advertisement would include:

- The job title.
- A very brief description of the job.

◊ The nature of the organisation's work.

◊ The geographical location of the job.

◊ The salary or wage range.

◊ The organisation's address.

◊ A specific person to whom applications must be made.

◊ A telephone, email or fax number for the candidates to use for contact.

◊ Qualifications and experience required.

◊ Any limitations the organisation may wish to place on the post.

◊ How the post should be applied for, such as filling in an application form or sending in a **curriculum vitae** supported by a letter of application.

◊ A deadline date for submitting applications.

Completion of job application form and letters of application

Employers will state in their advertisements whether the candidates are expected to contact the business and request an application form, or whether they should send in their CV and a letter of application.

Businesses may use their own application forms or standard ones, and they have the advantage of forcing the applicants to fill in each section so that the information about each candidate can be found in the same place and be readily compared. Application forms will require the candidate to give details of their educational and work experience, along with other information that relates to their suitability for the post.

A CV is a useful summary of a potential candidate's educational and work experience. There are many different ways in which CVs can be laid out, but they provide the potential employer with an idea of the background of the candidate and whether or not their experience and qualifications match those required for the job.

A CV is almost always accompanied by a letter of application. This is a standard business letter which gives the candidate the opportunity to state why they think they would be an ideal person to fill the post. It gives the candidate the chance to explain their interests and highlight parts of their CV that might be particularly relevant to the job.

Job description

A job description explains what the job involves and is useful for a business to match the right person for the job. The human resource department of a business will be involved in writing job descriptions for any vacancies that occur. A job description would include:

◊ The job title – the title of 'manager' or 'supervisor' might be included if the job includes the job-holder having responsibility for and authority over other employees.

INDIVIDUAL WORK
(5.18) ★ ★

Your tutor will give you a copy of the job description sheet shown in Figure 5.2. Look through the job advertisements in your local paper. Choose an advertisement for a job you think you would like to do at some time. From the advertisement, see if you can write a brief job description for the job involved. Choose an advertisement that has a lot of detail, although you might be able to think of some hidden duties that are not included in the newspaper.

If you cannot find any suitable job advertisements, choose from one of the following occupations and write your job description around that job role:

An office junior
Assistant to office manager
Receptionist
Accounts clerk
Mailroom assistant

You may find that talking to family, friends and colleagues will help you to complete the duties and responsibilities section.

 ◊ Where the job fits within the business – its position within the structure of the business.

 ◊ The tasks and activities that the job-holder will be required to carry out.

 ◊ The roles and responsibilities that are required of the job.

The amount of detail included on a job description will depend on the type of job that is being described. There will probably be more details given for a job with management responsibility than a job for a junior role with few responsibilities. Figure 5.2 shows the typical headings on a job description.

Figure 5.2
The typical headings in a job description

JOB DESCRIPTION
Job title:
Department/Function/Section:
Wage/Salary range:
Main purpose of the job:
Duties and responsibilities:
Responsible to:
Responsible for:

Person specification

As well as a job description, sometimes a business will draw up a person specification. This is more of a description of the kind of qualities the person should have to carry out the job satisfactorily. A person specification is the business's checklist of the ideal person for the job and will include a description of:

 ◊ The previous experience the person should have.

 ◊ The skills the person should have.

 ◊ The physical characteristics that may be necessary to do the job – including things like their height, weight, hearing or eyesight if those things could affect their ability to do the job.

 ◊ The qualifications required – a computer expert would need the qualifications to prove he or she could do the job.

 ◊ The personality and temperament required. This is important if the job involves working closely with other employees, customers or new employees, or leading a team.

 ◊ The level of motivation required – this is their ability, for example, to work alone and not be supervised and the pride they take in doing the job.

INDIVIDUAL WORK
(5.19) ★ ★

Go back to the job description in Group Work 5.18 and now, for the same job role, draw up a person specification. What qualities or attributes would the person need to do that particular job?

Prepare a list of criteria that you would consider to be essential, desirable or just required. These criteria may include some or all of those we have given you already, as well as some of the following:

• Current achievements (qualifications, driving licence, etc.)

• Aptitudes (social skills, listening, communication skills, legible handwriting)

• Interests (relevant sports or leisure activities)

• Personal circumstances (whether they are willing to work overtime or weekends, etc.)

• Physical attributes (appearance and ability to speak clearly).

Short-listing procedures

Employers will devote a considerable amount of time to recruiting employees and it is, perhaps, at the short-listing stage that many mistakes can be made. An employer cannot reasonably hope to interview all applicants for a particular post. They must select a number of candidates from the total number that have applied for the job. The employer will have already prepared a job description and a person specification and often these are used to compare applicants as part of the short-listing process. The employer will have decided how many people they wish to interview for the post and may set the target figure at no more than eight or 10.

The short-listing process is extremely important and each and every application needs to be looked at in some detail, as an individual who may not have the correct qualifications, for example, may actually be well suited for the job.

Employers therefore need a clear set of criteria to decide which applicants to include and which to exclude as they work through the CVs, letters of application and/or application forms and make a decision about each of them. The applicants that most closely match the requirements of the job will be invited to attend an interview. Those that do not match the criteria will be excluded and, dependent upon how busy the organisation is, may be sent a letter informing them that they have been unsuccessful on this occasion.

Normally an organisation will rank each of the candidates and the top group will be asked to come for an interview.

Use of identical interview questions for all candidates and candidate answer score sheets

Short-listed candidates will be invited to attend a selection interview or, perhaps, a series of interviews. Sometimes a business may invite a large number of potential candidates to a first interview and from this they will short-list those they wish to see a second time.

It is important that the employer makes sure that the individual that has made the application is actually the person attending the interview. This is not to say that impostors turn up for interviews, but in many cases a candidate who looks good on the application form may be a poor candidate in the flesh. Employers use a number of different ways in which to assess candidates, including:

- Observing the candidate at all times to see how they react to situations and different circumstances.
- Checking that the qualifications or references given by the candidate are genuine.
- Testing the candidate, perhaps by using multiple-choice tests, aptitude tests, scenarios or role plays.
- Asking the candidate probing questions about issues regarding their qualifications or experience that are unclear.

Increasingly, to make sure that the selection interviews provide equality of opportunity for all candidates, the interviewers will ask the same series of questions to each one. Normally the selection panel comprises a representative from human resources, the manager or supervisor for whom the candidate would be working and, perhaps, another existing employee who may be a trade union representative.

Each member of the selection panel will have been given the application details of each of the candidates prior to the interviews. This gives them the opportunity to read through the information and highlight any possible questions or queries about the candidate.

The panel will meet before the interviews and agree a series of questions and they may also prepare a score sheet for each of the major criteria outlined in the person specification. They will look through the applications first and score each candidate from the written information. They will then support this by scoring each of the candidates during the interviews. This ensures that all relevant information has been taken into account and that each panel member is using the same criteria to score each candidate.

Prompt letters of confirmation and decline

The successful candidate should be notified at the earliest opportunity. Generally it is not wise to contact the unsuccessful candidates until the successful one has confirmed that they will be taking up the post. It is worth remembering that the candidates are forming an opinion of the business whilst they are being interviewed and that a successful candidate may have changed their mind about accepting the position. If the employer has already told the unsuccessful candidates, only to discover that the successful one has turned the job offer down, this leaves the employer in a difficult position. The only course open is to re-advertise and incur all the expenses of recruitment once again. It is not unknown for successful candidates to accept an offer, then after a few days, during which an employer has contacted all the unsuccessful ones, they change their mind.

Anyone that has ever made an application for a job will have received a photocopied rejection letter. Others may have received a terse and brief telephone call to tell them they have been unsuccessful. In a great many cases, they will have received no contact at all. It is good practice for an employer to always contact unsuccessful candidates and give them feedback as to why they were unsuccessful at this particular time.

Some employers will make the promise to retain the details of unsuccessful candidates and state that they will be contacted if a suitable position for them arises in the future. In all cases, however, letters, telephone calls and other communications with unsuccessful candidates should be prompt and courteous. The employer should remember that the candidate has invested time and effort in making the application and attending the recruitment process. Also, if the employer promised to pay travel or other expenses, this should be done promptly when an expense claim form arrives from the unsuccessful candidate.

> **GROUP** WORK (5.20)
> ★ ★
> In pairs, write to one another a short, word-processed letter, telling your partner that they have been unsuccessful in applying for a clerical job with a large engineering firm. Think about what should be in the letter and how it should be phrased.

Illustration of appraisal procedures and documentation

Assessing the work performance of individual employees is usually the role of the human resource department. However, on a day-to-day basis, performance appraisal may be the concern of line managers and supervisors. Appraisal interviews should be a two-way process of feedback between the manager and employee. The aim is to improve performance through a joint problem-solving approach. The interview should be conducted in a pleasant and positive way throughout. The following should be considered by the organisation in their appraisal procedures:

- The employee should be given notice to allow for their preparation, possibly including a self-development review form (see Figure 5.3).
- A quiet room should be chosen and enough time allowed for the interview.
- Each side should prepare by considering the employee's previous appraisal and subsequent performance.
- Previous targets should be discussed at the start of the interview.
- Questions regarding what has gone well and what has not gone so well should be posed and answered.
- A summary of what has been achieved should be made at the end of the interview and the employee should be given time to read the appraisal documentation.

Employees should make the most of appraisal interviews and:

- Prepare before the interview, making notes of past performance results and anticipating any difficult questions.
- Not be modest about their strengths or put too much emphasis on weaknesses.
- Be clear about what support is required for future work, such as training, resources or time to reach targets.

The main purpose of appraisal interviews is to:

- Identify employee weaknesses.
- Identify employee strengths.
- Determine salary increases (in some organisations, however, appraisals are not linked to salary reviews).
- Determine who deserves promotion.

💧 Aid internal communication processes within the organisation.

💧 Determine staff development needs.

PRIVATE AND CONFIDENTIAL
STAFF APPRAISAL PROCESS
SECTION 1: STAFF ACTIVITIES RECORD FORM
Instructions: To be completed by the Appraisee and given to your Appraiser prior to the Appraisal interview. This form should be copied to the Head of Department (if he or she is not your appraiser) before the appraisal interview.
Name: Title:
Department: Post:
Grade:
Date of last appraisal/probationary review meeting:
Name of appraiser:
The sub-sections in this form are: Your role, Achievements, Review of objectives, Future objectives, Your manager, Personal development and Future development.
Your role
Please describe the main duties of your role.
Achievements
Please detail your achievements (what you think you have done well in your job). You can also refer to qualifications gained and additional work undertaken.
Review of objectives set at last appraisal (or last probation review)
You can use this section to evaluate your activities and indicate what you have completed in terms of your objectives over the last 12 months. You can comment on areas where previously-set objectives have or may not have been fully achieved.
Future objectives
Consider the major objectives that you expect to achieve in each area of your work and how you will measure your success. What do you believe your priorities should be for the coming year? Are there any new activites that you would like to undertake or develop?
Your manager
Is there anything you would like your manager to do in order to help you to improve your performance?
Personal development
Evaluation of training and development undertaken since last appraisal Please list the main development activities, whether formal or informal, that you have undertaken over the last 12 months.

Figure 5.3
An example of a self-appraisal form

Future development

Please indicate any areas of your work where you feel that you would benefit from guidance, training or development.

Signature of appraisee:

Date:

PRIVATE AND CONFIDENTIAL

STAFF APPRAISAL PROCESS

SECTION 2: APPRAISAL INTERVIEW RECORD

Part 1

Instructions: To be completed by the Appraiser following the Appraisal interview.

Name of appraisee:

Name of appraiser:

Head of department:

Date of appraisal interview:

The sub-sections in this form are: Appraisee's role, Activities and performance, Future objectives

Appraisee's role

Following discussion with the appraisee, please comment on the role of the appraisee as outlined in the Staff Activities Record.

Activities and performance

Following the appraisal interview, please comment on the activities and performance described by the appraisee in Section 1, with reference to the discussion themes attached at the back of this form and objectives set at the last appraisal (or last probationary meeting). You should discuss areas of performance including any areas that may require improvement, e.g. Administrative/Management activities, etc.

Appraisee's future objectives

Please specify agreed objectives for the next review period and any development needs that result from these (this can be used to inform Training and Development Needs Identification forms A and B). Objectives should be Specific, Measurable, Attainable, Resourced and Timescaled. Where areas requiring improvement are identified, an action plan should be agreed to address these areas.

Part 2

Instructions: The appraisee should review the comments made in the Appraisal Interview Record and make comments if appropriate. The document should be signed and returned within 14 days.

Appraisee's comments

I have read the comments made by the appraiser in the Appraisal Interview Record following my appraisal. I have nothing to add/wish* to add the following: (*delete as appropriate)

Appraisee's signature:

Date:

Appraiser's signature:

Date:

Head of Department

The Head of Department, where he/she is not the appraiser, is asked to sign below to indicate that the appraisal has taken place in a technically satisfactory manner and he/she has read the report.

Signature of Head of Department:

Date:

Figure 5.3
Continued

After the appraisal, the employee and appraiser will draw up an action plan that will cover all aspects of the interview. This will form the basis of the next appraisal interview. There will be an opportunity at this meeting for the employee to respond and offer evidence that issues identified as unsatisfactory in the previous appraisal interview have been rectified.

Personal staff development plan, annual performance reviews and implication for possible career development and orientation

The purpose of appraisal and its related documents is to identify key areas of an employee's qualifications, training and experience that need to be addressed in order to make them more efficient and productive. Obviously a business will be more inclined to approve particular training and development if it meets the business's objectives. Therefore, the training or personal development needs to be relevant to the work carried out by the employee.

Normally, an employee in consultation with their manager or appraiser will complete a staff development form (see Figure 5.4), which outlines the type of training or personal development recommended as a result of the appraisal.

INDIVIDUAL WORK
(5.21) ★ ★
Your tutor will provide you with a copy of the staff development form shown in Figure 5.4. Complete the form as best you can with a view to providing the qualifications you would need for your ideal job. Think about how many aspects of the training could be provided by an employer and how much of the training would have to be provided by a college or a training agency.

INDIVIDUAL TRAINING AND DEVELOPMENT
CONFIDENTIAL

Please duplicate this form as necessary. If you require further advice on issues raised in this form, please contact Human Resources.

Appraisee:	Appraiser:
Appraisee's signature:	Appraiser's signature:
Role/job title:	Date of appraisal interview:
Department:	

Training/ development area	Objectives of training/ development	Priority (i.e high, medium, low)	Preferred method of delivery	Timescale in which activity should take place (e.g. within 3 months)

Figure 5.4
An example of a staff development form

Identification of training needs and opportunities for personal development

As an alternative to advertising for external candidates for a post, an organisation always has the opportunity to find a current employee to fill that job vacancy. There are a number of advantages and disadvantages of what is known as internal recruitment. The advantages are:

- The individual knows a great deal about the organisation.
- The employer can save money on recruitment costs.
- Promotion is seen as a positive move by employees.

The disadvantages of internal recruitment are:

- Since the individual already knows about the policies and procedures of the organisation, they may not be able to offer any new ideas.
- External candidates tend to work harder in their initial period of employment.
- The individual that has filled the vacant job position will have to be replaced.
- In choosing one current employee, the organisation may overlook others that may be equally as suitable.

Advertisement of internal vacancies and promotion opportunities

Internal vacancies can be advertised by the business in various ways. Nearly all businesses have staff notice-boards and, rather like a job advertisement, brief details of the job vacancy can be posted here. Some businesses have staff newsletters, which could be used to advertise the internal vacancy. Other businesses, particularly with large numbers of staff, will also circulate memos or notices to inform employees of internal job vacancies. Increasingly, emails are being used as a replacement for memos.

It will usually be the responsibility of the human resources department to deal with enquiries regarding internal vacancies. They may well handle the applications very much like an external application. But the organisation has the advantage of already knowing a great deal about the potential candidates.

Some employees may apply for jobs with broadly the same salary and responsibilities, to expand their areas of expertise and skills. Other opportunities arise in organisations to gain promotion, particularly if a more senior member of staff has left the organisation. Since existing employees are probably far more experienced with the policies and procedures of the business than external candidates, the organisation will, in the first instance, try to recruit an existing member of staff to fill a more senior position. They will use similar short-listing and interview procedures to try to find the ideal candidate. If they fail to find a suitable candidate internally, they will advertise the post in the normal manner externally.

Equal opportunities and access to promotional opportunities

Under the terms of the various employment laws, all employees should have the right to apply for more senior positions. It is the responsibility of the employer, usually via the human resource department, to ensure that equal opportunity laws are followed, even in the case of internal applications for promotion. Remember that employers not only have a responsibility when they are dealing with external candidates, but they also have a responsibility once individuals begin working for them.

Clarification of potential personal aptitudes and related career options

The periodic appraisals or annual reviews should highlight any required improvements to an employee's skills or abilities. As we have seen, personal development plans can be designed in order to ensure that an employee gradually acquires the skills, experience and knowledge that will put them in a position to be able to apply for more senior posts in the future.

INDIVIDUAL WORK
(5.22) ★ ★ ★
Find out what the
following training-
related terms mean:

a) On-the-job training

b) Off-the-job training

c) NVQ

d) Professional
   development plan

e) Training-needs
   analysis.

Many employees learn new skills during the normal working process and will be able to rely on more experienced members of staff to help them through difficult parts of their job. Any manager or supervisor will be keen to ensure that the employees that work for them are as experienced and knowledgeable about their work as possible and should support any application by their immediate employees for additional training or development.

Larger organisations offer huge career opportunities, perhaps the ability to transfer from one area of the business to another, gradually gaining experience and qualifications along the way. Many good employers have comprehensive staff training events that are offered to all relevant members of staff. These training events give employees an opportunity to update their understanding of the job, acquire new skills and, in some cases, new qualifications.

INDUSTRIAL RELATIONS

The term 'industrial relations' refers to the ongoing dialogue or relationship between employers and employees, particularly regarding working conditions, rewards, job roles and other human resource-related topics. Also often known as labour relations, industrial relations usually involve an assessment of an employer's and their employees' ability or willingness to cooperate with one another on various matters.

Scope for conflict

Pay and conditions, individual and collective conflict and the changing nature of work

There is a wide range of potential problems or conflict between employers and employees. The purpose of any form of industrial relations is to try and resolve these conflicts and, as we will see when we investigate the role of trade unions, employee organisations have a key role to play in this.

Employees may face problems on a personal level, related to their pay or their working conditions. They may feel that they are not being sufficiently rewarded for their work or that the employer makes unreasonable demands upon them at work. Equally there may be problems with the actual working conditions, such as being forced to use inadequate equipment, poor lighting or hazards and risks in their working environment.

Usually the first stage is to bring up the problem with the immediate manager or supervisor. In the majority of cases, problems can be dealt with at this level, but if the situation is serious enough then it will have to be referred to human resources or a more senior manager. The problem only becomes a conflict when the two sides cannot agree on the best way forward. It is at this stage that both sides seek to resolve the situation in the most appropriate manner. It is also at this stage that, if relevant, a trade union may become involved.

Many problems at work, however, do not simply relate to one employee. They may have an impact on the entire workforce. When a single employee has a problem, then negotiations take place on an individual level. When several or all of the employees are concerned, this means that negotiations take place on what is known as a collective level. In other words, the problem or conflict affects all employees and the successful resolution of that problem will mean that all employees will follow what has been agreed.

Many problems and conflicts have arisen between employers and employees over changing working conditions. Many employers have changed their employees' working conditions in order to remain competitive. For shop workers, for example, this has meant opening on Sundays, which has had an affect on their home lives. Although they may be given an additional day off during the week, many of those working in retail do not feel that this has compensated them enough. Employers are keen to make Sundays a standard working day and not pay overtime to compensate the employees for losing what was a traditional rest day.

CASE STUDY   The importance of staff

Sunday working

From April 2004, workers in Scotland were no longer forced to work on a Sunday. A new law, the Sunday Working Bill, came into effect in Scotland and closed a loophole in the law that allowed Argos to sack some of its workers in Aberdeen for refusing to work on a Sunday. Shop workers in England, Wales and Northern Ireland have to give their consent to work on a Sunday. Because there had never been a ban on opening seven days a week in Scotland, workers were not protected until April 2004.

> **INDIVIDUAL** WORK (5.23) ★ ★
> Read the case study on Sunday working and then visit the BBC website at www.bbc.co.uk. Click on the news and then search for stories regarding Sunday working and the new law in Scotland.

The role of trade unions

Trade unions are fairly widely recognised across the country as the main way in which negotiations between employers and employees can take place. Trade unions have a number of key roles in dealing with issues related to their members, who are employees of various organisations. They carry out a multitude of different tasks, including:

- Protecting the wages and salaries of their members.
- Negotiating working hours and conditions.
- Monitoring health and safety.
- Providing a range of benefits, including pensions and unemployment pay.
- Representing the interests of their members in times of conflict with the employers.
- Lobbying government, employers and employers' associations to further the cause of their members.

> **GROUP** WORK (5.24)
> ★ ★
> Visit the website of the Trades Union Congress (TUC) at www.tuc.org.uk; and click on 'Unions' under 'About the TUC'. At the time of writing the Trades Union Congress had 70 member trade unions, representing around 6.5 million people. Use this page to find out the following:
>
> 1 What type of employee does AMICUS represent?
> 2 What is the BFAWU?
> 3 What has happened to the GPMU?
> 4 What is NATFHE?
> 5 What type of employee does NUT represent?
> 6 What is the T&G?
> 7 How many members does UNISON have?

Legal advice on employment terms: health and safety, collective bargaining (pay and working conditions) and issues of union recognition

Given the increasingly complex nature of employment, employees need to understand the variety of legislation which affects them. Trade unions provide their members with information and advice on the implementation, practice and reality of employment law. In doing this, the unions hope to put their employees on an even level with the employers. As it is often said, information is power and the absence of knowledge about employment law can be seen as a disadvantage.

Union representatives within an organisation will keep their members up to date with developments and pass on relevant information to their members. The constant interchange of information is vital in protecting members' pay and working conditions.

Trade unions will assist their members in understanding the implications of any contract of employment or new sets of policies and procedures proposed by the employer. They have specialist legal advice available to them to interpret even the most complicated documents.

Unions are also concerned with the health and safety of their members and will take an active role in assessing whether or not there are unacceptable risks and hazards in the workplace. They will put pressure on the employer to rectify the situation and, if necessary, will advise their members not to carry out particular tasks if they feel that health and safety matters are sufficiently serious.

Above all, trade unions enter into negotiations with the employer on behalf of their members. At a local level, trade union representatives will negotiate with senior management, as we will see in the next section. This is known as *collective bargaining* or *collective negotiation*. They seek to represent all of the employees and any agreement reached by the trade union officials will be binding on all employees.

In law, an employer does not have to recognise a trade union unless they feel that it would be beneficial to the business. In many cases, union recognition is beneficial because it means that collective negotiations can take place. Otherwise each employee would need to have their issues and situations discussed individually.

Organisations have different approaches to union recognition, including:

- Full recognition of a variety of different unions relating to different sections of the workforce.
- Recognition of a single trade union that represents all or the majority of their workers.
- The refusal to recognise any trade union.
- The establishment of a staff association instead of a trade union.

An understanding of key principles of negotiation

Personal negotiation and collective negotiation

Negotiation is a vital communication skill required by supervisors, managers and employer representatives, such as the human resource department. In dealing with disputes or possible conflicts, negotiation skills also become important for individual employees and representatives of employees, such as trade union officials.

At an individual level, negotiation can take place far more informally, perhaps a discussion between the employee and their immediate manager or supervisor can sort out any problems. They may also ask for a trade union representative or a colleague to accompany them to witness the conversation.

Negotiation is all about relative power. An employer has considerably more power than an employee and during negotiations, for there to be a fair and reasonable outcome, both sides need to put aside their strengths and negotiate for what is best for all concerned.

This is why, in many cases, in order to equalise the power between the employees and the employer, trade union officials step in to represent large numbers of employees. They will speak and negotiate on behalf of the employees from a position of strength as they represent so many people. As we know, it is in the best interests of both the employer and the employees that the situation is resolved as well as possible and to avoid the risk of the conflict becoming more serious.

Negotiations usually begin with a statement from both sides detailing how they view the situation. Both sides then suggest their solution to the problem. Usually the answer is somewhere in the middle. Both sides need to be aware that it is unlikely that the other side will completely agree to their solution to the situation. Therefore both sides need to be flexible and willing to move their position. What this usually means is that both sides state the extreme of what they propose, so that they can ensure that the final answer is as close to their actual viewpoint as possible.

Negotiations should be undertaken calmly and both sides should listen to the others' point of view and suggestions. Sometimes even the most difficult situations can be resolved quickly, but some may take days or weeks to reach a conclusion. In the next section we look at what happens if negotiations fail.

An understanding of the avenues for seeking redress of employment grievance

If an individual or a group of employees find it impossible to reach a satisfactory conclusion with their employer, then there is an opportunity to use independent organisations to help resolve the situation. Most commonly individuals will take their case to an Employment Tribunal, while groups of employees will enlist the services of ACAS (the Advisory, Conciliation and Arbitration Service).

GROUP WORK **(5.25)**

★ ★

As a group, think of a situation when you have negotiated in the recent past. Who have you negotiated with and how difficult was it to reach a conclusion?

Keyword

constructive dismissal – when the employee leaves their job due to the employer's behaviour

whistle-blowing – when a worker raises a concern about dangerous or illegal activity that they are aware of through their work

Employment Tribunals

Employment Tribunals (previously known as Industrial Tribunals) are independent bodies that hear complaints and make decisions on a range of employment issues. They are a less formal and more accessible way of settling employment disputes than the courts and around 130,000 complaints are raised with them every year.

There are Employment Tribunal offices in most major cities and all the administration of tribunal cases is dealt with from those offices. Tribunal hearings are also usually held in the Employment Tribunal offices.

Employment Tribunals hear complaints and appeals on over 70 different employment-related issues, including:

- Unfair and **constructive dismissal**
- Breach of contract
- Redundancy
- Sex, race and disability discrimination
- Equal pay
- Maternity rights
- **Whistle-blowing** (protected disclosure)
- Trade union rights.

WANT TO FIND OUT MORE?

Find out more about the work of Employment Tribunals by visiting their website: www.employmenttribunals.gov.uk.

INDIVIDUAL WORK
(5.26) ★

Using the Employment Tribunals website at http://www.employmenttribunals.gov.uk, find out where the nearest tribunal is located to your school or college.

ACAS

The role of ACAS (the Advisory, Conciliation and Arbitration Service) is to improve organisations and working life through better employment relations. It was founded in 1974 and since then has had experience in dealing with people in businesses of every size and sector. It is publicly funded, which ensures that they are independent, impartial and confidential. Every year ACAS helps employers and employees in over a million workplaces. It keeps up to date with today's employment issues such as discipline and grievance handling, preventing discrimination and communicating effectively in workplaces.

ACAS is involved in four main areas:

- Providing information and help via a helpline that takes 750,000 calls a year.
- Helping to resolve problems between employers and employees – it is successful in 90 per cent of cases.
- Helping to settle complaints about employees' right – around 70 per cent of cases that would be referred to an Employment Tribunal are resolved by ACAS.
- Running seminars and workshops to encourage effective working relationships.

ADAPTABILITY TO CHANGE

INDIVIDUAL WORK
(5.27) ★
Visit the ACAS website at www.acas.org.uk. Find out the following:

1 How does ACAS describe a contract of employment?

2 What is their arbitration scheme?

3 What regulations cover the 48-hour week?

As far as is reasonable, an employee should expect there to be some changes to their type of work and even, perhaps, to the working conditions. Businesses and technology are constantly changing to adapt to new challenges, opportunities and threats. This is true of commercial businesses, public organisations and even charities.

Whilst employees accept a job offer on the basis of a particular job description and job role, over time this job role may change and additional skills may be required, as well as additional duties that will need to be carried out. For the most part, employees cope with slow or gradual changes but, when they face extreme changes in their job role, they may run into difficulties, particularly if the job is radically different from what it used to be or they lack the skills to carry out the new role.

Understanding the potential for technological and structural change

The following set of headings are examples of the kinds of change that could take place. Obviously the use of machinery, including computers, can have a direct impact on the job roles of employees. Equally, a decision by an employer to relocate particular job roles abroad can be a major concern. Other issues also have an impact on employees, including mergers and takeovers, which involve the actual ownership and running of a business. Finally we will look at relocation, which has been a feature of businesses for several years as they seek to find a better location for their business, which can cut costs and provide access to a wider number of skilled employees.

E-business strategy

There are several sections in Unit 8 Business Online that specifically deal with the problems facing employees whose employers are shifting over to e-business as their major operation.

E-businesses are run via websites on the internet and therefore do not require the same types of employees as conventional retail outlets. Many of the transactions are automated by computer systems and the majority of the contact between the business and its customers is carried out electronically, by email.

Even an e-business, however, needs skilled employees, specialists who have sales skills and, of course, IT skills. Many e-businesses do not carry a great deal of stock so this means that warehouse facilities are no longer needed. Since the majority of the documentation is carried out electronically, there may no longer be a need for an administration department. Facts and figures about the business's revenues and expenditure will automatically be placed on computerised systems; therefore this reduces the work of accounts departments. With usually fewer employees, this also means that the work of human resources is cut down.

Outsourcing

Outsourcing refers to situations when a business chooses to employ another business, either in the same country or abroad, to carry out some of its operations. Many businesses, such as banks and insurance companies, have outsourced their sales teams and customer service work to countries such as India or China. Given the fact that wage and salary costs are significantly lower in these countries, a business can obtain huge savings by shifting their operations overseas. In recent months, however, there has been something of a backlash against outsourcing abroad as the quality of service to customers has dropped significantly when businesses have outsourced parts of their operations.

For an employee in a part of a business that is due to be outsourced there may be opportunities to obtain alternative work in another department in the business. This very much depends upon the level of skills and experience that the employee has and whether they are prepared to work in a different working environment. Many employees do not even have this option, however, as there is not sufficient or relevant work available in the business. They therefore face the prospect of having to find a new job. Employers must assist them in finding new work and compensate them for their loss of work according to how long the employee has worked for them.

Mergers and takeovers

Mergers and takeovers affect the ownership of businesses. A merger occurs when two businesses join together. They do this in order to control more of the market and, importantly for employees, to reduce their workforce because certain areas of their operations would be duplicated otherwise. This means that instead of having two of every department they only need to have one. That new, single department only needs to be big enough to cope with the work generated by the newly formed business. This means that in administration, accounts, human resources and in a host of other operations they can effectively halve the number of employees. This represents enormous savings to the new business.

Usually existing employees are graded when the merger takes place. Senior management and human resources carry out the grading. They identify key workers that must be found employment in the newly formed business. All of the other posts have to be applied for by the remaining employees. A selection process takes place on the basis of each employee's skills and experience and the best employees from either business are allocated to particular job roles. The remainder may find themselves without work and again it is the responsibility of the employer to assist them in finding work elsewhere, as well as to compensate them for their loss of work.

Takeovers take place when one business buys another business. They will usually purchase the business because it complements the type of work that the organisation already does. As with a merger, the employees of the newly acquired business may face job losses and, if not, then their jobs will certainly change. The employees become part of a much larger organisation and, once again, there will be a number of jobs that have been duplicated by the takeover. The business that acquired the other business will look carefully at the operations and make a decision as to whether or not all of the activities can be brought under one single operation, or whether it is advisable to keep the two separate.

Relocation

Sometimes a business may simply outgrow the premises in which they operate. In other cases, the original premises may no longer be suitable for various reasons – they may need more storage space, better access to the roads or rail network. On other occasions the cost of rent, rates or even maintaining the building may reach a point when it is no longer cost-effective to remain there.

Businesses will try to find premises that best suit their existing and future demands. Once they have reached the point where the premises are no longer suitable, they will seek premises elsewhere. While many businesses choose to remain roughly in the same area, to minimise disruption to their customers, suppliers and employees, others will move literally hundreds of miles away to more suitable premises.

Various parts of the country actively encourage businesses to relocate and offer incentives to these businesses in the form of grants, reduced rents and rates, and assistance in attracting new employees. Areas with high unemployment receive grants from central government and from the EU to help them attract businesses and thus reduce unemployment.

Local or even regional relocation of a business may not affect employees to a great extent. They may need to travel slightly further each day but the nature of their work may not change and the premises may be more suitable. Other employees face the prospect of having to move from the area in which they live in order to continue to work for their employer. Once again employers will identify their key workers. These will be individuals that the business feels they need to keep. They will be offered relocation packages. In other words the employer will either pay, or part-pay, the expenses of moving from the current location to the new location.

INDIVIDUAL WORK
(5.28) ★ ★

Visit the Portsmouth City Council website at www.portsmouth.gov.uk. Investigate the measures that the Portsmouth area has developed to attract businesses to their city. Answer the following questions.

1 What is their inward investment service?

2 What is the average cost per square foot of industrial premises in the area?

3 What is the phone number of their business services and development team?

Identifying information sources

To indicate such changes in the short and medium-term future, internal communications, local, regional and national news and trade journals

Many businesses and organisations decide to make changes that will radically affect their employees without consulting the employees before the decision has been made.

INDIVIDUAL WORK (5.29) ⭐

Visit the Flowers and Plants Association website at www.flowers.org.uk and under 'Industry info' click on 'Who's who'. Scroll down and find the section marked 'Press'. Select 'Floristry press' and press 'Go'. How many floristry trade journals are listed?

press release – a statement by a business outlining a news feature that can be used by the press to help them cover a story

Keyword

Businesses tend to take major decisions, such as those already discussed, in order to ensure the organisation's long-term survival and success. Many businesses feel that involving employees or trade unions before a decision has been made would cause unnecessary disruption to the smooth running of the business.

Having said this, a business would not wish for its employees to discover from another source that they are about to announce a major change that could affect them. Once a decision has been made, the first step is to communicate it internally. Perhaps the business will choose to call a meeting where they can inform all employees at the same time. In other cases individual departments or sections will be informed at specially held meetings. In other cases the business may choose to circulate a memo or email, or a special notice will be placed on the staff notice-board.

Once the employees have been informed, the business will usually find that someone has contacted the local, regional or national press. It will be the responsibility of a senior figure from the business to provide time for interviews, where they can explain what is planned and answer any queries or problems that either the employees or the local community feel are important.

Major changes to large businesses will find their way into the national press and perhaps TV and radio. Once again, a representative of the business needs to be prepared to explain the situation, the causes for the change, the likely benefits and any steps they are going to take in order to protect jobs.

Since a business not only has a relationship with its employees, but also its suppliers and customers, it is important for them to pass on a positive view of any proposed change. One of the many ways in which suppliers or business partners, for example, could be informed is to send a **press release** to the trade journals. Trade journals are newspapers and magazines that are designed and written to appeal to particular areas of industry, such as retailers, car dealers or building merchants.

Identifying the potential implications of such change

Any major change in the way in which an employer operates their business will have either a positive or negative impact on their employees. Some changes may offer much greater opportunities for employees in terms of their skill development and future employability. Other changes may be very negative and may lead to the employee being out of work and facing the prospect of having to find a new job. This section looks at the types of impact that major changes can have on employees.

Changes to working conditions

Many employees have faced changes in their working conditions as a result of their employer's drive to beat off the competition. As we have seen, many retail employees now find themselves in a position where they have to work the whole of the weekend. Other employees may find that their employer wishes to change their working hours. Many manufacturers or factories wish to run their machinery for 24-hours a day, 365 days of the year. This means that a proportion of their employees will work regular hours during the day, whilst others will get into work very early and leave at lunchtime. Others will start in the evening and finish in the early hours of the morning.

Sometimes these changes in arrangements actually suit employees and there has been a trend for employers to bring in what is known as a compressed working week. If, for example, an employee had to work 42 hours per week, instead of spreading out those hours over five days, they would work just three-and-a-half days. Each of the days would consist of 12 hours and the half day would consist of six hours. This means that the employee, although they are working for longer hours in a single day, have three-and-a-half days' leave per week.

It is not just working hours that can be changed. There may be changes in the way the employee actually carries out their work. Perhaps the introduction of new technology would change what may have been a paper-based job to an electronic-based series of duties. Jobs also change in manufacturing as new machinery and equipment are developed, making the jobs far more to do with checking and monitoring machinery, rather than doing actual physical work.

When employers expect their employees to change the very nature of their jobs, they usually provide retraining and assistance to help their employees make the transition.

Personal skills transferability and future employability

Employers are increasingly looking for people with skills that they can transfer to any job, for example:

- A willingness to learn
- Good verbal and written communication skills
- Self-motivation
- Team work
- Commitment
- Energy and enthusiasm
- Reliability and honesty
- Problem-solving and analytic ability
- Organisational skills
- Adaptability and flexibility
- Ability to meet deadlines
- Information technology skills.

This list may appear to be daunting and quite demanding, but employers are looking for employees that can display the widest possible range of skills. Increasingly, because even low-level job roles are more demanding, employees need to have a wide range of skills and show the willingness to learn new skills. This is known as multi-skilling, which provides employees with a broad range of skills that can be transferred from one job role to another. A prime example would be an individual who has used the Microsoft Office package for an administrative job and has sufficient typing skills to take on secretarial work.

If an employee is multi-skilled and has a wide range of transferable skills, then their future employment prospects are improved. Employers look for flexible, well-trained and highly skilled individuals who can adapt to various changes in their job roles as well as accepting and welcoming the need to continually update their bank of skills and knowledge.

Identifying opportunities for personal development

In the first instance, it is the employee that should identify any areas of knowledge or skills that they feel they need to add to or improve. Certain areas ideal for personal development will be highlighted, as we have seen, in appraisals or annual reviews. The personal development plans that arise from the appraisals will outline the key areas that the employee, supported by their supervisor or manager and ultimately the human resource department, feel are relevant to their job role.

In the meantime, other opportunities for personal development may arise, such as training courses either within the organisation or arranged by local colleges or training agencies. The human resource department will routinely inform employees of training opportunities and employees should also look in the local press and libraries for notices announcing training programmes in the area. Many of these external training programmes will either be paid for or subsidised by the employer. If this is not the case, then many of the courses have sliding scales of payment so that many of them are affordable to almost any employee.

CASE STUDY   On the move

Jess and Eve set up their IT training agency in the centre of London eight years ago. They have come under enormous pressure from competitors that have more staff and can offer a wider range of training courses. Whilst they have continued to be successful, Eve and Jess have found it difficult to convince businesses to let them put on training programmes for their staff.

The 50 per cent increase in the rent for their offices was the final straw. It did not mean that they would not make a profit, but it just added to the pressure. For some years they had both wanted to relocate to Suffolk, where they had enjoyed holidays and had a number of friends. They decided that they would move in five months and now had the problem of telling their employees.

Frank, Evelyn and Roger were all full-time members of staff. They carried out all of the administration work, accounts, marketing and liaised with businesses as well as trainers. They all live in London and would probably be reluctant to move. Eve and Jess knew that they needed Frank and Evelyn because they were key members of staff. They could replace Roger.

All of the other employees were taken on when a training programme was up and running with a customer. They used a pool of about 20 different trainers that were dotted around the country. Moving to Suffolk, therefore, would not cause problems for the majority of the trainers.

INDIVIDUAL WORK (5.30) ★ ★ ★
Read the case study and then suggest how they should go forward with their plans.

1 How should they handle telling their three full-time members of staff about their plans and their desire for two of them to move to Suffolk with them?

2 What should they tell their trainers?

3 What should they do about their current customers in London?

4 What should they do to find out whether there is a need for a training company in Suffolk?

5 What is the order in which they should do things?

Unit Revision Questions

1 State two types of implied terms.

2 State five things that should be in a contract of employment.

3 How many stages are there usually in a disciplinary procedure?

4 What is the standard maternity leave entitlement?

5 What is the difference between core and vocational skills?

6 What is a job description?

7 What year was the Data Protection Act brought into force?

8 What is internal recruitment?

9 Name three types of change that could affect an employee's working conditions.

10 What is multi-skilling?

UNIT 6

Introduction to Business Administration

This unit focuses on the importance of administrative processes in all organisations. Organisations rely on an accurate flow of information as well as the effective and secure storage and retrieval of that information. The information used by organisations is of great importance to decision-making.

This unit focuses on how organisations design and support their administrative systems and how they set up processes to make sure employees follow the procedures they have in place. This unit will require you to set up and operate a straightforward administrative system and you will also investigate why health and safety at work is so important.

This is an internally assessed unit and to cover the requirements of the unit you must:

- Investigate core administrative systems
- Consider threats to administrative effectiveness
- Examine the purpose of a simple administrative system
- Explore health and safety at work.

CORE ADMINISTRATIVE SYSTEMS

All businesses have core administrative systems to coordinate their activities and allow the decision-makers to plan for the future. Because businesses want to operate in an effective and efficient way, it is vital that they have immediate access to all the relevant information they need.

Information systems inevitably involve some form of filing, whether it is paper-based or computer-based. Businesses want to be able to monitor all parts of their systems, which are often designed so that they can easily be amended or evolved to meet changing needs.

Effectiveness is concerned with how the business achieves it goals and objectives. Systems play a vital role, as they are the means by which an organisation is able to operate as a whole. Organisations need not necessarily rely on their own employees to provide the design and running of systems. They may employ an outside specialist, an agency or a consultant.

Efficiency is described as the way in which the business uses its available resources in order to produce its outputs in the smoothest way possible.

Identifying and understanding the flow of key business information

However we describe administrative systems, we can identify a common thread within them. Each of the procedures in place within the business will consist of a simple process of turning inputs into outputs. Figure 6.1 explains this process.

The process part of the diagram can be split into two parts:

- The storage of the information (either in a paper-based filing system or by computer).
- The analysis of the information.

Inputs	Process	Outputs
The information received, via fax, telephone, order, money, etc.	The system by which the information is handled, e.g. input into a computer analysis, etc.	The supply of the response, e.g. letter, memo, report, telephone call, etc.

Figure 6.1
Turning inputs into outputs

So an administrative system can be defined as being one of two things:

- The activities carried out by managers to determine the aims and policies of the organisation.
- Control of the day-to-day running of the business.

Administrative tasks will be carried out at all levels of the organisation. In larger organisations an administration department will carry out administration, but in smaller organisations a single individual may carry out the administration. However, the basic purpose for these procedures, or administrative systems, remains the same:

- To provide support systems for all resources used by the business
- To keep records relating to all the activities of the business
- To monitor the performance of the business's activities.

The headings in this section of the unit describe the administrative systems businesses have in place to ensure that they have the resources they need to carry out their activities. We follow the flow of information through the businesses from the initial sales order to a supplier for materials, through to the request for payment from the supplier for those materials.

Sales orders

Unit 8, Business Online, covers the ways in which a business with an online presence provides its customers with the ability to order products or services via their websites. For the purposes of this unit, we will consider the paper-based ways in which a business obtains its requirements from its suppliers.

We already know that all organisations need to buy raw materials and services in order to produce or provide their own products and services. In order to obtain these materials or services, the business will have to complete documents requesting them. A business may want to purchase any of the following:

- *Materials*, which can take several different forms. They may be raw materials needed to produce products. They may, however, be headed paper to produce business letters or cleaning products used on the production line. These are known as consumables and will probably be ordered from the supplier using an order form.
- *Capital items*, which could be office furniture, new computer equipment, new buildings, etc. These are ordered in a different way to materials and a special purchasing system will be in effect within the business to deal with these.
- *Services*. To purchase a service from an individual or another business, it is necessary for the business to raise a contract. This contract would state the terms under which the work has been agreed and would be legally binding on both sides.

It is a business's purchasing department that would be responsible for buying materials or services for the organisation. This involves a series of processes and the completion of a series of documents. Once it has been decided which supplier will be used, the business will complete and send an order form.

The employee completing the order form will check the details with the supplier's catalogue and price list to ensure the details are correct. Then the order form will be sent to the supplier via fax, email or post. Sometimes, if an order is urgently required, the supplier would accept a telephone order, particularly if the business is a long-term customer. However, a completed order form would still have to be sent, as the suppliers would need this document for their own administrative systems.

An order form is a firm commitment that the business requires the materials. An example of a blank order form is shown in Figure 6.2.

From Figure 6.2 we can identify the information that the supplier requires from the business. Essentially the following information is included on the order:

- To – this is the address of the business buying the materials.
- Order number – each order placed will have a unique number. This information is vital to both the supplier and the purchasing department of the business, as we will see later.
- Date – every order placed must be dated.
- Delivery address – this may be different from the address of the purchasing business, as the materials may be required at a branch of their operations.
- Special instructions – these may include items such as the fact that the order had previously been telephoned to the supplier, or that delivery of the materials has been agreed by a certain date.
- Reference number – which may be the number of the item as stated in the supplier's catalogue.
- Quantity – the number of each item required.
- Description – identifies the exact nature of the item required.
- Unit price – the price of each item required.
- Amount – the total amount when the quantity and unit price are multiplied together.
- Authorised by – the purchasing business would have an individual, or a number of individuals, that are authorised to sign on behalf of the business.

It would be disadvantageous to a business if there were not an individual, or a group of individuals, who had the final say as to what could be ordered. This has to be someone

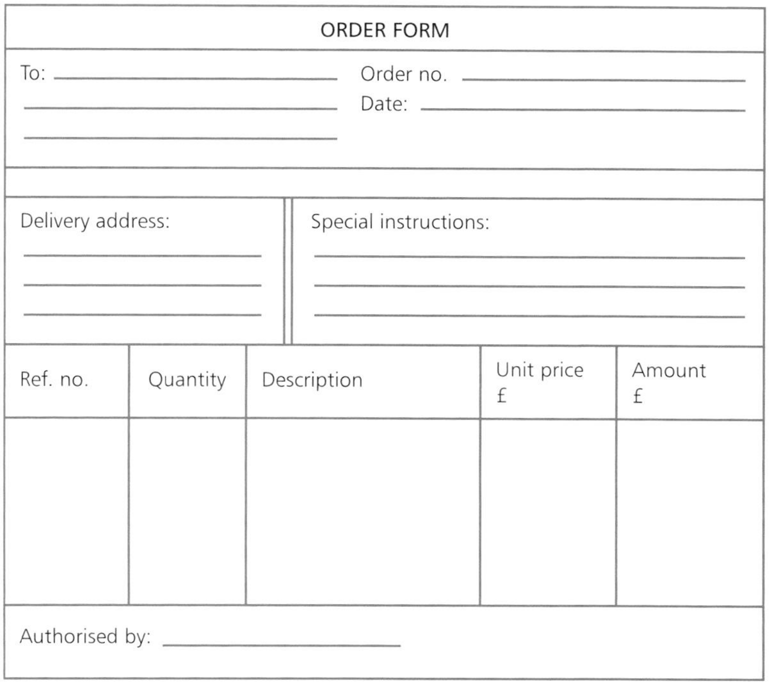

Figure 6.2
An example of an order form

with the right amount of authority within the business who knows its financial commitments. This person has to know what is needed and the urgency of that need. It makes sense that each department within the business has a person to authorise requirements, as they will have their own budget.

INDIVIDUAL WORK
(6.1) ★ ★

1 Produce your own order form and save it on a computer.

2 Imagine that it is one of your responsibilities to complete the order forms for your business. Complete your order form using the following information:

- Use the address of your school or college
- The order number is 1285
- Use today's date
- The delivery address is the same as the school or college address
- There are no special instructions
- You require the following:

  2 boxes of A4 paper (155) at £2.50 each
  4 boxes of staples (111) at £4.00 each
  3 packs of plastic wallets (75) at £1.50 each.

You will need this completed order for an activity later in this section of the book.

The order form is sent to the supplier's sales department, which has the main responsibility of creating orders for that business's products and services. Many organisations employ a large sales force that operates either on a local or regional basis. The greater the emphasis on selling to customers, the larger the sales force is likely to be. Those businesses that rely on advertising to stimulate interest in their products or services may have a smaller sales team. In terms of organising the efforts of the sales employees, the sales department will have drawn up a detailed sales plan that includes targets to be met by each area or region of the sales force. Also included in this will be the level of profit that can be expected from each and every product.

The key functions of the sales department's staff are to control and organise the selling and distribution of the organisation's products and services. The sales function may also be found within the marketing department of an organisation, but the sales operation will always be supported by administrative personnel and various sales representatives. As with any other managerial function, the sales manager will be responsible for the establishment and revision of systems that will ensure the smooth running of the sales operation. In addition, he or she may have specific targets to meet and must maintain budgetary control over these. Communication is a key feature of a good sales department, as the staff must be able to handle all communications with customers. They will also be responsible for the maintenance of any relevant records and exercise some control (via a credit controller) over the availability of credit to customers.

Dealing with customers requires the establishment of systems to efficiently handle enquiries and problems. These systems will also require the sales department to keep records of any enquiries made, orders received and other documentation that maintains an up-to-date record of customer transactions. Administration systems must be in place to ensure that the details of any conversation, negotiation or problem have been recorded accurately. This information, which is often held by the sales department, will include:

- The name and contact details of the customer
- Any discounts agreed with the customer
- The customer's **creditworthiness**
- Any specific customer requirements
- The customer's preferred delivery arrangements
- The average size of the customer's order
- The frequency of the customer's order.

Keyword

creditworthiness – the customer's history regarding the paying of money owed to the business. If the customer has missed some payments, the business might consider them to be less creditworthy and insist that an order is paid for immediately, rather than on credit

Production instructions

Once the order has passed through the hands of the supplier's sales department, it will often need to be handed over to the production department. This would be the case if the customer has ordered materials that are not held in stock, but which have to be produced for the customer.

The production department is involved in all functions that revolve around producing the products or services for the customer. They monitor the levels of wastage to ensure the most efficient use of their own resources and check the cost of their raw materials and parts purchased to make sure that profit margins are maintained. As new products are developed and technology changes, the production department will be responsible for purchasing all the necessary plant and equipment required, as well as organising the production process.

In consultation with the sales department, the production department must make sure that it can manufacture or supply customers with the quantity of products required at the time they have been requested. The tight monitoring of production levels means that the production department should know how long it would take to produce sufficient products to fill a particular order. Advance planning and close liaison with the sales department is vital to ensure that deadlines can be met.

Regardless of how many units of products are being produced, the production department is also responsible for the maintenance of quality. Each product must meet a number of strict quality standards and must, to all intents and purposes, be exactly the same every time.

Once the contents of the order have either been produced or selected from the supplier's warehouse, they are then packaged and prepared for delivery to the customer.

Delivery advice

The supplying business will need to have a record of what has been prepared for despatch to the customer, but the customer will also need some documentation to check against their order. A *despatch note*, also known as a *delivery advice note*, is sent to the customer when the goods are despatched and a copy will also be attached to the product's packaging or included inside the package.

The person receiving the products may not have a copy of the original order form, so all they will do is check that the delivery advice note states correctly what has actually been delivered. They will then complete a *goods received note*, which is used to update the stock records and to check against the original order before paying the supplier's invoice.

INDIVIDUAL WORK
(6.2) ★ ★
To find out more about quality standards, visit the website of the British Standards Institute at www.bsi-global.com. Find out the following:

1 What is a kitemark?

2 What are CE markings?

3 What is a BSI benchmark?

DELIVERY ADVICE   No. _____

To: _____

_____   Your order no. _____

_____   Date: _____

The following items have been despatched today by rail/company van/post:

Quantity   Description   No. of packages

_____   _____   _____

_____   _____   _____

_____   _____   _____

I certify that the goods have been received today.

Signed: _____   On behalf of: _____

Date: _____

Figure 6.3
An example of a delivery advice note

GOODS RECEIVED NOTE		No. _____
Date received	Order no.	Delivered by
Quantity	Description	No. of packages	Stores ref.
Received from	Entered in stock	Received by
_____ Supplier	Date _____ Initials _____	_____ Storekeeper

Figure 6.4
An example of a goods received note

INDIVIDUAL WORK
(6.3) ★ ★
Look at Figure 6.4.
Consider each of the
headings in turn and
suggest your own
reasons why these
would appear on this
document.

If the number of boxes or packages does not tally with the items actually delivered, it could be that any of the following have occurred:

- *Goods missing* – this could be because the supplier was out of stock, or it could have been an oversight on the part of the warehouse. The supplier would need to be contacted, as would the accounts or finance department of the purchasing business, so that they do not pay for what they have not received.

- *Extra goods* – any items that were not stated on the original order form but were listed on the goods received note should be returned to the supplier.

- *Incorrect goods* – any goods received that were incorrectly sent would have to be returned to the supplier.

- *Damaged or faulty goods* – the supplier would have to be notified immediately and replacement goods requested.

Invoices

Once the products have been delivered to the purchasing business, the supplier will send their invoice. This will list the quantity and description of the goods sent, as well as the total amount owing. The invoice will also state a date by which a payment should be made, and will list any discounts made available to the purchasing business. The purchasing business will check the invoice against the order form and the goods received to ensure that they all tally. They will check that the:

INDIVIDUAL WORK
(6.4) ★ ★ ★
1 Produce and save a
copy of your own
invoice, using Figure
6.5 as a guide.
2 Complete the invoice
for the goods you
ordered on your
order form in Activity
6.1. The additional
information you need
is:
• The invoice
number is 568.
• Use today's date for
the invoice.
• The terms are 10
per cent discount.
• The goods were
despatched two
days ago.
• VAT should be
calculated at 17.5
per cent.

- Order number is correct
- Goods listed match those delivered
- Quantity listed matches that delivered
- Price listed matches that quoted
- Calculations are correct
- Discounts are as agreed.

All invoices contain the term 'E&OE' at the bottom. This stands for 'errors and omission excepted' and helps to ensure that the supplier can send a further invoice if a mistake is found on the original one.

It is to the advantage of the supplier to send out the invoice promptly, so that payment is made as quickly as possible. How quickly the customer pays an invoice will depend on the terms under which it ordered the goods. It may want to take advantage of a prompt payment discount, or be entitled to a cash discount.

The VAT will have to be calculated on the invoice.

- VAT is charged on the goods and the delivery charge.
- VAT is added to the total price of the goods, less any discounts available.

```
┌─────────────────────────────────────────────────────────────────────┐
│                              INVOICE                                  │
├─────────────────────────────────────────────────────────────────────┤
│  To: _____      Invoice no. _____       │
│      _____      Date: _____       │
│      _____      Terms: _____       │
│                                                                       │
│  Your order no. _____     Despatch date: _____        │
├──────────┬──────────────────┬──────────────┬──────────────┬──────────┤
│ Quantity │ Description       │ Unit price   │ Total price  │ VAT      │
│          │                   │              │              │          │
│          │                   │              │              │          │
│          │                   │              │              │          │
│          │                   │              │              │          │
│          │                   ├──────────────┴──────────────┤          │
│          │                   │        Gross value          │          │
│          │                   │   Less trade discount       │          │
│          │                   │     Net value of goods      │          │
│          │                   │     Plus VAT @ ____%         │          │
│          │                   │        Invoice total        │          │
│ E&OE     │                   │                             │          │
└──────────┴───────────────────┴─────────────────────────────┴──────────┘
```

Figure 6.5
An example of an invoice

Payment advice

Once a month, often at the end of the month, the supplier will send a *statement of account* to each of its customers. This statement will list the transactions that have taken place between the two businesses. It will show the totals of each of the invoices sent to the customer, plus any payments made by the customer during the month. The balance shown at the end of the statement is the amount of money the customer owes the supplier.

Statements of account are a supplying business's advice to their customers that payment is now due and they are important to an organisation for two reasons:

- They keep a check of what a customer still owes.
- They keep a check of what is still owed by the business.

Very often, when a customer pays a supplier, they will do so by different methods, including:

- *Cheque* – these are more commonly used by smaller businesses.
- *BACS* – this is the Bankers Automated Clearing Service and is a system that allows a business to transfer its funds from their own account to another business, or an employee. When the funds leave the account of the customer they are automatically credited to the account of the supplier.
- *EDI* – this is Electronic Data Interchange and is a system that allows instant payment.
- *Credit transfer* – this allows the customer to issue a payment order to their bank, instructing it to transfer funds into the supplier's account.
- *Standing order or direct debit* – where the customer instructs its bank to pay a fixed amount to the supplier each month.

If payment is made to the supplier via an electronic method of payment, it is normal for the customer to send a *payment advice* to the supplier. This advice will notify them that funds have been transferred directly into their bank account.

INDIVIDUAL WORK
(6.5) ★ ★
Consider your order form and invoice prepared in two previous activities. If you were transferring funds to the bank account of the supplier of this order, what information would you need to give them on the payment advice? Why do you think it is necessary to give them this information?

Understanding the nature of different information sources

As we know, maintaining an efficient and accurate recording system of business activity is essential to all forms of businesses. Records are kept for four main reasons:

- *To fulfil statutory (legal) requirements* – laws are in force that require different types of businesses to keep records of their transactions for VAT and tax purposes, and information for investors, customers and employees.

- *To assist in future planning* – records are maintained to allow managers to make decisions on the basis of past experience.

- *To provide evidence of transactions* – in order to track all income and expenditure relating to a business's activities, including:
  - purchases made
  - sales made
  - dates of transactions
  - organisations and individuals with whom transactions have been made
  - payments received and pending
  - personnel records
  - stock levels
  - staff training and development
  - accurate minutes of meetings.

- *To monitor performance* – an organisation must attempt to identify any problems arising from its business activities and have in place a system that can highlight these.

To carry out all four of these crucial activities, a business will use a number of different information sources. The following headings highlight the sources of information.

Emails

Communication sent by email offers the benefit of being virtually paperless, but when the destination terminal is busy it can be stored and sent later. Larger organisations have their own network, which is known as an *intranet*. It is only accessible by the organisation's employees or those with the business's authority to use it. An *intranet* is like the internet, but it has a firewall that stops unauthorised users from accessing it. Businesses use the intranet to share information between users.

Email offers a variety of common features, including:

- Terminals to prepare and store messages.

- Communication links with other work stations within the network.

- A directory of addresses.

- A central mailbox.

- A system that dates the message.

- A function to note that the message has been received.

- A facility to multiple-address so that all members of a particular group are sent the message simultaneously.

- A prioritising system that identifies messages as important or routine.

- A storage facility that keeps in the memory those messages that have not yet been received.

- Rapid, paperless transmission.

Letters

In addition to the actual content of a letter, there is a wealth of information in any business letter. As we have seen, business letters have the organisation's full trading name, address, company registration number or charity number, contact details (telephone, fax and email) and may well also have the names of the directors of the business.

Letters from customers, even if they are letters of complaint, ca
information about the products or services being offered that may
considered by the business in the past. Since many businesses do ı
contact with their customers, even complaints are considered valı
information.

Minutes of meetings

As already mentioned in Unit 4, the minutes of a meeting should represent a true
account of what was discussed during the meeting. They recount any discussion topics,
any action to be taken on a specific area of discussion, which member of staff is to take
that action and by what date. Minutes also identify any motions that have been voted on.

Minutes of meetings, therefore, provide useful information for a number of people
within an organisation, or those from outside that have an interest in the activities of
the business and are authorised to receive a copy.

Drawings

Statistical diagrams and drawings can display complex information in a way that is easy
to understand. This makes them a powerful communication tool for many
departments in an organisation, including:

- The accounts department, who would be able to present information to the
  decision-makers in the form of graphs, charts and tables.
- The sales department, who would be able to present sales figures from a variety
  of different regions or representatives in the form of graphs, charts and tables.
- The marketing or research and development department, who could portray
  their vision of a new product, brand logo or design to the decision-makers of
  the business.
- The human resource department, who could recount complicated
  information about a large number of employees in this way.

This method of communicating information has some advantages over the spoken or
written word, including:

- Much more detail can be expressed.
- The audience is likely to be more interested in a drawing, chart or diagram,
  than in a long, complicated verbal or written explanation.
- The information, which is usually produced and stored on computer, can be
  easily updated should the need arise.
- Charts, diagrams and drawings can be printed or photocopied onto an
  overhead transparency sheet or displayed on a screen via computer, so that
  large numbers of individuals can be informed at one presentation.

Spreadsheets, budgets and projections

Businesses can gain vital information from the data they store on their spreadsheets.
They will use spreadsheet software, such as Excel, to forecast:

- The business's spending budget
- Details of each department's spending budget
- Production schedules
- Cash flow forecasts (see Unit 3).

Taken together, this budgeting and forecasting information can provide the
organisation with clear and unambiguous sets of figures on which to base their
forward planning.

Database records

Databases are based on the idea that a common pool of information can be organised
in such a way that all those using the system can be satisfied. Therefore, instead of each

department within a business keeping and maintaining its own set of files, they are grouped together to form a database. Such databases have advantages over traditional filing systems:

- There is no unnecessary duplication of information, which is more economical and is also more effective in keeping information up to date.
- There is less chance of inconsistency of information.
- Comprehensive information is more readily available.
- Any enquiries can be dealt with on demand, rather than going through the normally tedious process of obtaining files.

There are two main types of database system:

- *Centralised systems*, where all the processing of information is carried out by one computer. This central computer is responsible for processing the information, even though it may be linked to terminals. This means that each of the departments within a business may have their own terminal, but the information is stored by and retrieved from the central computer.
- *Distributing systems*, where the individual departments' terminals can carry out some of the information processing. These terminals have their own storage and retrieval programs, so information can be input and manipulated on them, rather than just on the central computer.

Database software, such as Microsoft Access, has the following features:

- Data can be stored in the form of records that either relate to one individual or to an item.
- The department setting up the database can decide what will be included.
- The information can be sorted in a variety of ways, including alphabetical, chronological and numerical order.
- Information can be extracted from the database as a list or records, an individual record, a group of records or one particular category of the records.
- The database information can be imported into Microsoft Word and included in other documents, such as a report.

Depending on the type of business and its main activities, information could be stored on a database in order to provide the business with some of the following information:

- The details of the business's customers
- The details of an organisation's members
- The details of a doctor's or dentist's patients
- The stock levels in a warehouse
- The business's supplier information.

Customers' sales histories and profiles

Another important source of information for a business is data about their customers' buying habits. A business will have a record of the frequency and amounts together with the types of products or services purchased by any of their customers. To begin with this information will be useful as the business might be able to predict how much, when and what the customer may purchase in the future.

Many businesses use a form of profiling when they investigate their customers' sales histories. They will rate particular customers, perhaps as frequent, regular, occasional or one-off customers. Each of these groups of customers will have their own particular characteristics. Perhaps the customers are businesses of a particular size of type. By profiling the key customer types, the business will be able to create targeted marketing messages to them in order to encourage the customers to buy more frequently or to inform them of new products or services being offered that may be of interest to them.

Address books

We already know that an email address book is a valuable source of information, but so too is the more traditional method of storing addresses. Regular contacts will be stored in alphabetical order and all relevant information can be obtained, for example, the business's main contact in another organisation, their company's main address, branch details, the contact's telephone extension number and email address.

INDIVIDUAL WORK
(6.6) ★ ★

Make a copy of this table and complete it by filling in the gaps.

Type of information entering a business	How the information is processed by the business	Type of information that may leave a business
Fax		
Telephone		
Email message		
Business letter	Filed in a filing cabinet	A reply or response in writing or via the telephone
Money from a customer		
Bill from a supplier		

Identifying and understanding methods of information communication

Businesses will try to use the most effective method of communication for transmitting messages, both to their employees and to those outside the business, such as customers and shareholders. The most appropriate method of communication depends on factors such as speed, cost, the need for feedback or the need for a written record.

Any form of communication involves an exchange between a sender and the receiver of that information. But the way in which a business is structured can also affect its channels of communication. It will very much depend *where* decisions are made. An organisation with many layers of management in its structure (a **hierarchical** structure), will have its decisions made at the top. An organisation with only two or three levels of staff is known as a *flat structure*. These businesses are usually quite small and all the staff will know one another. Another type of organisational structure is the *matrix structure*, which allows teams to be created to undertake particular tasks. This method allows individuals to be brought together and for communication to be straightforward.

Let us look at the different ways a business can communicate information. (Unit 4 Business Communication covers the verbal and written communication methods in much more detail.)

Keyword

hierarchical – a very formal type of organisation with various layers of managers and supervisors

Verbal communication

Verbal communication is also often referred to as the spoken word or oral communication. Businesses use verbal communication in a variety of ways on a daily basis. The different types of verbal communication are illustrated in Figure 6.6.

Document-based communication

Communication that involves the production of a document is also known as written communication. Figure 6.7 shows the main forms of written communication within most business organisations.

Some written communications are specifically internal, such as memos and notices that are placed on staff notice-boards. The remainder could be for both internal and external use.

Email messages, although sent electronically, can also be printed out so that a copy of the written communication can be stored in a conventional filing system if required.

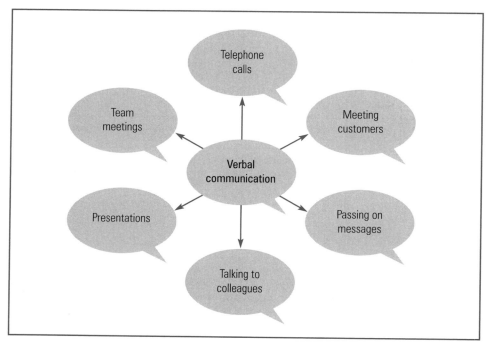

Figure 6.6
Types of verbal communication

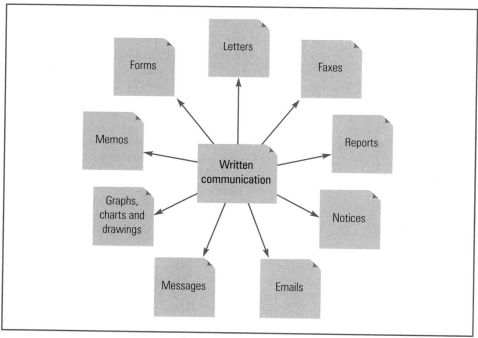

Figure 6.7
Types of written communication

Via EDI

Electronic data interchange (EDI) is a computer-to-computer exchange of business information. It enables electronic commerce (e-commerce) because businesses can exchange information much faster electronically and cheaper than using paper-based systems.

Research suggests that EDI will grow an average of 7.7 per cent per year until at least 2007. In 2001 alone the total value of products and services purchased worldwide was worth $1.8 trillion, compared with business-to-business e-commerce systems, which totalled $0.5 trillion. EDI has been around for 20 years and it is only recently that businesses are beginning to shift over from EDI to e-commerce. The problem is that businesses remain loyal to EDI because they know, understand and trust it. It may take some years before e-commerce systems catch up and then overtake EDI.

GROUP WORK (6.7)

★ ★

In pairs, suggest three advantages for a business using EDI.

Storage and retrieval

The safe and secure storage of information and the easy access or retrieval of that information is imperative if an organisation is to function successfully and efficiently.

The term 'storage and retrieval' can often be confusing when one has not worked in an office. In fact, they mean 'filing'. This word can also cause a reaction – often one of groans and moans! Filing is often thought to be boring and routine, and, in essence, it is. Nowadays, however, storage and retrieval also includes the computerised systems of storing and retrieving information.

Another word for filing is 'indexing'. Obviously filing involves a logical and effective way of recording documents and storing them in an efficient system, which will allow the easy retrieval of that information when required.

Filing is the basis of record-keeping and entails the processing, arranging and storing of the documents so that they can be found when they are required. The documents are placed in consecutive order and preserved in that system until they are required for reference. This can be carried out in any number of locations – a telephone directory is an index of alphabetical names and addresses. Your own address book is also a method of indexing in alphabetical order.

Paper-based filing systems

So what are the basic techniques required to ensure that the storage and retrieval of information and documents is efficient? Let us look at this in some detail by considering the following points that help you adopt good filing practice:

- Ensure that the papers which have been passed for filing have been marked in some way to indicate that they are ready for storing.
- Sort the papers into order so that they are grouped in the required way.
- Remove any paperclips and staple documents together – this will ensure that they do not get separated during the filing process.
- Each individual file should be in date order, with the most recent documents at the top or front.
- Be neat with the documents – curled edges can easily become torn.
- File daily if possible – this makes it less of a chore and also ensures that the files are up to date.
- Follow organisational procedure regarding 'out' or 'absent' cards. These are cards that are inserted into a file if the paperwork contained in the file has been removed by a member of staff. The card will indicate who has the file, when they took it and when they should return it to the filing cabinet.
- Follow up all overdue files regularly when they have been borrowed by another member of staff or department and not returned them on time.
- Use a cross-reference system whenever a file is known by more than one name. It is often necessary to update files, for example when an organisation changes its name, or when a personnel file changes name because the member of staff marries. This could cause confusion as some people may still refer to the file, or look for it, under the old name. For this reason, a system has to be in place which enables the person searching to find it without too much difficulty. The cross-reference slip would be placed either in the old or in the new file, directing the person seeking the file to the correct place.

◆ Thin out the files when necessary. There will be an organisational procedure regarding the length of time documents are held in the system. When they become obsolete or out of date they may be transferred to the archives. This is an additional storage area where files are stored in boxes in case they are required for reference. The archives could be in another room or even in another building. We look at archiving in more detail later in this unit.

◆ Be aware of health and safety regarding filing cabinets. For example, always close drawers after you have used them, and lock drawers and cabinets before leaving the office at night.

◆ Always ask for help if you are unsure where something should be filed, and do not be afraid to offer ideas if you think the system could be more efficient with some improvements.

The alphabetical method is the filing of documents according to the first letter of the surname. It is the most common method of classification used in businesses. This is normally the first letter of the surname of the correspondent. In a human resource department, files could be arranged in alphabetical order, determined by the first letter of the surname of the member of staff.

Some rules for alphabetical filing include:

◆ Take the first letter of the surname and then each letter after that, for example:

Black, Brian
Blake, John
Blakemore, Margaret.

◆ If the surname is the same, place the first name or initial in alphabetical order, for example:

Smith, David
Smith, John
Smith, William.

◆ If the surname and the first name are the same, file by second name or initial, for example:

Jones, Brian A
Jones, Brian D
Jones, Brian P.

◆ Treat surname prefixes as part of the name and all names beginning with M', Mc or Mac as if they were spelt with Mac, for example:

McBride, Angus
McGregor, William
MacMasters, Peter.

◆ File all 'saint' surnames beginning with St as if they were spelt 'Saint', for example:

St John, Ian
St Luke's Church
St Mary's Hospital.

◆ Ignore titles, for example:

Brown, Sir Andrew
Grey, Lady Jane
Simpson, Major David.

◆ Ignore words like 'The' and 'A' in the name of an organisation, for example:

Card Shop, The
Office Equipment Centre, The
Tea Shoppe, The.

◆ Numbers should be filed as if spelt in full, for example:

55 Club, The (would be filed under 'f' for 'fifty')
99 Boutique, The (would be filed under 'n' for 'ninety')
111 Association, The (would be filed under 'o' for 'one').

INDIVIDUAL WORK
(6.8) ★ ★
Place the following list of names in alphabetical order:

Hutchinson, David
Conway, Malcolm
Hunt, Peter
Woodhouse, John
Jackson, Nick
Sutherland, Joshua
Hewitt, Ernest William
Hewitt, Diane Elizabeth
Canwell, Stuart
Canwell, Alun
Hurle, Peter
Aliffe, Burt
Smith, Marie
Smith, Delphine
Wright, Susan
Canwell, Rosie
Greene, Susan
Green, Samantha
Leggett, Michael

A quick way of putting a list into alphabetical order is to put them into numerical order first, by writing the number of the position the entry will be in an alphabetical list next to the relevant entry, and then writing the list out again in numerical order.

The numeric classification method of filing is linked by means of index cards to the alphabetic method we have just looked at. Each document or folder is given a number and these are filed in number order. The information contained within the files is sorted into alphabetical order. The index cards contain the number of each document or folder and a summary of what is contained in that document or folder. They are also filed numerically. The index cards act as a short-cut method to finding information, rather than looking through whole files for specific information, such as contact names for a company.

Chronological filing means that documents are stored according to the date, again with the most recent date being at the front or top of the file. Travel agents are likely to use this classification method of filing, as they receive travel documents for their customers. The documents would be filed in date order, either of the customer's departure date, or of the required payment dates. A sales representative might also use the chronological system of filing paperwork according to the dates they have arranged meetings with customers.

Too many files in the filing system can be a waste of valuable space and a waste of paper. There are some organisations, however, that have no option but to create a new file for each new name that is encountered, for example hospitals, doctors and dentists have to have all the information about individual patients in one file.

The term 'archiving' means storing away old files in another location, for example another room, cupboard, storage area or another building belonging to the business. Archiving does not mean throwing away. Old files might only be temporarily old. They may be needed again in the future and only need to be archived until they become current again.

There will be procedures in place that have to be followed, mainly because someone with authority will have to decide when a file becomes an old file. An file could be an old file if, for example, the information in it:

- Relates to a previous customer or business the organisation used to deal with
- Relates to an employee who has now left the business
- Is now out-of-date information.

On a regular basis, the timing of which will be set down in the organisation's procedures, someone will go through the filing cabinets to take out those that need to be placed in the archive area. A note will be placed in the filing cabinet to identify the fact that the file has been transferred to the archive, just in case someone looks for the file in the future.

Obviously, the main purpose of filing paperwork away is being able to find it again when it is needed, either by yourself or by someone else. Being able to find the right information from a filing system is known as retrieving information and this would be done to:

- Add more information to the contents of the file
- Obtain some information from the contents of the file.

If someone takes individual documents from a file, they may go missing forever. You should never allow just one or two pages to be taken from a file unless:

- Most of the information contained in the file is confidential and the person needing the one or two documents cannot see the rest of the confidential information.
- The information contained in the file is much too large to take away.

There are some golden rules for making sure that information from a file does not get lost or refiled in the wrong place:

- Record the fact that information has been taken from the filing cabinet by inserting an 'out' or 'absent' card in its place.
- Use a log sheet to record the fact that the file has been borrowed, who took it and when they took it, where they have taken it to and when they have agreed to return it.
- Keep information on the log sheet up to date and chase up any files that are not returned when they were agreed to be returned.

Databases and directories

All information stored on computer must also be protected. Organisations are more likely nowadays to use this method of filing their records because it is easier to store and retrieve documents. They must ensure that:

- Back-up copies of documents are made and stored safely.
- Passwords are used by the staff using the computer, and these should be changed regularly.
- User codes are used if necessary. Only those who are authorised to access the information know these codes, and they often only relate to specific files or documents stored.

It is important that information stored on a computer system (known as data) is organised correctly so that vital details can be found quickly and used by the managers of the business straightaway. Many businesses have chosen a specific data-handling system because it has a number of different facilities that are useful to their own particular range of activities. However, the use of computerised systems has its own set of advantages and disadvantages.

The business will have chosen their system for the preparation, storage and retrieval of data for a number of different reasons. They will then train the employees who will be using this equipment and software so that they are aware of the importance of:

- *Accuracy and checking* Given the fact that any computerised system is only as accurate as the data it receives, there is always the possibility that the information is inaccurate as a result of human error. Obviously, more sophisticated data-handling systems will have a series of checks and double-checks to identify potential errors. Accuracy is of paramount importance if the organisation is to rely upon the system, especially given that many decisions will be made on the basis of the information that it handles.
- *Cost* Most organisations will use data-handling systems in order to cut costs. Bearing in mind that there will be significant costs related to the initial buying and setting up of the system, there needs to be a point at which the data-handling system gives good value for money to the organisation. This can be measured in terms of either the time that can be saved in using the system or the reduction in the number of employees. At other times, cost-cutting benefits could also include the fact that sales are not lost, products are always in stock, or employees are paid the correct amount of salary. The more time that can be saved by not having to repeat tasks or sort out problems, the more money that will be saved.

INDIVIDUAL WORK
(6.11) ★ ★
We have now looked in some detail at the ways in which businesses can store their information, paper-based and electronic, and retrieve it at the right time, by the right person.

Compile two tables, one for paper-based storage and retrieval and the other for computer-based storage and retrieval. Each table should have two columns headed 'Advantages' and 'Disadvantages'. Complete the table with your thoughts about the two methods. Which method has the most advantages?

Speed and accessibility In most cases, the use of data-handling systems means that information can be processed much faster than it could using a manual system. Provided they can rely on the system, employees are free to concentrate on other areas of the business's activities, for example customer service issues or the development of a new product or service. Many organisations have to operate within very strict deadlines, particularly in the banking industry where many millions of financial transactions have to be processed on the same day.

Understanding how administrative systems provide precise and timely information for management decision-making

Senior management decision-makers need to have constant access to up-to-date and accurate information that can assist them in controlling and directing the business. There are three key areas of a business, common to most businesses, which are responsible for implementing administrative systems that capture this data. The following headings give more detail about these three key areas.

Sales figures

The sales and marketing department of a business is responsible for keeping accurate figures on sales achieved. For many businesses this is what is known as the bottom line. In other words, the value of the sales accomplished by a business ultimately determines how much profit it will make. The sales department will, as we have seen in Unit 3, have budgets. These are targets that they are expected to meet and exceed.

One of the first things that the organisation requires is a measure of how sales figures compare to budgeted sales targets. This will show how the business is performing.

Sales figures can be complex as they can include any of the following:

- Actual sales made where payment has already been received.
- Sales that have been made but the money has not been received as the customer has been given credit terms.
- Expected sales based on conversations with customers and expected future orders.

Depending upon the type of business, there are a number of different ways in which sales data can be captured and then added together to give total sales figures for the day, month or week. These include:

- Cash register totals
- Invoices paid, cross-referenced to cheques and other payments received
- Invoices sent out but not yet paid.

INDIVIDUAL WORK
(6.12) ★ ★
Adam Reynolds runs a small DIY business. He has cash-paying customers and also deals with the building trade. At the end of the day, he totals the amount in his cash register and discovers that he has £456 in cheques, £383 in credit and debit card payments and £108 in cash. Two of his customers have also come in and paid invoices totalling £804. Adam has also sent out six invoices that are not due for 30 days for a total of £2,284. How much money has Adam actually made today?

Profit statements

The accounts department of a business prepares profit statements. A profit statement is calculated by subtracting the total costs of the business from its total revenue. This means that the accounts department needs to have access to all information regarding revenues and costs. An accounts department can create this profit statement at any point, but usually at the end of a month, quarter (every three months) or the end of the financial year.

The profit statement provides a snapshot of how well the business is performing. It can be used to compare the amount of profit being made with that being made at the same time the previous year. It gives the business's decision-makers an opportunity to see how well the business is performing and whether they need to make adjustments to improve the level of profit.

Collecting together the necessary paperwork to create a profit statement is a complex task. It requires the accounts department to have access to all invoices, a log of payments made to the business, purchase order forms and any other documentation relating to income or expenditure of the business. Assuming that the accounts department can assemble or be given this information, then they will first create what is known as a balance sheet. This shows the total income and expenditure of the business, along with any assets the business may own. From this, they can work out how much profit (or loss) the business has made.

INDIVIDUAL WORK
(6.13) ★ ★

Adam has just worked out his total revenues and costs for the month. His total sales figures were £20,500. It cost him £8,400 to buy the products he has sold to his customers. In addition his rent and rates for his shop have cost him £1,400. His telephone bills and various other costs amounted to £306. He pays himself £2,000 per month and his wage bill for Arthur, the only other person that works for him, was £804 for the month. What was Adam's total profit before tax for the business?

Staff turnover rates

In the course of a month or a year, a business may lose a number of members of staff, for various reasons. They may also take on a number of new members of staff. Staff turnover measures the number of staff leaving and joining the business in a given period of time.

The human resource department, or personnel, would be responsible for maintaining these figures. They will know exactly how many employees work for the business, how many have left and how many have joined.

Staff turnover is an important measure of how satisfied employees are with a whole range of issues surrounding their work. Employees can leave for a huge number of reasons, including being offered better employment elsewhere, feeling under-valued, feeling over-worked or believing that they are not being paid enough money. Employees can also leave because of serious problems at work, perhaps they have been given warnings for being late and, in some extreme cases, they may have been sacked.

It is the human resource department's responsibility to note how many employees have left, and why, and then, of course, to replace them.

Staff turnover is usually shown as a percentage. If, for example, a business has 20 employees and five leave over a period of time, they would have a staff turnover of 25 per cent. If, however, a business had 100 employees and half of them left in a year, they would have a staff turnover of 50 per cent.

Businesses try to keep their staff turnover down to the barest minimum as they know that experienced employees are valuable to them and that it is often difficult to find suitable replacements.

The business's decision-makers will use staff turnover figures as a measure of how well the business manages and values its employees. Key employees will need to be rewarded and persuaded to remain with the business and the decision-makers may opt to increase their wages or benefits if they fear that staff turnover is too high.

Understanding the need for information security

There are many pieces of confidential information contained within different files. These may include:

- Personal information about employees, which would be filed in the human resource department or the accounts and finance department.
- Financial information about the business or department in which you work.
- The plans of the department in which you work or the business as a whole.
- Customer information, such as names, addresses, or the amount of money they spend with your department or business.

As we have discussed elsewhere, confidential information must be kept secret and secure. If filing cabinets contain confidential information you must make sure that:

- The files are never left unattended on a desk.
- The files are never taken into any areas of the business that are not involved in the information contained in the folders.
- The contents of the files are never discussed with others from the business or outside of the business.
- The files are never lent to anyone who does not have permission to access to them.
- The filing cabinet drawers are locked and the keys kept safely.
- The old files remain confidential when they go to the archives.

Any unwanted files should be shredded rather than placed in wastepaper baskets or recycled.

Personnel records

The main function of the human resource department is to recruit the new employees and organise them so that they perform the roles that the organisation needs to meet its objectives. The human resource department is also sometimes known as the personnel department.

They closely monitor the selection of new employees. But this is not the end of the function of the human resource department. They also try to ensure that suitable employees are trained and developed adequately and, if particular employees are suitable, they also try to ensure that they are given more responsible and often better-paid jobs (promotion) within the business.

Close contact is kept with all the other departments of the business to make sure that the employees are receiving the right kind of training by organising:

- The induction of new employees – telling them about the organisation when they first start.
- Training – perhaps to include how to use new technology.
- Retraining – perhaps when an employee's job has been moved from one department to another.

The human resource department is also responsible for keeping all employee records, including details of:

- Holiday entitlements – amount of holiday already taken and the number of days the employee has left to take.
- Sickness records – the number of days the employee has taken off due to illness.
- Qualifications of each employee.
- Experience of each employee, both before joining the business and whilst working for the business.
- Wage or salary of each employee.
- Pension details for each employee.
- Confidential reports from the employees' line managers or supervisors.
- Details of the training each employee has undertaken.

All confidential information of this kind has to be carefully stored by law. The Data Protection Act 1998 lays down rules for human resource departments as to who can see such information and the way in which it is kept by the business.

The human resource department is also the main negotiator on behalf of the business in matters relating to trade unions and employee associations. They negotiate about general problems, for example regarding pay and the working conditions of employees.

When an employee leaves an organisation this is known as termination of employment. The human resource department is also involved in this procedure and

they ensure that the employee receives all relevant documents relating to the way in which they are leaving. Employees could leave an organisation for a number of different reasons, including:

- ◈ Retirement – when they have reached the age where they are entitled to receive a pension and wish to give up working.
- ◈ Redundancy – when the business has decided that the employee's job is no longer required and they are not required in another department of the organisation.
- ◈ New job – when employees simply decide to move on to another business.
- ◈ Dismissal – when the employee has behaved in a way that is not acceptable to the business and is asked to leave.

Financial performance reports

Because a business's competitors would be very interested to find out about how well, or otherwise, a business is performing financially, it is vital that all work carried out within the business's accounts department is kept confidential. A leak outside the business, or often to other departments of the business itself, could prove to have a drastic effect on the business's ability to be competitive.

The finance or accounts department of an organisation supervises all matters involving money. Computers and calculators are used extensively. Sometimes the finance department is split up into two further sections:

- ◈ The financial accounting section handles the day-to-day accounting procedures. They keep track of all money coming into the business and all money going out of the business.
- ◈ The management accounting section concentrates on analysing the financial figures and trying to predict, or forecast, how much the business will earn, and how much the business will have to pay out, in the future.

The finance department will record and monitor:

- ◈ Sales of the business's products or services.
- ◈ Purchases the business has made to make their products or provide their services.
- ◈ Manufacturing costs – how much it is costing the business to make their products.
- ◈ Running costs – how much it is costing the business to keep running, for example their lighting and heating bills.
- ◈ Dividends to shareholders – how much the business is paying those people who have bought shares (private limited companies and public limited companies).
- ◈ Wages and salaries – how much the business is paying its employees.
- ◈ Departmental and organisational budgets – how much each department is spending and how much the whole organisation is spending. A budget is often worked out for each separate department. In order to stick to their budget, the department would have to provide the finance department with details of what they have earned, what they have spent and on what it has been spent.

The finance department would use this information to find out whether or not the business is making a profit. They check that the business's revenue is greater than the costs.

The directors, shareholders and senior managers of the business need the information the finance department calculates. The finance department gives this information to them in written documents, including balance sheets and profit and loss accounts. By law, the finance department has to keep written records of all financial decisions taken by the business, including records of all sales made and items purchased.

New product designs and competitor analyses
Working closely with the marketing department, which is k
business's competitors' products and services, the researc
department would attempt to come up with new products

The main function of the research and development de
up with new products or services. It also has to come up w
effective way of producing them. It will, after carrying out
designs and proposed ways of producing the product to t'
The production department will then take over the responsibility of putting the
product into production.

On a routine basis, the research and development department will test samples of
the products being manufactured to ensure that they are of a high enough quality to
meet the standards set by the business. They also have to meet the different quality
standards set down by the government.

The research and development department will also test the products of the
business's competitors. They will do this to find out how they have been manufactured
and whether the business's products compare favourably to them. They will also keep
a close eye on any new technologies that become available to see if these would
improve the business's design and production processes.

INDIVIDUAL WORK
(6.14) ★ ★

You work for a business that is about to move offices and have been asked to sort out
and distribute archived files stored in a cupboard. Where would you send the
following documents and folders?

a) The attendance record and pay details of Susan Dodd, who left the business eight
years ago

b) The projected sales figures and actual sales figures of three products that are no
longer offered by the business

c) Some concept drawings for a product that was researched and developed 10 years
ago

d) A folder containing information about three major competitors in your local area.

THREATS TO ADMINISTRATIVE EFFECTIVENESS

Poor communication is a threat to administrative effectiveness. There are a number of
reasons why communication fails to be effective. Some of them will not be obvious
until a problem occurs, but most will have an effect on administrative effectiveness.
Some of the problems are avoidable if the communication methods are thought
through properly. In other cases the problem will remain until something dramatic is
done to improve it.

Barriers to communication are problems between the sender and the receiver of
the information. In other words, a block of some sort exists which stops the message
getting through or stops it getting through in the intended way. Some common
barriers to communication are:

- *Lack of training* If employees are not trained to use the different ways of
communicating, then they will either make mistakes or not be able to use that
form of communication at all. Training in the use of equipment and the ways in
which communications should be written or spoken are essential. These forms of
training and ways of doing things will often be part of organisational procedures.

- *Lack of information* One of the most common barriers to communication is not
having all the information that you need to make a decision or to help someone
make a decision. If, for example, a customer called a business and asked for the
price and availability of a product and was told that it was out of stock, a sale would
be lost. If the employee who had taken the call had known that the warehouse had
just received a delivery of that product, then the sale would have been made.

💧 *Personal relationships* One of the most common reasons why communications are ineffective within an organisation is that individuals either do not like one another or do not understand one another. Personal likes or dislikes may mean that employees will avoid one another, even if this means that information is not passed on between them and has a bad effect on both their own work and the business itself. This is a very difficult barrier to deal with but may be solved by either getting to the root of the problem between the two individuals or changing the job role of one of them so that they do not have direct contact with one another. An alternative to this is for the business to attempt to help them to get along better by giving them some team-building training.

💧 *Faulty systems* There may be a problem with the organisational procedures and something in the process has been forgotten which causes a barrier. Perhaps one part of the whole process of dealing with an order has not been considered and this causes a blockage and prevents the customer receiving the product or service.

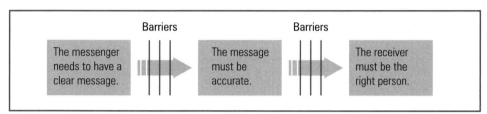

Figure 6.8
Barriers to communication

Barriers to good communication might include:

💧 Writing something down incorrectly

💧 Not hearing the customer's request correctly

💧 Losing important notes or documents

💧 Not telling the right person about a problem

💧 Having too many other things to do

💧 Not realising the importance of the query.

Identifying and understanding administrative errors

Inaccuracies and discontinuities
Administrative errors can take a number of different forms, including:

💧 A cheque sent for the wrong amount of money

💧 A file placed in the wrong place in the filing cabinet

💧 A letter sent to the wrong person

💧 An invoice completed incorrectly

💧 A computer fault that stops an email message being received

💧 A diary entry being forgotten

💧 Work being copied inaccurately

💧 The agenda of a meeting not being sent to all involved.

GROUP WORK (6.15)

We have given you eight possible administrative errors, how many more can you think of? This should be easy as there are lots of things that can go wrong.

Checking, correction and prevention
It is vital that organisations have efficient and effective procedures to ensure that errors and inaccuracies do not creep into their administrative systems. They need to collect, store and distribute huge numbers of documents, and there is little point in doing any of

this if the documents are incomplete, inaccurate, illegible, unchecked or unreliable. There are five key reasons why there may be problems with documents. These are:

- *Document completion* This may seem very obvious, but a document needs to be completed. A bank will not accept a cheque, for example, that is not signed. An incomplete invoice or order form will cause problems for those who have to deal with it.

- *Accuracy* Documents must be completed accurately. One incorrect figure or word could cause problems. Addresses, for example, need to be accurate, otherwise post can go astray. Many organisations keep duplicate, or even triplicate, copies of documents in order to check back to see whether they were filled in correctly.

- *Neatness* Everyone thinks that their handwriting is perfectly legible, but this is not always the case. Business needs to ensure that someone else can actually read any handwriting on documents. In Europe, for example, they put a line across their 7s to make sure that it is completely different from the number 1.

- *Checking* All documents need to be checked before they are circulated. The person completing the documents should normally do this. The problem is that it is difficult to see one's own mistakes, so it is a good idea to get another person to check the work.

- *Reliability* As we have already seen, many organisations produce their documents in duplicate or triplicate. This means that there will be several copies of the same document circulating around the organisation. It is highly likely that some areas of the business may not check the accuracy and reliability of the document and rely on information from it, so it needs to be accurate, correct and reliable.

INDIVIDUAL WORK
(6.16) ★ ★
Think of as many things as you can that could be inaccurate or incomplete on a cheque. How many different things does a person have to write on a cheque in order to make it valid and acceptable by a bank?

Importance of related legislation: Data Protection Act 1984 and 1998

Since 1984, the Data Protection Act has offered some protection for the individual whose details may be held on the computer of any organisation. In 1998 the Act was revised to incorporate the European Union Directive that stated: 'any person, organisation or business wishing to hold personal information about people, must register with the Office of the Data Protection Commissioner'.

The amount of information held on computers about each individual person is growing because of the increasing use of computers to store information. Under the Data Protection Act 1998, everyone has a right to see information about themselves that an organisation holds on their databases.

Those companies that keep information about individuals must register with the Data Protection Commissioner. It is possible to see a list of all the companies who have registered in any major public library.

The register will have information on:

- The type of information the company holds
- The purpose for which it is used
- Where the information came from
- Who might be able to see this information.

All sorts of businesses might hold information about people, including:

- An insurance company may have information about people's health and lifestyles.

- A motor insurance company will have information about drivers' records in relation to accidents, traffic offences and the kind of car that each individual drives.

- A supermarket that has a loyalty scheme may have a great deal of information about individuals' buying habits and how much is being spent in a given period of time.

💧 A credit card company will also have a lot of information about people's buying habits and their attitude to credit.

💧 A health centre will have a great deal of information about its patients' health and lifestyles.

The information contained could be very valuable to some businesses. It could also seriously damage the reputation of an individual if the information is inaccurate or if some information falls into the wrong hands.

It is possible to find out what data is being held. To do this it would be necessary to:

💧 Ask the Data Protection Commissioner for a list of businesses that hold data about individuals.

💧 Write directly to the business to ask them to send details of the information that is held.

💧 Wait to receive a copy of any information held.

The Data Protection Act 1998 gives the individual the right to know what information is held about them. It also provides those businesses that hold information with a set of data protection principles that control how information can be stored and used. These principles are:

💧 Obtain and process the information fairly and lawfully and for clearly specified purposes.

💧 Hold only the information that is adequate, relevant and not excessive for the purpose it is held.

💧 All information held must be accurate and up to date.

💧 Only keep the information as long as it is required.

💧 Do not use or disclose the information in any way that is different from its original purpose.

💧 Give individuals access to information about themselves and, where appropriate, correct or erase the information.

💧 Take appropriate measures to ensure data is secure against loss, damage or unauthorised and unlawful processing.

💧 Do not transfer data to countries that are outside the jurisdiction of the EU.

If a company is found to be in breach of these principles, action can be taken against them.

Data can be used in certain circumstances, such as:

💧 Preventing or detecting crime and catching or prosecuting criminals

💧 For the assessment and collection of taxes due to the government

💧 Health education and social security matters

💧 Household, personal and family matters.

> **INDIVIDUAL WORK**
> **(6.17)** ⭐
> Visit the website of the Data Protection Commission at www.dataprotection. gov.uk. Find out what kind of information can be obtained.

Major threats to the integrity of an administrative system

It is not just employee error that can have an impact on the effectiveness of administrative processes. As we will see in this section, numerous threats can come from outside the business and others are unavoidable problems that have to be planned for even if their occurrence is unlikely.

Fire, vandalism and malicious damage

Fire can threaten an entire business and can, as a result of an electrical failure inside the business or a deliberate attempt to burn the premises, destroy all records. Many businesses store their archive material off-premises, but this does not protect the ongoing records, particularly paper documents and information that may be stored on computers. This is why, particularly with electronic documents, backing-up or copying systems should be put in place, as we will see later in this section.

The business may be the victim of a break-in and, whilst the business runs the risk of items of equipment and property being stolen, the vandals may choose to smash up computers and other equipment. Again backing-up information, together with a more elaborate security system, can prevent this from being quite so disastrous.

Malicious damage is a deliberate act of vandalism to destroy something that belongs to the business. This could be an act carried out by an employee or a former employee, or perhaps a complete stranger to the business.

Software viruses

A virus is a computer program that tries to reproduce by attaching itself to other software programs (hence the name 'virus'). When a program is run that is infected by a virus, the virus is also activated and has an opportunity to damage data or to spread. Some viruses deliberately cause damage to data.

Viruses can spread via hard disks, floppy disks, and shared folders accessed across a network. Typical viruses include:

- *Boot sector viruses* Rather than infecting computer programs, these viruses infect special hidden system areas of disks known as the boot sector or the partition sector. They are transferred from PC to PC on floppy disk.

- *Macro viruses* infect files, but files normally considered to be data files rather than software. A macro virus or logic bomb may be present in a Word-for-Windows document (DOC file), template (DOT file) or Excel spreadsheets (XLS file). These files may contain 'autoexec macros'; that is, a sequence of instructions that are run automatically when the document or spreadsheet is opened. The macro may be designed to cause damage and to infect other documents, templates or spreadsheets.

- *Trojans* are malicious computer programs that pretend to be some other beneficial computer program, such as a game or useful utility. They rely on people being tricked into running them. When a Trojan is run it may appear to do nothing, or do what it claims to, but at the same time it is secretly doing something else such as deleting your data files or compromising the security of your computer.

- *Back-door programs* are a type of Trojan that, if the user is tricked into running them on their computer, will open up a 'back door' that will give anyone else on the internet complete control over your computer. They can copy, delete and change files, obtain passwords and capture keystrokes as the user uses their computer on the internet.

- *Worms* spread automatically by exploiting security vulnerabilities. Once released, a worm spreads automatically from one vulnerable system to another.

Some worms or viruses spread by email. If an email is just plain text there is no way that the act of reading a plain email message can cause a computer to become infected with a virus. However an email may be infected if it is sent in HTML (like a web page, with formatting) or if there is an attachment with the message. Attachments can be programs containing Trojans, software viruses or documents containing macro viruses. The computer will be infected when the user opens or views the infected email attachment or HTML message. The ILOVEYOU virus was an example of a virus spread in an attachment. The attachment was disguised so that it looked like a harmless text file, but was actually a virus that ran when you double clicked on it.

Virus hoaxes circulate widely by email. These are messages purporting to warn the user about a virus that spreads through email and urges them to pass the message on to everyone you know. They are often dressed up with impressive-sounding technical nonsense to make the victim believe the message. In general, be suspicious of emails that suggest the user should pass them on to everyone they know – they are nearly always junk chain letters.

Hardware failure

Hardware failure is rare and it cannot be predicted or avoided. The aim of the business that suffers a hardware failure is to detect and resolve it quickly to ensure that their operations are not disrupted. Data is exposed when there are hardware failures. The most common are computer or disk crashes. Random failures may take place, such as a cup of coffee being dropped onto a computer.

CASE STUDY **NHS communications disrupted by hardware failure**

The NHS Information Authority and the national programme for IT suffered a 'major hardware failure' that caused 'server disruption in communications' in September 2003.

The organisations are responsible for the government's £2.3 billion investment in NHS IT. The failure was revealed in NHSIA board minutes. The disruption took place on 1 and 2 September, and affected 600 staff working for the NHSIA and the national programme for IT.

A spokeswoman for the NHSIA said the majority of incoming e-mails received during this time were fully recovered. 'A proportion of NHSIA and national programme for IT staff have alternative e-mail facilities so the impact, although serious, was not catastrophic,' she said.

The incident occurred following a single hard-disc failure on one of the NHSIA's two Exchange servers, which was followed by failures in a second hard-disc, motherboard SCSI card, a SCSI cable and a tape back-up drive. The NHSIA has since added two back-up servers as a safeguard against future disruption to its e-mail system.

GROUP WORK (6.18) ★ ★

Has your school or college suffered from a hardware failure? What happened and was the data backed up? Discuss the implications to your school or college if this did occur.

Hacking

A hacker is a computer programmer who enjoys exploring computer systems. Hackers consider the security on business computer systems to be a challenge and will use any means to break into those systems. In some cases, hackers only wish to prove that they can break into a system, whilst others search for secret information or try to erase the data on a business's computer system.

A *firewall* is a program or piece of hardware that checks information coming into the computer through an internet connection. If the information does not pass routine checks, then it will not be allowed through the computer. Firewalls filter and analyse data that could cause damage to the computer. Firewalls also prevent hackers from gaining access to data stored on a computer system.

Setting up appropriate security measures

Contingency, back-up storage, retrieval procedures and facilities

Many businesses use tape back-ups to protect their data. Tape back-up is low cost and reliable, but the data on the tape is only as useful as the last time it was backed up, so the back-up procedure needs to be a regular process. In large organisations, it is impractical to back up large amounts of data all the time. As an alternative, businesses may locate their servers, which are their main computers, in another location and perhaps have a second set of servers that automatically back up from the first set of servers. This is usually adequate if there are individual hardware failures, but it still leaves the data exposed as the only safe copy of the data is on one of the servers.

Increasingly businesses use a form of real-time back-up. This sends data to an external server run by a service provider. In the worst case scenario, if all of the businesses systems break down due to hardware failure, then all of the information that had been stored or was ongoing when the failure happened would be saved on the service providers' back-up systems.

CASE STUDY Data disaster

The majority of data disasters are fairly straightforward, including corrupted disks, faulty back-up, human error, power cuts, fire, flooding and theft. Human error is still responsible for most data losses. In fact, humans cause 30 per cent of data loss by accidentally deleting files, failing to back up data or maliciously destroying data. Many businesses do not have a disaster recovery plan and of those that do, only 25 per cent of them ever bother to test them. Many business advisors recommend that businesses take their data storage and back-up more seriously and that businesses need to be educated about disaster recovery solutions. This area of IT looks to be one of the major growth areas in coming years. With 80 per cent of all disasters caused by people or process failures, the remaining 20 per cent result from technological or environmental failures.

INDIVIDUAL WORK
(6.19) ★ ★ ★
Employees have access to a great deal of sensitive data and computing power on their desktops, so expensive mistakes are often inevitable. Suggest three ways in which a business could recommend to its employees better measures for protecting the business's data.

SIMPLE ADMINISTRATIVE SYSTEMS

Much of the information for this section of the unit has already been considered either earlier in this unit or in Unit 3 Business Communications. The IVA for this unit requires you to describe and/or recommend a simple administrative system for a small business. The focus, therefore, of this part of the unit is practical. Where appropriate, you will find additional information about areas not already covered, such as travel arrangements, maintaining diaries and using the internet for research.

Key information flows

As we have seen, many parts of an organisation are interrelated and they rely upon one another to pass on, process, action, store and retrieve information. We have also seen that many businesses use paper documents, whilst others have made the shift, at least in part, to electronic documentation. Regardless of whether it is paper or electronic-based, the communication channels between the different parts of the organisation still need to be maintained and vital information needs to be stored safely and retrieved when required. This means that different parts of the organisation will be responsible for generating documentation, processing that information, acting on that information and then storing it so that it can be retrieved as needed at some point in the future.

Communication channels and storage and retrieval facilities

INDIVIDUAL WORK
(6.20) ★ ★ ★

Bermuda IT Systems Ltd is a small business that provides computer systems to other businesses.

- Pamela runs the sales department. She receives orders from customers, which she copies and sends to Clive. She then creates an invoice, which she sends to the customer and copies to Hamish, who runs accounts.
- Clive, when he receives a copy of the order, prepares a delivery note, which he places on the goods to be despatched. When they have left the warehouse for delivery to the customer, Clive sends a copy of the delivery note to Hamish and one to Pamela to confirm that the delivery has been made.
- Hamish, after having matched up the invoice and the delivery note, adds this to the customer account and every month sends out a statement to the customers, and if necessary a reminder note for payment.
- Pamela stores copies of customer orders, invoices and delivery notes from Clive.
- Clive stores orders matched with delivery notes.
- Hamish stores invoices, delivery notes, customer account details, statements of account and reminder notices.

1 Draw up a simple chart showing the movement of documents around the business.

2 How might the business be able to cut back on its storage of their paper-based documents?

3 How might they make retrieval of the documents more effective?

Monitoring systems and customer queries

INDIVIDUAL WORK
(6.21) ★ ★

At Bermuda IT Systems Ltd, Pamela in the sales department runs what she calls a three in-tray system to deal with correspondence and customer queries. She has labelled up three in-trays: one is marked 'Immediate', the second 'This week' and the third 'Sometime'. When she receives a telephone call, letter, fax or email (which she prints out), the correspondence is placed in one of the trays. She throws the junk mail away. Important correspondence or queries are placed in 'Immediate'. Correspondence and queries that can wait for a day or two are put in 'This week'. Everything else goes into the 'Sometime' tray.

It is Monday morning and as usual Pamela has a pile of mail. She will place all the junk mail into her other system, known as 'bin'.

1 Where should she put the following correspondence and queries?

   a) An email marked 'Urgent' from a customer that wants her to ring before lunch

   b) A catalogue sent to her by a computer supplier that she has not heard of before

   c) A returned letter containing one of her own invoices, marked 'Address not found'

   d) A jiffy bag with three printer cartridges and a note from a customer saying they are the wrong cartridges

   e) A letter asking for a copy of Bermuda's catalogue to be sent

   f) A letter from a sales rep telling her that he will be in the area at the end of the month and would like to visit her

   g) A statement of account from a supplier

   h) A poster and calendar from a supplier.

2 What do you think Pamela's actions should be with each item of the correspondence?

Organising routine travel arrangements

Before any travel arrangements can be prepared, you need to find out whether the person travelling has any particular requirements. They may have a preferred route or method of transport, they may wish to travel at a particular time of day or may wish to avoid air travel or ferries. When considering possible routes to a particular destination there are a number of alternatives. The further afield the destination is, probably the quickest and most direct route is by air. Isolated destinations are often difficult to get to and the traveller may have to make detours, stopovers or change aircraft to reach them.

Even rail and coach travel offers a number of different routes. Travellers may not necessarily want to go directly from the point of departure to the destination. They may wish to stop over and include an extra visit on the way. Certainly in the UK and for closer destinations in Europe, a car probably offers the most flexible and personalised opportunity for travel. If the traveller is the one driving the vehicle, then there may also be a number of alternative routes. There are a number of travel route programmes available free on the internet, such as the one offered by the AA. Options could include:

- The quickest route
- The shortest route
- The scenic route
- The motorway route
- The route using only A and B roads
- The route least likely to present traffic hold-ups.

For business travel, the traveller will probably need to be at a particular place at a particular time. By looking at the route, it should be possible to work out when the traveller needs to leave in order to reach the destination at the right time. It is also worth remembering that travelling at particular times of the year can involve additional complications. During the summer or during holiday periods more people are on the move and the traveller is likely to encounter delays. The final consideration is that foreign travel will involve a change in time. Many countries are ahead or behind the UK (UK time is known as Greenwich Mean Time (GMT)).

If the traveller is going to a destination abroad then there may be some other considerations to take into account. These include:

- *Health* Vaccinations and inoculations are required to protect the traveller against certain diseases in some countries. Travel agents are a useful source of information about what needs to be done regarding health before travelling abroad. Health insurance is vital for travellers going to destinations abroad, particularly those outside the EU. Within the EU, European visitors can use the domestic healthcare of the country they are visiting.

- *Insurance* It is advisable to take out travel insurance to cover medical fees, accidents and loss of personal belongings. This can be arranged through a travel agent or an insurance broker.

- *Passports* A traveller must check that their passport is still valid. Some countries will not allow entry if the passport has nearly expired. Normally passports cover a 10-year period and are available from the Passport Office.

- *Currency and traveller's cheques* Obviously if the traveller's destination is an international one, it is advisable to take some foreign currency. Most of the countries within the EU use euros. There are usually a large number of banks and exchanges that will change British pounds into the currency of the country being visited. Many of the banks also accept credit and debit cards, and local currency can be drawn out using their cash machines. Many travellers prefer to take a small amount of a foreign currency and the rest of their currency in traveller's cheques. These can be obtained from a bank or a travel agency and are either in British pounds or American dollars.

- *Visas* If the traveller plans to travel outside the UK or the EU, they may need a visa to enter the country. The Foreign and Commonwealth Office Travel Service can provide information about visas. They also have important information about over 200 countries and issue travel warnings and advice to travellers visiting these countries.

Business travel is an extremely important part of normal business operations. Many thousands of people take business trips every week. They may be visiting customers or suppliers, attending meetings or special events. A business traveller may, therefore, need to take a number of other documents and items with them, including:

- Briefing documents about the destination they are travelling to and the businesses that they will be visiting.

- Sales literature, including brochures and catalogues.

- Samples of products or descriptions of services.

- Display equipment, such as CDs, DVDs, posters and other marketing material.

- Business cards to be distributed to customers and suppliers as necessary.

- Addresses, contact names and telephone lists of all customers, suppliers and other businesses or individuals the traveller may be visiting.

Many businesses have now recognised the importance of business travel and the following points are worth bearing in mind:

- Around 80 per cent of all businesses have a formal travel policy and 75 per cent of these businesses have preferred ways in which they organise air travel, hotels, car hire and rail travel.

- Around 75 per cent of businesses use a travel management company to organise their business travel.

- Around 85 per cent of businesses do not book their travel electronically.

All airlines, rail operators and the vast majority of hotels have websites or agents that work on their behalf to allow travellers to book tickets or reserve rooms. This is also true of car hire – many of the major car hire businesses, such as Avis and Hertz, have websites that allow the traveller to hire a car near their home or business and leave it at their departure airport. A traveller can also hire a car for the duration of their visit and return it to any of the car hire centres.

INDIVIDUAL WORK
(6.23) ★ ★ ★

Two people wish to leave Ipswich and travel to Prague for the following day. They need to be in Prague by 14.00.

1 Using the internet, and assuming that they can get to any east or south-east airport in the UK, find them a suitable return flight (they expect to stay in Prague for three days).

2 Find them a hotel near the centre of Prague.

3 Book them the use of a car for the duration of their stay in Prague. (You should end the procedure at the point where you are asked for your method of payment.)

Producing an itinerary confirming contact arrangements

An itinerary is a summary of the details and plans for a visit, including all times, accommodation and methods of travel. If a visit is a particularly long and complicated one, the itinerary will be very detailed and might consist of many pages. In such a case, a briefer version containing only essential information could be printed onto cards so the traveller can carry these in his or her pocket for easy reference.

The essential list for any itinerary needs to be drawn up after the following information has been gathered together:

- The dates for the travel and the accommodation needed.
- Preferences about travel method and types of accommodation.
- The times and dates of meetings and appointments.
- Whether any seats need to be reserved or car hire included.
- Whether the travellers have passports or need visas, insurance or any other documents.

ITINERARY

For Susan Grafton
25 January 2---

Monday 25 January 2---
Depart:	Norwich	09.30
Arrive:	London Liverpool Street	11.05
Hotel:	Regent Palace	
	Piccadilly Circus	
	London	
	Tel: 020 7273 6290	

Seminar: At the hotel
Registration	12.30
Lunch	13.00
Interpersonal skills	14.00
Afternoon tea	15.30
Plenary session	15.45
Close	16.30

Theatre: The Adelphi Theatre	20.15

Tuesday 26 January 2---
Seminar: At the hotel
Dealing with customers	10.00
Coffee	11.00
Role-play exercises	11.30
Lunch	13.00
Aggressive callers	14.15
Afternoon tea	15.30
Plenary session	15.45
Close	16.30

Depart:	London Liverpool Street	18.00
Arrive:	Norwich	20.00

Figure 6.9
An example of an itinerary

An itinerary should include:

- The dates of the travel and a breakdown of where the travellers need to be at any particular time during the visit.
- Departure and arrival times and include addresses and telephone numbers as required.
- Details of each booked arrangement, including table bookings at restaurants and entertainment.
- Every aspect of the traveller's journey, including the return trip.

In order to support the itinerary the person organising it will have to ensure that:

- Any relevant tickets have been booked and are given to the traveller.
- Car hire details have been passed on.
- Insurance documents are ready.
- Any certificates relating to vaccinations or inoculations are carried.
- Passports and visas have been checked.
- An information pack about the area has been prepared.
- Taxis or hire cars for transfer to the airport or hotel have been arranged.
- Appropriate money is available, either in traveller's cheques, foreign currency or the business's debit or credit cards are carried.

The itinerary should be as complete as possible and a copy should be given to each traveller. An ideal itinerary would take the following points into consideration:

- It should not be too tight and the travellers should be allowed some time to themselves.
- It should take into account that time differences will affect the traveller if it is a long-distance or international destination.
- Allow time for delays in transport, particularly during holiday times and poor weather conditions.
- National, religious or local holidays and festivals should be taken into account as they may affect travel arrangements.
- It should always use the 24-hour clock and state that it is local time.
- Time should be allowed for waiting for connections at airports and ports.
- It should include flight numbers as well as check-in, departure and arrival times.
- If flying, the correct terminal should be stated.
- If travelling by rail, the correct platform number should be stated (if known).
- The name, address, fax and telephone numbers of each of the hotels booked should be included.
- Suggest times when it would be appropriate, given the time differences, for calls to be made to the traveller.
- A copy should be kept by the person organising the travel so that they know where the traveller will be and when to contact them if necessary.

CASE STUDY Rachel's European tour

Rachel has a busy week in front of her. Over the next five days she must visit five European cities to meet with business partners. She needs to be in Cologne at 11.00 on Monday. She has to be back in London on Monday evening for a meeting with her business's director. She has to be in Paris for a meeting at 14.00 on Tuesday. On Wednesday she heads for Madrid where she has a meeting at 10.30. She then travels to Lisbon on Thursday where she must attend a meeting at 12.30. On Friday she needs to be in Athens for a meeting at 13.00. She hopes to be home by no later than 20.00. Luckily Rachel only lives 20 minutes away from Gatwick Airport and since all of the meetings are in the centre of the cities she is visiting she does not need a hire car.

INDIVIDUAL WORK (6.24) ★ ★ ★
Is Rachel going to be able to do this? Have a look on EasyJet's website and find out whether her proposed itinerary is possible or not. If it is not possible, what changes would you suggest that she makes to her itinerary so that she can visit all five cities?

Operating manual and electronic administrative systems

Organisational skills are very important to anybody who works in administration. In the business world, disorganisation can lead to time wastage and mistakes, some of which might potentially damage the business. Organisational skills include:

- Keeping a neat and tidy desk area.
- Keeping a diary of dates and times when meetings should be attended. A record should also be kept of any expected visitors (who may be customers or prospective customers) to the organisation.
- Having an efficient way of storing and retrieving documents, whether this is paper-based or on a computer system.
- Having a follow-up procedure in place so that documents are always available at the correct date and time.
- Managing time efficiently. Time management does not just apply to those people who are in authority and have many responsibilities at work, it is important for everyone to monitor how they use their time at work.
- Having a 'to do' list. This list can be weekly and/or daily and should list the duties that have to be carried out. Prioritising duties or tasks and then ticking off those completed is very satisfying and a finished list is a good way to end the day.

Maintaining a diary and operating calendaring software

Planning does not just involve daily or even weekly routines. Sometimes you may have to plan weeks or months in advance. The simplest way of achieving this is to put up a wall chart or planner in the office. Deadlines can be written on this chart or a variety of stick-on symbols used to highlight particularly important dates in the future.

Increasingly, people use personal digital assistants. These are mini-computers which have a function that allows information regarding deadlines to be entered and will alert the user to the fact that deadlines are coming up. They can also alert the fact that someone needs to be in a particular place, at a particular time so meetings or appointments are not missed.

As an alternative to the usual form of diary, some organisations may use an electronic diary method of logging appointments and meetings. This information can be stored either on the main computer system, a laptop or a personal organiser. The electronic diary enables the user to scroll forwards or backwards by day, month or year. It can store around five years' worth of days and dates. It is used to store provisional or confirmed appointments, holiday periods and set reminders for particular days, weeks or months in the future. The electronic diary can also be used to detail appointments, cross-reference appointments or tasks.

There are very few people who are well organised all the time. Such people are very self-disciplined and keep their work area neat and tidy and have lists of things that are waiting to be completed. They also do work in a strict order, rather than concentrating on work which they enjoy doing.

Without some organisation, work can become chaotic and put unnecessary pressure on an individual. It is therefore important to become organised at work in order to:

- Be able to find what you need.
- Not keep everything in your head, but on paper, where you can use it to remind you.
- Make the best use of your time.
- Finish jobs more quickly.
- Be more confident.
- Be less stressed.
- Be more efficient.

INDIVIDUAL WORK
(6.25) ★ ★

How well organised are you? Try to answer these questions as honestly as possible.

1 How messy is your bedroom at home?

2 If you have a work area at home, or at work or college, just how much have you managed to push into your desk drawers?

3 How forgetful are you? Do you rely on trying to remember things rather than writing down what you have to do?

4 If you had to go shopping for various items, would you write down a list or would you try to remember what it is you have gone out to buy?

5 Have you a clear idea about what you have to do each day?

6 How do you prefer to pass on messages to people?

7 When was the last time you lost something important?

8 How often do you have to search for clean clothes, or clothes that are not crumpled, in the morning when you are getting dressed?

9 When was the last time you failed to get a piece of coursework in on time?

10 Would you know where to find your National Insurance number if you needed it immediately?

Using the internet effectively

Focused research, investigations and sourcing

The internet provides access to a wealth of information on countless topics contributed by people throughout the world. The internet is not a library in which all its available items are identified and can be retrieved by a single catalogue. In fact, no one knows how many individual files reside on the internet. The number runs into a few billion and is growing at a rapid pace.

Anyone with basic technical skills and access can publish on the internet. It is important to remember this when you find websites in the course of your research. Some sites demonstrate an expert's knowledge, some may be updated daily, while others may be outdated. As with any information resource, it is important to evaluate what you find on the internet. Making sure that the information is correct and useful can be tricky, the following list gives some guidelines:

- How reliable and free from error is the information?

- Are there editors and fact checkers?

- Can the sources be verified?

- Is the information free of grammatical, spelling, and other typographical errors?

- Are charts and graphs clearly labelled and easy to read?

- Is there a bibliography or links to other useful sites?

- What are the author's qualifications for writing on the subject?

- Who is responsible for the web page? Can you trace the source to a person, company, organisation, institution, etc? Is that source reliable?

- Is the information presented with a minimum of bias?

- Are the biases of the person, company, organisation, institution, etc. clearly stated?

- Is any advertising clearly separated from the informational content?

- Is the content of the work up to date?

- Is the publication date clearly indicated?

- Are there dates on the page to indicate when the page was written, when the page was first placed on the web, and/or when the page was last revised?

💧 Are there any other indicators that the material is kept current?

💧 What topics are included in the work?

💧 To what depth are topics explored?

💧 Is there any indication that the page has been completed? Or is it still under construction?

💧 Is the entire work available on the web or only parts of it?

💧 Is it clear what topics the page intends to address?

💧 Does it succeed or has something significant been left out?

There are a number of basic ways to access information on the internet:

💧 Go directly to a site if you have the address. If you know the internet address of a site you wish to visit, you can use a web browser to access that site. All you need to do is type the URL in the appropriate location window. URL stands for Uniform Resource Locator. The URL specifies the internet address of the electronic document. Every file on the internet, no matter what its access protocol, has a unique URL. Web browsers use the URL to retrieve the file from the host computer and the directory in which it resides.

💧 Browsing home pages on the web is an interesting way of finding desired material on the internet. Because the creator of a home page programs each link, you never know where these links might lead.

💧 Explore a subject directory. An increasing number of libraries, companies, organisations, and even volunteers are creating subject directories to catalogue parts of the internet. These directories are organised by subject and consist of links to internet resources relating to these subjects.

💧 Conduct a search using a search engine. A search engine allows the user to enter keywords relating to topics and retrieve information about internet sites containing those keywords. Search engines have the advantage of offering access to a vast range of information and resources located on the internet.

Organising meeting arrangements

You will find full details of organising meeting arrangements in Unit 4, but again in this section you need to display your ability to make meeting arrangements. As a practice run for your IVA, you will need to carry out a series of connected tasks that ask you to organise meeting arrangements.

Room booking

Once a date and time for a meeting has been decided, the organiser will also need to know how many people are expected to attend, as this will determine the size of the room needed. Some businesses have rooms available for meetings, but in many cases meetings can take place outside the workplace, perhaps at a local hotel or conference centre. This will have the distinct advantage, as far as the organiser is concerned, of being able to deal with the other issues we consider later, particularly refreshments and the necessary facilities for the meeting.

Signposting

Not only will the individuals attending the meeting need to know exactly where the meeting will be held and when, but they will also need some assistance in finding the right room once they meet the location. It is standard practice, if the meeting is being held on the business's premises, to have a clear sign in the reception area, directing those attending to the room. Arrows and signs can be placed at junctions of corridors to ensure that the delegates find the correct room. Hotels and conference facilities provide a similar service and the signposting will be their responsibility.

INDIVIDUAL WORK (6.26) ★ ★

Using an internet search engine such as Google, find out the following:

a) The number of MPs in the UK Parliament and the name of your MP

b) The address of the local Business Link office

c) The lowest-priced airline ticket from any London airport to Paris

d) The website address of Guide Dogs for the Blind

e) The birth and death dates of Winston Churchill.

Reception

The meeting may need a reception area where the delegates report. Each delegate can be ticked off on the list of those due to attend and be issued with badges, information packs and any other information required. They can also be directed towards the refreshment area and shown their allocated place at the meeting. If the meeting is taking place on the business's premises, then the staff on reception duty will usually undertake this role. A sign will indicate to the delegates that they should report to reception and the receptionist can give information and directions to the delegates. Delegates may need passes to enter the business premises and these can be distributed at this point.

Refreshments

Coffee, tea, water and perhaps soft drinks should always be available to the delegates on demand. Usually an area is set aside where they can help themselves to refreshments or they can be served by a member of the catering staff. Hotels and conference centres usually lay on this facility for each meeting, but if the meeting is taking place on the business's premises, then this needs to be organised in advance.

Distributing preparatory information

Delegates will probably have been sent information packs regarding the topics to be discussed at the meeting, but there is no guarantee that they will have either brought them or have read them. At the reception area information packs can be distributed to each delegate as they arrive. They should contain any relevant documents, including an agenda and a programme of the events, breaks and expected finish time for the meeting.

Note-taking, minute preparation and distribution

Delegates will want to make their own notes about the discussions taking place in the meeting. It is usual practice to provide them with either a pad or a few sheets of paper and a pen. Any notes that they take will be in addition to the official notes being taken by an individual who assumes the role of meeting secretary. This individual will take notes in order to create the official minutes of the meeting, if these are required.

As it is usual practice very early on in the agenda of a meeting to look at and approve the minutes of the previous meeting, this is an essential task. The minutes need to be an accurate record of what was discussed at the meeting and detail any decisions made. As the previous meeting will have determined many of the items on the agenda of a future meeting, there will be indications in those minutes of work or research that has to be done for the meeting they are now attending.

The minutes of the previous meeting will be amongst the documents distributed to delegates when they first arrive. This will give them an opportunity to look through those minutes to check to see whether or not they are an accurate record.

GROUP WORK (6.27)

A group of 30 local Business Studies teachers and lecturers have been invited to your school or college to discuss how they run this course.

1 Find out where meetings such as this could take place in your school or college.

2 Who would deal with the administrative side of setting up the meeting and preparing the documentation?

3 Where would the reception area be located and would the delegates need passes or badges?

4 How would note-taking materials be provided? You can assume that one of your own teachers, lecturers or administrative staff would be responsible for the minute-taking.

5 Who would organise the refreshments?

HEALTH AND SAFETY AT WORK

All organisations have a responsibility to provide their employees and their customers, or visitors, with a healthy and safe environment. This does not just mean making sure that slippery floors are cleaned immediately so that nobody falls over. There are many government imposed laws (legislation) and regulations that identify what an employer and the employees have to do to ensure the environment, both inside and outside the organisation, is kept safe, hazard-free and healthy.

All employers are legally bound by an important series of Acts of Parliament regarding health and safety. Some of these are general, in that they apply to most businesses, but others are more specific in that they relate to organisations that deal, for example, with chemicals or toxic substances, or those involved in the manufacture or handling of food. Obviously, if an employer does not comply with these laws, then the business will be in jeopardy. If the requirements of the different legislation are found to have been broken by an organisation, the employer could be faced with court action and be considered to have been negligent.

Identifying common health and safety hazards

Piles of books, filing cabinets, computers and their associated cables all add to the chance of an accident occurring in any office situation. But what, exactly, is the difference between a hazard and a risk?

- A hazard is something that is likely to cause you or one of your colleagues, or a visitor to the business, some potential harm. A good example of a hazard is a trailing cable from a piece of electrical equipment, such as a computer or a photocopier. If the cable is attached to the skirting board, as it should be, or hidden under the flooring, then the risk of an accident is quite low.

- A potential hazard becomes a risk if there is an increased chance of an accident occurring. For example, if the cable trails across a room or across a regularly used route, then there is a high risk of someone tripping over it.

Obviously it is in everyone's best interests that the risk of injury from potential hazards is reduced to the absolute minimum. To achieve this, an employer would carry out regular *risk assessments* and would rely on the employees of the business to report any new hazards or an increase in the degree of risk involved. However, if these risk assessments are non-existent within a business, or are not carried out satisfactorily by the employer, the Health and Safety Executive operates an advisory service which the business can use.

When we consider what may or may not be hazards in an office environment, it is important to remember that a hazard is not necessarily a risk. So, in other words, there are some hazards that, if dealt with correctly, will never become a serious risk to the employees. On the other hand, there are some hazards that, if not dealt with quickly enough or correctly, would easily become a risk. There are a variety of areas within an office environment that could cause a potential hazard. These include:

- *The use of any machinery or equipment*, mainly because these are run by electricity, which is a potential hazard in itself. The machinery or equipment could develop a faulty plug, the cable could be inappropriately trailed across a room or there could be a problem with the socket into which it is plugged.

- *The use of materials or substances*, for example items with sharp edges, heavy or bulky items and poisonous substances, such as ink or cleaning fluids. The safe storage of such items is essential, particularly if they are bulky or heavy, and they should be easily accessible to the user. They should never be left in a place where they are likely to cause an obstruction, should always be stored in the correct containers and never used if they have become out of date.

- *Unsafe working practices and behaviour* If accidents are to be prevented, then it is important that all employees adopt the right approach and attitude to safe working. Areas of work that come into this category are general office safety, fire prevention, and regular maintenance of machinery as well as the lack of care by some employees.

INDIVIDUAL WORK
(6.28) ★
Look at the website of the Health and Safety Executive at www.hse.gov.uk. What information do they give businesses about making sure they are working safely? Print out a copy of any sheets they provide a business with.

- *Dealing with accidental breakages and spills* All spills should be immediately dealt with in order to reduce the risk of an accident, either from a fall or from the liquid coming into contact with electrical equipment. Breakages, too, are a possible risk in that an unknowing passer-by could either cut themself on, or trip over, the obstacle. The same risk of falling also applies to uneven or worn floors, which should be reported as soon as identified as being hazardous.

- *General office environment* This aspect of health and safety really covers the overall level of hygiene within the office environment, for example adequate ventilation, general cleanliness and toilet/washing facilities available to employees.

When does a hazard become a risk? A potential hazard only becomes a risk if there is an increased chance of an accident occurring.

It makes sense then that a person is unlikely to be able to identify a risk if they are unaware of the potential hazards. Employees have to be aware of the hazards and potential hazards around them when they are at work and also be aware of what to do if a hazard develops into a risk.

If accidents are to be prevented, it is important that the right approach and attitude is adopted at all times and that precautions are taken whenever possible to avoid accidents. Although the main responsibility for ensuring safe working practice is with the employer, via safety committees and safety officers or representatives, ultimately it is up to the individual employee. Some of the common office tasks undertaken can cause temporary or longer-term problems, such as the well-known Repetitive Strain Injury (RSI). This can be very painful and cause long-term damage to joints and bones. However it is not just the incorrect posture or repeated movements whilst using a computer or keyboard that need to be considered here.

In most offices, a variety of electrical equipment is used on a regular basis by a number of different members of the staff, for example the photocopier or the fax machine. Something as simple as removing a paper-jam from the photocopier could place an untrained or less-than-confident individual in some danger. Equally, actually using the photocopier in the wrong environment could also be a potential hazard.

Legislation

We have discussed already the fact that organisations have to comply with health and safety legislation and that, if they are found not to be doing so, they stand the risk of court proceedings or closure. It is important to know what this legislation actually covers and the number of laws that relate to an administrator.

The legislation was initially brought into force in the early 1970s in order to try to reduce the number of accidents occurring in the workplace and it has done this effectively ever since.

Health and Safety at Work Act 1974

The Health and Safety at Work Act 1974 (HASAWA) is probably the most well-known and important Act. The duties of the employers are based on the principle of 'so far as is reasonably practicable'. This means that risks need to be balanced against the costs and other difficulties of reducing a risk. The Act requires employers to use common sense and take suitable measures to tackle potential risks and employees to take reasonable steps to ensure their own safety and that of others.

The requirements included in the Health and Safety at Work Act 1974 apply to all workplace environments, however large or small. It applies to anyone who is on the premises including employees, managers, customers and even contractors who are involved in maintenance or temporary work.

The Act states that:

- All employers must ensure the health, safety and welfare at work of all their employees as far 'as is reasonably practicable'. Specifically this includes:

  - All entry and exit routes must be safe.
  - There must be a safe working environment and adequate facilities for the welfare of staff (somewhere to make a drink, toilet facilities, a quiet area).
  - Equipment must be safe and well maintained.

EMERGENCY EXIT

- Transportation and storage of all articles and substances must be done safely.
- Protective clothing must be provided.
- There must be clear information, instruction and training on health and safety with adequate supervision of issues to do with health and safety.

- Where the business has five or more employees, there should be a written statement on health and safety policy for the business. The statement should be written by the employer and continually updated to include any changes. This document must be circulated to all employees.

- The business should allow a trade union to appoint safety representatives who must be allowed to investigate accidents or potential hazards and follow up employee complaints. Safety representatives should be given time off to carry out their duties. All employees must:

  - Take responsibility for their own health and safety.
  - Take responsibility for the health and safety of others who may be affected by their activities or actions.
  - Cooperate with their employer to meet health and safety requirements.

WANT TO FIND OUT MORE?

The website of **Her Majesty's Stationery Office** at www.hmso.gov.uk gives further information about all legislation.

Control of Substances Hazardous to Health Regulations 1994

These regulations have been introduced to make sure that organisations control the use of chemicals and other substances that could cause harm to people, for example solvents that can be extremely harmful if they are inhaled. It also states that the employer must ensure that employees handling these substances are fully aware of the dangers that they present to them.

Procedures

Dealing with workplace accidents and emergencies, recording and reviewing accidents and incidents

Despite the fact that the office environment is a much safer place to work than say a building site, accidents still happen to people when they are at work. However, the majority of hazards are low risk. Consider it from a practical point of view:

- A hazard can be something quite small that can easily be put right without a risk to anyone.
- There may be set business procedures to follow that reduce the risk of injury to anyone.
- There could be set business procedures to follow that protect all those on the business's premises.
- There could be set procedures to follow that eliminate or control the degree of risk involved.

Although employees need to be vigilant, employers would not want to have a continual stream of reported problems. Not everything is a potential risk, so it is important that only the most important issues are dealt with officially. Each organisation will have its own set of procedures in place for their employees to report problems of a health and safety nature. Usually there will be someone within individual departments that should be contacted initially for minor issues, or it could be that a supervisor should be aware of the issue.

Apart from the minor health and safety issues that need reporting, there is also the possibility that an accident or other type of emergency may occur. Organisations will have reporting procedures in place and it could be that the witness to the accident would have to take any of the following actions:

- Call a member of staff who is trained in first aid
- Call the emergency services
- Deal with the situation themselves until help arrives
- Complete an accident report form and enter the details in the accident book.

All organisations like to keep a record of any accidents that occur on their premises and many are governed by legislation to do so. This means that an *accident report form* would have to be completed for any injuries to individuals whilst they are on the premises. In addition to this, an *accident book* is usually held in the reception area or in the first-aid room for a company employing more than 10 employees and each incident should be logged in this. Businesses use these records of accidents, or often near accidents, to try to improve their levels of health and safety. They will also monitor the nature and cause of all accidents or incidents to try to make sure that their organisation is not suffering more of these than the national average for their industry. Obviously, if you are at the scene of an accident, it is important to remember not to move anything until either the first-aid member of staff or the safety officer arrives on the scene, as they will need to make a full report of what happened.

All organisations require their employees to report accidents in the workplace and the main reasons for this reporting procedure are to ensure that:

- Any insurance claims can be made. If a person is hurt at work, they will need to prove that it happened there and not somewhere else. So if the incident has been logged at the time, this will provide evidence for them.

- Additional precautions can be taken in the future. An accident might reveal risks that had not been considered before.

The accident report form or the accident book will require vital information that details the nature of the accident and allows the person completing it to give a full explanation of the situation. An accident report form will require information on:

- The employee's full name
- The employee's home address
- The particulars of the accident, for example date, time and place it occurred
- The treatment given
- The name of the person giving the treatment
- Whether or not the individual required hospital treatment
- The nature of the injury
- The names of any witnesses to the accident
- A description of how the accident occurred
- The nature of the activity being undertaken at the time of the accident.

There are a number of important issues that the organisation will want to glean from the accident report form, including:

- Was the person involved in the activity authorised to do what they were doing? This has a bearing on who was to blame for the accident. If the person was not authorised, then the employer may not be liable for the injuries.

- Was the accident caused by machinery? The employer and the safety inspectors would want to know whether the machine was safe to be used, being operated correctly and with the recommended safety guards in place.

- Has an accident of this kind happened before? There would have to be an investigation if it was a commonly occurring accident.

Any employee witnessing an accident should remember the following about reporting:

- Take in as much information about the accident as quickly as they can.
- Identify any dangers to themselves, the injured person or others that may appear on the scene.
- Decide whether they can handle the situation themselves or whether they need to summon help.
- If necessary, get help as quickly as possible.

INDIVIDUAL WORK
(6.29) ★ ★

1 See if you can look at your college's accident book. If you can, pick out the five most common reasons for accidents happening at your college.

2 Now go back to the www.hse.gov.uk website and find their five most common reasons for accidents occurring in the workplace. Do their reasons match in any way those you have identified from your college's accident book?

It is important when dialling 999 to:

- Give the emergency services your telephone number
- Tell them exactly where the accident has occurred
- Tell them the nature and seriousness of the accident
- Tell them the name, ages and sexes of the injured people, if you know them
- Tell them about any hazards that they might encounter when responding to your call.

Do not put the telephone down until the control officer clears the line.

Dealing with emergencies and following the organisation's set procedures for doing so can be somewhat different to dealing with an accident. When we consider emergency situations, this really covers the need to evacuate the premises for one of several reasons, including:

- Fire
- Equipment malfunctions
- Gas leaks
- Contamination risks
- Security alerts.

The organisation's set procedures for dealing with emergency situations will determine actions in such cases if the need arises. Also, some industries are more prone to suffering from emergency or evacuation situations, for example those that have public access, banks, building societies and government buildings or any buildings attached to a factory that may have a fire or a contamination threat.

The reasons for implementing emergency procedures are the same as for accident monitoring, in that the organisation would want to reduce the risks involved both to people and to the workplace. Let us look at the reasons for evacuation in a bit more detail:

- *Fire* Obviously it is important to keep inflammable items away from any sources of ignition and to keep all fire doors closed. Most procedures will insist on the activation of a fire alarm and/or contacting the emergency services, but stress that the employees should not attempt to tackle a fire themselves. Some fires are the result of arson and not always accidentally started.

- *Equipment malfunctions* Lots of things can, and do, go wrong with machinery, although regular servicing and maintenance can avoid this. However, if there is a significant malfunction, this could result in the evacuation of a part of the building within which it is housed to avoid injuries to those employed within that area.

- *Gas and water leaks* A gas leak is a danger that should not be ignored. A gas leak could result in an explosion or a health risk in that those within the premises could inhale the gas. Water leaks can be equally dangerous, particularly if the water comes into contact with the electricity supply.

- *Contamination risk* This is particularly relevant in businesses using chemicals when there have been accidental emissions and when there is a risk that poisonous substances, or substances hazardous to health, have been released or are believed to have been released. Often the evacuation of the premises is a precautionary measure because the employer would want to protect employees and would want to ensure the risk is removed before anyone is allowed back into the premises.

- *Security alerts* These are, unfortunately, more common than they used to be. Security alerts and threats to the premises of an organisation can come from both inside and outside the company. Those coming from the inside can include the theft of goods by one of the employees and could result in evacuation in order that all staff can be searched. Threats from outside the organisation can come from:
  - Robberies or burglaries, which often result in some form of violence to those working within the organisation.

- Bomb threats, often carried out in order to either threaten a company or to make a political statement.
- Activists and spies, who are capable of entering the premises in order to do damage, tamper with the site or steal information.

INDIVIDUAL WORK
(6.30) ★
How many times in the last year has your organisation had to be evacuated because of an emergency situation? Find out this information and include details of any fire drills or evacuation drills you have been involved in.

Emergency procedures and practice evacuations aim to make sure that, in the event of a real emergency, quick, clear thinking is the key to safe evacuation of a building or the vicinity of a potential accident. There are a number of things to remember if involved in an emergency situation:

- Move swiftly to get out of the building or at least out of immediate danger and try not to panic.
- The last person to leave the room should close the door. This is a way of double-checking that a room has been cleared of personnel and if a fire is the emergency then it will help to prevent it from spreading.
- Be aware of notices that give the location of the fire assembly points and fire exits.
- Follow the emergency procedures in operation in the workplace.

Enhancing workplace health and safety

According to the Royal Society for the Prevention of Accidents (RoSPA), there are around 350 fatalities to workers and members of the public at work. In all, around 29 million working days are lost each year due to accidents. They also give the following figures for accidents and health and safety matters:

- In the UK there are 1.6 million workplace injuries every year as well as 2.2 million cases of ill-health caused or made worse by work.
- Health and safety failures currently cost the UK's employers up to £6.5 billion every year.
- The maximum penalties for breaching health and safety legislation are unlimited fines and up to two years in prison.
- The rate of fatal and major injuries in firms employing fewer than 50 employees is over twice the rate in firms employing more than 1,000 people.
- Around 60 per cent of fatal injuries to workers occurred in construction, transport and storage, agriculture, forestry and fishing.
- Amongst the most common kinds of accident involved with fatal injuries are: falling from a height; being struck by a moving vehicle; and being struck by moving or falling objects.
- Slips and tips account for 42 per cent of major injuries to employees (local authority sectors) and half of all non-fatal injuries to members of the public.
- Stress-related illness is estimated to account for about 20 per cent of reported cases of occupational ill-health (about 500,000).
- Car and van drivers who cover 25,000 miles a year as part of their job have the same risk of being killed at work as coal miners. Work-related driving is one of the biggest single causes of all reportable accidents.
- Around 1.2 million people suffer from back pain and repetitive strain injuries caused by their work, amounting to 9.9 million working days lost each year.
- Between 50,000 and 100,000 cases of skin disorders caused by work are reported each year.
- Some 6,000 employees suffer burns at work each year.
- Some 1.3 million workers are exposed to noise levels above 85dB, which puts them at risk of damage to hearing.
- Some 400,000 people are believed to be suffering from asthma caused by their work. There are around 1,000 new cases each year.
- 2,000 people suffer accidents involving chemicals each year.

INDIVIDUAL WORK
(6.31) ★
Visit the RoSPA website at www.rospa.org.uk. Click on 'Occupational' and answer the following questions.

1 How many businesses each year receive a RoSPA Occupational Health and Safety Award?

2 What advice do they give to small businesses on health and safety?

RoSPA goes on to suggest that only 40 per cent of workplace accidents are reported and that 70 per cent of accidents could actually be prevented.

Preventing accidents and emergencies, professional risk assessment, review of working practices, staff training, benchmarking against best practice and investment in improved facilities

It is obvious how important health and safety legislation is to both the employer and the employees of a business. But how would anyone know whether a business is complying with the legislation? The local council or authority has the right to inspect the business premises at any time to ensure that adequate and appropriate health and safety procedures are in place. In addition, the Health and Safety Executive also has inspectors who visit business premises to examine equipment and machinery. They also have the power to enforce the requirements of the different Acts of Parliament concerning health and safety.

A business owner must contact the local authority when the business first opens and inform them of the organisation's intention to trade in the premises. There are further steps the employer has to take when first starting the business:

INDIVIDUAL WORK (6.32) ★

Where is the Health and Safety at Work poster displayed in your school or college? Why do you think they have chosen to display it in this particular place?

- Contact either the Environmental Health Department and/or the Health and Safety Executive (depending on the type of business activity).
- Take out employer's liability insurance and obtain a certificate of this insurance.
- Display the insurance certificate within the premises of the business.
- Draw up a health and safety policy for the business.
- Display a Health and Safety at Work poster within the business premises.
- Carry out a risk assessment and keep a record of any potential health and safety risks within the business.

The main requirements of the different health and safety legislation require the employer to, at least, comply with the following:

- Provide a safe working environment (safety).
- Provide adequate welfare facilities for employees (health).
- Ensure all entrances and exits to the business premises are safe (emergencies).
- Ensure all equipment and systems used within the business premises are safe (protection).
- Ensure all equipment and systems used within the business premises are regularly serviced (maintenance).
- Ensure that all items needed for the handling or the storage of the business's products are safe (warehousing).
- Ensure that any dangerous or toxic materials used by the business are housed in safe containers (secure storage).
- Provide instruction, training and/or supervision to all employees regarding safe working practices and the use of all materials (educational programme).
- Investigate and promptly deal with all accidents by identifying their causes (accident prevention).

Naturally, with the responsibility for health and safety sitting very squarely on the shoulders of the employer, most organisations are very keen to improve their record and to protect their employees. They are also aware that they need their employees to be health and safety conscious and to assist them in ensuring a healthy and safe environment. Many do this by:

- Setting their employees practical goals to reach health and safety standards.
- Encouraging their employees to work together and cooperate in a safe manner.
- Encouraging their employees to accept responsibility for health and safety matters.
- Identifying key members of staff to deal with health and safety matters.
- Regularly addressing health and safety issues and encouraging staff to improve.
- Ensuring all staff are aware of health and safety issues through an initial induction programme and suitable training courses as and when required for updating purposes.

The major cause of accidents within the workplace tends to be attributed to employees working in an untidy and careless manner. Having said that, the employer also has to take responsibility for ensuring that employees have all the information they need to work in a safe manner, and eliminate the risks to themselves, their colleagues and visitors to the organisation. This information could take several forms. The employer needs to ensure that staff:

- Are familiar with all equipment being used.
- Are trained in health and safety matters.
- Have access to manuals or handbooks relating to equipment or machinery being used.
- Are clear about safe working practices.
- Are familiar with the health and safety policy of the business.

It would not be appropriate to list here the common risks that people face in the course of their work in an office environment, but these are the main risks:

- Injury to part or parts of the body, including injury to the eyes from chemicals or particles, the ears from loud noise, and the body from falling objects or from slipping.
- Fire.
- Contamination.
- Electric shock.

So the main way to avoid these risks is to have a policy in place that covers all aspects and reduces, but hopefully eliminates, them as far as possible.

Apart from the prevention of accidents aspect, an organisation would try to ensure that there are certain individuals who have a specific duty to minimise risks. Having said that, no prevention scheme is completely foolproof and everyone has the responsibility to maintain vigilance and avoid the possibility of a potential hazard becoming a risk.

This policy will be revised and updated on a regular basis by senior management and from these revisions the employees will be made aware of the business's codes of practice. The safety policy will be a written account of how the business intends to train and instruct its employees on health and safety matters and how it will keep a record of its procedures for reporting accidents and emergencies.

Depending on the size and complexity of the organisation, the codes of practice will include:

- A detailed account of how employees should act in the event of an emergency
- A detailed account of how employees should act in the event of an accident
- A list of trained first-aid personnel within the business
- The location of the first-aid room
- A list of named safety representatives or members of a safety committee.

In larger organisations a safety committee is set up and in smaller businesses a safety officer or safety representative is designated. These individuals will keep the management of the business informed of any changes in government legislation regarding health and safety and inform them of any problems within the business that could mean they are not complying with these laws. In addition they will also strive to prevent or reduce risks by ensuring that:

- All the relevant employees are issued with and are using personal protective equipment. This would be issued to anyone dealing with toxic or otherwise dangerous materials or substances.
- All machinery and equipment is being used in accordance with the manufacturer's safety instructions. This is particularly relevant when the use of safety guards is recommended.
- The premises is adequately ventilated. This is important when hazardous fumes or smoke is involved in the business's activity. Extractor fans and machinery to circulate the air can ensure that sufficiently good air quality is maintained at all times.

INDIVIDUAL WORK
(6.33) ★ ★
Did you receive any training about health and safety when you first joined your college? If so, did you receive any written confirmation of what you had to do in the case of fire or emergencies? Perhaps you had some training of this kind during your induction period? Read through anything you might have been given at this time so that you refresh your memory about what you were told.

  ◊ Suitable fire extinguishers and/or fire blankets are available throughout the business's premises.

  ◊ Safety warning signs are clearly marked. These need to be displayed prominently so that employees, customers and visitors can easily see them.

  ◊ Sufficient individuals are trained to deal with first-aid situations. Under the Health and Safety at Work Act 1974 the employer is required by law to make sure that qualified individuals are available.

  ◊ Employees are adhering to the business's safety policy by carrying out safe working practices. It is no good having a safety policy in place if the employees are not working safely!

Very often the business's safety policy will be an integral part of a new employee's contract of employment, which will be issued on starting the job. In addition the safety policy is sometimes included as a written statement in the business's charter or promise to its customers. For example, a college would include its safety policy in its communication with new students, who are, in effect, the college's customers.

  If an organisation is complying with the legislation laid down by the government, then there will be a number of individuals within the business who have certain responsibilities. They will have been given this role not only to ensure that the management is aware of all health and safety issues, but also so that all employees know who to contact when it becomes necessary.

INDIVIDUAL WORK
(6.34) ★ ★

Imagine that you are the office manager. You have received the following list of complaints from some of the office assistants about the general safety in the office:

a) There are not enough cleaning materials for the computers.

b) The office is not ventilated adequately because the windows are sealed closed.

c) The photocopier is giving off a strange smell.

d) When other members of staff are talking on the telephone it is very noisy.

e) You cannot always see the computer screens properly because the sun shines in the windows and onto the screens.

f) The rubbish bins are not emptied very regularly and sometimes they do not get emptied at all.

For each of the points, decide what you should do to improve the situation.

Unit Revision Questions

1 What is an invoice and which parts of a business receiving an invoice would be interested in it?

2 What are minutes?

3 What is EDI?

4 Which part of a business might create a profit statement?

5 How might a business check inaccuracies in letters before they are posted?

6 What is a hacker?

7 What is meant by 'back-up'?

8 Why might a traveller need a visa?

9 What is HASAWA and when did it come into effect?

10 What is the difference between a risk and a hazard?

Sales and Customer Service

This unit aims to help you to understand sales and customer service activities. Sales and customer service are controlled by a number of different legal and regulatory guidelines that all sales employees must observe. This unit will look at pre-sales preparation and how to acquire customer service skills. The unit also looks at after-sales service, which is a vital part of customer service aimed at encouraging repeat sales.

   This is an internally assessed unit and to cover the requirements of the unit you must:

- Explore sales promotion techniques
- Investigate effective pre-sales preparation
- Examine effective sales practice
- Consider effective after-sales service.

SALES PROMOTION TECHNIQUES

Sales promotions aim to improve the sales of a product in two main ways. Firstly, the sales should increase dramatically during the campaign, but secondly, once the campaign is over, the new level of sales should remain higher than it was beforehand. This is best illustrated by considering Figure 7.1.

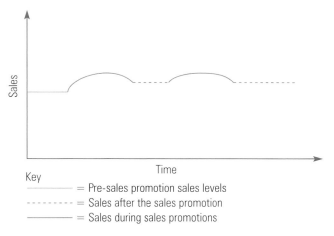

Key
———— = Pre-sales promotion sales levels
- - - - - - - = Sales after the sales promotion
———— = Sales during sales promotions

Figure 7.1
The effect of sales promotion

Designing a sales promotion

Format, style, use of materials, key messages, intended outcomes, product unique selling points, sales locations and additional product information

Sales promotion is an example of a *below-the-line* marketing activity, i.e. it is a discrete (not so obvious) marketing method, like public relations. Compare this with advertising which is considered to be *above-the-line*, i.e. it is an overt (open or obvious) marketing method. Usually, the sales promotion effort is concentrated either *on pack* (on or within the packaging) or at the **point-of-sale**.

Before we consider some sales promotion techniques, we should fully consider the functions of sales promotion campaigns, which include:

- To encourage stockists to order the product or existing stockists to increase their orders. If the stockist believes that the sales promotion will generate demand (or extra demand), then they may be more inclined to consider the product. The sales promotion aimed at the customer (end user) rather than the stockist directly, would normally be supplemented by specific trade deals as an extra incentive (these would include special discounts or sale or return deals, etc.).

- To encourage the customer to try the product or increase their level of purchasing. Typically, these sales promotions are used in the food industry. Examples of this approach include free samples of one product on a different product (perhaps a powdered milk product attached to a coffee jar) or a simple 'two for the price of one' promotion. Again, the purpose of the exercise is either to aid the launch of a new product or to boost the sales of an existing one.

- To counteract the effects of the competition. When a competitor either launches a new product or is running a sales promotion for an existing one, there is the danger that some of the market share could be lost. In order to 'spoil' the competitor's campaign, the organisation could introduce a simple sales promotion (such as a special price or a two-for-one deal) and attempt to maintain their share of the market.

- To improve the distribution network and enhance the sales representative's journey cycle. If the campaign works, the supplier will be able to acquire more customers in a given area and vastly improve the efficiency of the sales representative's journey cycle by having an increased number of customers in the territory.

- To revitalise or relaunch a product that has become rather stale in the eyes of the customers. The product or service may be performing reasonably, but a sales promotion could positively improve the customers' perceptions of the product and give a useful boost to the sales.

Some of the more common forms of sales promotion include:

- *Free samples* – either given out in a retail outlet, attached to another product, on the front of a magazine or posted through customers' letter boxes.

- *Cut-price special offers* – products would be despatched with pre-printed price reduction flashes on the packaging.

- *Two for the price of one* – either two products attached to one another, or the price of one of the items is deducted at the point-of-sale (checkout).

- *Free gift on pack* – a version of a 'premium offer', either on or in the pack, given out at the cash desk or the packaging itself (tin boxes for tea bags, storage jars for coffee, etc.).

- *Free gifts on proof of purchase* – requiring the customer to collect a number of tokens or wrappers which can then be exchanged (by mail) for a range of gifts (free or at a reduced price).

- *Self-liquidating premiums* – the customer receives a coupon on the pack offering a reduction in price for the next purchase of the same product.

- *Competitions* – a variety of different 'games' of skill and judgement such as completing the slogan, putting the features of the product in order of importance, answering various questions and matching the coupons, etc.

- *Personality-based promotions* – linking the product with a well-known personality (such as Gary Lineker and Walkers Crisps) or a particular event (such as Coca-Cola and Euro 2004). Normally the personality promotions will be backed up with a competition or a coupon collection exercise.

Any sales promotion campaign needs to be supported by a concerted effort on all fronts. In other words, the organisation needs to have the following in place before the launch of the campaign:

- The customer response structures need to be in place (applicable if the customer has to contact the organisation as an integral part of the promotion).

- Sufficient stocks need to be available in the outlets and in reserve to cater for demand.

- The sales representatives should be well briefed so that they can brief the retailer.

- Any response mechanism should be clear and easy to use by the customer.

- Special point-of-sale materials should have been created and distributed to retailers.

- The on-pack messages need to be clear and stand out well.

- The promotion needs a good 'catchy' title.

- The distributors and retailers should be given incentives to be part of the promotion (perhaps short-term additional discounts would be appropriate here).

Sales promotions are often referred to as 'push and pull' strategies (see Figure 7.2).

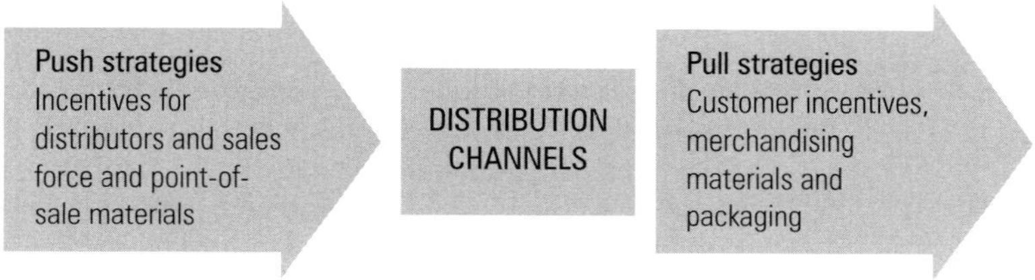

Push strategies
Incentives for
distributors and sales
force and point-of-
sale materials

DISTRIBUTION
CHANNELS

Pull strategies
Customer incentives,
merchandising
materials and
packaging

Figure 7.2
Push and pull strategies

Obviously, either during or directly after the sales promotion campaign, the organisation will need to assess its effectiveness and impact on the sales of the product. Typically, the following criteria would be used:

- The increase in sales volume of the product.

- The number of new customers created.

- The repeat purchase rate of customers.

- The profit per unit during and after the promotion.

- The performance of the promoted product against a similar product that did not have a promotion.

- The attitude, or change in attitude, towards the product (both the customer and the retailer).

- The additional profit gained from the new purchasers of the product.

- The sales revenue, profit and volume of sales against the promotional costs.

- The increase in the number of retailers stocking the product.

- The improvements in the distribution system and the sales representative's journey cycle as a result of the promotion.

- The effect on goodwill (both customers and retailers).

- The increase in the amount of point-of-sale materials/displays used by the retailers.

We have already considered the main benefits of the sales promotion as far as the customer is concerned. We will now look at the incentives that can be used to encourage both retailers and sales representative involvement. We begin by looking at the retailer, who would be offered:

- Extended credit terms

- Retailers' associated competitions/promotions

- Cash discounts
- Case bonuses (such as one extra box for every 12 ordered).

Sales representatives would normally be offered:

- Cash payments for achieving sales targets attached to the promotion
- Prizes (such as holidays, etc.) for particular target achievements
- 'Best salesperson of the month' prizes
- Team prizes for the best-performing region.

Finally, an integral part of the sales promotion and, for that matter, a vital role of the sales representative's regular visits to a stockist is to provide (and encourage the use of) a variety of different window displays, point-of-sale materials and other merchandising tools. These promotional tools would include:

- Point-of-sale materials, including posters, leaflets and aisle banners.
- Shelf-strips, which can either be attached along the shelf or be used to stick out to attract attention.
- Posters designed for windows and doors.
- Freestanding or wall-mounted displays.
- Dump bins (floor or shelf-mounted containers).

INDIVIDUAL WORK
(7.4) ★ ★

During your next visit to a supermarket or large store, look out for point-of-sale materials. What kind is being used? Is it well placed and does it attract your attention?

Usually, the retailers' use of point-of-sale materials may entitle them to an extra discount or incentive. These materials not only help to increase the sales of the product in the outlet, but also greatly enhance the prospect of being allocated shelf space in an increasingly competitive market. Despite the attendant difficulties of convincing the outlet to use the materials, the sales representative will see these materials as another useful tool in the battle to obtain orders.

Organising a sales promotion

As we have seen, a business may have several reasons for launching a sales promotion. In this section we will look at the various choices and the preparation that needs to take place before launching, or even designing, the promotional campaign.

Above-the-line and below-the-line methods

Traditional advertising media such as press, radio and TV are known as above-the-line. Non-traditional media such as sales promotions are known as below-the-line. In many respects, these are redundant phrases as all marketing work is now considered in an overall campaign and there is no longer a distinction between the two. Campaigns are now described as going *through-the-line*.

Below-the-line elements of marketing include:

- In-store vouchers and special offers.
- Loyalty card offers that encourage repeat purchases or encourage someone to purchase a product that they would not normally buy.
- Competitions, both in-store and on the back of packaging.
- Packaging which is used to attract the buyer's attention.

Above-the-line marketing includes:

- The press, including newspapers and magazines – the advertisements can be very detailed.
- Television advertising that reaches large audiences.
- Radio advertising, there are many new national, regional and local independent radio stations to reach particular audiences.
- Cinema advertising – effective, with good sound and colour, often used to test advertisements that will later be screened on television.
- Posters and billboards which can be sited near road junctions, shops, travel centres and other locations where there is a large amount of passing 'traffic'.

- The internet – the newest form of advertising and quite effective if it reaches the right kind of audience.
- Mobile advertising, which includes trucks and lorries bearing the names and messages of shops and businesses. This also includes the increasing trend to send text messages to mobile phone users.

Competitor analysis

The purpose of competitor analysis is to look at the external challenges and opportunities a business may face. There are many reasons why it is advisable to find out about the competition before launching any new sales promotion or other activity. These include:

- The business can discover its own advantages, in other words the reasons why customers do business with them instead of the competition. The purpose of this is to then communicate this competitive advantage to win new customers.
- It can analyse any current issues and the competitors' products and services may create new ideas or improvements in the businesses product or services.
- The business might discover that there are some categories of customers whose needs are not being met.
- By looking at the competition, the business is better able to understand the market. Perhaps a successful competitor offers reduced prices at a particular time of the year.
- The market may simply have too many competitors and the business can avoid making a costly mistake in throwing money into a promotion that will have little effect on the market.

To carry out competitor analysis, a business will need to carry out research to:

- Discover the names of competitors, including any that might be competitors in the near future.
- Make a summary of each competitor's products, including where they are sold, quality, advertising, staff, distribution methods, promotional strategies and customer service.
- Try to assess the competitors' strengths and weaknesses from the customers' point of view and identify which of the weaknesses the business can exploit.
- Try to work out the competitors' strategies and objectives. An ideal starting point is the annual report. There is other readily available information on the internet.
- Find out the current strength of the market – it might be growing or it might be stable at this time.

Competitive analysis can be undertaken in several ways. These are the most common:

- Researching the competitors on the internet, particularly their own websites, and news stories about their successes and failures.
- Secret personal visits to their location to see how the employees interact with customers. What do their premises look like? How are their products displayed and priced?
- Use the sales staff to talk to customers as they interact with the same kind of customers as the competition. What is their view of the competitors?
- Analyse the advertisements and promotions of the competition. This should give the business clues about the kind of market they are targeting, along with their market position, product features and benefits as well as prices.
- Attend speeches or presentations made by representatives of your competitors.
- Look at trade show displays to see how the competition displays their products and services. What kind of customers do the trade shows attract?
- Written sources including general business publications; marketing and advertising publications; local newspapers and business journals; industry and trade association publications; industry research and surveys and annual reports.

INDIVIDUAL WORK (7.5) ★ ★
Think about two very similar products, such as Pepsi-Cola and Coca-Cola. We already know that Coca-Cola is the most popular soft drink, but Pepsi-Cola is constantly trying to catch them up. Suggest at least three ways in which Pepsi-Cola could run a campaign to try to take some of Coca-Cola's market.

Market sensitivity

Market sensitivity is a measure of how customers react to marketing activities and, in this case, sales promotions. It is a measure of how many new customers can be attracted to the product or service as a result of the sales promotion. Obviously, a business would want to test to see how effective the promotion might be before they actually launch the promotion itself. There are a number of different ways in which this can be achieved including:

- They could make some mock-ups of the sales promotion materials and show them to a group of people selected to represent the type of customers that the promotion is aimed at.
- They could show mock-ups of the promotion to retailers and other business customers and see what their reaction is to the sales promotion.
- They could ask their own sales representatives to comment on the sales promotion.
- They could try out the sales promotion in a small area of the country and gauge the reaction to it before they launch the promotion across the country.

Types of promotional appeal

Obviously one of the main purposes of any sales promotion is to attract the types of customers identified by the business as being prime targets. The promotional activities need to appeal to them in order to draw their interest. It should not be forgotten that there is a high likelihood of the competitors running similar promotions at the same time, so the promotion needs to stand out.

Typical forms of appeal are designed to use images, personalities, TV shows, characters and other means to attract the customers. A product designed for children would tend to use cartoon characters, pop stars or children's toys as a main part of the sales promotion, possibly offering stickers, small toys, photographs or posters. A promotion aimed at gardeners might use well-known TV gardeners, whilst a DIY product might feature a famous TV designer.

CASE STUDY Sales promotion with London Zoo

London Zoo is the UK's top wildlife attraction and it is a good bet that it will be the best known among your customers too. With its lively, fun and educational image, a London zoo promotion can help your brand be noticed in a crowded marketplace.

Animal themed promotions are attractive to both adults and children, and with the benefit of the high-profile London Zoo name, logo and expertise, your promotion will work hard for you.

London Zoo promotions can help increase sales, differentiate a product from a competitor's or create awareness. You will most likely want to develop your own promotion specifically tailored to your commercial objectives, but built around an animal theme. We can help you in this, and will work closely with you to set up the ideal promotion for you.

The zoo offers the following forms of sales promotion in association with organisations:
- On-pack promotions to increase visibility
- POS promotions

- Animal-related competitions with animal facts and prizes
- Collector schemes with an animal theme to encourage repeat purchase and loyalty
- Business-related activities and events on the zoo's site or on the business website
- Licensing programmes including the endorsement of the zoo's logo as a well-known charity to build loyalty and sales
- Product sampling opportunities to the zoo's ABC1 visitors.

INDIVIDUAL WORK (7.6) ★ ★

Read the case study and answer the following questions.

1 What is meant by 'on-pack promotions'?

2 What does 'licensing programmes, including the endorsement of the zoo's logo' mean?

3 What are product-sampling opportunities?

4 What does 'ABC1 visitors' mean?

5 Suggest at least three products that would benefit from an association with London Zoo or a similar organisation.

WANT TO FIND OUT MORE?

Visit the website of the **Advertising Standards Agency** and find out more about their work and the code of practice at: www.asa.org.uk.

Advertising Standards Agency guidelines

The Advertising Standards Authority (ASA) is an independent organisation that polices the rules laid down in the advertising codes. It is the self-regulatory body for advertisements, sales promotions and direct marketing in the UK. The ASA administers the British Code of Advertising, Sales Promotion and Direct Marketing (the CAP Code) to ensure that advertisements are legal, decent, honest and truthful.

The code covers such forms of promotion as premium offers of all kinds: reduced prices and free offers; the distribution of vouchers, coupons and samples; personality promotions; charity linked promotions; and prize promotions of all types.

CASE STUDY Tango advertisement taken off air

In November 2004, the Advertising Standards Authority (ASA) chairman, Lord Borrie QC, asked broadcasters to remove an advertisement for the soft drink 'Tango' from the TV schedules following complaints from members of the public. The ASA was investigating concerns that the advertisement may lead to emulation, by children, resulting in harm. Lord Borrie, after careful consideration, exercised his powers to have it taken off air pending the outcome of the investigation.

The advertisement, 'Tango Pipes', featured a young man wrapped inside an orange-filled carpet and laid on top of several large concrete pipes. The man rolls down a hill, crashing into a tree and is then hit by the concrete pipes resulting in the oranges exploding over him.

The ASA took over responsibility for broadcast advertising regulation on 1 November 2004 and received four complaints about the commercial. The complainants include relatives of a boy who was killed in an accident whilst playing with concrete pipes. They believe the advertisement depicted dangerous behaviour and could result in emulation by children who see it.

INDIVIDUAL WORK (7.7)

Read the case study on the banning of the Tango advertisement and then visit the website of the ASA at www.asa.org.uk and find out whether there have been any further bans in recent months.

Sale of Goods Act 1979/1995

According to the Sale of Goods Act 1979, traders must sell goods that are as described and of satisfactory quality. If consumers discover that products do not meet these requirements they can reject them and ask for their money back. They can also ask for a repair or replacement or claim compensation.

The Sale of Goods Act has been replaced by the Sale and Supply of Goods to Consumers Regulations (2002). Under the new regulations, consumers can now demand repair, replacement, partial or full refund on any goods that were faulty or defective at the time of purchase. Consumers no longer have to prove that the goods were faulty when purchased; instead the retailer will have to prove that they were not.

Supply of Goods and Services Act 1982

This law states that certain terms are implied in every transaction for the transfer of goods and that the goods must:

- Correspond with the description given
- Be of satisfactory quality
- Be fit for the purposes.

Consumer Protection Act 1987

The Consumer Protection Act 1987 safeguards consumers from products that do not reach a reasonable level of safety. The main areas dealt with are:

- *Product liability* The Act allows injured persons to sue producers, importers and own-branders for death, personal injury or losses. Defective products are defined as being those where the safety of the product is not such as persons generally are entitled to expect. On the other hand, a product will not be considered defective simply because it is of poor quality or because a safer version is subsequently put on the market.

◆ *Consumer safety* The law requires producers and distributors to take steps to ensure that the products they supply are safe, that they provide consumers with relevant information and warnings, and that they keep themselves informed about risks. Safe products are defined as being products which under normal or reasonably foreseeable conditions of use present no risk or only the minimum risk compatible with the product's use, and which is consistent with a high level of protection for consumers.

Consumer Credit Act 1974

The Consumer Credit Act 1974 regulates consumer credit and consumer hire agreements for amounts up to £25,000. Its protections apply to agreements between traders and individuals, sole traders, partnerships and unincorporated associations, but not agreements made between traders and corporate bodies such as limited companies.

The law covers:

◆ The form and content of agreements.

◆ Credit advertising.

◆ The method of calculating the Annual Percentage Rate (APR) of the Total Charge for Credit.

◆ The procedures to be adopted in the event of default, termination, or early settlement.

◆ Extortionate credit bargains.

A new Consumer Credit Bill was announced in November 2004. The key benefits of the new law will be that it will:

◆ Protect consumers and create fairer and more competitive credit.

◆ Improve consumer rights and redress, give power to consumers to challenge unfair lending and more effective options for resolving disputes.

◆ Improve the regulation of consumer credit businesses by ensuring fair practices and, through targeted action, to drive out rogues.

◆ Make the law more appropriate for different types of consumer credit transaction by extending protection to all consumer credit.

Trade Descriptions Act 1968

The Trade Descriptions Act 1968 aims to prevent misleading descriptions of all goods and services. The Act protects consumers from misleading or false descriptions of goods.

The law applies to suppliers, manufacturers and retailers of goods, as well as services, facilities and accommodation. The law states that it is the business's responsibility to ensure that the goods, services, facilities and accommodation sold or provided are not falsely described. Legislation on misleading prices was made under the Consumer Protection Act 1987.

Monitoring promotional effectiveness

Since many sales promotions, especially consumer-oriented ones, result in direct consumer responses, a business can track their effectiveness relatively easily. Many sales promotions are designed to encourage the customer to sample the product. This is one of the most popular types of consumer promotions. A business will want to know how effectively it induces consumers to actually buy the product once they try the sample.

A business will look for what is known as the *promotional bump*. There will be an increase in sales during the promotion; this is expected, as it will hopefully attract more customers to sample the product during the length of the campaign. The key point arrives when the promotion is over. What happens to demand when there are no more products out in the market with the sales promotion? This is where the bump comes in. The business should see a sustained rise in the number of products sold as some of the customers that tried the product during the promotion will continue to buy the product after the promotion.

INDIVIDUAL WORK
(7.8) ★★
Read the information regarding consumer protection laws and then answer the following questions.

1 You purchase a CD player from a local shop using your credit card. Four weeks later it stops working. What can you do?

a) Nothing – it is just bad luck

b) Go back to the store and reject the item

c) Try and fix it yourself.

2 A relative has bought you a games console for your birthday. You open it straightaway and it appears to be faulty. What are you entitled to?

a) Nothing, it should have been checked at the shop

b) A full refund, but only the relative can take it back

c) The shop has to offer you a replacement.

The customers, who were not customers before the sales promotion, have switched brands from a competitor and have now become customers of the business. This was precisely what the business intended when they launched the sales promotion. The trick is now to keep those new customers as well as the original ones and build on the growth with the next sales promotion and advertising.

CASE STUDY Muscular Dystrophy and Somerfield

The Muscular Dystrophy Campaign and the Somerfield Group developed a successful sales promotion to help raise brand awareness as well as essential funds. During 'Muscles for Muscles' awareness week in May 2004, a sales promotion was run on flower bouquets which raised a fantastic £12,000.

'The sales promotion that we ran with the Muscular Dystrophy Campaign on a bouquet of flowers was a huge success. The bouquets were very popular with our customers and flew off the shelves. The charity understood the needs of Somerfield and were efficient to work with,' said Peter Neuman, Flower Buyer for the Somerfield Group.

> **INDIVIDUAL** WORK (7.9) ★ ★
> Next time you visit a supermarket, note down how many sales promotions are in action at the time. How would you categorise them? What measures of success do you think the businesses are looking for?

Dealing with complaints

As you will recall, the ASA polices sales promotions run in the UK. Their code must be followed by a business running a campaign. The sales promotion must:

- Be legal, decent, honest and truthful.
- Be conducted equitably (even-handedly), promptly and efficiently and be seen to be dealing fairly and honourably with consumers.

CASE STUDY Avon and Hoover get it wrong

An advertisement boasted that it was 'too good to be true'. It offered a free mobile phone for every £15 spent on cosmetics and proved the claim to be exactly right – Avon did not have enough mobile phones to give away.

Thousands of shoppers tried to take advantage of a free voucher for a phone from an Orange shop in return for spending £15 on skincare products. The Advertising Standards Authority (ASA) upheld 27 complaints about the fiasco even though the company had included small print in the offer stating 'subject to availability'.

What angered the watchdog particularly is that the firm continued to promote the offer even when it must have known that there were insufficient phones to meet demand.

The offer started in February and ran until the end of April 2004. Avon admitted that it had based its estimates on previous offers for less popular, cheaper items but nevertheless had doubled the number of items available in case demand was high.

'We told the promoters to take greater care when estimating demand for free gifts on the basis of previous promotions and to take immediate and unambiguous action to minimise disappointment in the event that demand for future promotional items exceeded supply,' said the ASA.

Avon said it had apologised to unhappy customers and offered them the chance to buy a skin cream at half price instead. Avon eventually promised everyone a phone – even if it meant waiting until new stocks were available. But some complainants had been waiting for six weeks and had not been told when to expect their gift.

The most disastrous sales promotion was the Hoover promotion in 1993 and 1994 offering two free flights to the US and Europe for anyone spending more than £100 on a product. The offer was massively over-subscribed and 600,000 people claimed the flights.

Hoover had to spend £48 million on flights to meet the terms of the offer. The company's European president, William Foust, and two other executives lost their jobs.

> **INDIVIDUAL** WORK (7.10) ★ ★
> Find out more about these two poorly organised sales promotions. What lessons should they teach other businesses before they launch their own sales promotions?

◈ Be run in line with accepted principles of fair competition and not bring the industry into disrepute.

◈ Operate in line with the spirit, as well as the letter, of the rules.

A business running a promotion is expected to make an informed estimate of expected demand before the promotion starts, and to have sufficient promotional products and resources available to meet that demand, and despatch goods within 30 days. Phrases like 'subject to availability' do not relieve a business of these responsibilities. All promotions should clearly state all the limitations and conditions associated with them, including the closing date and anything likely to influence a customer's participation in it. Complex rules should be avoided.

Customers are entitled to replacement goods or an immediate refund – the full cost of which falls on the promoter – if they receive damaged or faulty goods. Consumers must be able to keep the full business name and address after sending off the application form for the relevant promotion.

On average, the ASA receives around 1,500 complaints each year regarding promotions.

PRE-SALES PREPARATION

In order to succeed, businesses must be alert and responsive to the needs and preferences of today's consumers who are more demanding and discerning than ever.

This also means that the business needs to be creative, delivering quality and value for money. Consumers now expect the highest possible standards of customer care. This means proper policies and procedures for dealing with enquiries and complaints, should things go wrong. It requires staff who are properly trained and equipped for dealing with customers with special needs and those from minority and ethnic backgrounds. The business needs to have a sound working knowledge of consumer rights and entitlements. Finally, a business needs to put all of these factors into action.

Understanding consumer protection legislation

Many businesses do not provide any customer information about their policies for refunds, complaints and customer care. In many cases, where information is provided, the nature of it and how it is provided, is very much dependent on the size of the business.

Larger businesses may have a website, although many do not use them to provide customer information. On the other hand, smaller businesses are more likely to provide customer care information by advice at point-of-sale. All businesses use printed material like leaflets and brochures to some extent.

Customers need to have confidence in the products and services they buy and also in the business that they are dealing with. Information about the business and its customer care policies should be readily available and easily accessible.

Generally, business awareness of consumer protection legislation is poor. Many businesses are unsure if there is a specific body dealing with complaints for their business or industry. There is enormous confusion about the roles and responsibilities of various agencies.

In a recent survey, over half of businesses had never heard of some of the organisations involved in consumer protection and had no idea how to contact them. Overall, smaller businesses tend to be less aware than larger businesses.

It is important that businesses are familiar with consumer protection arrangements generally and not just the bodies relevant to their business. It also means that employees need to be aware and it is the responsibility of the business to inform them and keep them up to date with the legislation.

> **INDIVIDUAL WORK**
> **(7.11)** ★ ★
> How might a retail store or chain ensure that its sales staff is kept up to date with consumer protection legislation?

Business and retail customers and professionally trained buyers

Many businesses do not just deal with retail customers. A shop that sells stationery, for example, may be geared up primarily to deal with retail customers that come into the store. They will, however, often supply a number of local businesses with their stationery requirements. Depending on the size of the business, some of the sales staff may only deal with retail customers, whilst others will deal with the local businesses.

Businesses tend to buy in greater quantities than retail customers and they may also have accounts with the business and be given credit terms. Businesses as customers are keen to purchase their products and services at a good price, as well as expecting a high level of customer service. An organisation that supplies other businesses with products and services, therefore, will encounter professional business buyers that will often wish to negotiate prices, delivery, credit terms and discounts.

Supply constraints

It is not always possible for a business to have adequate stocks of products to meet the demands of its customers. Retail stores, in particular, are reliant upon their suppliers to be able to deliver products as and when they are ordered. It is therefore likely that from time to time certain products will not be available for immediate delivery or pick-up. In such cases, the sales staff need to find out when the products may or may not be back in stock and to clearly explain to the customer that it is possible to order the product, but that the delivery date needs to be checked.

Some customers will want to purchase and take products away immediately, and it is the role of the sales staff to try to make the sale, even if the products are not in stock, rather than risk the customer purchasing the product elsewhere. Customers must be told if a product is not in stock. They will expect to be given a firm date as to when the product will be available and also wish to be advised if that date changes. If the product is not in stock by the promised date, then the customer may seek a refund or cancel their order.

Product knowledge

Just as sales staff need to be aware of the business's policies on dealing with customers and have a knowledge of consumer protection legislation, they also need to be seen as an expert, or at least knowledgeable, about the products that they are selling. Customers will often ask sales staff for their opinion of various competing products. They will ask about features and benefits of each of the products so they can make a more informed choice before deciding which to buy.

Many businesses have a policy towards this service to customers and will often steer the customers to products that provide the business with a greater profit margin.

Business customer sales histories

If a business deals with other businesses, then they will have fuller and more accurate records of the previous purchases made by those customers. These customer records will contain the following information:

INDIVIDUAL WORK
(7.12) ★★
Using Microsoft Word, design a simple customer record card for business customers. It should contain spaces to include all the information listed here.

- How often they make purchases
- How much they are likely to spend in a single order
- What kind of products or services they buy
- The names of the buyers
- The address and contact details
- The method of payment
- Any delivery requirements
- The discounts offered.

Pricing policies

Normally, retail customers only receive discount from shops if the products have already been discounted by the store and are available at that price to anyone. When a store deals with business customers, however, they will have a range of discounts, usually dependent upon how important the customer is to the business. Usually, the larger the amount spent by a business customer, the higher the discount offered.

A business does need to ensure that each product's price covers all of the costs incurred by the business in buying it from a supplier and selling it. The business will then add its profit margin to the product. The amount of profit can, of course, differ if the discounts offered to businesses are different. Obviously the higher the discount, the lower the profit margins made on each of the products.

The business customer records will detail the amount of discount normally given to that business. A business may actually ask for a larger discount than usual, and in such cases it would be the responsibility of the manager to decide whether or not this additional discount can be given.

Customer service training

A significant number of businesses currently do not provide any training for their staff in customer care. The vast majority of larger businesses tend to provide training of some kind. Small and medium-sized businesses, on the other hand, are less likely to do so.

Where training is provided, this tends to be either general or in areas such as the business complaints handling policies. Less training is provided in areas such as consumer rights, dealing with people with disabilities or from ethnic minorities, dealing with older consumers and people with children.

Once again, the level of customer service training depends on the size of the business, with larger businesses much more likely to provide staff training of this nature. Businesses do realise that better staff training will eventually be reflected in increased consumer satisfaction.

Many businesses aim to increase and develop their staff training. This applies in particular to small and medium-sized businesses where less training is provided at present and where levels of business knowledge and awareness are lowest.

The vast majority of businesses do need to provide more staff training in dealing with customers from disability, ethnic and other minority backgrounds.

Different clients and range of customer requirements

In the course of a normal day, sales staff in a retail store will have to provide assistance to a wide variety of different customer types. Not all customers will be alone. Many will be part of a group comprising people of different ages. Younger people respond to a less formal approach and want more of a relaxed interaction with the sales staff. Older customers may want a more respectful and professional approach.

Sales staff also need to be aware of the fact that they could easily offend customers from different cultural backgrounds. All customers need to be treated with respect. Some have different dress codes and preferences. Non-English-speaking customers can present a challenge to sales staff, although increasingly in many stores important information, particularly regarding customer service, has been translated into different languages. Essentially, a business may have the following types of customers:

- Single individuals may well be better-off than married couples or those with children. Very often these individual customers are younger, so the business will be keen to ensure that they become long-term customers. They will also bring in friends and, in later years, their partners and/or their children.

- It is common for families or groups of adults, or even groups of children, to become regular customers. Families make up the majority of the population and they consume many different products and services. The store needs to be family-friendly and, perhaps, provide baby-changing facilities or even play areas for the children.

- Customers will be of different ages and the store will have to cope with their different demands. As mentioned, younger people are reasonably happy with an informal approach, but older people like to be addressed and dealt with more formally.

- People from different cultural backgrounds can either be UK citizens or visitors from overseas. We live in a multicultural society and businesses need to be aware, particularly in cities and larger towns, that there will be considerable numbers of individuals and groups from different cultures.

- People with disabilities will need to be able to enter and move around the store easily. People with visual impairment may need assistance. Those with literacy or numeracy difficulties may require help reading signs or information on products.

Negotiation skills, courtesy and efficiency

In addition to customers needing advice about different products, a sales assistant's role is ultimately to persuade the customer to part with money in exchange for the products. Sales assistants consider it a failure, having had a conversation with a customer about a range of products, for that customer then to leave the store without making a purchase and, perhaps, buying the products elsewhere. Whilst sales staff need to be aware of how they provide customer service, their primary goal is to sell products.

Some customers may need encouragement and persuasion before they decide whether to purchase a product or not. To successfully make a sale, a sales person needs to:

GROUP WORK (7.14)
★ ★

1 Why might it be important to a retail business that their customers feel valued and that the staff care?

2 What are the implications to the business if the customers do not feel valued and the staff give the impression that they could not care less about them?

- Establish a rapport with the customer.
- Find out what the customer is interested in.
- Describe the major benefits of the product.
- Overcome any objections to purchasing the product.
- Answer any questions about the product, price, delivery or any other matter that could leave the customer undecided.
- Close the sale. In other words, they have to convince the customer to buy the product now.

Most customers will need help and assistance. Sometimes the help may be of a practical nature, such as demonstrating how a product works. Whatever the nature of the request for assistance, sales staff always need to be polite and appear willing to help. However small the request for assistance might be, customers must feel that they are valued and that the staff actually care about them.

Referral procedures

In some cases, a situation may arise with a customer that cannot be resolved and the situation will have to be passed on to a more experienced or senior member of staff. Referral procedures differ from store to store, but usually there is a senior or experienced sales person available to ask for advice or to take over the situation.

Typical referral situations include:

- A customer with a complaint that cannot be dealt with using the normal complaints procedure.
- A customer who is abusive or rude.
- A customer asking about aspects of the product that the sales staff are unable to answer.
- A customer making requests that are outside the authority of the sales staff.

Return and exchange policies

Normally a business will have a policy which will allow a customer to return the item for an exchange or refund if they are not completely satisfied with their purchase. Usually, all articles in saleable condition are accepted for credit or exchange within 30 days of purchase. Cash refunds will be made only to the purchaser.

Some businesses will adopt a more complicated policy. If the goods are damaged or faulty, customers will need to contact customer services as soon as possible. Customer services will then arrange a replacement or a refund. Usually, customers will need to contact customer services and arrange for the goods to be returned within seven days for a refund.

INDIVIDUAL WORK
(7.15) ★ ★
Find out about the returns policy in one of your local stores.

Security personnel

Many stores prefer store detectives to uniformed guards so that thieves do not know that they are being watched. Store detectives are highly skilled at blending into the background inside stores. Their role is to observe customers' behaviour by acting like

WANT TO FIND OUT MORE?

Useful information on store detectives and uniformed guards can be obtained from the **International Professional Security Association (IPSA):**
Northumberland House Business Centre
11 The Pavement
Popes Lane
Ealing
London W5 4NG
Tel: 020 8832 7417
www.ipsa.org.uk

INDIVIDUAL WORK
(7.16) ★★
Visit the IPSA website and answer the following questions.

1 When was IPSA formed?

2 What are its purposes?

3 What kind of members, individuals and organisations, does it have?

normal shoppers and not arousing suspicion. If they see a customer stealing from the store, then they will follow the customer until they have shown they have no intention of paying for the goods, and then arrest them for theft.

Policies within stores differ, but the detective may detain the offender until the police arrive, or may issue a formal warning and banning order and then escort the offender from the premises.

Store detectives are ideal for larger stores with poor CCTV coverage. When a store is too big for a uniformed officer to observe all areas, a store detective will generally be more effective.

Store detectives need to have:

- A mature, responsible and honest nature
- Good observational skills
- Strong verbal and written communication skills
- The ability to handle sensitive situations
- A polite and helpful attitude
- A good level of personal fitness
- The confidence to challenge or tackle people when necessary
- The ability to use initiative and make quick decisions.

Uniformed security officers act as a deterrent to criminal activity, and provide a useful link between a business and its customers. Often the first person a customer will see when they enter a shop is the security guard; therefore first impressions are absolutely vital.

Preparation of the physical sales environment

In this part of the unit, we turn our attention to the place in which sales representatives or shop assistants carry out their duties. The physical sales environment refers to the place in which sales people and customers meet.

As we will see, the layout of stores can either determine how comfortable both groups are, or can be designed to ease the flow, aid security measures or simply make the premises more accessible.

Accessibility, furnishings and décor

By law, all stores open to the public have to have disabled access. This means that ramps and lifts have been constructed to comply with these laws. Ramps and lifts are, of course, of great value to people with small children and to older people.

Access is important. It should be easy for the customer to enter the shop and not have to hunt around for the entrance. Often the doors to shops are kept open or work electronically with sensors to detect movement outside.

Once inside the store, the customer needs to have enough space to move around. There must be sufficient room between the isles or products and everything needs to be clearly marked. Many larger stores have floor plans and notices telling the customers where certain items are located. Supermarkets have signs above the aisles to show the customers where to find regularly purchased items.

The store should be at the right temperature, it should have sufficient lighting, and customer service points and cashier tills need to be marked. In addition, the store needs to mark the emergency exits and, if they have any, the customer toilets.

The layout of the store is usually designed to encourage the flow of customers. Stores will avoid locating several regular-purchase products in the same place to prevent bottlenecks. They will locate these products around the store, also in the hope that as customers pass other products they will buy them as well.

The look of the store is also important. Many chains have a common look to all of their stores and indeed the layouts are very similar. Colour, use of lights, carpets, rest areas and other features are all designed to help the customer feel comfortable. This means that they will not rush and they will make decisions about purchasing products in a more relaxing environment. Stores hope that by making their customers more relaxed, they will buy more and come back more often.

INDIVIDUAL WORK
(7.17) ★ ★
Think about one of the stores you visit on a regular basis. How is it laid out? Are things easy to find? Does it make you feel more comfortable?

Use of music

Many retailers use music to help customers feel relaxed and believe that they are in familiar surroundings. In 1995, in the UK alone, royalty payments (paid to music companies and their artists for non-broadcast commercial use of music) amounted to £53.8 million. Research on music and consumer behaviour has, however, almost completely ignored the potential effect of in-store music on purchasing and particularly on product choice.

One study investigated the purchasing of German and French wines and it was discovered that a musical 'fit' has a huge influence on product choice. Four French and four German wines were displayed in a supermarket drinks section. The wines were matched between the countries for their price and dryness or sweetness. Each of the four shelves contained one French and one German wine and appropriate national flags.

The position of the wines on the shelves was changed halfway through the two-week testing period. French and German music was played on alternate days from a tape deck situated on the top shelf. Shoppers buying wines from the display were asked by two researchers to complete a questionnaire.

French wine outsold German wine when French music was played, whereas German wine outsold French wine when German music was played. Questionnaire responses indicated that the French music made customers think of France and the German music made them think of Germany.

Future research is planned to investigate the effects of music relative to silence, or relative to the effects of music from a country that does not produce wine.

INDIVIDUAL WORK
(7.18) ★ ★
What kind of music, if any, is played in your favourite store? What effect does it have on you?

Health and safety hazards

All employees need to be clear about the responsibilities they have to make sure that the store operates in a safe and careful manner. Just as it is easy for members of staff to injure themselves at work, it is also possible for customers to have accidents in the shop.

Routes around the store need to be kept clear. Cables, products that have not been put on shelves, or displays and any other obstacles need to be cleared from areas through which the customer traffic passes. In many stores selling electrical goods, there is an additional hazard from trailing wires, the electricity supply itself and children with drinks close by.

There can be a huge number of potential hazards to customers in any retail store. The business will need to have insurance in order to cover them for claims by customers should they injure themselves or their property whilst on the premises. The business will be held responsible if customers are injured and staff training would normally include instructions about ensuring customer safety.

Market competition and buyer behaviour

All businesses, as we have seen, face competition from a large number of other businesses. All businesses need to be aware of the activities of the competition. In a retail environment, this may mean a competitor having a wider range of products, selling products at a lower price, being more accessible to customers or simply having a better reputation. All of these factors can affect the sales and the behaviour of buyers visiting the store.

If the business fails to react to actions taken by its competitors, it runs the risk of not attracting as many customers. If the customers are not entering the store, then the sales staff cannot sell products to them.

The competition could be offering their customers any of the following, which will affect the way customers view the business and have an influence on where they choose to shop:

GROUP WORK (7.19)
★
As a group, think about at least two of the nearest supermarkets that you visit. How do they compare? Which is the most suitable for customers, using the list here as a guide?

- More convenient parking, close to the store, with disabled and parent/toddler parking spaces.
- More advertising in the media to attract customers to the store.
- A sale or discounted prices on various products.
- A wider range of products.
- Packing, car loading and delivery services.

- A wider range of services to customers, including refreshment area, children's play area, more tills, a good supply of trolleys, wider aisles, clear signposting.
- More and better-trained staff.

SALES PRACTICE

Effective sales practice is vital to all retail businesses. The business will have procedures in place to make their staff aware of the ways in which they require customers to be dealt with. The following headings explain in more detail what a business's procedures might require of their staff when dealing with customers.

Meeting and greeting customers

When using face-to-face communication, it is possible to see the other person's body language. Important face-to-face communication considerations are:

- Be polite.
- Be helpful.
- Make them feel valued – try to use the customer's name during the conversation so they feel special and remembered.
- Try not to be distracted by losing eye contact and looking elsewhere, or by fiddling with clothes or pulling at hair.
- Let the customer finish the conversation.
- Always leave with a smile and say goodbye.

Dealing with telephone calls is different because:

- Explanations can only be in words – there is no body language to reinforce what is being said.
- Attitude is expressed by the voice – the way one speaks and phrases used are the only way that the caller gets an impression of attitude.

Voices sound different on the telephone to the way they do in a face-to-face conversation. Those answering the telephone on behalf of the organisation should use a good telephone technique, which includes:

- Answer the telephone as quickly as possible – do not let it ring for ages before picking it up. Even if the person who normally answers that telephone is busy, someone else should answer their phone and help the caller in any way they can.
- The telephone should be answered with 'Good morning' or 'Good afternoon'. This is not just to be polite, but indicates to the caller that the phone call has started.
- The name of the person answering, or the name of the organisation or department in which they work, should be given. This tells the caller that they are through to the right section and are talking to the right person.
- Get into the habit of answering the telephone with the hand not used for writing. This leaves the writing hand free for jotting down any message or notes.
- Always have a pen and paper next to the telephone. Some organisations give their employees telephone message forms to use. These will have a series of different headings to remind the employee about the questions they may need to ask of the caller.
- If the telephone call involves finding out more information for the caller, then it may mean that they cannot be helped straightaway. If this is the case, their name and telephone number should be taken and once the information has been found out, they should be called back straightaway.
- If the telephone call is not for the person answering the call, they should give the caller some options:
  - Can someone else help them?
  - Can a message be taken?
  - Can someone else call them back when they are free to do so?

INDIVIDUAL WORK
(7.20) ★ ★
How much more difficult would it be to explain a product over the telephone compared to demonstrating the product to a customer face to face?

Asking appropriate questions and listening to customer answers

There are a number of important things to consider when having a face-to-face conversation or talking on the telephone (both are forms of verbal communication). You need to consider:

- The way you speak, for example whether you make yourself clear, or whether you use slang during your conversation.
- The pitch and tone of your voice.
- The way you listen and pay attention to what is being said.
- When not to speak or interrupt.
- What questions to ask.
- Body language – this can give someone who can see you an idea of what you are thinking . Body language can also help you to explain something.

GROUP WORK (7.21)
★ ★

How good are you at reading body language? Sit opposite a partner and see if you can express different feelings just by the expression on your face. Try showing each other the following expressions, but do not use any words:

anger	boredom	disapproval
annoyance	happiness	fear
shock	polite smiling	irritation

Body language is very important in face-to-face communication, more so than when speaking on the telephone because the two people having the conversation cannot see one another on the phone.

When having face-to-face communication with people a mixture of both verbal (spoken) and non-verbal (body language) communication is used. There are two considerations here:

- Being able to read other people's body language.
- Being aware that your body language can be read by the other person.

GROUP WORK (7.22)
★ ★

How good a listener are you?

1 In pairs, get your partner to tell you about a recent TV programme they have watched. They should talk to you for at least three minutes about this programme. Now you have to tell them everything that you can remember about what they said. Did you remember most of it or did they have to remind you about some things?

2 Now swop roles and repeat the exercise.

Listening is important in both face-to-face communication and for telephone calls. We all listen to a great number of different people during one day. But not many of us could remember exactly what has been said to us in each one of those conversations. That is why, when you are at work especially, it is a good idea to take notes during an important conversation. This helps you to remember what has been said later in the day.

Effective sales presentations

Sales staff play a crucial role in convincing customers to part with money for products and services. They do this by having sales conversations with the customers. These can take place either face-to-face or via the telephone. In many organisations the terms 'salesman', 'saleswoman' and 'salesperson' have now been replaced with titles such as 'sales adviser', 'sales counsellor', 'sales consultant' or 'sales representative'. There are a number of different types of presentation, including:

- *Sales promotions*, which as we have seen encourage customers to make repeat purchases, build up long-term customer loyalty and encourage new customers to visit the store. They include price reductions, vouchers, coupons, gifts, competitions, lotteries and cash bonuses.
- *Sales seminars*, which are usually aimed at the sales representatives themselves or business buyers. They provide information about the products and services, along with a demonstration. They explain how complaints and faults are handled and are aimed at improving the awareness of the products and services, as well as helping customers to understand more about the business.
- *Product launches*, which are also aimed to broaden the appeal of particular products or services and, in some cases, the opening of a new store. Product launches can take place at exhibitions or displays. In other cases, sales reps would demonstrate the product, perhaps in a location other than the store

itself. An example would be in the main public area of a shopping mall. These are aimed to attract customers to the store or to try new products and services.

Sales presentations are supported by a number of different forms of display, which are designed both to make the product more attractive and the store more interesting. Examples of displays that support sales presentations are:

INDIVIDUAL WORK
(7.23) ★ ★
On your way home from school or college, note down how many different advertising messages you see. Where are they directing you to go to purchase products and services? What made you notice them?

- 🖌 *Window areas* These can include posters stuck to the glass or boards in the window area, a pelmet with the product's name pasted along the edges of the window, empty product packs attractively stacked, life-size cut-outs of product characters or personalities and illuminated displays with flashing lights. They are designed to be eye-catching and striking and attract customers into the store.

- 🖌 *Point-of-sale* This is the area near the cash tills. Examples include cut-out displays that move with the air current and are suspended from the ceiling, posters announcing special offers, a pelmet along a shelf, empty packs, dump bins placed near the tills with a selection of products, wire stands for smaller products, portable displays and dispenser boxes for leaflets and brochures.

- 🖌 *Public places* These are areas away from the store where significant numbers of potential customers pass by. These could include illuminated displays, display stands, leaflet dispensers, video screens and TVs.

- 🖌 *Advertising sites* These would be placed near areas where potential customers visit or pass, including bus and railway stations, airports, buses and trains or outside buildings.

Non-verbal communication

Non-verbal communication is body language. The key points of body language are:

- 🖌 *Facial expressions* These are the most common form of body language and we should always be aware of what our face is telling someone else. For example:
  - A smile can make a big difference when you meet someone.
  - Our eyes can widen when we are surprised and narrow when angry.
  - Our eyebrows move upwards when we do not believe something and lower when we are angry or confused about something.
  - We can look bored if our mouth is pouting.

- 🖌 *Gestures* We use our head and hands a lot when we agree or disagree with something. We can gesture to:
  - Agree with someone by nodding our heads.
  - Disagree with someone by shaking our heads from side to side.
  - Greet someone from a distance by waving our hands.
  - Give someone directions by pointing with our finger.
  - Giving someone the 'thumbs up' sign to let them know everything is OK.

- 🖌 *Posture (the way we sit or stand)* This can also tell others a lot about what we are thinking or how we are reacting to someone else.
  - Sitting well back in a chair with ankles crossed gives the impression of being relaxed or confident.
  - Sitting on the edge of a seat gives the impression of being nervous.
  - Standing straight with head high gives the impression of confidence.
  - Standing slumped with shoulders down gives the impression of being depressed or lacking confidence.

- 🖌 *How close one gets to other people* Apart from shaking hands, we do not often get close to people we meet at work. Most people have an invisible circle around them that they prefer others not to enter. This means that they may feel uncomfortable if others get too close to them. Getting too close to someone else's face can be a sign of aggression.

- 🖌 *Whether one is sitting or standing* Someone who is seated and having a conversation with a person who is standing up can often feel 'lower' in importance than the one standing.

- 🖌 *Eye contact* It is important to have eye contact with the person you are talking to. Eye contact shows the other person that you are giving them your full attention and often helps them to understand what is being said. Sometimes it is possible to get a better idea of how someone is going to react by looking into their eyes. Be careful though not to 'stare' into someone's eyes as this can be a sign of aggression.

Supplying appropriate information

Customers will need a range of information to help them choose and buy products or services. They will expect the staff to be able to give them all the information they need. Sales staff, therefore, need the following skills in order to provide the correct information:

- They must understand what is being asked.
- They must be able to provide the information or know where that information can be found.
- They must understand that any request for information is important, both for the customer and for the business.

Sales staff need to be fully trained in order to at least appear to have the information readily to hand. The information needs to be relevant and explained in the shortest possible time.

Preparing quotes and estimates

It may be the case that the customer asks for a quote. This means that the sales rep has to state the actual price of the product, the date of delivery and any discounts that the customer may be able to receive. Business customers, in particular, will ask for quotes as they get quotes from several suppliers before deciding which business to purchase their products from.

An estimate usually refers to a service, rather than a product. This is because the cost of providing the service may be different in every situation. An example would be a retail store that sells and installs kitchen units. The price of each of the units may be clear, but the price to actually fit the units may differ from customer to customer. It is rather like preparing a quote, but this time the sales rep needs more information from the customer, perhaps regarding the size of the kitchen, where electricity points are and where the water supply comes into the room. Having received this information, an estimate, which is a best guess at the likely price to provide the service, can be made.

Pace of interaction

The sales representative's main responsibility is to sell products or services. They must therefore make a decision about to how long to spend with each customer. The customer may not wish to be rushed, but while the sales rep is busy with one customer they cannot deal with another customer. It is, therefore, part of the sales rep's role to judge how quickly they can deal with an individual customer and bring the conversation to a successful sales conclusion. A fine balance has to be maintained: a customer does not want to feel rushed, but other customers do not want to have to wait too long.

Customers with special needs

As we have seen, when we looked at different types of customers, some may have special needs, including people who have:

- A disability or who use a wheelchair
- A visual or hearing impairment
- Literacy or numeracy difficulties
- Small children
- A first language which is not English.

Many larger stores deal with all of these different types of customer with special needs, but others have to deal with the situation as and when it arises. Disabled people, for example, might need a seating area or wheelchair access; people with visual impairment may need to be directed to particular parts of the store. People with hearing impairment might need products to be demonstrated rather than explained. People with literacy or numeracy problems or a poor understanding of English may benefit from a demonstration rather than an explanation.

People with small children will not only need easy access, but may also need baby-changing facilities or, perhaps, a play area.

Following up sales leads and sales administration

A sales lead is when a customer makes an enquiry about a product or service, but does not follow it up with a purchase. The business will have taken note of their name and contact details. If the customer does not come back to make a purchase after a day or two, the business will contact them to see if they can convince them to make the purchase.

Many businesses receive enquiries from customers on a daily basis. They will ask about the availability of products, their price, delivery charges and whether the products are in stock. Each of these contacts made with customers represent a potential sale and businesses have a number of different methods of following up these leads to try to achieve a sale.

In the normal course of daily activities, a sales department would have to deal with a number of administrative duties. These include:

- Handling correspondence and responding to telephone contacts with customers
- Keeping and updating customer records
- Arranging customer visits and reporting back on meetings with customers
- Taking, progressing and monitoring orders
- Processing invoices
- Preparing quotations and estimates
- Keeping records of sales targets and actual figures.

Typical activities will vary according to the business in which the sales representative is working, but may include:

- Maintaining loyalty from existing customers through regular review visits.
- Calling on potential customers to demonstrate products and attempt to win new markets.
- Ensuring that they fully understand customers' businesses and requirements.
- Acting as an information channel between a company and its products and existing/potential markets.
- Contacting clients by telephone to negotiate terms of an agreement and using persuasion skills to conclude the sale.
- Gathering market and customer information.
- Staffing trade exhibitions and demonstrations.
- Negotiating variations in price, delivery and specifications.
- Advising on forthcoming product developments and discussing special promotions.
- Trouble-shooting in matters of documentation, delivery, service and parts.
- Visiting retail and wholesale outlets.
- Checking quantities of goods on display and in stock.
- Determining the appropriate order and negotiating with the manager.
- Recording sales and order information and sending copies to the sales office.
- Reviewing own sales performance.
- Making accurate, rapid cost calculations.
- Feeding back to employers any information gathered on future buying trends.

Warehouse and distribution

The main function of warehousing and distribution is to coordinate the movement of products and services in and out of the business. In situations where an organisation provides a delivery service to customers, it is essential that the most efficient and cost-effective routes are chosen.

A distribution manager will usually run the *distribution centre*. He or she is responsible for designing, running and maintaining a cost-effective centre to ensure that products arrive at the business in a suitable state and at the right time, and are sent out to customers in the same manner.

The distribution manager would usually work in close cooperation with the sales department, as it will be the distribution manager that has to make sure that any promises made by sales staff to customers are fulfilled. The distribution manager, therefore, usually controls all of the warehousing and storage and is supported by two other managers:

- *The transport manager*, who deals with all aspects of delivery. He or she works in close cooperation with the distribution manager, the warehouse manager and the sales department. It is this person's role to ensure that deliveries to customers are made when promised.

- *The warehouse manager*, who is responsible for the smooth running of the storage of products kept by the business. He or she will also be responsible for accepting deliveries of products from suppliers. Sometimes the warehouse manager may have to organise the collection of products from the store to be brought back to the warehouse for delivery to customers. The warehouse manager has to ensure that the warehouse is well organised, that products can be found and that there is an accurate record of how many of each product are in stock.

GROUP WORK (7.26)
★ ★
Assuming a warehouse is not located behind a retail store's premises, where would a warehouse be ideally located to carry out its functions of accepting deliveries, storing products and delivering them to customers?

Dealing with more than one customer

As we have seen, the demands on a sales rep's time can mean that several customers may be waiting for assistance. We have also seen that the sales rep has to pace their interaction with each customer to suit that customer's needs, but also be aware of the fact that there are other customers waiting.

It is possible for a sales rep to deal with more than one customer at the same time. Different parts of the sales process can be reached with each customer. If, for example, a sales rep has already convinced a customer to purchase a product and is just waiting for someone to bring the product from the warehouse, this customer can be left until this has happened and the rep can move on to another customer. Perhaps they can take their money at the till, show them the products and explain that they will return when they have had a chance to look at them in their own time.

Closing a sale

Closing a sale is the ultimate goal of a sales rep. A sale is closed when the product has been exchanged for payment (or promise of payment in the case of a credit sale). To reach this stage, the sales rep will have dealt with any objections, queries or questions the customer has posed, and convinced them to make the purchase.

Once the sale is closed, the sales rep will always ask whether there is anything else that they can help the customer with. They will thank the customer and the interaction with the customer at this stage will be over. As we will see, however, it is valuable for the business not to end the relationship with the customer at this point. As far as the sales rep is concerned regarding this particular sale, their role is now over. But they may well have interaction with the customer in the near future.

Repeat purchases

Satisfied customers mean repeat business and recommendations from those customers to other potential customers. If a customer has left the store happy, they will continue to buy their products from that business. This is known as *repeat business*. The retail store will want customers to keep coming back and also to bring their friends and family along with them. Ultimately this will mean the business will have more customers. If the customer has had a good experience with the business, they are more likely to recommend it to others. Customers that have come to the store after

INDIVIDUAL WORK
(7.27) ★ ★
Think about your favourite store. Do they run any schemes to reward you if you recommend another person to become a customer? If they do not, what could they reasonably offer you to do this on their behalf?

recommendation may well become regular customers themselves and recommend the business to even more people.

Some businesses offer vouchers and discounts to their existing customers who recommend other customers. This is an incentive to encourage them to talk about their experiences with the business and to convince others to make purchases from that business.

Customer contact details and following up a sale

Many businesses carry out transactions with their customers and the only information they retain is a cheque or credit card receipt. This means that they have not captured any information about the customer that could be of value to them in the future. Some businesses, however, take a different approach.

In retailing, a large number of individual stores and chains have customer loyalty cards. To receive one of these cards, the customer has to complete a form, stating their name, address and other contact details. Each time the customer uses their card, the business puts the details of their transaction with the business onto the customer record database.

Tesco, for example, runs an extremely successful customer loyalty card system. The card rewards customers that make repeat purchases from them. Their customer database is sophisticated and is able to identify the key products purchased by each individual customer. They then generate individual statements, vouchers and offers to match the buying habits of the customer. In this way, Tesco can reward customers for being loyal, give them incentives to purchase more products and introduce new products that might be of interest to the customer by offering them at a discounted price.

When dealing with business customers, particularly those that have credit terms, a business will have to retain contact details. Invoices, statements of account and reminders need to be sent out from time to time. In addition to this the business will use their customer contact database to generate letters to all their customers, telling them about new products and services or special offers. Again the business can target particular customers and design the special offer or information to suit their buying habits.

CASE STUDY Customer loyalty cards

Around 70 per cent of UK consumers have customer loyalty cards, and many have customer loyalty cards from several competing businesses. Customer loyalty cards are the fastest-growing modern point-of-sale development. Customers are spoilt for choice and switch brands or businesses far more easily than before. Customer loyalty cards need to clearly give the customer benefits. As far as the business is concerned, they not only need to ensure that records are kept up to date, but they also need to know which customers have the highest levels of loyalty. Businesses can use loyalty cards to focus on their most profitable customers and then they need to gear up their business to serve these individuals.

INDIVIDUAL WORK (7.28) ★ ★
Read the case study and then answer the following questions.

1 Why might an individual choose to have more than one loyalty card?

2 How might a business encourage a customer with a loyalty card who has not purchased for some time to return and purchase again?

3 Should a business waste time trying to attract back lost customers or should they concentrate on their profitable ones?

AFTER-SALES SERVICE

After-sales service recognises the fact that the organisation's relationship with the customer does not end with placing the product in a carrier bag and taking their money. The organisation will be keen to provide:

- Friendly and supportive advice, either in-store or via a helpline
- Stocks of spare parts
- An efficient maintenance service.

These features are designed to encourage the customer to make repeat purchases with the business. In addition to the provision of repairs, maintenance and advice, after-sales service has become an integral part of a business's marketing and customer service provision.

Customers expect after-sales service and often this will be a deciding factor when making the decision about which business to choose for their purchase.

Nationwide or international dealer network information

Many retailers are part of a chain, which means that after-sales service can be delivered at any location where the chain has an outlet, regardless of where the product was purchased. If, for example, a customer purchased a product in Glasgow whilst on holiday, they could return the product, if it proved faulty, to a branch nearer their own home. This form of nationwide network provides a far more convenient way for customers to receive after-sales service.

Manufacturers also have similar arrangements. They will have a network of dealers, possibly across the globe. So someone who has purchased a car from a London dealer will be able to obtain after-sales service from another dealer in France if they were there when a problem occurred.

Other businesses use the services of independent dealers to carry out their repairs and after-sales service, particularly if they do not have outlets of their own in a particular area.

Preparation for returns

Any outlet in a chain, or indeed part of a dealer network, needs to be prepared to provide after-sales service to customers. This service must include the ability to repair, replace or even give a refund, depending on the circumstances. The returned item will eventually find its way back to its original manufacturer, but at the point of contact with the customer it is the member of the retail chain or the dealer that will have to carry out the necessary interaction, customer service and after-sales service with the purchaser.

Dealing with complaints

Customer dissatisfaction may lead to complaints and requests for assistance. Reasons for dissatisfaction can include:

- A product or service which is either faulty or not suitable
- A product which the business does not stock or which is out of stock
- Poor service
- A problem which no one seems able to assist the customer with.

Most businesses have a formal complaints procedure for customers who are dissatisfied. It is usual practice for complaints to be referred to a manager who has the power to act on them and make an on-the-spot decision to deal with the situation. There are some key points to remember in the event of a complaint:

- Do not interrupt. Give the customer the opportunity to explain the situation.
- Always appear to be sympathetic to the customer.
- In particularly complicated cases, make sure that all details are written down.
- Check with the customer the main points of their complaint.
- Even when the customer is rude or abusive, stay calm and polite.
- Refer the matter to a senior member of staff if necessary.
- Never give the customer a vague answer or an unbelievable excuse.
- Do not directly blame another member of staff.
- Do not lose your temper.
- Remember, it is a problem as far as the customer is concerned and it should be taken seriously.

◇ Always tell the customer exactly what is happening, particularly if this involves having to refer it to another member of staff.

◇ Never make promises which cannot be kept by the business.

An organisation that is concerned with improving its customer service will carefully check all the complaints they receive. They will want to know how often different customers complain about the same thing. If they find that complaints about the same subject occur regularly, then they will attempt to improve the situation. Often they will have a special form that customers have to complete. Reading these forms will help the organisation's managers to decide if the service can be improved or if extra services can be introduced to improve customer satisfaction.

In carrying out their business activities, many organisations will receive a number of written complaints from their customers. In response, the organisation would have to write back to the customer. Depending on the type of complaint, this could be a simple letter of apology, or it could involve:

◇ The letter plus an offer of a refund.

◇ The letter plus an offer to replace faulty products or services.

◇ The letter plus an offer of a cash payment to reimburse the customer for any problems or inconvenience.

Obviously an investigation into the complaint would have to be undertaken by the organisation. They would be interested to find out whether the complaint was a result of some action by an employee or group of employees. If this were the case, then they would want to reassure the customer that the individual would be suitably disciplined.

Even if, after their investigations, the organisation discovers that the customer has no real cause for complaint, they would still want to respond to the customer. Often they would:

◇ Apologise to the customer for the fact that they have found cause to complain.

◇ Make a 'token' offer to the customer. This could be a voucher to be spent at the organisation in the future. They would do this so that the customer felt satisfied with the way the organisation had handled the complaint and to maintain 'goodwill' with the customer.

All letters of complaint should be handled as quickly as possible. Even when an enquiry or investigation has to be undertaken before a solution is found, the customer should be kept informed as to what the organisation intends to do and when they intend to do it.

Repairs and replacement parts

A customer complaint might occur some weeks or months after the original purchase. Usually, in the early stages after a purchase, a customer will demand and the business will give them a replacement or a refund. After a certain point, however, it is more likely that the product may need repair. Depending upon how long ago the purchase was made and whether it is covered by a guarantee or warranty, the retail outlet will take the responsibility of sending the faulty product back to the manufacturer, who would carry out the repair and then send it back to the retailer, who in turn will inform the customer that the repair has been carried out.

Other businesses run repair services that require a specialist to visit the customer and carry out the repair on site. The cost of the repairs would be covered under the guarantee or warranty of the product, if this has not expired. The problem arises when the product is no longer being made and replacement parts become difficult to obtain. The manufacturers of products, such as cars, washing machines and television sets, hold a small stock of replacement parts for products that they no longer manufacture. Local repair services, either employed by the manufacturer or retailer, can obtain these parts direct from the manufacturer, although this process takes time.

Positive and negative recommendations and publicity and identifying sources of customer dissatisfaction

As we have seen, a positive experience from a customer can lead to their making a positive recommendation to others about the business. A negative experience with a business can result in customers warning other people not to use the business.

The average customer with an unresolved complaint will tell nine or 10 people; 13 per cent tell more than 20 people. For every one complaint received, the average business has 26 unhappy customers it never hears from; six of these customers have problems that are considered 'serious' problems. Up to 70 per cent of complainers will return to a business if their complaint is resolved. Up to 95 per cent return if the problem is resolved quickly.

The main reasons behind customer dissatisfaction are:

- Uncaring, negative attitude of employees and management
- Upset with the treatment they received
- Failure to return customer calls
- Employees not given the power to make decisions
- Poor handling and resolution of complaints.

These can be summarised under the following headings:

- Performance of the staff, business or product
- Unrealistic expectations of the staff, business or product
- Misunderstandings.

In order to deal with these issues, a business needs to realise that:

- The customer is the most important person in the business.
- The customer is not dependent on the business; the business is dependent on the customer. The business therefore works for the customer.
- The customer is not an interruption of work. The customer is the purpose of the work.
- It is the employees' job to satisfy the needs, wants and expectations of the customers and, whenever possible, resolve their fears and complaints.
- The customer is the lifeblood of the business and deserves the most attentive, courteous and professional treatment the business can provide.

All of these reasons can be addressed by making sure that customer service is delivered to the highest possible standard, that products and the level of service are accurately described and that any information given to the customer is correct. In other words, better and clearer interaction with customers can handle the majority of reasons why a customer can become dissatisfied.

GROUP WORK (7.30)
★ ★

1 As a group, explain any after-sales service you may have had to ask for from a business. What was your experience of that after-sales service? Did it leave you with a positive or negative image of the business?

2 Individually, try to find a customer care and after-sales service leaflet or brochure from a business local to you. Many supermarkets and retail chains have customer service information available. Argos is a good example as they give their customers a refund and exchange policy.

Unit Revision Questions

1 What is the difference between above-the-line and below-the-line marketing methods?

2 What is the ASA?

3 What is the value to a business of maintaining customer sales histories?

4 In which year did the Consumer Credit Act become law, and what is APR?

5 How might music aid sales?

6 State three health and safety hazards to customers in a retail store.

7 What is sales administration?

8 What is the difference between warehousing and distribution?

9 Briefly define after-sales service.

10 Give three key reasons for customer dissatisfaction.

UNIT 8

Business Online

This unit looks at the ever-growing opportunities for businesses in conducting their sales and marketing via the internet. It will look at some of the different types of online business activity that allow customers to view products, buy online and even customise a product. The unit also looks at the various advantages and disadvantages of an online presence and how this fits in with particular businesses' aims and objectives. It also asks you to implement an online presence as part of a feasibility study for a business.

This is an internally-assessed unit and to cover the various aspects of the unit you must:

- Explore a range of online business activities
- Investigate the benefits of an online business presence
- Examine potential disadvantages of an online business presence
- Consider the business feasibility of going online.

ONLINE BUSINESS ACTIVITY

It is difficult to assess the value of internet-based business throughout the world. Some estimates suggest that the total value of electronic commerce worldwide has already exceeded $208 billion. Of this, around 88 per cent is commerce between businesses. Growth areas include wholesale and retail, estimated at around $89 billion per year.

Consumer online expenditure is around $26 billion per year and growing year-on-year as more households buy computers and start buying products and services over the internet.

CASE STUDY Get into the net

Some 20 million Britons were predicted to do their shopping on the internet during 2004, according to a report from IMRG (an e-commerce trade organisation).

IMRG estimated that UK shoppers would spend £17 billion online in 2004, rising to £80 billion by 2009. The Chief Executive of Tesco said: 'You only have to look at the business we did last December to see how fast the online operation is growing. We did as many sales in December as we did in the whole of 1998.'

According to Sainsbury's Bank, which has seen a 600 per cent increase in internet banking customers over the years 2000–03, banking services are due the next big increase in revenues. The bank predicts a big increase in the number of financial products purchased online. The bank's Chief Executive said: 'People are becoming increasingly time-poor and this has been a significant factor behind the growth of online banking and supermarket banking in general.'

Sainsburys estimated that there was a 31 per cent increase in online purchasing of financial products in 2003 and that this was set to continue. Some three million UK adults now buy their financial services online.

INDIVIDUAL WORK (8.1)

★ ★ ★

1 If the approximate population of the UK is 60 million, what is the average spending per person predicted for 2004 and 2009, based on the figures given in the case study?

2 If three million adults bought their financial products online in 2003, what will be the figure in 2004, assuming that the increase was the same as in the previous year?

Auctions

Auctioning items is no new thing, but it has become an extremely popular activity online. In auctions, the seller sets a low starting price and a group of buyers bid gradually higher prices until a winner is announced.

Today a large part of e-commerce is comprised of online auctions, selling practically anything to worldwide buyers every day of the week. There is an increasing number of auction sites, but the largest is eBay.

eBay was founded in 1995 and the site quickly grew into an online marketplace for individuals and businesses to buy and sell items. Initially, eBay was the site to buy and sell collectables and antiques, but now there is virtually no limit to the range of products on sale on the site. On average there are around 12 million items for sale in some 18,000 categories. In 2002, eBay sales reached nearly $15 billion, the site levying a percentage on each item listed and a small percentage of the final sale price.

Online auctions tend to be person-to-person, business-to-business or business-to-customer sales relationships. Both new and used items are posted, usually with a picture, description and a warranty or guarantee, as well as shipping information.

After the auction closes, usually after five to seven days, the bidder with the highest price wins and is contacted by the seller to finalise the transaction. After a transaction is completed both buyer and seller are asked to leave a feedback rating about each other's performance. Future buyers can then gauge a seller's credibility by using these feedback ratings.

The buyer and the seller can remain anonymous, buying and selling under assumed names. This sometimes causes problems when there are disputes. Purchasing through online auctions does entail a certain amount of risk for both buyers and sellers. Problems can include broken items, items different to what the buyer expected, stolen items being sold, and even stolen credit cards being used for purchases. The most common problem is either the seller, or more often the buyer, failing to get in contact once the auction is over.

Online auctions have radically changed the way in which individuals and businesses buy products and services. An individual or business with internet access anywhere in the world can now be involved in the buying and selling of products and services to anyone else anywhere else in the world. It seems certain that the trend will only grow in future years.

Banking

The number of individuals in the UK who use online banking is another difficult figure to assess. At least seven million people use online banking facilities and recent research suggests that this figure may be doubled.

With over 60 per cent of the UK population using the internet, digital TV and new-generation WAP mobile phones, the trend is definitely towards greater numbers using online banking services.

Many banks have been closing branches, reducing the number of their employees and establishing call centres out of the UK, but there has not been a sudden rush by account holders to adopt online banking as their sole form of banking services. Indeed, other research has shown that only 40 per cent of those who do not use online banking would be interested in doing so in the future.

Recent trends include the possibility of making payments by email rather than by writing a cheque. This is a highly popular option for those who use the internet on a more regular basis.

The number of online banking customers seems to be growing at a rate of around one million a year, with the online banks concentrating on new services and products to offer customers. Banks are keen, for cost reasons, to move as many of their customers as possible away from the expensive high street branches to online customers.

The banks have suffered a backlash against the closures of their high street branches and the cutbacks in staff at these banks. However, it has meant that many customers, who can, have been driven to do most of their banking online. Many financial specialists believe that the fact that the banks have failed to give good service in the high street has led to many people using the online services instead, which will mean that the banks can save enormous sums of money and continue their cuts in the number of employees.

Banks have recently begun to realise that online banking is no substitute for high street banks and that many people actually want to deal with the financial matters face-to-face rather than on the telephone or by a series of online form filling and emails. Banks are beginning to look for a balance between high street banks and online interaction with their customers.

Chat rooms

Chat line users are amongst the heaviest users of the internet. A chat room is a place on the internet where people with similar interests can meet and communicate by typing messages to one another on their computers.

The vast majority of people in chat rooms are there for genuine reasons and there is an incredible amount of learning and sharing occurring each minute of each day on a global basis. Chat rooms are a popular method of communication for young people.

Messages that are typed in by a user appear instantly to everybody who is in that chat room. Some chat rooms are 'moderated' – certain messages are not broadcast because they do not conform to the standards set up by the operator of the service. Reasons for a message being blocked could include: discussion off the topic, bad language or repeat messaging especially of undesirable or obscene text, known as 'flaming'.

CASE STUDY Internet chatters

A recent survey by NetValue found chatters to be online more than 17 days a month, and also discovered chatters to be heavy users of other internet protocols, particularly audio-video streaming (used by 54 per cent of chatters), secured connections (92 per cent) and instant messaging (59 per cent). Not surprisingly, chatters send and receive more than twice as many emails as the general internet population. Male chatters send and receive more than three times as many emails as the general male internet user.

Chatters clicked on an average of 4.8 banners in one month, which is almost double that of the general internet population, and their unique page views are also more than double the overall internet population.

'When it comes to defining the typical chat room participant, there is no significant gender gap in the percentage of chat users,' said Jim Hatch, president of NetValue. 'However, there are considerable differences in their demographic profiling. For example, 8.1 per cent of female chatters defined their occupation as professional, compared to 27.1 per cent of male chatters. Additionally, female chatters spend two more days per month chatting than do males.'

More than half (50.7 per cent) of female chatters are under age 35, according to NetValue's research, and more than half (56.2 per cent) are older than 34. Perhaps alluding to the popularity of chat with teenage girls (whose long-recognised domination of the telephone may be evolving to include chat), nearly 20 per cent of female chatters earn $0 to $5,400 annually. Almost 22 per cent of male chatters are in the $27,000 to $36,000 bracket.

The internet sectors with the highest concentration of chat users are the personals, with more than 16 per cent, and the movie sector (15 per cent). Science and technology (14 per cent); the family sector (13 per cent); and the adult sector (12 per cent) are also popular with chatters.

INDIVIDUAL WORK
(8.2) ★ ★
What do you understand by the following terms used in the case study?

a) Internet protocols

b) Audio-video streaming

c) Secured connections

d) Instant messaging.

The majority of chat rooms, however, remain 'open' – messages are posted automatically with no human intervention. People can often enter a chat room without any verification of who they are.

Gambling

Internet gambling is a fast-growing industry with estimated 2003 revenues of more than $4 billion. There are around 1,800 e-gaming websites around the world, the majority of which are based in offshore locations in the Caribbean.

In the UK, the government-commissioned Budd Report recommended more open gambling laws, including the laws concerning online gaming. The UK liberalisation plans have attracted a great deal of interest internationally both from conventional casinos, with talk of Blackpool becoming the Las Vegas of Europe, and in the online field.

The major UK bookmakers all now have substantial online operations. Ladbrokes, William Hill and Coral have all gone heavily into the sports betting market, which only requires a betting licence. Most sites also offer casino games, although these casino game sites cannot currently be hosted in the UK and so are hosted offshore.

CASE STUDY Online betting

Sportingbet is a pure online operator and has grown rapidly to be one of the largest operators in the world, with 608,000 customers in 150 countries. Their turnover to their year end March 2002 was £991.5 million up from £324.7 million in 2001 with a profit before tax of £5 million compared to a loss of £4.2 million in 2001. Betfair, which matches bets between private individuals, has also experienced substantial growth since its launch.

INDIVIDUAL WORK (8.3) ★ ★
Read the case study and answer the following questions.

1 If Sportingbet has 608,000 customers in 150 countries, what is the average number of customers per country?

2 What is meant by 'turnover'?

INDIVIDUAL WORK (8.4) ★ ★
Visit the website of Total Jobs, just one of the many online job search services, at www.totaljobs. com. How would you use this service to find a job as a trainee manager in retailing in your region of the country?

The growth of online gambling has not been confined to the internet. Interactive TV and mobile operators see gambling as providing a profitable source of content for new channels. Channel 4 has launched www.attheraces.com, which combines live racing with the ability to bet on the races interactively. BSkyB offers interactive betting services, which are becoming a substantial source of revenue. Orange has signed up with www.ukbetting.com to offer a range of betting services to their mobile users.

Job searches

Online job searching has become one of the ways of finding a career. Internet technology allows searches for job openings as they occur. Many organisations now invite online applicants, which allows them a much wider geographical range of potential applicants.

Many career-hunting sites allow applicants to submit their CVs directly to the companies, making the application process much easier. Most search pages can even provide helpful information on relocating after being accepted for the job. There are many ways to find a career, a job and a future, just by looking online, but some aspects of the internet are not the best bet for career searching.

Many organisations have realised that there is enormous competition to find the right person for a job and this is a major reason why so many advertise their posts online. There still needs to be follow up after the application has been made, perhaps by interview or by telephone. In a recent survey, only 4 per cent of internet users stated that they had found their jobs online.

Many organisations use the internet to find employees because it saves money and time. However, many key positions are not easy to find online, and both organisations and employees have found that there is no substitute for networking, research and applying in person.

Last-minutes services

In an increasingly busy 24-hour, 365-day working world, customers around the globe value their free time and want to spend it in the most productive or relaxing manner. As a result, several online services have sprung up on the internet to take away the need to trudge around shops looking for the best price or that ideal present for a difficult friend or relative.

In a world where many people have both busy work and home lives, last-minute services provide the answer to their lack of time to spend looking for gifts and holidays. On these sites, a bewildering range of products and services are displayed and the user only has to specify the type of product or service they are looking for within the criteria offered on the website. Criteria, such as price, time, colour, brand name and a host of other choices, narrow the search parameter and allow the user to choose and pay online.

CASE STUDY lastminute.com

lastminute.com was founded by Brent Hoberman and Martha Lane Fox in 1998. The website (www.lastminute.com) was launched in the UK in October 1998. Following the success of the UK site, localised versions of the website were launched in France, Germany and Sweden in September, October and December 1999 respectively. An Australian version of the website was launched in August 2000 in conjunction with travel.com.au, the joint venture partner for Australia and New Zealand. A further joint venture agreement was signed for an operation in South Africa in May 2000. In December 2000, lastminute.com further expanded its European presence to seven countries with the official launch of websites in Italy, Spain and The Netherlands.

lastminute.com aims to be the global marketplace for all last-minute services and transactions. Using the internet to match suppliers and consumers at short notice, lastminute.com works with a range of suppliers in the travel, entertainment and gift industries and is dedicated to bringing its customers attractive products and services. lastminute.com carries almost no inventory risk, selling perishable inventory for its suppliers and, where appropriate, protects suppliers' brand names until after purchase.

lastminute.com seeks to differentiate itself by generating some of the lowest prices for many travel and entertainment deals, and by packaging and delivering products and services, such as restaurant reservations, entertainment tickets and gifts, in convenient, novel and distinctive ways. It also aims to inspire its customers to try something different. Since 1998, the company believes that it has developed a distinctive brand, which communicates spontaneity and a sense of adventure, attracting a loyal community of registered subscribers. Recent research conducted by BMRB showed that lastminute.com is the second most recognised e-commerce retailer in the UK. In September 2004 the company had over 9.3 million subscribers globally.

INDIVIDUAL WORK
(8.5) ★ ★
Read the case study and answer the following questions.

1 What do you understand by the term 'joint venture'?

2 What do you understand by the term 'distinctive brand'?

3 What is a registered user?

WANT TO FIND OUT MORE?

Visit www.lastminute.com and find out how the business is performing at the moment.

Procurement and sourcing

E-procurement is the purchasing of goods and services using the internet. E-procurement systems are designed to simplify the procurement process by reducing unnecessary administrative tasks and paperwork. In theory, this should improve the purchasing cycle.

Electronic supplier catalogues provide customers with a single searchable source of products and services. Orders created by users are sent electronically to the respective suppliers for action and delivery.

Procurement is one of the most complex decisions an organisation has to face. Sourcing suppliers and procuring goods at the right price can take a long time, much of it wasted hunting for the right supplier and the right products and services. E-procurement offers an online platform for buyers and suppliers to interact and reduce the cycle time of procurement.

While e-sourcing allows the buyer to analyse, purchase and identify opportunities at a better price, e-procurement allows the buyer access to direct and indirect goods and services. Forecasts estimate that the total amount spent on the e-procurement of goods and services globally will have reached $520 billion by 2004.

The major advantages of e-procurement and e-sourcing are that:

- On average a business can negotiate a 14.3 per cent reduction in goods and services costs.
- It cuts sourcing cycles in half – in other words it takes half the time to find the right products or services.
- It reduces sourcing administration costs by nearly 60 per cent – it takes less people less time to find the right products and services.
- It shortens time-to-market cycles by 10–15 per cent – a business buying products and services can then sell the products and services to their own customers much quicker.
- It enhances the ability to identify, evaluate and negotiate with new and foreign supply sources – it is no longer the case that a business has to buy from a local or even national supplier, they can 'shop' for products and services around the world.
- It improves product quality – a business can always buy the best they can afford, not just what is available.
- It improves and strengthens supplier relationships – by dealing with more suppliers the business can forge a close relationship with those that provide the best products or services.

- It identifies and standardises in 'best practices' in sourcing – a business can learn from the experiences of other businesses in carrying out e-procurement and e-sourcing the right way.
- It improves the expertise and competency of sourcing professionals – those involved in the sourcing will quickly learn the problems involved.
- It improves intelligence on suppliers and markets – the business will be able to access more information about their competitors and the markets they serve.

CASE STUDY E-sourcing success

With more than 80 per cent of leading businesses using e-sourcing technologies, cost and performance benefits can vary greatly. According to a new study, businesses sourcing more than 80 per cent of their spending can achieve high savings.

'E-sourcing best practice leaders are applying strategic sourcing to a broader portion of overall spending and generating – and keeping – more cost savings,' said a spokesperson. 'The secret to their success is that they apply process discipline and flexible negotiation methods to their sourcing process. Leaders also have secured top-level executive support to secure resources and enforce compliance for their sourcing programs.'

INDIVIDUAL WORK (8.6) ★ ★ ★
Read the case study and answer the following questions.

1 What is meant by 'process discipline'?

2 What is meant by 'flexible negotiation'?

3 What is 'executive support'?

Product supply

The supplying of products is an enormous business on the internet. Not only do consumers purchase a wide range of products from a variety of different online companies, but other businesses purchase their own consumables and other products essential for their work.

UK online shopping revenues increased by 50 per cent in 2003 and, for the first time, more goods and services will be bought using credit cards and debit cards than cash.

As far as consumer spending is concerned, the UK spent £200 million online in 2003, still a fraction of overall spending, but the figure is expected to grow over the coming years as internet security improves and users gain confidence in e-commerce systems.

Consumers are not only embracing online shopping, they are also increasingly keen to conduct all types of transaction via credit card rather than cash. This degree of progress has pushed the UK to the forefront of credit-card security technology.

The number of payment cards being used grew by 9 per cent to 160.6 million in 2004. In 2005, total plastic card use, including business spending, will top £269 billion, against £268 billion of cash payments. In 2005, personal credit and debit cards alone are expected to overtake cash payments.

Surprisingly, although plastic spending has increased, credit and debit card fraud actually fell in 2004 for the first time in eight years. This is partly attributed to increasing security measures, such as the £1.1 billion investment in chip and PIN technology by UK card issuers.

CASE STUDY Boom in online shopping

Internet shoppers spent an average £770 each in 2004 on goods and services, according to a survey by YouGov, commissioned by Alliance & Leicester.

The survey found that almost 50 per cent of shoppers bought a holiday, flight or hotel stay over the internet, while 45 per cent purchased CDs and other forms of music online. Thirty-nine per cent of those polled by YouGov said they had bought shoes or clothes over the internet and 34 per cent had purchased electrical items. Eighty-seven per cent of shoppers said they had bought much more on the internet in the last year than they did five years ago, the survey found. Over a third of those polled said they buy goods and services online every couple of weeks.

INDIVIDUAL WORK (8.7) ★ ★
Read the case study and answer the following questions.

1 What was the average spending per month on online shopping?

2 What was the most popular purchase online?

3 Why might there have been such a large increase in the number of people buying online compared to five years ago?

Research

While the majority of consumers research products online, they make their purchases in actual high street stores. Around 65 per cent of internet users regularly practise this 'cross-channel shopping', and 51 per cent purchase something this way every three months. Cross-channel shoppers are younger, wealthier and more experienced online. They purchase a wide variety of products, with the category of books/music/DVD/video games being the most popular (64 million cross-channel transactions last year).

Around half of cross-channel shoppers switch brands before they purchase offline, and spend an average of £80 on additional products once they are in the store. Ultimately, the average cross-channel shopper spends £238 on products they research online and buy offline, which adds up to £5.6 billion per year.

It is not only customers that carry out online research; it is a growing area of marketing and market research. Internet research is a global phenomenon with estimated spending of £416.5 million. Experts suggest an annual growth rate of more than 250 per cent.

Some types of online marketing research are pure products of the internet era. These include:

- Measurement of website audiences and 'surfing' activity
- Testing of the effectiveness of online advertising
- Gauging reactions to websites themselves.

Around 75 per cent of internet research spending is devoted to better understanding of attitudes and activities of consumers, while 25 per cent is spent on business-to-business efforts.

It is possible to compare offline (traditional forms of research) and online research:

- Online research is cheaper than offline research as offline research is labour-intensive.
- If the questionnaire is designed with care, data quality is high in online research.
- Geographical coverage is unlimited in online research.
- Automated online research has low interviewer bias (the interviewer does not have to interpret the answers given) compared to offline research.
- Time for data entry or data arrangement is reduced in online research.
- Sampling is accurate and controllable in offline research.
- The researcher has high control over interviewee in offline research, e.g. the interviewer can clarify problems on the spot and make questions easier to understand for the interviewee.

Most online research is generally carried out through web pages and emails. Web surveys can incorporate radio buttons, data entry fields and check boxes, which help researchers to take responses from respondents easily and according to requirement.

CASE STUDY Buying online research

Only a few years ago, buying market research reports involved the purchase of a complete hard-copy report. Today, publishers are offering web access, through their branded sites, to reports, databases and immediate downloading of reports or extracts. Many businesses are now offering extracts — the so-called 'slice and price' option — to broaden the customer base to those who are willing to pay £20 or more for a specific piece of information, such as market size or competitor details, but are unwilling to pay for the complete report. These 'slice and price' options are usually based around chapters or sections of reports. Credit card payment makes the transaction simpler.

Datamonitor, for example, has packages for markets such as healthcare and IT. Datamonitor's core product is no longer its off-the-shelf reports but its Strategic Planning Programme that costs £20,000 a year for a single user licence. This gives access to reports, weekly briefings, analysis and interactive forecasting models.

INDIVIDUAL WORK (8.8)
★ ★
Read the case study and then visit the following websites:
www.marketresearch.com
www.mindbranch.com
www.ecnext.com.
What kind of products and services do they offer?

There is also a growing market in the sale of online research. Many marketing organisations carry out research and then sell on the results to businesses. Some of the information can be accessed by paying a subscription to a particular website, whilst other reports can be purchased as digital documents or hard copies from the research service business.

Games and music

Recent figures show that gaming is becoming more and more popular in the UK. In 2002, the UK spent over £1 billion on their passion for the games. Things have come a long way from the first game, 'Space War' (1961), and now over a thousand new games come into the shops every year.

The new hardware and software is not cheap and the main age range for game players is 24–34. These people played with video games from a very young age and now have the money to buy the latest games. Men and boys are still the main players and buyers, but more girls are showing interest. There are many new games coming out that are aimed at women or young girls.

In the 1960s, many young people went to the cinema, but videos led to the closure of many cinemas, but only now are cinemas making a comeback. Buying or renting videos was the main pastime in the 1980s and 1990s. Now, the UK spends more money on computer games than on videos (and DVDs) or going out to the cinema. Gaming is the number one choice for very large numbers of people.

A few years ago, a software program called Napster was created and then closed down for allowing the illegal sharing of copyrighted material, mostly music files. Conservative estimates put the number of Napster users at 40 million just 18 months after it was created and with no real advertising.

Napster was allowing access to music for free, much of it months before it was available in shops, but such a high figure indicated to the music industry that there was a keen appetite for a new way of accessing music. The media giant BMG effectively bought Napster for a reported $55 million. Napster may not be what it was, but other services persist such as Audio Galaxy, Morpheus, Grokster and KaZaA. A recent survey by the BPI (British Phonographic Industry Ltd) suggests that around five million people in the UK download over one billion tracks a year using peer-to-peer file-sharing

CASE STUDY Subscription vs pay-as-you-go

Subscription-based services are now available that offer many of the features of Napster-type programmes with the difference that they are completely legal, if not free. Internet music subscription services are widely available from MSN, Freeserve, HMV, BT and many others. The most common pricing structure is 500 credits for a £4.99 monthly fee. With these credits, users have a choice: stream tracks at a cost of 1 credit each, download tracks for 10 credits each or burn to CD for 100 credits. The pricing encourages users not to create physical copies of the music, but instead access them on demand. The tracks downloaded using subscription services are encrypted so they cannot be played by others or by non-subscribers. This process is referred to as DRM or Digital Rights Management. This last point is a vital shift: if these services prove popular, in the future you will not buy music but instead it will be rented.

INDIVIDUAL WORK (8.9) ★ ★
Read the case study and then, using a search engine, find out the names and web addresses of five major providers of downloadable music. What are the payment options for users? Which offer the most value for money and flexibility for users?

OD2 (On Demand Distribution), the company providing the infrastructure and management of many of these services, acknowledges that for older consumers this is an unfamiliar concept. Younger users are not put off, according to OD2; as the market matures so acceptance of 'renting' will grow. The issue for many music lovers, however, is the commitment to a perpetual subscription as the downloaded tracks become useless once your subscription to a service ends. On a per track basis, these services are certainly cheaper, but their success depends on a shift in consumer thinking.

Some providers offer songs for download on a pay-as-you-go basis, most notably Apple. Launched at the end of April 2003, and only available to US users, the Apple iTunes shop sold over 1 million tracks in its first week of operation.

What is certain is that buying and downloading music from the internet is here to stay. It will change the way audiences think about buying music and it will lead to changes in the home: media servers delivering content to wirelessly networked stereos does not sound as far fetched as it did just a few years ago.

programs. They create 126 million CDs using computer CD-writers. Despite such huge figures, the exchanging of music files allowed by these programs is illegal. Some suggest that the lack of legitimate music online has forced people to use alternative sources.

By 2003, there were signs that the music industry was beginning to catch up. In April 2003, EMI was the first of the big five record companies to make the majority of its music available online (90 per cent or around 140,000 tracks). As the number of broadband connections rises, the UK is beginning to see the new way of purchasing music becoming the accepted standard. Legitimate downloads are now tracked to create a weekly chart, a sign of growing acceptance. It is predicted that almost 20 per cent of all music sales will be in digital format within 10 years. There are two ways of buying and downloading music from the internet, by subscription or pay-as-you-go.

Virtual property tours

A simple search engine query reveals over 600 sites offering virtual property tours. Largely, the online tours are provided by a wide variety of different estate agents as a back-up to the more conventional visit to a property.

Virtual tours allow anyone with internet access to view what they would see if they were actually visiting a property. This form of technology has been available using IPIX and other 360 degree virtual tour imaging systems for several years. Virtual property tours are being used by an increasing number of estate agents and property agents abroad to give prospective buyers and tenants an easy opportunity to view properties before they make a personal visit.

CASE STUDY Abrexa UK

Abrexa UK (www.abrexa.co.uk) is a search engine that uses an age rating system to provide visitors with a clear warning about the suitability of websites, in the same way that films have age classifications.

This unique feature allows parents to easily spot sites unsuitable for their children. It also allows adults to make an educated decision about whether to visit a website. The age rating takes into consideration swearing, sexual content, violence and drug references.

It uses these icons next to search results:

U	Especially designed for young children
PG	Parents should use their discretion
12	Not suitable for under 12s
15	Not suitable for under 15s
18	Not suitable for under 18s
X	Very strong adult content.

INDIVIDUAL WORK
(8.10) ★
Visit the Abrexa website at www.abrexa.co.uk and find out more about the age rating system they use. How useful would the system be to restrict access for children?

Supply of digital information

The advent of powerful personal computers and the internet resulted in a rapid growth in digital information. Anyone can create contents using his or her own personal computer and make it available on the internet. Many high-quality data sources are also available online within a single click of the mouse.

The growth of digital information, however, has brought in tremendous challenges in managing, organising and accessing such information.

Sectors

Just like regular businesses, the internet has a wide range of different businesses offering a wide range of products and services in both the public, private and voluntary sectors of the economy.

Obviously, there are many thousands of organisations and businesses that operate either solely on the internet or have websites to support their other activities. In this section we will look at three examples of different types of organisation and how they fit into each of the three major sectors.

With the increasing use of the internet, organisations and businesses cannot afford to ignore the importance of having a website for their customers or clients to access. The development of websites takes into account the following factors:

- The use of the internet increased from 72 per cent in 2002 to 77 per cent in 2003.

- More than half of those that connect through the internet (56 per cent) use a broadband internet connection.

- The adoption of broadband more than doubled since 2002.

- In 2004, 43 per cent of all organisations adopted broadband compared to only 17 per cent in 2003.

- E-mail adoption increased from 66 per cent in 2002 to 77 per cent in 2003.

- Adoption of websites increased from 50 per cent in 2002 to 57 per cent in 2003.

- Adoption of a Local Area Network (LAN) increased from 30 per cent of organisations in 2002 to 37 per cent in 2003.

- At a sector level, IT leads with an average technology adoption level of 91 per cent across internet access, website, email and LAN, followed by finance and insurance (74 per cent). Hotels and restaurants (36 per cent) and retail and wholesale (43 per cent) lag behind in their average adoption of e-business technologies.

- Smaller organisations and particularly micro organisations (0 and 1–4 employees) are far less likely to adopt e-business technologies.

- In 1–4 employee organisations there is an average technology adoption level of 61 per cent across internet access, website, email and LAN, compared to 71 per cent within 5–9 employee organisations and 92 per cent within 50+ employee organisations.

Public sector

NHS Direct Online is a website providing high-quality health information and advice for the people of England. It is unique in being supported by a 24-hour nurse advice and information helpline.

Key services offered on the website are:

- A self-help guide – an easy-to-use guide to treating common health problems at home. Using a Body Key, you can identify your symptoms and by answering simple step-by-step questions, work out the course of action that is best for you.

- A health encyclopaedia containing over 400 topics covering illnesses and conditions, tests, treatments and operations. Illustrations or photographs support many topics.

- Information on illnesses or conditions, including sections covering diagnosis, prevention, complications and treatment. Information about tests, treatments and operations explain why they are necessary, when they can be done, why they should be done, when they should be done, how they are performed, results, recovery and future prospects.

- A searchable database of hospitals and community health services, GPs dentists, opticians and pharmacies.

Private sector

Amazon was one of the pioneers of online sales. Amazon.co.uk is the trading name for Amazon.com International Sales, Inc. and Amazon Services Europe SARL. Both companies are subsidiaries of Amazon.com, one of the leading online retailers of products. The Amazon group also has online stores in the United States, Germany, France, Japan and Canada. Amazon.co.uk has its origins in an independent online store, Bookpages, which was established in 1996 and acquired by Amazon.com in early 1998.

Amazon.co.uk is famous for selling books, but they also sell millions of other products including cameras, coffee machines, DVDs and CDs.

Voluntary and non-for-profit sector

Charity Choice is an encyclopaedia of charities on the internet, listing over 9,000 organisations in the UK. The Charity Commission's website has a list of registered UK charities, including links to the web addresses where available. The National Council

> **INDIVIDUAL WORK**
> **(8.11)**
> Using the website
> www.nhsdirect.com
> find out the answers to
> the following questions.
>
> 1 What do they
>   recommend when a
>   baby has a rash?
>
> 2 What is the nearest
>   pharmacist to your
>   home?
>
> 3 Using the Best
>   Treatments options,
>   what is
>   recommended for
>   back pain?
>
> 4 What is HealthSpace?

CASE STUDY   What you can do on Amazon

- Browse and search for specific products by subject area — books, music, DVD, video, electronics and photo, software, PC and video games, home and garden, toys and games, gifts, auctions and zshops.
- Sell your stuff at Amazon.co.uk Marketplace.
- Buy gift certificates or send items gift-wrapped as presents.
- Create a wish list and never receive an unwanted gift again.
- Find out 'Your Recommendations' and discover what's 'New for You'.
- Join Amazon.co.uk Associates and earn money by selling Amazon products from your own website.

INDIVIDUAL WORK
(8.12) ⭐
Using the list from the case study find out more about the following Amazon features.

1 What is a wish list?

2 What are the advantages of becoming an associate and how is this done?

3 What is a zshop?

INDIVIDUAL WORK
(8.13) ⭐ ⭐
Using the internet, visit www.charitychoice.co.uk.

1 What is the purpose of this website?

2 How many UK-based maritime charities are there and how many of them have their own website?

3 What is the Charity Choice Directory?

for Voluntary Organisations (NCVO) is the umbrella body for English voluntary organisations. Its website has over 2,000 members listed in its links to the voluntary sector online.

The World Development Movement is just one of the many thousands of charities. Its website at www.wdm.org.uk details its work worldwide. It was founded in 1970 and operates in partnership with other organisations in the UK and around the world. Its primary goal is to tackle the underlying causes of poverty. They try to persuade decision-makers to change the policies that keep people poor. They carry out research and promote positive alternatives.

Levels and types of online presence

First and foremost, a business needs to define the specifications for its website content. There are two major kinds of content to be considered, static or dynamic content, summarised in Table 8.1.

The theme of the website needs to be designed to deliver the most appropriate intended image. Apart from the content, endless possibilities exist to maximise the return on the investment made by the business:

- Increased exposure of the website can be obtained by submitting to thousands of search engines around the world.
- Registered site viewers can generate a highly accurate and targeted source for online marketing activities.
- An online ordering system, built on the foundation of the online product and customer data infrastructure, can effectively transform order processing online.
- A website eliminates issues such as time difference for global enterprises and allows better tracking of ordering and shipping by both customers and administrators.
- Global coverage and timely delivery of important business information increase as internet usage grows.
- A business's online presence grows as usage increases.

Table 8.1
Static and dynamic website content

Static content	Dynamic content
Company identities, including logos, slogans, corporate messages, etc.	A database has to be set up. The data will include important information such as product categories, codes, description, sizes, colours, materials, prices, images, etc.
Company information, including history, organisation, company culture, personnel, contact information, etc.	Database design has to coincide with the display format and design of your online storefront.
Business information, including ordering procedures, shipping, credit terms, etc.	Consideration also will be given to incorporate ease of updating the data to minimise the cost of ongoing maintenance of the data.
General product information, including quality, material, sizing guide, what's new, etc.	

Passive brochure ware

A website can either be a dynamic tool focused on achieving a specific set of business objectives, or it can be a passive electronic brochure telling visitors what the business is, where it is, what it does and when it is done.

Most shop websites today take the passive brochure ware approach. Although generally not very effective, this type of site can help keep the shop's image current and offer some convenience to existing customers.

A dynamic website features helpful, frequently updated content that keeps customers returning to the site. A dynamic website offers what is known as 'actionable' tools that allow the business to communicate with their customers.

Independent shops and small chains have always suffered from limited choices for promoting their businesses, providing convenient solutions to customers and increasing their profit margins. Many argue that a dynamic website can be the most cost-effective solution for achieving these objectives. Most shop websites in use today are only passive brochure ware types because the cost of creating and maintaining a dynamic site has been prohibitive. Easier and more affordable tools to create dynamic websites are now available and passive brochure ware websites are becoming a thing of the past. A dynamic website is clearly the best choice for helping independent shops and small chains maintain a competitive edge.

Complementing offline services

If a business is successful online, then why might it be so important to have an offline, or conventional, presence? Customers seem to think that it is important, as recent research has uncovered.

A physical 'bricks and mortar' presence is still important to many consumers. Around 50 per cent of all customers rated having a physical offline presence as 'very or somewhat important', with only 15 per cent stating that it was not important at all. Offline presence as an influence on the purchase decision appears to be declining; although 35 per cent of customers stated they would be more likely to make a purchase from a website if the brand had a physical offline presence, 34 per cent said it would not affect their purchase decision.

It was the youngest group (the under-25s) that placed the most importance on a physical presence, with 61 per cent rating it as 'very or somewhat important'. Men and women showed virtually identical attitudes toward online shopping and purchases.

Mail order

The simple fact that internet-based businesses are not conventional stores means that they need to deliver the majority of their products and services by mail order. At the top of the list of complaints received by Trading Standards officers around the UK are the non-delivery of internet goods and mail order problems.

In theory, customers are protected by the Sale of Goods Act 1979 and the Consumer Protection (Distance Sales) Regulations 2000. When a customer buys goods over the internet or by mail order, they enter into an agreement with the seller. These agreements are called 'contracts'. A contract gives details of the main points the customer agreed with the seller (e.g. what they are buying and how much they have to pay). A contract does not have to be written; it may be verbal or partly verbal, partly written.

When a customer buys goods from a mail order or internet company, delivery should be within a reasonable time. Often, the seller will specify a certain date. The customer has a right to reject the goods and claim a refund (for late delivery). After October 2000, if the seller does not deliver on the promised date, or within 30 days, the customer is entitled to reject the goods and receive their money back. But in most cases, buyers are willing to wait a little longer.

The law allows the customer to return them (for any reason) if they change their mind about buying them. Normally, they should make the cancellation in writing, within seven days of delivery. The word 'goods' includes things like cars, toasters, washing machines, food and even animals. Computers, computer disks and computer games are also 'goods'.

Online transactions

As we will see later in this unit, there are a number of different methods used to enable online financial transactions to take place. Primarily, customers will use credit and debit cards as well as direct fund transfers.

Many businesses use the expertise of professional website designers to find online transaction solutions including online credit card transactions and product cataloguing. These can be incorporated into the web design and development services to produce a fully functional e-commerce site, which is easy to use for both the customer and the supplier.

Interactive customisation

Increasingly online businesses focus on customer interaction, with an emphasis on organisation and ease of navigation, to make sure they have a pleasant experience with the website.

To complement this, businesses also concentrate on the customer's interface. These interfaces allow the customisation of websites to appeal to their customer's needs. **Cookies** offer an innovative means to collect data on the demographics and behaviour of web users. Site visit statistics can be estimated more accurately by using cookies; cookies also allow the customisation of websites without making the user reset preferences every time the site is revisited.

Main channel of business activity

In 2000, the merger of AOL and Time Warner created the first big 'clicks and mortar' company. 'Clicks and mortar' describes the union between internet growth and traditional levels of profit.

When the merger was announced in January 2000, internet and online companies were fashionable investments and hugely capitalised in many cases. Their revenues, though growing fast, are still generally small.

In 2001, the second-largest toy retailer in the US, Toys R Us, reported a bigger than expected loss, after a major store refurbishment programme hit sales. However, online sales at the company's toysrus.com site more than tripled to $29 million versus $8 million in the previous year, thanks to an alliance with Amazon.com.

> **Keyword**
>
> **cookie** – a small text file that is placed on the user's hard drive by a web server. It is a code that is uniquely the user's and can only be read by the server that sent it

> **INDIVIDUAL** WORK
> **(8.14)** ★
> Visit a website, such as www.amazon.co.uk, and register as a user. See what options there are to customise the page to suit your tastes and interests. Visit the same website on another occasion and see if it has 'remembered' your customisation.

CASE STUDY **Amazon and Waterstone's**

In 2001, the UK's biggest bookshop chain, Waterstone's, passed over its e-commerce operations to rival Amazon.co.uk.

The move, which cost 50 jobs, increased Amazon's grip on the increasingly lucrative online book market. Waterstone's continues to have an online presence but Amazon provides orders and technological expertise.

The British book chain had about 200,000 registered online customers compared to more than three million on Amazon. The new Amazon-powered site was launched in time for the Christmas rush and promoted in Waterstone's stores. Waterstone's reduced its online division to a skeleton staff that continues to provide editorial content for the new site.

> **INDIVIDUAL** WORK (8.15) ★ ★
> Read the case study and then answer the following questions.
> 1 Why might Waterstone's have decided to give their online business over to Amazon?
> 2 What does a 'skeleton staff' mean?

BENEFITS OF ONLINE PRESENCE

The benefits of web presence for any business are increasing as more and more business communications are made online. The internet has reached its full maturity to become the new medium of choice with its huge advantages over the conventional media.

The internet will see its next stage of development as businesses move their commerce activities totally online. Many creative marketing and sales approaches that use the power of online business have been proven in recent years, with great results, translating into increased productivity as well as profitability. The internet offers great promise for businesses that are determined to be the pioneers in their industries in utilising it as the platform of conducting their businesses.

A product showroom website is an effective approach for a business to start its web presence. Having an online product showroom immediately gets their investment working for the business. An electronic storefront maximises business presence and minimises costs. New product information can be updated in a matter of hours and made available to customers all over the world. These and many other advantages of being online are advancing businesses ahead of their competitors.

Global round the clock visibility, expansion of market presence and equality of presence

Reports show that 95 per cent of all web traffic flows through the major search engines. So, positioning is the main key to the success of any business online. Standard search engine registry techniques and traditional print advertisements are often not enough because of the billions of different web pages. Research also shows that only around 1–3 per cent of users view listings past the first three result pages.

The cost of a business acquiring its own **domain name** is a relatively simple and affordable investment, which in turn gives the business vast and ongoing global exposure on the internet.

The internet simplifies internal and external communication through the use of email and of the worldwide web (instant global mass communication). It allows any business to:

- Collaborate with colleagues and customers anywhere in the world.
- Publish information to a global audience.
- Gather information from global sources.
- Research competitors from anywhere in the world.
- Research and gain greater knowledge of potential customers from anywhere in the world.
- Provide innovative and improved customer service and support 24 hours a day with FAQs (Frequently Asked Questions with answers) and online order taking. This can greatly reduce communication times and improve customer relations.
- Sell products and services 24 hours a day, locally, regionally, nationally and globally.
- Purchase products and services 24 hours a day and enjoy 24-hour technical support from suppliers.
- Reduce information and distribution costs, as document files can be instantly transmitted around the globe via email and world wide web.
- Increase market share without increasing advertising budget, by taking advantage of this low-cost, far-reaching, high-impact advertising media. The internet can deliver a real return on investment.

Remember that websites can be fully interactive; visitors read information on products or services and then fill in a form which automatically informs the business of their enquiries. This allows advertising, online order taking, online payments and customer support.

Websites provide a level playing field on which small or medium-sized businesses can compete with their larger competitors. This is because, for a few hundred pounds, a small business can have the same global exposure on the internet as a multinational spending tens of thousands of pounds.

The internet is a low-cost advertising medium because websites can contain rich multimedia promotional material, visible all around the world.

Rapidity of response to customer interest

E-commerce can help provide the business with additional profits. Not only will business make significant cost savings, but they will also have increased flexibility and rapid response to customers' needs, providing customers with new opportunities to enhance their activities and opening new market opportunities.

Keyword

domain name – a website's address on the internet. It needs to be registered by a business, organisation or service, just like a business name. It allows potential customers to find easily the business's web address and website

---

INDIVIDUAL WORK

(8.16) ★

Visit www.approved index.co.uk. Find a web developer in your area and see what the costs are to develop a website.

Customers now demand:

- Access to a service regardless of service provider
- The ability to give and receive information or to make a complaint
- The ability to carry out a transaction, book or pay for something
- An efficient response to enquiries
- Responsive helplines and extended opening hours.

Customer expectations are continuously increasing. Loyalty is a thing of the past as customers seek out products and services that are best able to satisfy their requirements. Responding quickly to customer interest in products and services is advantageous to a business because:

- On average it costs between five and six times more to attract a new customer than to keep an existing one.
- A business can boost profits from 25 per cent to 125 per cent by simply keeping 5 per cent more of their existing customers.
- Only one out of 25 dissatisfied customers will express dissatisfaction.
- Happy customers tell four or five others of their positive experience.
- Dissatisfied customers tell nine to 12 others.
- Two-thirds of customers do not feel valued by those serving them.

Analysis of online competition and keeping up with the competition

Competitive Intelligence (CI) is an important task undertaken by all businesses. Competitive analysis allows a business to fill gaps in their knowledge about what competitors have been doing, are doing or even could be doing. It enables the business to confirm, or deny, rumours and uncover the truth about what is happening in their competitive environment. The business aims to provide itself with in-depth analysis on competitor firms, enabling them to build a complete picture that can be used in their planning processes.

In a business world, which operates continuously, keeping up with the competition has never been more important, but it has also never been easier. The internet provides a wealth of free intelligence including market reports, white papers and free research of every kind. It is no longer the case that only large corporations can afford specialised market research.

Often, a business will find a source and a trail to follow and then it is a question of clicking from one site to another. If a business is trying to find information about a specific industry, they begin by thinking about the types of organisations that would collect that information.

If a business is hoping to get an edge on the competition, it is logical to check out their websites. Most businesses have websites and they are an excellent starting point for research. On the websites, the researcher will be able to find information about the company's mission, financials, staff, experience and markets, and recent press releases they have issued.

Government sites are another excellent resource. Most of the counties maintain websites packed with information. Search engines, such as Google, provide some very useful results.

Overall, the internet is a useful source for free research, but businesses need to know the drawbacks. The research may take time and, above all, sources need to be checked. Where does the information come from? What date was it written or posted on the website?

Responsive integrated supply chains

The ability to operate an efficient and highly responsive, **integrated supply chain** is emerging as the key competitive advantage in business.

INDIVIDUAL WORK (8.17) ★★
Using Google or another search engine, find out how many websites have information on the following businesses:
a) The Body Shop
b) Nelson Thornes
c) British Telecom
d) French Connection
e) Parker Pens.

integrated supply chain – a fully working chain of supplier and customers who work in close contact with one another to reduce the time delays for orders and deliveries

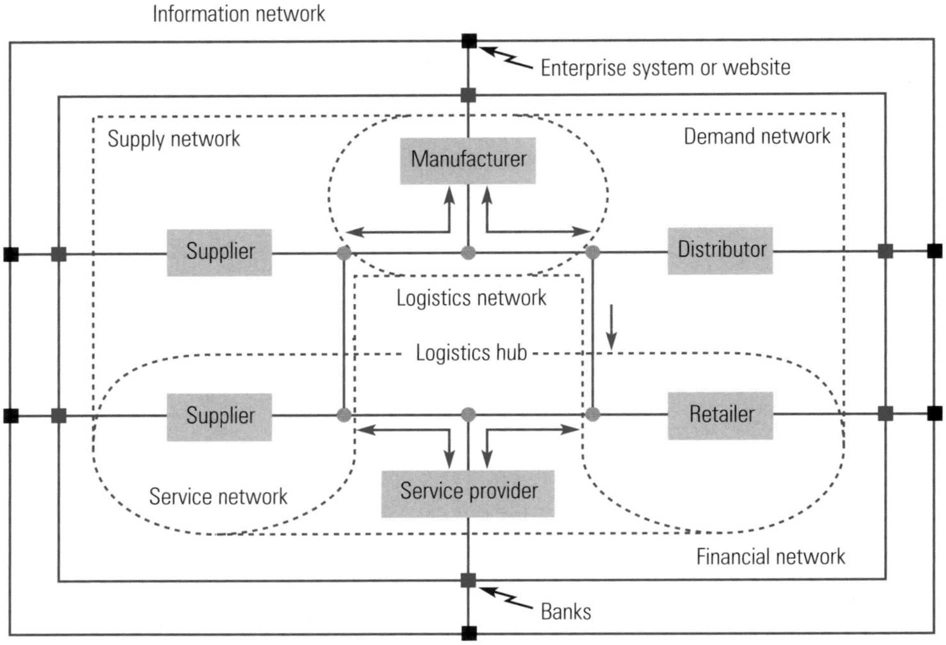

Figure 8.1
An integrated supply chain

An efficient supply chain network should provide:

- An ability to source globally.
- Online, real-time information networked around the organisation (and perhaps wider).
- Information management across, rather than only within, the organisation.
- An ability to offer products globally.
- Improved customer response times.
- Lower stock levels.
- Shorter 'time to market' for new products.

Keyword

extranet – an extranet site is one that can only be accessed by a user group in the 'outside world', such as customers

It is vital to ensure that the various organisations involved in the supply chain are working together at the same time and to the same ends. A responsive supply chain needs information to flow freely from organisation to organisation. Electronic Data Interchange (EDI) has for a number of years allowed high-speed, secure, communication across such boundaries. For a number of reasons, EDI has only been adopted by the largest manufacturers – it seems to have been regarded as expensive and unfriendly. The **extranet**, the web-based information service, is now operating securely across a number of organisations.

Extranets are particularly useful because they:

- Are based on standard web-servers and browsers, so most organisations have much of the hardware required.
- Provide access to information 24 hours a day.
- Can allow members of the extranet community to input information, saving both time and error.
- Can allow direct access to the information by end customers.

INDIVIDUALWORK
(8.18) ★ ★

Visit the Opportunity Wales website containing information on extranet services at:
www.opportunitywales.co.uk (click on 'Online Guides' and 'Intranets and Extranets').
What are the main advantages for a business using an extranet compared to an intranet?

Punctual deliveries

When a business becomes a part of an integrated supply chain, it should have direct contact with all of its suppliers. They will know when the business might need additional raw materials, components, products or services, as they will be aware of their stock levels. This means, in theory that the suppliers should always be in a position to deliver to the customer. This also means that all of the businesses down the line of the supply chain will be able to keep reasonable stock levels and that the supply chain will not break down just because one of the partners is not able to supply their customers.

Access from a wide range of devices

Although computers are the primary tools used to connect business, suppliers and customers, there are increasing moves towards providing other forms of access. One of the early developments was the laptop computer, which can be connected to the internet via connections provided, for example, in airport lounges, and of course mobile phones.

Mobile communications devices, such as the new-generation mobile phones and personal assistants, provide businesses with a means by which they can remain in touch with the suppliers and for their own customers to contact them.

MOST is a wireless sales management application designed to improve business efficiency. By using handheld PDAs (personal digital assistants, i.e. handheld computers), MOST ensures constant communication between the sales teams and the business itself. It has a number of key advantages including:

- Orders can be taken in real time.
- Paper orders are eliminated.
- Products can be chosen by the customer from a dropdown menu or by scanning in a bar-code.
- The PDA will confirm that the order has been received.
- The order can be relayed in real time by **GPRS**.
- Discounts can be built into the system, either on a per-customer or individual salesperson basis.
- Order and customer histories can be viewed.

Real-time ordering enables the business to:

- Eliminate transcription errors
- Improve stock control
- Remove the paper trail
- Speed up invoicing
- Build up a database of purchase history and management information.

E-procurement and sourcing

As we have seen, e-procurement is the purchasing of goods and services using the internet. E-procurement systems are designed to simplify the procurement process. They reduce unnecessary administrative tasks and paperwork and improve the purchasing cycle process flow.

Electronic catalogues are loaded onto the online application to provide customers with a single searchable source of products and services. The orders created by users are sent electronically to the respective suppliers for action and delivery.

This process includes:

- Selecting the supplier
- Submitting formal requests for goods and services to suppliers
- Getting approval from the buyer
- Processing the purchase order
- Fulfilling the order

Keyword

MOST – Mobile Ordering and Sales Terminal
GPRS – General Packet Radio Service, enables networks to offer 'always-on', higher capacity, internet-based content and packet-based data services. This allows internet browsing, email on the move, powerful visual communications, multimedia messages and location-based services

WANT TO FIND OUT MORE?

To find out more about the MOST systems visit: www.synergixps.co.uk and click on 'Products' to reveal a list of items.

- Delivery
- Receipt
- Payment
- Shipping.

E-sourcing also involves the electronic procurement of products. The process is more automatic, especially dealing with contracts and processes. The systems include applications, decision-support tools and associated services used to identify, evaluate, negotiate and make purchases. E-sourcing's primary aim is to efficiently determine the mix of suppliers, products and services that can deliver the lowest total-cost solution while meeting business objectives.

E-sourcing auctions work like an eBay auction in reverse. The business holding the auction goes online not to sell to the highest bidder, but to buy goods from the bidder with the lowest prices and best terms. The buyer typically invites only a handful of suppliers that have been checked first before they participate. In these auctions, several suppliers compete to supply the item. The suppliers enter bids lower than the current lowest bid. At the end of a predetermined period of time, the customer will choose a supplier based on a number of factors, including the lowest price.

INDIVIDUAL WORK
(8.19) ★ ★
Visit the Ariba website at www.ariba.com/.
Find out more about their e-sourcing options and solutions.

Online order tracking

Being able to track orders, from the moment they are placed to final delivery, helps a business to control the way they operate. Depending on the particular system, benefits can include:

- Better service – customers and suppliers can check the progress of orders themselves.
- Cost savings – order tracking can interact with stock control processes, which means the business can reduce stock wastage (they are also likely to avoid over- and under-orders from their suppliers).
- Trust – offering the customer real-time online order tracking helps show the business as an open and honest operation, increasing customer trust in them.
- Just-in-time production/delivery – shared order status lets customers and suppliers reduce lead times.

A business needs to decide what level of online order tracking it needs and may ask the following questions:

- Should they simply use the built-in order tracking offered by many online couriers?
- Would they benefit from an integrated order tracking system of their own?

It is important that the business chooses the right approach to match their capabilities as well as their requirements. Ineffectual order tracking can be worse than no order tracking at all.

A business needs to decide whether they need a simple order tracking system (built-in order tracking), solely to cover deliveries, or a more complex system that will become an integral part of their overall business management system (integrated order tracking).

Built-in order tracking is ideal if the business only wants to track part of their business process, such as the delivery stage. This is the easiest type of tracking system to set up. There are two main options as shown in Table 8.2.

In order to implement a built-in order tracking system, the steps shown in Figure 8.2 need to be taken.

Integrated order tracking systems are useful if the business is supplying complex products. They will need to integrate their order tracking with their internal processes. This will allow the business to track orders from the moment the sale is made. The fully integrated system should allow the features outlined in Table 8.3.

Table 8.2
Types of built-in order tracking system

Type of built-in tracking system	Description
Delivery order tracking	Many online courier companies, such as TNT, UPS, etc., offer this as a free service. Customers will need email facilities to receive the shipment number and internet access to visit the courier company's website.
Website functionality	If the business already has a storefront website set up to handle sales electronically, then the 'shopping cart' software will usually be able to incorporate tracking data from a courier service.

Implementing integrated order tracking systems is more complicated. Many businesses carry out the following research before implementing their own systems:

- They try out order tracking used by other businesses, such as Amazon, to see how it works and what information is made available to the customer.
- They try out online couriers to see how their systems work.
- They look at some of the integrated tracking systems available and see how they work.
- They then look at the options and try to decide what would best suit them.

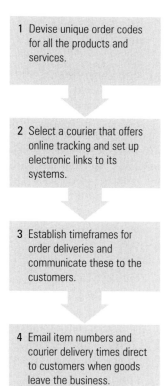

1 Devise unique order codes for all the products and services.

2 Select a courier that offers online tracking and set up electronic links to its systems.

3 Establish timeframes for order deliveries and communicate these to the customers.

4 Email item numbers and courier delivery times direct to customers when goods leave the business.

Figure 8.2
Implementing a built-in order tracking system

Table 8.3
Features of integrated order tracking systems

Features of the integrated tracking system	Explanation of purpose
Status reports	Whether an item is on back order, in production, at the warehouse or in transit
Real-time inventory information	The business will know precisely what is and what is not in stock and will be able to tell when products or components are due to arrive from suppliers.
Customer receipts	These can be generated to confirm purchase details, plus shipping and handling charges.
Data transfer	The XML (eXtensible Mark-up Language), the universal internet communication, will help ensure smooth data transfer.
Order histories and audit trails	These allow the business and the rest of the supply chain to monitor the flow of goods.

WANT TO FIND OUT MORE?

Visit some of the following websites to find out more about online order tracking.
Couriers with online tracking systems:
www.ups.com
www.tnt.com
www.dhl.com
Suppliers of online tracking systems:
www.exe.com
www.descartes.com
www.ovum.com
www.tradestream.com.

Once they have chosen a suitable system, the following steps are taken:

1 They try out the system by tracking a simple order through all of its stages. This should reveal any potential problems with the system.

2 They link up their main processes (such as manufacturing products using a number of different components) to the tracking system.

3 They give their customers access to the system so that they can track their own orders.

4 They link up suppliers to the system.

Reduced overheads and labour costs

As we have seen in Unit 3, most businesses aim to keep their overheads to a minimum and make the best use of the employees they need. If, as we will see, a business chooses to be mainly or wholly an internet-based operation, it can save on many of the costs that are unavoidable in conventional businesses.

By using the internet and solutions provided by the internet, a business can drastically reduce its costs in a number of different ways (remember that overheads refer to costs, which are fairly constant regardless of how busy or quiet the business is at any particular time):

- Administration is reduced as the majority of the documentation needed is electronic, which means that fewer administrative employees are needed.

- The premises used by the business can be located anywhere. Therefore the business does not need to pay for expensive high street premises with high rents and rates.

- The business may not need to purchase machinery to make products as it may be cheaper to source them anywhere in the world with guaranteed deliveries using an integrated supply chain system.

- As production machinery may not be necessary, a business may not need to employ skilled workers to carry out the production.

INDIVIDUAL WORK
(8.20) ★ ★
Visit some of the websites featured in the 'Want to find out more?' box. Which system would suit a small business that supplies second-hand books online?

Reduced stockholding

Stock levels of products that sell well can be kept under control by using sales analysis and automatic order generation procedures.

Sales history can be used to identify products where there are excess stocks to satisfy customer demand. By identifying products that have not sold since a selected date, a business can evaluate the pricing and their relation to different manufacturers' products within the same range. The business can then take the necessary action to promote the sale of these products.

Improved cash flow through fewer bad debts

A bad debt is an amount of money owed by a customer that the supplying business (the creditor) has no realistic chance of ever receiving. In theory, many businesses running online operations will not have customers who do not pay for products or services, unless they offer credit terms. Offering credit terms means offering the customer a specified period of time to pay the invoice for the products and services supplied.

Since many online businesses only deal with consumers rather than business customers, this problem does not emerge as a major concern. Payments, as we will see, are usually made by credit, debit and automated payment systems. This gives the seller a degree of security and assures them of payment provided they have followed the correct procedures.

Online businesses dealing with other businesses face the same kind of problems with bad debts as conventional operations.

CASE STUDY Bad debts

Scope Net Graphics is one of many small and medium-sized companies that suffers the problem of frequent late payments and, in the case of some customers, no payments at all.

'On a number of occasions, it has almost led to the company going under,' admits Michael Bowles, managing director of the small reproduction/graphics firm based in Kent.

With a turnover of £130,000, Scope Net Graphics always has to chase clients before receiving a settlement and is generally waiting on outstanding payments totalling between £25,000 and £30,000.

Michael Chambers, managing director of BACS Payment Schemes, offered the following advice:

'The late payments problem is clearly a big concern for the business and highlights a nationwide issue. Many SMEs [small and medium-sized enterprises] across the UK regularly face cash flow problems, and clearly legislation alone is not sufficient to instigate real change.

Practical steps such as offering discounts to early payers and running credit checks on those that consistently re-offend will go some way towards curbing bad payment practice, although in the long term perhaps you should consider a more strategic approach.

With the increasing popularity of automated payments, services such as Direct Credit [where large and small organisations can make payments by electronic transfer directly into bank or building society accounts] already offer a robust and reliable alternative to traditional settlement methods. They can go some way to regulating your cash flow and reducing administrative costs.

By actively encouraging the use of such practices, you may also find that you develop stronger customer relationships, diverting the focus away from debt and back towards core business areas.'

INDIVIDUAL WORK
(8.21) ★ ★ ★
Read the case study and recommend a course of action for the business.

Freedom of low cost location

Assuming that the business has access to good-quality internet connections, then the actual physical location of the business does not have to be a great concern. The business also needs to have access to a reasonable supply of skilled employees and not be too far from major centres of population to make attracting new employees to the business a serious issue.

In addition to the lower-cost location, the business may also be able to claim various incentives from the local government, particularly if the unemployment level is high in the area.

Deliveries to the online business from suppliers do need to be taken into consideration as remote areas are often more difficult to get to and further away, thus increasing the costs to have products delivered to the door. The Scottish islands, for example, suffer from this problem and couriers and delivery services charge an additional fee to cover the extra expense of servicing these areas.

Affiliations with ISPs and portals

Internet Service Provider (ISP) affiliate programmes are extremely popular and provide affiliates with income. The most successful ISPs online have well-established brands and high brand awareness levels online. The most well-known ISPs are BT, Wanadoo, Tiscali, NTL and Virgin. They, and other ISPs, offer internet connection via narrowband (fixed telephone lines) or broadband (see page 276). ISP affiliate programmes exist for both types of internet connection.

CASE STUDY Anyone fancy a move to Cornwall?

Cornwall is one of the most sparsely populated areas in the UK. Less than half a million people are scattered over England's second-largest county, and no single town comprises more than 25,000. Like London, it is a place where five miles is frequently a very long way – but for different reasons.

Because of the fragmented, almost exclusively rural population, this is a place where the Digital Revolution, with its non-reliance on major economic centres, could bring genuine renewal amid widespread unemployment. It is also a place that does not have a dozen New Media agencies cropping up within a couple of streets. Instead, they have the Digital Peninsula Network – an organisation of about 130 Cornwall-based digital professionals, aiming to encourage a community spirit and to share expertise among companies as much as 70 miles apart.

When businesses decide to move to Cornwall from central London, it is about more than escaping the hideous rents and beer prices, and finding an office near the beach. The businesses felt that they were actively demonstrating their faith in the technology.

In short, they believed there was very little they could offer their clients in London (not to mention Europe and the US) that they could not do just as well from the sunny South West – and probably do it cheaper too.

**INDIVIDUAL WORK
(8.22)** ★ ★
Read the case study on Cornwall and answer the following questions.

1 What does the 'Digital Revolution' mean?

2 Find out what the Digital Peninsula Network does at www.digitalpeninsula.com.

3 What is a 'digital professional'?

It is estimated that 90 per cent of the UK will have access to broadband by the end of 2004. Broadband pricing is very competitive and dropping closer to narrowband prices. Customers are increasingly choosing broadband as their internet connection. There are currently over three million broadband users in the UK. With around half of the UK households and two-thirds of businesses connected to the internet, this leaves a massive potential market open to broadband services.

Broadband affiliate programmes offer a high reward for all new sign-ups to the affiliate programme. Affiliates can target a wide range of potential customers, from those looking for cheap broadband to those customers prepared to pay high prices for extremely fast services, such as online gamers.

Affiliate programmes are often misunderstood.

- An *affiliate* is a 'referrer' or website that promotes a product in an effort to earn revenue.
- A *merchant* is someone who owns a product and is sharing revenues with an affiliate, based on the affiliate's performance.
- Affiliate programmes aim to send targeted traffic to websites.

Essentially, there are three basic affiliate programmes. The first two are the most common:

- Pay Per Click (PPC) – when an affiliate is compensated for sending traffic to the merchant.
- Pay Per Sale – when the merchant compensates the affiliate if the referral generates a sale or purchase.
- Pay Per Lead – when the merchant agrees to pay for a lead (a potential customer), which is very uncommon because it is subjective and up to the merchant.

The most common forms of affiliate websites tend to provide information, entertainment and content services to their customers. The most common online merchants sell products, goods and services online. These are programs which allow affiliates to earn money based on the visitors to the affiliate's site who click through to another's website. Some pay a small amount for the 'click through' and others provide a percentage of sales when a visitor 'clicks through' to your site and buys a product or service on the other party's site.

Affiliate programmes allow a business to pay and track incentives from other websites that send web surfers, leads or paying customers to their website. Commissions based on purchases made by traffic sent from the referring website can be paid. Besides a commission, an affiliate can receive a flat fee, or other incentives, for all valid transactions it refers that generate a sale or lead.

In order to be a successful affiliate, the affiliate site needs either to have lots of traffic or target a specific audience, frequently one not available to the merchant.

Affiliates need to have a tracking system. Typically sales can be tracked by using an HTML code, which is placed in a shopping cart or on the 'order confirmation'/'thank you' page. Cookies can also be used which are created when the customer clicks on a banner advertisement.

Pay-per-click (PPC) search engines (also known as a portal) offer the marketing option called 'pay per click' to users. The search engine guarantees the placement of a small advertisement on the search results page for a specific keyword or keywords in return for a specified payment, but only when a visitor clicks on that advert.

The advertiser pays nothing to appear on the results page. They only pay the amount they have agreed to when someone actually clicks on their advert and is taken to their website.

A PPC listing on a search engine results page typically consists of a title, which usually is the business's website name or perhaps a short heading (around 50 characters) and also a short (no more than 200 characters) description of the service offered by the business or some promotional wording. Some PPC search engines strictly control the text that can appear in the listing, while others are more open to using the advertiser's own text. Examples of PPC search engines are Overture, Google AdWords, FindWhat, GoClick, Search123 and LookSmart.

Some PPC search engines determine the ranking of a business on the results page by the amount a business pays per click. Examples of PPC search engines which use this type of ranking system are Overture.com and FindWhat.com. The highest ranking goes to the highest bidder.

Accessibility for users

The Disability Discrimination Act 1995 (DDA) requires service providers to ensure that disabled users are not disadvantaged by designs that fail to take account of their needs.

If a business provides products, facilities and services to the general public and has not taken steps to make sure they are accessible to everybody, it may be discriminating against people with a disability under the terms of Part III of the Act.

According to the Disability Rights Commission, one in seven people in the UK suffer some form of disability and many people experience some loss of sight and manual dexterity particularly as they get older. Missing out on these customers by not designing a website they can use could lead to lost sales.

Businesses realise that by improving accessibility, they will make a service easier for all customers to use. It will also project an image of a business that cares about all its customers and provides very good publicity.

A business can improve the accessibility of their website themselves, but there are many organisations which can offer advice, such as:

- *Audits* – internationally recognised standards and checklists for website accessibility can identify how accessible the website is now.
- *Customised guidelines* – as organisations often find it helpful to have their own in-house accessibility design guidelines, the advisers offer internationally recognised guidelines and disability specific guidelines.
- *Design* – advisers can help with design, involving disabled users at any stage of the design process to ensure that any new designs fully incorporate their needs and prevent any costly design mistakes.
- *User testing* – advisers have access to a network of disabled users to test the website.
- *Training courses* – advisers can also offer training courses for employees to help integrate accessibility.

The key benefits of increasing accessibility are that:

- It helps meet legal obligations under the Disability Discrimination Act 1995.
- It often makes the website easier to use by all visitors.
- Sales may improve and the image of the business may be improved.
- Easy access helps to improve loyalty.
- Major issues such as screen reader problems can be identified early in design before modifications become expensive.

WANT TO FIND OUT MORE?

To discover more about affiliate programmes and PPC search engines, visit **The Affiliate Mega Guide** at: http://affiliate megaguide.com.

INDIVIDUAL WORK
(8.23) ★ ★
Visit the Affiliate Mega Guide site and answer the following questions.

1 What is an autoresponder?

2 Does it matter where you are in the world as far as the affiliate programmes are concerned?

WANT TO FIND OUT MORE?

Visit the website of the **Disability Rights Commission** to find out more about the guidelines for websites: www.drc-gb.org.

In February 2003, the Disability Rights Commission (DRC) published its revised Code of Practice on rights of access to goods and services for disabled people. The Code uses 'goods and services' to describe all products and services that are provided to the population and specifically includes websites in this description.

Businesses must take reasonable steps to ensure their websites are accessible to people with a wide range of disabilities. The DRC publishes guidelines on its website (www.drc-gb.org) about how to make sites accessible for all types of disabled users. The Code uses a wide definition of 'disabled', so it could potentially have a wide-reaching effect.

Popularity of internet salons and cyber cafés

Two fast-growing trends in global culture are coffee and computers. Cyber cafés put the two concepts together and have created a new social trend.

Cyber cafés are cafés, bars, bistros and restaurants where a customer can eat, drink and use computers to email and browse the internet. The main purpose of a cyber café is, however, to provide computer access to customers.

WANT TO FIND OUT MORE?

Visit the **Cyber Cafés** website at www.cybercafes.com to find out how many registered cafés there are in the world.

If you are travelling, cyber cafés (known as internet salons in France) are the best way to communicate with friends and family at home by email. Beyond the UK, cyber cafés have become global. While London, Manchester and Liverpool have been the most affluent in cyber café culture, the rest of the UK has numerous venues of cyber café culture.

As the trend toward internet access via cyber cafés and internet kiosks spreads across the globe, there are progressively more and more potential customers coming online everyday. This means that even in the lesser-developed countries, customers have access to the internet and therefore have access to businesses online.

Developments in broadband

Narrowband is available to all UK households and businesses in the UK with a fixed telephone line. This is still the most popular and cheapest way of getting online in the UK, but the speed of connection is slower than broadband.

INDIVIDUAL WORK
(8.24) ★
Visit
www.cybercafes.com
and find out:

1 How many cafés are listed in Togo?

2 How many cafés are listed for the Philippines?

Narrowband customers have the option of either unmetered access (paying a flat fee each month regardless of actual time online) or metered packages (essentially pay-as-you-go). Prices in the narrowband market are extremely competitive. Customers are increasingly looking for a suitable package, a trusted name, price, value and level of service.

Broadband take-up over Digital Subscriber Line (DSL) and/or cable modem now has the potential to reach 80 per cent of UK homes and businesses. Three million households and small businesses have already taken up a broadband service – with around 40,000 households and businesses a week installing a new broadband connection.

Narrowband internet access is available to anyone with a phone line, but 90 per cent of households are now connected to a broadband-enabled exchange, allowing them to subscribe to higher-speed, always-on services. However, BT estimates that 3 per cent of these households are located too far from the enabled exchange to be able to receive a broadband service using current technology. This is a particular problem in rural areas. BT has stated that the percentage of households connected to a broadband-enabled exchange will rise to 99.6 per cent by the end of 2005.

Government support

According to the government, their policy on broadband is:

'The Government believes that rapid rollout and adoption of broadband across the UK is important to both its social and economic objectives. In February 2001, the Government published *UK Online: the Broadband Future*, which set a new target for the UK to have the most extensive and competitive broadband market in the G7 by 2005 with significantly increased broadband connections to schools, libraries, further education colleges and universities. This target is about getting the UK's broadband environment right for business and consumers, as well as ensuring that

regional development agencies – set up in England to assist economic development, promote efficiency, investment and competitiveness, as well as attracting employment and the development of skills in their areas. There are nine regional development agencies

Keyword

public sector organisations gain optimum benefit. Extensiveness means extending broadband networks to households throughout the country, including those in rural and remote areas. Competitiveness means providing consumers with value for money, and a wide variety of product choice in the market.'

In simple terms, this means that the government is committed to developing and implementing a strategy for meeting these goals in close consultation with key players in the private and public sectors, in particular by:

- Establishing a UK online Broadband Stakeholder Group (BSG), to be chaired by the e-Minister.
- Developing through the **regional development agencies**, complementary strategies at local/regional level.
- Assisting the regional development agencies in this by establishing a fund of £30 million over 2003–05 to support them in taking forward innovative schemes to meet local requirements.

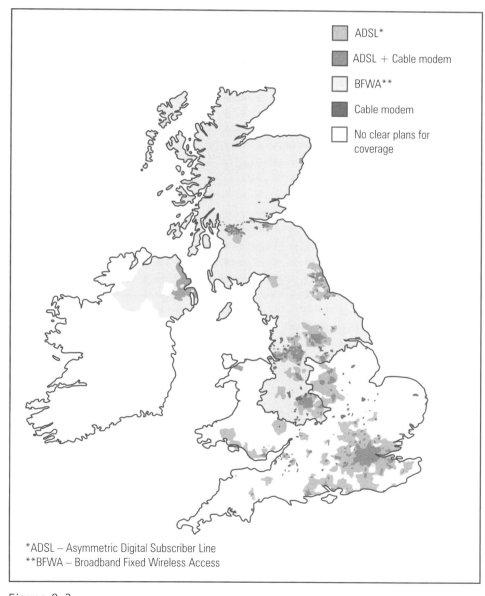

ADSL*

ADSL + Cable modem

BFWA**

Cable modem

No clear plans for coverage

*ADSL – Asymmetric Digital Subscriber Line
**BFWA – Broadband Fixed Wireless Access

Figure 8.3
Anticipated broadband coverage by 2003

INDIVIDUAL WORK
(8.25) ★ ★
Visit the website of the Broadband Stakeholders Group (BSG) at www.broadbanduk.org. Who are the BSG and what is their purpose?

Secure credit card payments

There are three main methods of online payment available. Credit card payments are the most popular, followed by internet transfers and third-party payments. An internet transfer is when a customer pays directly through their online banking system into the online store's account. A third-party payment involves a third party such as a bank, which enables the customer to make a payment directly into the online store's bank account. Although similar to internet transfers, third-party payments occur at the same time that the customer makes their online purchase.

From a customer's point of view, each payment method has its advantages and disadvantages, but regardless of the payment method used, a shopper does not carry any risk when it comes to online fraud.

> **WANT TO FIND OUT MORE?**
> Visit the website of **NoChex** to find out about their services for businesses: www.nochex.com.

Table 8.4
Online payment systems

Payment system	Website	Explanation and costs to business
Paypal	www.paypal.com	Paypal ensures a secure payment system with merchant accounts. The charges for this service are 2.2% + 20p on your transaction so a £100 transaction would be approximately £102.40. This is the only cost that occurs with this service. Paypal also offers free listing on their index of shops. The Paypal shop index can be found at paypal.com. Customers can set up a Paypal account to pay for goods.
WorldPay	www.worldpay.com	For merchants that sign up to WorldPay Direct for their internet payment system, the following transaction processing charges apply: £50 set-up fee + £145 annual fee, which also includes three free currencies (additional currencies by arrangement).
Credit cards		4.5% Merchant Service Charge on credit card transactions. Note that this is the *only* fee charged, there are no additional charges payable to banks or other third-party organisations.
Debit cards		50p charge per debit card transaction. There are no additional charges payable to banks or other third-party organisations.
NoChex	www.nochex.co.uk	This British payment system is a free checkout service for your website; they also provide email-based payment. The checkout is on industry standard SECURE (128 bit SSL) web page, which can be branded to include a company logo.
Netbanx	www.netbanx.com	Entry level £75 + VAT. One product at a fixed price. Ideal for subscription services with one fixed price. NetBanx provides generic authorisation and decline pages. The merchant is responsible for maintaining the HTML payment form initially supplied by NetBanx. Intermediate level £125 + VAT. Set-up for two to 10 products, each at a fixed price, with one selectable for payment, e.g. a subscription to a service sold either monthly, weekly or annually would constitute three separate products.

INDIVIDUAL WORK
(8.26) ★
Visit the NoChex website and answer the following questions.
1 What is the charge per transaction for a sole trader?
2 What are merchant tools?

Low cost availability of web authoring tools

Competition has driven down the prices of the tools needed to create websites. Table 8.5 shows a selection of some of the cheaper alternatives.

Table 8.5
Web authoring systems

Web authoring system/website	Features
Adobe GoLive CS www.adobe.com Click on 'Products' and 'Web publishing'.	Adobe GoLive CS software is designed to create professional websites, and it is easy to use with other Adobe software. Setting up new pages is simple using the WYSIWYG layout view and simply dragging a layout grid onto a new document and setting the required width. Text can be formatted using HTML tags or by using GoLive's dedicated CSS Editor, which allows the user to create and edit their own styles with real-time visual feedback. GoLive's comprehensive sets of authoring features are ideal for those working in a print and graphics environment. The product's integration with Adobe's Creative Suite can provide a very powerful, all-in-one solution.
Dreamweaver www.macromedia.com Click on 'Dreamweaver' under 'Products'.	Macromedia Dreamweaver is a WYSIWYG system which allows users to see how the pages look before they are uploaded. It is also possible to work with HTML using a single click. The HTML is colour coded so users can track them in a split screen with the design. Dreamweaver has CSS support and a tool to help users build CSS documents that is easy to use and understand. Positioning styles are also available so that the site is XHTML compliant. Opening files such as CGI and Perl is much easier with Dreamweaver as there is a built-in colour coding for PHP, ASP.Net and XML. Dreamweaver offers all the power and control that a designer could want, combined with the speed and production tools useful for developers.
BBEdit www.web.barebones.com	BBEdit, provided by Bare Bones Software, Inc., is a text and HTML editor available for Macintosh only (non-WYSIWYG). This editor offers great functionality and control over HTML code. As a powerful text editor, it offers features such as multiple undo, multi-file find and replace, the capability to read all DOS/Unix/Mac files up to 2 GB in size, and more. At the same time, acting as an HTML editor, it offers HTML specific features such as floating tool palettes, syntax colouration, and HTML syntax checking. Using this editor with a browser is as simple as clicking a button, allowing one to view a web page as it is created.
Microsoft Front Page www.microsoft.com/frontpage	Microsoft's FrontPage is a WYSIWYG system that allows users to create and build dynamic and sophisticated websites. The biggest advantage is that users will be familiar with Office tools. New layout and graphics tools make it easier to design exactly the site needed and at the same time enhanced publishing features and options help users to get the web pages online quickly and simply. FrontPage also has wizards for interactive and dynamic features including live links to databases, discussion forums, search forms, hit counters and navigation bars. Using Microsoft Windows SharePoint Services and Windows Server 2003 connected to FrontPage, it is possible to modify and present live data from a range of sources, including XML, to build rich, interactive data-driven websites in a WYSIWYG editor
Nvu www.nvu.com	Nvu is designed for Linux Desktop users as well as Microsoft Windows and Macintosh users. It uses WYSIWYG for editing of pages, making web creation straightforward. Nvu has integrated file management via FTP. Users simply log in to their website and navigate through the files, editing web pages on the fly, directly from the site. It has reliable HTML code creation that will work with all of today's most popular browsers. It is possible to jump between WYSIWYG Editing Mode and HTML using tabs. Tabbed editing is used to make working on multiple pages much more user friendly. It has powerful support for forms, tables and templates. It is claimed that Nvu is the easiest to use, most powerful Web Authoring System available for Desktop Linux, Microsoft Windows and Apple Macintosh users.

> **INDIVIDUAL** WORK
> **(8.27)** ★ ★
>
> Visit at least three of the websites mentioned in Table 8.5 and note down at least three major features of each system.

POTENTIAL DISADVANTAGES

As with any business, establishing a website and an online business has its disadvantages. For every advantage mentioned already, there is a downside. As the website is accessible by anyone with an internet connection around the world, the chances of difficulties, either with attacks on the website, fraud or bad publicity are magnified. Compare the potential dangers of an online business and a small business based in a high street and the opportunities for things to go wrong are numerous.

Exposure

Web defacement is just one of the many perils facing websites. It is carried out by hackers who gain access and change the contents of a website. The messages that hackers leave behind vary from merely placing their alias or logo to replacing the original contents with whatever content they wish, similar to how traditional graffiti is written.

Research in 2004 revealed these alarming figures:

- Eighty-five per cent of businesses (primarily large corporations and government agencies) detected computer security breaches within the last 12 months.

- More respondents (70 per cent) cited their internet connection as a frequent point of attack than cited their internal systems as a frequent point of attack (31 per cent).

- The number of those citing their internet connections as a frequent point of attack rose from 59 per cent to 70 per cent.

- Ninety-seven per cent of respondents have websites.

- Ninety per cent of those attacked reported website vandalism, up from 64 per cent in 2003.

- Seventy-eight per cent reported denial of service, up from 60 per cent.

Hostile chat rooms, negative publicity and defamation

Businesses may often find themselves victims of a very different form of attack – from hostile former customers, employees or activists who have a problem with either the products or services offered by the business or the way in which it does business.

Hostility and negative publicity can be very damaging to a business. Even if the root cause of the problem is based on facts, a business can find it very difficult to prevent rumours from circulating. The internet has thousands of chat rooms, and a poor opinion of a business or a website expressed in a chat room can do immense damage. Worst of all, it is very difficult to stop the rumours from spreading.

Any business that might face this kind of problem needs to be aware of what they can do. Used properly, the internet can help a business to respond to its customers and critics:

- *The business needs to have a plan.* Many businesses do not have a working and detailed crisis communications plan.

- *The business needs to maintain an online presence.* It needs to post the latest news on their website. They may not be able to control the electronic rumour mill or a hostile chat group, but they can contribute concrete facts to the conversation.

- *Someone needs to be the key figure.* This person needs to represent the business and have the confidence of the rest of the organisation. They will be the public face of the business during the crisis.

- *Ensure that the website works.* The business needs to make sure that interested parties can access accurate information and be able to find the latest news or the media section on the website.

- *The business needs to be able to learn from a crisis.* It needs to look at the situation after it has been dealt with and see what could have been handled better.

In a crisis, a business needs to put the internet to work to help protect its reputation and in the end try to build better relationships with customers and other important groups.

Payment security and unfamiliar trading conditions

Some 90 per cent of internet fraudsters get away with their crimes – the police are unable to deal with this new type of retail crime. Around 57 per cent of companies state that they have reported frauds to the police, but 53 per cent encountered a lack of interest. Only 9 per cent of frauds reported by online retailers to the police result in prosecution.

> **INDIVIDUAL WORK**
> **(8.28)** ★ ★
> Using an internet search engine, find out about the *Noah v AOL* case in the USA.

Recent research has shown that around 70 per cent of companies thought that the internet was more risky than other routes to market, with the majority of respondents experiencing an increase in fraud on the internet during 2004. Some 52 per cent of online traders claimed that internet fraud was a problem for their organisation and 55 per cent said it was a growing problem.

Retailers seem to become aware far too late when they have been victims of fraud. Almost half of the companies (48 per cent) reported that it could take more than a month before they are made aware they were victims of card fraud. A further18 per cent said it took up to seven weeks.

It seems that many fraudsters are hard at work, with 40 per cent of companies being hit by the same fraudster more than once, with 18 per cent saying that they had been hit three times by the same fraudster before the fraud was detected and the account closed. Around 11 per cent of respondents admitted that thieves had hacked into their site. Only 15 per cent of companies said they had automated systems for detecting fraud. The vast majority still employ expensive and inaccurate manual processes. Only 52 per cent use any external data to verify a customer's name and address.

Fraudsters have realised that methods of prevention are currently so inadequate they need spend little time or effort covering their tracks. Less than 10 per cent of fraudsters bother with a redirection service at the goods delivery address, and only 10 per cent make the effort to set up a false telephone account.

In order of incidence, the most common features of card fraudsters are:

- 'Using a real name at a real address but not the cardholder's name' – this shows that fraudsters will typically copy identities of previous residents associated with the premises from which they are operating.

- Next most common is using 'cardholder's name at a real address but not the cardholder's address'. It suggests that the fraudsters often have information about the real name of the cardholder.

- Third most common with 'false name at real address' exposes the interception or illegal generation of credit card numbers.

- Finally, 'cardholder's genuine name and address, but parcel delivered to another address' shows that certain fraudsters will hijack not only the card number, but also the cardholder's real identity and address, creating the illusion of a completely genuine transaction.

In 58 per cent of cases, businesses thought that the fear of fraud was a significant barrier to successful trading on the internet.

INDIVIDUAL WORK
(8.29) ★ ★
Find out the latest figures on internet fraud and suggest reasons why customers might be frightened to leave their credit card details online.

Dealing with increased market interest

Flexibility is the key to dealing with increased market demand. It is a problem stepping up operations to cope with increased demand, but a problem that all businesses welcome.

Businesses tend to try to match any increased demand by either installing new systems or employing more staff. The business needs to be sure that whilst coping with increased demand, they are certain that this new level of demand will continue into the future. A business does not want the expense of purchasing new equipment and taking on more employees only to discover that the increased demand is temporary and that it falls back to the old levels of demand.

Vulnerability to hostile attack

Contrary to what might be assumed, hostile attacks are currently the least significant cause of system crashes and problems. Environmental disruption and operator error are the biggest sources of problems followed by software problems and then hostile attacks.

On the other hand, the number of hostile attacks is increasing, roughly doubling each year. Occurrences of operator errors and design and implementation errors are increasing at a slower rate, while the occurrence of problems due to environmental disruption remains constant.

While businesses will focus on hostile attacks, trustworthy systems need to be able to tolerate not only such attacks, but also factors from the other three categories:

◇ Environmental disruption (loss of electricity, etc.).

◇ Operator errors (errors made by the users).

◇ Design and implementation errors (software, downloading and installation problems).

Denial of service

In a denial-of-service (DoS) attack, an attacker attempts to prevent legitimate users from accessing information or services. By targeting the business's computers and their network connection, or the computers and network of the sites they are trying to use, an attacker may be able to prevent the business from accessing email, websites, online accounts (banking, etc.), or other services that rely on the affected computer.

The most common and obvious type of denial of service attack occurs when an attacker 'floods' a network with information. When a user in the business types a URL for a particular website into their browser, they are sending a request to that site's computer server to view the page. The server can only process a certain number of requests at once, so if an attacker overloads the server with requests, it cannot process the request.

This is a denial of service because the user cannot access that site. An attacker can use spam email messages to launch a similar attack on the business's email account. Whether the user has an email account supplied by their employer or one available through a free service, such as Yahoo or Hotmail, each user is assigned a specific quota, which limits the amount of data they can have in their account at any given time. By sending many, or large, email messages to the account, an attacker can use up the quota, preventing the user from receiving legitimate messages.

In a distributed denial-of-service (DDoS) attack, an attacker may use the business's computer to attack another computer. By taking advantage of security vulnerabilities or weaknesses, an attacker could take control of the computer. The attacker can then force the computer to send huge amounts of data to a website or send spam to particular email addresses. The attack is 'distributed' because the attacker is using multiple computers, including the business's, to launch the denial-of-service attack.

Unfortunately, there are no effective ways to prevent a business being the victim of a DoS or DDoS attack, but steps can be taken to reduce the likelihood that an attacker will use their computer to attack other computers by:

◇ Installing and maintaining anti-virus software.

◇ Installing a firewall, and configuring it to restrict traffic coming into and leaving the computer.

◇ Following good security practices for distributing email addresses.

◇ Applying email filters to manage unwanted traffic.

CASE STUDY WorldPay under attack

In November 2003, the internet payment system WorldPay was under attack from unknown hackers, disrupting thousands of online retailers around the world. WorldPay's payment and administration networks were flooded with computer-generated requests, which clogged its system and slowed transactions.

This was a 'denial of service' attack. WorldPay said its service to customers had been 'adversely affected'.

However, WorldPay stressed that transactions were still being processed – albeit more slowly than usual – and that the security of data had not been compromised.

'We realise it is disrupting our business and our customers' business and we apologise

unreservedly for that,' said a spokesman.

In an email to customers, WorldPay said it was doing all it could to combat the attack. 'While such attacks can be anticipated to some extent, it does take time to identify and deal with the exact nature of a particular attack which can also change several times, over several days,' the company said.

Owned by the Royal Bank of Scotland, WorldPay has 30,000 clients around the world. These range from multinational firms such as Vodafone and Sony Music Entertainment to numerous small online retailers. WorldPay operates in more than 70 countries. It accepts payments on credit cards including Visa, Mastercard and American Express.

INDIVIDUAL WORK (8.30) ★ ★
Read the case study and find out what happened and how it was resolved. Have there been any other recent major denial of service attacks on businesses?

Potential unpopularity with staff and the outsourcing of key functions

Many businesses are considering outsourcing work abroad. This means shifting jobs from the country in which the business is operating and developing a similar operation abroad. The first consideration is that the labour costs abroad can be a fraction of those in the home country, for example the cost of an average employee in the UK might be £14,000 but in India it could be as little as £1,400.

An example of what could go wrong if costs are the only main consideration is the case of the consultancy business Sapient. They located around 40 per cent of their staff in new offices based in New Delhi. The business was expecting savings on the salaries and wages of around 50 per cent, but discovered that they were only saving 20 per cent. This is because there are numerous hidden costs in employing people abroad.

Salaries abroad are certainly cheaper, but often exclude bonuses paid in an attempt to reduce employee turnover, along with employees' accommodation costs. Added to this, employees abroad with the necessary skills to help run an online business are in short supply which means that their pay will be higher than normal. It is expected that these skill shortages will mean that, in the short-term, wage costs in India and China will rise by around 25 per cent.

Software which runs perfectly well on computers at home may not work on systems abroad. The reservation system of Hilton International, a major hotel chain, relocated abroad and immediately ran into software problems. Instead of costing £3 million to develop at home, the new system created abroad cost £2.3 million after 54 weeks of development.

There are also other problems with locating operations abroad including political stability. India's problems with Pakistan have brought the two countries close to war in recent years, which creates uncertainty for businesses relying on IT staff based there.

Table 8.6 looks at the hidden costs of outsourcing abroad.

Table 8.6
The hidden costs of outsourcing abroad

Hidden cost	Explanation
Transition	A business cannot expect the overseas operation to work well from the beginning. The outsourcing service will need to understand the operations and processes and this may take some time.
Communications charges	If the business is videoconferencing or telephoning, their communications costs with the overseas office will inevitably be higher than for a local office, especially with a leased line.
Travel and accommodation	Interviews and meetings will require travel.
Staff management	Depending on the nature of the work being outsourced, offshore offices could leave local staff without work. Managing retraining or redundancy will create costs for the personnel department.
Management and governance	There will be new rules and regulations to deal with as different countries have different laws related to businesses.
Inflation risks	Wages and salaries for offshore staff will not stay the same forever. In addition, current salary rates in the emerging outsourcing markets, such as China, Vietnam or Mauritius, are increasing.
Business continuity	Political problems abroad may affect operations.
Security changes	Sending sensitive information overseas creates dangers.
Hidden labour costs	Bonuses paid by Indian companies to prevent staff leaving. Employee accommodation costs.

CASE STUDY Unions and outsourcing

Since the mid-1990s, outsourcing has been a considerable concern to trade unions, particularly in the banking sector. The unions identified a number of key reasons why banks were choosing to outsource.

Working in and with emerging economies was cheaper than in the UK and other Western nations and there was a supply of well-educated, technically literate people in the emerging economies.

Many of the banks were looking for short-term savings and advances in technology meant that thousands of jobs and entire sectors of industry could be relocated. Added to this, time and geography were no longer barriers.

Unions also recognised a trend. Just as manufacturing was relocated to the cheapest area in the past, so the 'new' industries were following. Outsourcing was a growing problem – while India currently dominated the outsourcing industry, it was expected that China and other nations would follow.

At the same time, emerging nations were aggressively marketing the benefits of relocating call centres. Many other IT functions and corporate organisations were not only 'shipping out' existing functions, but were planning new projects and expansions overseas, creating a situation where future jobs are 'lost' to the UK before they ever existed.

A union spokesman said: 'We need to challenge some of the fundamentals. Global competition has undergone a step change. New technology makes many areas of work relocatable to anywhere in the world at, literally, the switch of a button. We now face a different competitive model than we thought. But this isn't going to fade away. Nor is it restricted to low-skilled work. It is wrong to think this is just a challenge at a low skilled level. The challenge for us as unions, and for government, is how do we compete to maintain growth? All economies, including developing nations are entitled to compete. Protectionism is not the answer. Raising the skills level is essential and necessary, but it is not in itself enough. We need to challenge the business model so companies can't unilaterally decide to follow the lowest cost route. We don't accept that it is inevitable. This is not just happening in India. The challenge will also be from China, Africa and Asia – anywhere that can establish technology and a workforce'

INDIVIDUAL WORK
(8.31) ★ ★

Read the case study.

1 What did the spokesperson mean by 'protectionism'?

2 What is meant by 'companies can't unilaterally decide to follow the lowest cost route'?

Financial uncertainties

Investment costs of hardware, software and program adaptation and set-up expenses offset against uncertain future revenue

A business which has either already established itself as an online operation, or one that is expanding, faces financial uncertainties at every turn. A huge amount of new businesses fail in their first year simply due to the fact that they over-estimate their income compared to their actual spending.

Whilst the costs of computer hardware have crashed in recent years, a fully integrated system using the latest technology is still a considerable investment in the future. While computer hardware platforms are increasingly powerful, roughly doubling in capability every 12 to 18 months, the hardware manufacturers are seeking to maintain or expand their turnover coupled with falling hardware costs. Businesses may need as many as five applications open simultaneously, meaning that the need for ever more powerful machines continues.

Businesses also use terminals – basically a network of computers rather than 'stand alone' machines. These too have distinct cost-saving and efficiency benefits including:

- Hardware costs are lower as users can share printers and other office hardware equipment.
- The business can be more efficient as a network allows information to be shared by all employees.
- Communication between employees is much easier with the use of applications such as email.
- A centralised security system makes it almost impossible for outsiders to break into the system.
- Users can access their files from a remote location.
- Internet access is improved, more cost-effective and secure.

In May 1998, the 11 original member states of the European Monetary Union (EMU) formally announced a plan for the adoption of a single European currency, the euro. Organisations within participating countries needed to modify their single-currency systems to behave as dual-currency systems for the duration of a three-year transition period before full change over to the single euro currency in 2002. The first phase of the euro transition took place in 1999 and entailed software adaptation costs exceeding $150 billion. This is just one of the expenses that can cause problems for businesses.

BUSINESS FEASIBILITY

In this part of the unit we turn our attention to the processes that need to be undertaken in order to develop an online presence for a business. The term 'feasibility' refers to the website's potential effectiveness or success as far as the business is concerned.

Implementation issues

In this section we will look at the various implementation issues and the switching over of operations from an offline to an online presence.

Difficulties of e-business implementation, potential requirement for customisation, desired extent of online operations and changing user specifications for desired service levels

Implementation refers to how the business is proposing to develop an e-business operation. It requires a number of phases:

- *Business planning* What problems will the e-business solve? How can the business best integrate any e-business with its existing information communication technology systems? How long will it take for the e-business to provide enough profit to cover the costs of its development? How can the business gradually improve the e-business service by stages?

- *Requirements of the e-business* What will the e-business need to be able to achieve? Will it simply be a catalogue or can customers purchase and make orders? How sophisticated does the ordering process have to be? How big will the website need to be? Is the desired name available? Which ISP will host the website? Are there standard templates that could be used, produced by another business that would suit the business's purposes?

- *Customisation* There are standard software systems and website designs, but will these suit the purposes of the website? Is it possible to see a mock-up of the website and for various options about its design to be discussed? Is it possible for the business or the individuals designing the website to thoroughly test all of its functions and links within the site at the earliest possible stage?

- *Installation* Does the business already have a suitable information and computer network to cope with the demands of the e-business? What new hardware and software needs to be purchased?

- *Integration* Can the e-business systems be fully integrated into the current ICT system? Are there any problems of compatibility?

- *Data conversion* What data needs are there for the new system? Can existing customer data be transferred to the new system? Is it possible to crash test the system using sample customer details?

- *Testing* The e-business system needs to be thoroughly tested, even taking into account the most ridiculous thing a customer or visitor to the website might do. Is the website clear? Can the customers navigate through the website, view products, make orders and then review their order status?

- *Training* A user training manual needs to be written and anyone that will be involved with the new e-business needs to be fully trained and shown exactly how the system works.

- *Post-implementation* After the website has been up and running for a few days, but no more than a month, customers and employees using it need to be interviewed in order to assess their reactions. Are there improvements that can be made? What is the feedback in general from customers? Does the system live up to the expectations of the business?

INDIVIDUAL WORK
(8.32) ★ ★
Assume you are a small business wishing to establish an online presence. What would be the best way to detail all of the stages chronologically that you would have to work through in order to get the website up and running.

◆ *User support* Customers and employees will need ongoing support, particularly if parts of the website are changed and processes differ.

Desired speed of change

Switching from a predominantly offline form of business to an online business is not always in the hands of the business itself. In this section we will look at the various other factors that will influence and determine how fast the transition can be from offline to online.

It is important to remember that, in assuming that the business is already operating as an offline business, all normal operations have to continue while the website and implementation process is being developed. Changing over can only happen when everything is in place to make that transition.

Pace set by competitors

Some businesses are trend-setters or market leaders. They are the first businesses to move into new markets or devise new ways of selling their products or services. There always has to be one business that takes the plunge first. Most of the competitors will wait and see how effective these changes have been for the pioneering business before deciding to move in that direction themselves.

Other businesses take a different view and keep a close eye on developments within their competitors' businesses. As soon as their key competitors develop new systems online and are able to access a wider range of different customers they know that by not responding quickly they will lose some of their market share. If a pioneering company manages to get ahead in the development of their website and online presence whilst the others are still waiting to see what might happen, they will have a huge advantage.

Adaptability of key staff

As we have seen in this unit, all businesses have a number of key members of staff that are absolutely essential to them, no matter which direction the business is moving in. These are employees that know key information, have important contacts and, above all, have the skills, expertise and loyalty to the business that employers would find difficult to replace.

From the outset the business needs to ensure the support of its key members of staff and make plans to retrain them if necessary. The key members of staff in most modern organisations have the essential ICT skills. They may not be proficient in dealing with online business transactions and customer interaction. This can all be addressed with gradual, but intensive, retraining. A business would seek to include its key staff in the decision-making, particularly regarding how the online operation will work. It can learn from their experiences and the key members of staff may be able to suggest solutions or head off possible problems in the future before they have even occurred.

Potential redundancies and industrial relations problems

We have also seen in this unit that the establishment of an online operation can lead to a reduction in the number of staff needed by a business. Expensive premises and large numbers of administrative staff are just two of the key savings that businesses can enjoy by shifting from a more traditional style to an e-business. Any potential losses in members of staff have to be handled with great care.

Some members of staff can be redeployed in other parts of the organisation, even if this means that they need retraining. Huge job losses, however, present a very different problem. If the majority of the employees realise that they have no part in the future plans of the business, they have nothing to lose from causing the maximum amount of disruption to the business.

Although it is not necessarily a solution, many of these problems can be offset if the employees and trade unions are included in the conversations at the earliest possible stage. This gives the maximum number of employees the opportunity to seek employment elsewhere. Those that the business may wish to retain are also given an opportunity to retrain and become more proficient with the information systems to be used in the new e-business.

We have also seen that when many businesses change to an online presence, they have a tendency to outsource many of their operations. This does leave existing employees without a job. Businesses need to support these employees and assist them in obtaining work elsewhere, as well as compensating them financially for their loss of work.

Timescale for effective online operation and transition from offline activities

A business changing to online operations will usually set itself a date by which the new operation will be 'live'. As the online operations are being developed, the business will gradually move its current offline activities to online activities. Once the necessary systems are in place, all paper documentation and records can be transformed into electronic formats.

Various parts of the transition can take place simultaneously. The sales department, for example, could be entering all its customer records and sales histories onto databases, whilst the warehouse changes to an electronic stock control system. Gradually the manual paper-based activities will be transformed into electronic versions.

Once all of the operations have been converted, the business will then be in a position to launch the online operation. They would be foolish to consider doing this before all of these necessary elements are in place.

Benefits of increased sales or service supply and anticipated timescales of benefits

The obvious hope of a business transferring over to an online operation is to have a greater market presence and the ability to attract a wider variety of customers. Businesses tend to look at the probable benefits of a radical change such as this in the short, medium and long term. They will not expect to cover all the costs of transition to an e-business immediately.

- In the short term, they will be looking for increases in sales, which should prove that the decision was a good one.

- Gradually the sales will build and in the medium term, possibly after a year or two, the development costs of the online business will have been covered. The business, at this stage, will be pressing on and expanding its range of services to customers online. By this stage they will also have had experience with the system and may have adapted it to suit their own needs and those of their customers more closely.

- In the longer term, the business will, hopefully, have achieved a greater market share and will be enjoying increased sales, as well as attracting more customers by continually updating and developing its online presence.

Competitive disadvantage of not going online

Several studies have aimed to discover why businesses may be reluctant to switch their operations to an online business. Many businesses still run an offline and an online service to their customers.

A business may choose not to totally commit themselves to an online presence because:

- They do not believe that the business would be more successful if they made this investment.

- The business is too small and already under pressure to fulfil its customers' needs without the added pressures of more customers achieved via an online business presence.

- They believe that their entire computer system would be open to attack and that they do not trust the security measures that can be used to protect their own data and that of their customers.

- They are quite happy with the processes as they already are and see no need to adapt to an online presence when their existing systems work as well as they do.

- They cannot forecast the level of demand and are unsure whether there would be any increased demand.

- Their profit margins may already be low and the additional costs of online transactions may not make new business cost effective.

- They do not have sufficient resources to fund any switching costs from offline to online. They may believe that the software and hardware requirements in terms of cost are too high.

As we have seen, there are considerable benefits in establishing an online presence, yet many businesses still choose to run offline and online operations alongside one another. Traditionally, many retailers in particular have relied on high street stores. They have come under severe competition from online businesses that can offer products and services far cheaper because they do not have as many overheads as a high street store. Since many of these businesses feel that they are relatively secure as a high street operation and can compete with local or regional stores, they wish to retain this presence in the high street, whilst attempting to compete with online businesses at the same time.

An example of this is the group that owns Dixons, Currys and PC World. All three parts of the organisation have high street or superstore presence around the country. They provide a comprehensive range between them of electrical products. At the same time they also offer the same range plus additional products and services online.

CASE STUDY Constructing construction websites

In the UK around 42 per cent of construction businesses have their own company website and around 75 per cent of these sell their products and services online. Twenty-four per cent of them said that they had set up their websites to attract new customers. Nineteen per cent said the reason was to retain their customers, whilst 14 per cent thought it was an important part of providing a quality service.

Only 4 per cent of construction businesses thought that having a company website was vital for their success. Forty-seven per cent thought that having an e-business was good for their image as far as customers and suppliers were concerned. Forty-four per cent said that being online opened new markets and opportunities for them.

When asked where they would make a major investment, only 11 per cent said they would spend it on developing an e-business. Nineteen per cent said they would spend it on a new IT system and 29 per cent said they would spend it on buying new vehicles.

The most common reasons for not going online were lack of time (20 per cent) and 8 per cent that said there was no need for them to go online.

INDIVIDUAL WORK (8.33) ★ ★
Read the case study and then answer the following questions.

1 Do you think that lack of time is a sufficient reason for not establishing an online presence?

2 Do you think that some of the businesses are correct in saying that there is no need to have an online business?

3 Why might having a website be important for the business's image?

Unit Revision Questions

1 What is e-procurement?

2 What do you understand by the term 'passive brochure ware'?

3 How might a business analyse competition online?

4 How might a business reduce its overheads and labour costs by shifting to an online operation?

5 What are ISPs and what are portals?

6 How does the government support the development of broadband?

7 What do you understand by the term 'denial of service'?

8 What is user customisation?

9 What are the implications for employees of a business transferring solely to online operations?

10 State three reasons why a business may choose not to have an online presence.

Starting Up a New Business

This unit looks at the steps involved in setting up a new business. There are hundreds, if not thousands, of opportunities and good ideas but many fail if the preparation is not right.

The unit looks at the necessary steps involved, including the legal and financial requirements. You will also learn how to complete a business plan using sources of advice and guidance. The unit also looks at the vital personal qualities you would need to become a successful entrepreneur.

This is an internally assessed unit and to achieve the requirements of the unit you must:

- Investigate market opportunities for a possible new business venture
- Consider the minimum legal and financial requirements
- Complete a draft business plan
- Explore the personal qualities of a successful entrepreneur.

MARKET OPPORTUNITIES

Market opportunities represent chances for businesses to be able to identify demand (need) for products and services and then supply them. The identification of particular demands can be complicated and the business needs to be sure that it is geared up to be able to satisfy these demands should it find a worthwhile opportunity. A business will begin, as we will see, by looking at its own strengths and weaknesses. It will then examine the opportunities and threats presented by the market and the competitors. The business needs to understand as much as possible about the market and in particular the trends of the market. It will achieve this by carrying out research. Some research can be purchased or is available on the internet through government agencies. Other more focused research may need to be undertaken by the business itself.

A business also needs to be clear as to the current business climate, which means that it must predict what other businesses might be doing and how ready customers may be to buy products and services from them. Above all, it needs to examine the amount of competition there already is in the market and judge whether it is the right time to enter that market.

Products and services in potential demand

Customers' needs, wants, desires and requirements change all the time. Anticipating what will be needed in the future is quite an art. The first task of an organisation is to try to identify what the customers want and not what the organisation thinks they want.

The overall market demand for products and services are often beyond the direct control of an individual organisation. Needs are generated by the public in any region or market and they are often unique to that market. They are quite easy to measure. The main factors affecting demand can be categorised as follows:

- *Economic factors* – the influence of the economy.
- *Geographical factors* – weather, for example, can have an effect on which products or services are demanded.
- *Demographical factors* – for example the age, average household size and composition of the market.

- *Socio-cultural factors* – trends that affect a customer's motivation.
- *Comparative price factors* – the value of the product or service to the customer in relation to their spending power. Factors in this category include inflation, wage levels and the cost of raw materials in the market.
- *Mobility factors* – the customers' willingness or ability to travel in order to visit a particular retail outlet or location.
- *Government or legislative factors* – the legal consideration as to whether there are government rules and regulations about particular product or service development.
- *Media communication factors* – the media have a powerful influence over the demand for products and services. Although expensive, advertising via TV, radio and in the press can have a huge audience.

Demand also responds to changes in the supply of products and services. Supply is an important consideration of demand and demand is an important consideration of supply.

INDIVIDUAL WORK (9.1) ★ ★

1 If you worked for a business that offered holidays abroad to its customers, which of the following would you consider important?

   a) Better-quality furnishings in hotels
   b) Soundproofed rooms
   c) Better heating and ventilation in rooms
   d) Better bathroom facilities
   e) Bigger rooms
   f) Better lighting in rooms
   g) Better food on the plane.

2 You probably think that all of these are important. But not all can be done immediately. Put them in order of priority.

Customers demand that their requirements are met. They are always looking for the benefits that a product or service can offer them. A business will want to ensure that they have:

- The right product available
- At the right price
- In as many places as possible
- In stock at all times, both in the warehouse and in the retail outlets.

As we will see later, businesses will carry out market research in order to monitor customer reaction to its products and services so that it can build a profile of customer expectations.

Some of the more obvious expectations of customers can be addressed as a matter of course. Organisations can identify the key expectations relating to their particular area of business, including:

- Accurate and reliable information about the product or service.
- Prompt and courteous advice and feedback regarding questions about the product or service.
- Wide availability of the product or service.
- Consistency in the quality, style, colour or other standardised features of the product or service.
- Reliable and responsive **after-sales service**, maintenance or technical back-up after the purchase of the product or service.
- Good, competitive prices that encourage customers to return to the same organisation for their products or services.
- A consistent public image of the business that does not undermine or embarrass the customer.

Keyword

after-sales service – a customer service provided by a business after the sale of the product or service has taken place

INDIVIDUAL WORK
(9.2) ★ ★

In a number of activities throughout this unit you are going to be taking the same role. You have come up with a brilliant idea, which you want to call 'Swan and Fable'. The product or service can be whatever you want it to be. There are no instructions at this stage.

The first task is as follows:

1 Decide what your product or service is going to be.

2 Decide whether there is a demand for your product or service.

3 What might be your target market?

INDIVIDUAL WORK
(9.3) ★ ★

You now need to consider the feasibility of Swan and Fable. Your tasks are:

1 Consider who your likely customers are.

2 What are your likely start-up requirements in terms of skills and resources?

3 Draw something that represents what your product will look like or explain how your service will be of use to the customers.

So, to ensure that there is potential demand for its products and services, a business will need to make sure that what they produce is what the market wants and needs. They will want to do this for a number of reasons, including:

- To generate income from sales or produce a profit for the business.
- To maximise the benefits to the business of increased sales, more profit and creating a good image.
- To manage the effects of any forthcoming changes, such as political, legal, economic, social or technological.
- To allow them to coordinate their activities in order to meet their aims and objectives.
- To enhance customers' perceptions of the organisation, product or service.

Products and services to match skills and resources

At the outset it will be important for a new business's owners to assess their skills and to be aware of the resources available to them. They may have ideal visions of what they want to do in the future, but without adequate skills and resources they will not succeed in such a competitive world. Essentially, the skills they would need are the ability to:

- Evaluate their own strengths and weaknesses
- Work independently or with other people
- Plan
- Manage their time effectively
- Set targets
- Review progress
- Make decisions
- Solve problems.

We look at all these skills in more detail a little later in this section.

Resources are even more fundamental. Central issues are the coordination and organisation of resources currently available or those that are required. Resources can be:

- *Human* – the person starting the business and the skills of others needed.
- *Physical* – including premises, machinery and equipment, stock and materials.
- *Financial* – how much capital they have available and where they would get any additional finance that may be needed.

Niche possibilities

A niche market is a specialised market that is not often targeted by larger organisations. The products sold to a niche market are often tailor-made so competition is low and high prices can be charged. Marketing and selling products and services to a niche market often requires a very different approach to those adopted for larger markets, or mass markets. There are likely to be fewer customers in a niche market and this means that they will require the product or service to be precisely what they require.

SWOT analysis

Unit 2 Exploring Key Business Pressures gives a detailed account of a SWOT analysis and how it is used by a business to plan and make decisions that will direct them towards meeting their objectives and dealing with any changes.

SWOT analysis is an effective way of identifying strengths and weaknesses, and of examining the opportunities and threats faced. Carrying out an analysis using the SWOT framework helps to focus activities into areas where there is strength and where the greatest opportunities lie.

Strengths include:

- ◆ The advantages the business has over the competition
- ◆ What the business does well
- ◆ The relevant resources the business has access to
- ◆ What other people see as the business's strengths.

Weaknesses can be both internal and external and include:

- ◆ Areas that could be improved
- ◆ Things the business does badly
- ◆ Things the business should avoid.

Opportunities could include:

- ◆ Any good market opportunities facing the business
- ◆ Any interesting trends the business is aware of.

Useful opportunities can come from such things as:

- ◆ Changes in technology and markets
- ◆ Changes in government policy related to the business's operations
- ◆ Changes in social patterns, population profiles, lifestyle changes, etc.
- ◆ Local events.

A useful approach to looking at opportunities is to look at a business's strengths and judge whether these are likely to open up any opportunities. Alternatively, the business could look at its weaknesses and judge whether they could open up opportunities by eliminating the weaknesses.

Threats to a business are the obstacles that they face, including:

- ◆ What their competition is doing.
- ◆ Changes to the required specifications for their main activities, products or services.
- ◆ Changing technology.
- ◆ Bad debts or cash-flow problems.
- ◆ Their own weaknesses.

INDIVIDUAL WORK
(9.4) ★ ★

1 Do you foresee Swan and Fable being marketed into a niche?

2 Complete a SWOT analysis (see Unit 2) for Swan and Fable.

Market trends

It is vital for a business to understand its markets and its customers. Providing they do understand who they are selling to and why those customers purchase products and services from them, the business can begin to understand how future demands might move.

Markets and customer tastes and demands change constantly. A business needs to keep track of these movements to ensure that they can match the predicted market trends as and when they occur. This is difficult to do as it requires the business to invest time, money and effort in market research.

Use of primary and secondary market research

To find out about market trends, consumer confidence and what the competition is doing, a business will carry out market research. This research can be broken down into two types: primary research and secondary research.

When a business has to obtain the information themselves, this is known as primary research, or field research. There are four methods of primary research:

- ◆ *Personal interview* – a representative of the business stops people in the street to ask them questions face to face.
- ◆ *Telephone interview* – very similar to a personal interview, but the interviewee is asked questions over the telephone.
- ◆ *Postal survey* – a business sends out a letter and a questionnaire and asks the respondent to send their completed questionnaires back to the business.
- ◆ *A panel* – asking the same group of people a range of questions over a period of time in order, for example, to check their attitudes.

Table 9.1 shows the advantages and disadvantages of the different methods of primary research.

Table 9.1
The advantages and disadvantages of different methods of primary research

Method of primary research	Advantages	Disadvantages
Personal interview	• There is a high response rate as people do not often refuse to answer. • A questionnaire is easy to analyse. • Any questions misunderstood can be explained. • The respondent does not have time to consider their answer so responses are likely to be more truthful.	• The cost is often high because of the interviewer's time. • If the respondent is in a hurry they may not give full consideration to the questions. • Interviewers will need training. • Collecting the information can take time.
Telephone interview	• It is a quick way of getting through a lot of interviews. • The interviewers can stay in one place. • Costs are relatively low because travel is not involved. • People are easily accessible.	• You cannot interview people that do not have a telephone. • You cannot tell a respondent's approximate age without asking. • People may be annoyed at being disturbed and may not pay attention. • The interviewer cannot provide identification.
Postal survey	• A wide selection of the population can be reached. • It is relatively cheap. • Interviewers do not have to be trained. • Specialist groups, such as readers of particular magazines, can be reached. • Answers may be more considered and not rushed.	• Not everyone will respond. • Questions could be misunderstood. • It is expensive to keep an up-to-date mailing list. • It can take a long time for all responses to come back. • The person the questionnaire was intended for may not be the one in the household to complete it.
A panel	• It gives a good indication of trends. • Valuable background information about the members of a panel can be obtained. • It is easy to judge whether or not external factors have influenced the members of the panel.	• External factors, such as a death or a family problem, could affect the respondent's opinions. • The respondents may not behave as they normally do because they are being observed. • It is expensive because panellists will have to be rewarded and/or replaced if they leave.

INDIVIDUAL WORK
(9.5) ★ ★
Visit the website of the Office of National Statistics at www.statistics.gov.uk. What information do they supply that could be useful to you in determining the current trends related to Swan and Fable?

So, primary research can be expensive and time consuming. Before an organisation goes to this expense, it should consider what information is already available. Secondary data, as this already available information is known, can be sourced from a variety of different places and can be much cheaper than carrying out primary research.

Secondary data can be found in local libraries and in many reference books, as well as via the internet. This information can show local, national and regional trends, as well as statistical information.

Current business and consumer confidence and market competition

In carrying out market research, a business will try to make some kind of judgement about their potential share of the market. In other words, they will need to seek information about their competitors' businesses and their products. This will enable them to position their product and set pricing levels. Many small businesses operate in a market where there are lots of suppliers and no single individual organisation has more than about a 5 per cent share.

Being able to measure market share is much easier than being able to take market share from competitors. To assess the level of competition, a business needs to consider:

- What are the competitors' products?
- How many do they sell?
- How have they performed in the last few years?
- What organisational structure do the competitors adopt?
- What are their sales techniques?

- How do they manufacture the products?
- Who are their main customers?
- What is their delivery service like?
- What is their customer service like?
- How good is their after-sales service?

Market size is also a key feature. A business can measure the potential demand for a product in financial terms or by the number of units that could be sold.

It is important for a business to measure their market potential, which is different from market size. Market potential refers to the probable growth or lack of growth of the markets. In order to find out about potential customers, a business will:

- Send questionnaires to potential customers.
- Follow leads from a list of individuals that may have approached the business as a result of receiving correspondence from them in the past.
- Follow leads from existing customers who may have referred potential new customers to the business.

In doing this kind of research about potential customers, a business will have to make sure that they record all the information they have gained, devise a system with which they can follow up responses from customers. In addition they will have to make sure that all potential customers receive regular updates and information about the business.

Before a business can collect statistical data on its market for a product or service, it needs to know which market that is. To define what the market is, they need to decide:

- Whether their market is a consumer, industrial or professional one.
- Whether age, sex, family size or marital status is the basis of the customer target group.
- Whether the product or service relies on the local area alone.
- Whether a customer's social status is important.
- Whether the customer's frequency of purchase is an important factor.
- Whether the target market is influenced by fashion or current trends.
- Whether the target market is influenced by the price of the product or service.
- Where the target market currently purchases their products or services.
- Whether the target market requires fast and frequent deliveries.
- Whether the target market requires a high level of after-sales service.

The business's suppliers would also be a valuable source of information as they could provide the business with some analysis of potential customers that would allow the business to investigate the nature of the products or services they desire.

INDIVIDUAL WORK
(9.6) ★ ★

1 You now need to think about your Swan and Fable product or service in terms of the market will it be aimed at.

a) What do you think are some of the characteristics of your potential customers?

b) Is your product or service aimed at a market that has lots of competition?

c) If so, who would be your main competitors? What do you know about them?

2 Carry out some research within your own group and some of the staff at your school or college. Design a questionnaire aimed at finding out whether your product or service would be attractive to your respondents. Ask them how much they would be prepared to pay for it and whether or not they already use a similar product or service. If so, where do they buy it and why do they do so?

WANT TO FIND OUT MORE?

To find out more about the **Federation of Small Businesses,** visit their website at: www.fsb.org.uk.

INDIVIDUAL WORK

(9.7) ★ ★

Visit the Federation of Small Businesses website. Click on 'Regions' and find the nearest branch to you.

Possible new business ventures

Self-employment

The number of self-employed has been steadily rising since around 1986. By the end of 2003, the number of self-employed in the UK had almost reached 300,000. The 2003 figures show an overall increase of 8.9 per cent, some 8.6 per cent for men and 9.7 per cent for women. There are now in excess of 200,000 men in self-employment and roughly half that figure of women.

When a new business is starting up, the individual will need to undertake considerable forecasting and forward planning at the outset. They will have to convince potential providers of finance, such as banks and other financial services, that they have an effective business plan and that their new enterprise has a reasonable chance of success in the future.

The Federation of Small Businesses was formed in 1974 and now has over 185,000 members. It promotes and protects the interests of the self-employed and owners of small businesses. The FSB runs a helpline, which receives around 100,000 calls a year.

As we will discover in the next section, the self-employed often start up their businesses as sole traders or partners. Self-employment can be undertaken in virtually all types of industry, including building, catering, cleaning, IT, gardening, hairdressing, plumbing and window cleaning.

LEGAL AND FINANCIAL REQUIREMENTS

Legal requirements

Choosing an appropriate business structure

There are three basic types of business ownership; sole proprietorship (sole trader), partnerships and limited companies.

Sole traders

Around 63 per cent of all UK businesses are single-person enterprises known as sole traders. Many people choose this business structure as it can be the easiest to set up and run.

Registration of a small business is very straightforward, the record-keeping is simple and the owner keeps all the profits after tax. Operating as a sole trader gives the business owner a chance to test their market before getting involved in more complicated forms of business structure. The major drawback is that if the business fails, then any losses will have to be found by the owner. Sole trader businesses have a single owner and that owner has complete control over the business.

The law does not make a distinction between the business and the sole trader. This means that the owner has unlimited liability. Unlimited liability means, in practical terms, that any business debt has to be paid from the owner's personal wealth if the business fails. It is usual for the business to cease trading when the owner chooses to retire or dies. In many cases, however, the business may be passed on to a relative or sold.

Most sole trading businesses are small, with low turnovers and either no or very few employees. At present, there are around 3.7 million sole trading businesses in the UK and of that total around 2.3 million of them are sole traders with no employees. Sole traders include plumbers, hairdressers, electricians, small retail stores and a host of other types of business in almost every conceivable area of work. The largest groups of sole traders are in the construction business (builders and allied trades) and this accounts for around 24 per cent of the 2.3 million sole traders with no employees. The next largest group provide business services and these account for some 18 per cent of the total.

Many sole traders operate under the name of the owner, but others choose a different name. It is not a legal requirement to register a business name. Contacting the National Business Register can be the best way to do this, but it is best to avoid certain words such as 'international', 'federation' and 'registered', as these are restricted words under the Business Names Act 1985 and the Company and Business Names Regulations 1981. Companies House and the National Business Register have full lists of words that are restricted and will tell you how to gain approval to use them.

As with any business name, you must be careful not to use a name that is similar to an existing business. The first thing to do is to look on a search engine on the internet. You can also check (at no cost) with the National Business Register, the Trade Marks Register and the Patent Office as well as the limited companies names index at Companies House.

As a sole trader, you must register as self-employed with the Inland Revenue within three months of starting up or pay a fine. The three-month limit starts from the last day of the sole trader's first month of trading.

The key issues of a sole trader are summarised in Table 9.2.

Partnerships

A partnership is created when two or more people decide to form a business. There have to be at least two people and a maximum of 20 in a partnership. The partners receive a percentage of the profits in line with the percentage of the total investment they put into the partnership.

The partners are responsible for all of the debts of the partnership – not just the debts incurred by them as a partner, but the debts incurred by all partners. Creditors can demand that the partners surrender their own assets to cover the debts of the partnership.

There are several advantages of forming a partnership. These include:

- Partners are able to share the burden of running the business, provide support and help deal with the problems.
- The partners can take it in turns to run the partnership, which helps reduce the stresses of running a business on your own.
- The partners will have a broader range of skills, knowledge and experience.
- Each new partner adds to the mix of skills, knowledge and experience.
- Decision-making can be easier as the different partners bring with them a range of experience and views on each decision that needs to be made.

The main disadvantages of partnerships are:

- As a partnership, each of the partners has less freedom to make decisions on an individual basis.
- The partners may have different views on what they want to achieve and what the objectives of the partnership should be.
- Some of the partners may wish to put much of the profit back into the partnership in order to grow, whilst others will be looking for a better income from the partnership.

Table 9.2
The key issues of a sole trader

Key issues	Explanation
Management and raising finance	The owner makes all the decisions on how to manage the business. The owner raises money for the business out of their own assets, and/or with loans from banks or other lenders.
Records and accounts	The owner has to make an annual self-assessment return to the Inland Revenue. The owner must also keep records showing their business income and expenses.
Profits	Any profits go to the owner.
Tax and National Insurance	As owner is self-employed, the profits are taxed as income. The owner also needs to pay fixed-rate Class 2 National Insurance contributions (NICs) and Class 4 NICs on profits.
Liability	As a sole trader, the owner is personally responsible for any debts run up by the business. This means the owner's home or other assets may be at risk if the business runs into difficulties.

- As all of the partners have a say in the decision-making, the process can be slower.
- Conflict between partners can take up time and effort which should be spent on building up and running the business.
- Partners may resent the rewards a partner receives if that partner is not seen to be working as hard as the others.

The key issues of partnerships are summarised in Table 9.3.

Private limited companies

Many small businesses choose to set themselves up as a private limited company. A limited company is a separate legal entity, owned by its shareholders and run by the director(s).

There are two main ways of setting up a private limited company:

- *Ready-made company* You can buy an off-the-shelf limited company – a company that has already been formed and already has a company name. The company can be available within two hours, which means you can trade almost immediately. All that will be required is the name(s) of the director(s), the name of the company secretary and the company's proposed address. The cost for a ready-made company can range from £85 to £135.

- *Tailor-made company* To set up a private limited company, you will need to select a name for your limited company then you will need to check if the name is available. You then need to appoint at least one director for the company. (This can be anyone who is not an **undischarged bankrupt** or who is disqualified by court from holding a directorship.) You then need to appoint at least one secretary. (If you are the company's sole director you cannot also be the company secretary. You therefore need to appoint a company secretary who can be a spouse, relative or friend to take on this role. No formal qualifications are required.) The next step is to establish a registered office. (This is the address where letters and reminders from Companies House will be sent to you. The address can be anywhere in England and Wales, or Scotland if your company is registered there.) If you change your registered office address after **incorporation**, the new address must be notified to Companies House on Form 287. A private limited company can be set up with a company registration agent. Prices start from about £100 to £138.

Keyword

undischarged bankrupt – an individual who has been declared bankrupt and has not yet paid off their debts

incorporation – the procedure by which a business registers itself at Companies House and becomes a legal entity. It is also known as registration or formation

Table 9.3
The key issues of a partnership

Key issues	Explanation
Management and raising finance	Partners usually manage the business, although they can delegate responsibilities to employees. Partners raise money for the business from their own assets, and/or with loans. It is possible to have 'sleeping' partners who contribute money to the business but are not involved in running the business on a daily basis.
Records and accounts	The partnership and each partner makes annual self-assessment returns to the Inland Revenue. The partnership keeps records showing business income and expenses.
Profits	Each partner takes a share of the profits.
Tax and National Insurance	Partners are classed as self-employed and taxed on their share of the profits. Each partner also pays fixed-rate Class 2 National Insurance contributions (NICs) and Class 4 NICs on their share of the profits.
Liability	Each partner is personally responsible for all debts incurred by the partnership. This means their homes or other assets may be at risk if the business runs into problems.

The main advantages of setting up a limited company are:

- *Limited liability* – the shareholders will not be held personally liable for company debts.
- *Separate entity* – the company has its own legal identity separate from the shareholders and officers.

The key issues of private limited companies are summarised in Table 9.4.

Table 9.4
The key issues of a private limited company

Key issues	Explanation
Management and raising finance	A director or board of directors must make all of the management decisions. Shareholders, borrowing and retained profits provide the finance. Public limited companies can raise money by selling shares on the stock market, but private limited companies cannot.
Records and accounts	The accounts must be filed with Companies House. An annual return (form 363s) is sent before the anniversary of incorporation each year. The form must be checked, amended and returned to Companies House with a fee. The directors and secretary are responsible for informing Companies House of changes in the structure and management of the business.
Profits	Profits are distributed to shareholders in the form of dividends.
Tax and National Insurance	Companies must pay corporation tax and must make an annual return to the Inland Revenue. Company directors are employees of the company and must pay Class 1 National Insurance contributions (NICs) as well as income tax. If the company or organisation has any taxable income or profits, it must tell the Inland Revenue that the company exists and that it is liable to tax.
Liability	Shareholders are not personally responsible for the company's debts, but directors may be asked to guarantee loans to the company.

> **WANT TO FIND OUT MORE?**
>
> Visit the site of the **British Franchise Association** at: www.british-franchise.org.

Franchises

One option in setting up a business is to buy a franchise. This means that you buy the right to run a business that the franchisor has set up. Typical examples of franchises are McDonald's, The Body Shop and KallKwik. For small businesses, the franchise tends to be retailing and eating establishments or providing a service such as cleaning.

The key advantages and disadvantages of setting up franchises are summarised in Table 9.5.

When choosing a franchise, many people use the services of an independent adviser. It is important to make sure that the franchisor is a member of the British Franchise Association. An accountant can check the forecasts of sales given by the franchisor.

The key issues of franchises are summarised in Table 9.6.

Table 9.5
The advantages and disadvantages of franchises

Advantages	Disadvantages
• You get more help and advice starting up and running the franchise than you would get on starting your own business. • You start with a reputation and under a well-known name. • You get a ready-made product or service that is established.	• You may be less free to develop in your own way. • You may have to start fairly big – maybe too big for you if you have no experience. • You have to pay an ongoing management fee.

Table 9.6
The key issues of a franchise

Key issues	Explanation
Management and raising finance	It is the franchise agreement that usually sets out how the franchised business should be run. The franchisors usually provide management help and training to franchisees as part of the overall package. 　　It is the franchisee that has to find the money needed to start up the business. In some cases, the franchisors offer a loan.
Records and accounts	The records and accounts depend on the business structure chosen by the franchisee. In addition to the regular legal requirements, the franchisors will need to see detailed financial records.
Profits	Franchisees usually pay a share of their turnover to the franchisor. This reduces the profits and these are distributed according to the legal structure of the business.
Tax and National Insurance	This depends on the business structure chosen by the franchisee.
Liability	This depends on the business structure chosen by the franchisee.

Business registration

It is quite simple to form a company. Ready-made companies can be bought for quite a small sum of money and although the company may already have a name, this can be changed for an additional small fee.

All businesses have to register with the Companies Registration Office. This involves some form filling and a further fee. It is advisable that this is done through a solicitor if a limited company is being formed.

Companies House holds the public records of more than a million companies. Its four main functions are to:

- Incorporate and dissolve companies.
- Examine and hold documents presented under the Companies Act 1985 and 1989 and other legislation.
- Make this information available to the public.
- Exercise certain powers in relation to companies on behalf of the Secretary of State for Trade and Industry.

Once the registration of the business (incorporation) has been completed, every business is required to provide the following information to Companies House:

- An annual return
- Its registered address
- Notification of a change in the company's directors
- Notification of a change of company secretary
- Details of its directors and shareholders
- Annual (yearly) accounts.

Companies House attempts to ensure that this information is available to any individual wishing to gain access to it. In doing this, the organisation helps to provide peace of mind for its customers, suppliers, creditors and shareholders.

As businesses are required to meet this registration obligation, this means that Companies House can provide up-to-date and accurate information. If a business fails to register with Companies House, the directors can be liable for fines, as can the business.

INDIVIDUAL WORK
(9.8) ★ ★

1 Investigate at least five partnership firms in your local area and try to discover the number of partners in each of these businesses. What advantages do they have over sole traders?

2 If you were starting a business, what kind of qualities would you be looking for in your partners?

INDIVIDUAL WORK
(9.9) ★

Visit the website of Companies House at www.companieshouse.gov.uk.
　　Click on 'Web check'. Type in the name of a business local to you and this will enable you to click on the name from a list.

1 When was this company formed?

2 What is its official address and company number?

Use of solicitors

For a new business, choosing the right solicitor can be as important as choosing the right bank. Solicitors tend to specialise in different areas of the law, but most partnerships have a small-business specialist and one that can give advice on starting a new business. Sometimes businesses choose larger firms of solicitors in order to benefit from the combined skills and expertise of the individual partners. Solicitors offer valuable advice on many of the following concerns for a new business venture:

- The legal forms of business
- Personal guarantees
- Employment law
- Debt collection
- Terms and conditions of contracts
- Terms and conditions of lease agreements
- Franchise agreements
- The patenting of products
- Registered trade marks.

Key legal constraints

Using a solicitor will assist a business in ensuring they are complying with the required laws that are in force for anyone that begins trading or starts their business operation. Businesses are required to ensure that they have complied with various legal guidelines. The following is a checklist of the legal aspects that a business should consider as an essential part of their business planning:

- What are the current planning consents or authorised uses of the premises to be used by the business?
- Do the premises meet Health and Safety at Work regulations?
- Do the premises meet fire regulations and do they have a current fire safety certificate?
- Do the products conform to the Weights and Measures Act 1985?
- Do the products conform to the requirements of the Trading Standards Office?
- Do the products conform to the Environmental Health Office requirements?
- Is there a possibility that the business may breach any environmental protection laws?
- Do any aspects of the marketing or advertising effort breach the Trade Descriptions Act 1968?
- Do any aspects of the marketing or advertising effort breach the Consumer Credit Act 1974?

Employment law requires that particular attention should be paid to providing a contract of employment for all those who work for the business and that they pay attention to the laws concerning discrimination.

Health and safety regulations have become an increasingly complex area for businesses to consider. A business must ensure that it complies with the Health and Safety at Work Act 1974 in the following respects:

- Providing safe machinery and equipment.
- Ensuring that regular maintenance is undertaken.
- Ensuring that all operating procedures for machinery and equipment are carefully monitored.
- Ensuring that safe methods of handling potentially dangerous or hazardous materials are adhered to.
- Ensuring that employees are well supervised at all times.
- Providing healthy and safe working conditions.
- Ensuring that the access to and exit from the premises is safe, unblocked and clearly marked.
- Ensuring that any visitors to the premises encounter a safe environment.

Employer's liability insurance covers a business against claims that may be made by employees who have suffered injury in the course of their work. The term 'employee' is a broad one in this respect, as it covers all of those individuals that are under contract in some way to the business.

Customers are becoming increasingly aware of environmental issues and consequently certain businesses will cite environmental considerations as being key objectives. Specific environmental policies that may be adopted include the:

- Use of environmentally friendly products and processes
- Careful disposal of all waste
- Use of energy-efficient heating systems
- Use of biodegradable packaging materials.

The Environmental Protection Act 1990 and its implications for UK businesses have been supported by a number of European Union Directives. These attempt to ensure that businesses take full account of their social and environmental responsibilities at all times. These laws, coupled with considerable customer pressure, have caused businesses to re-evaluate many of their costs of production. When considering environmental concerns, a business will try to examine the following aspects of its activities:

- Do any activities involve environmental risk?
- Do any of our processes involve environmental risk?
- Do we use any materials that are environmentally suspect?
- Do our products have a detrimental impact on the environment?
- What type of waste do we produce?
- What level of waste do we produce?
- Can we implement cost-effective ways of eliminating pollution?
- If we establish environmental policies, will it make us more efficient?
- Is there a real public or customer demand for environmentally sound products?
- What environmental protection legislation could be expected in the future?
- Do we have systems and procedures in place to ensure we comply with existing or expected legislation?
- Can we improve our image to the public by implementing environmental practices?

The Trade Descriptions Act 1968 relates to the products and services that a business supplies. This legislation states that:

- A product must comply with its description.
- A product must be capable of performing to the levels claimed by the manufacturer.
- Faulty products should be replaced or a refund made to the customer without exception.
- Products should meet all existing safety standards.
- An organisation faces prosecution if it is found to be selling unsafe products.

INDIVIDUAL WORK
(9.10) ★ ★
Another piece of legislation that governs the activities of a business is the former Sale of Goods Act 1979 and 1995 that has now been replaced by the Sale and Supply of Goods to Consumers Regulations 2002.

Find out what a customer can now demand if products they have bought from a business are faulty.

Financial requirements

Planning the financial resources of a new business involves considering:

- The amount of capital available from the owners of the business
- The source of any additional finance needed.

Before any business can begin its operations, it needs start-up finance to pay for essential items. The organisation will need a variety of different pieces of equipment or assets, such as vehicles, premises, shop fittings, machinery, land and working capital.

Initial start-up capital

The majority of small businesses do not require significant funding to get started. Around 25 per cent only need around £10,000 for their initial start-up capital. This does reflect the fact that very few new small businesses are involved in manufacturing. Most small businesses use a combination of funding rather than one single source.

The most frequently cited sources for funding are (with the most frequent first):

- Foregoing salary
- Personal savings
- Loan from family and/or friends
- Private company investment
- Bank overdraft facility
- Business Angel investment
- Princes Trust loan/grant
- Venture capital investment
- Short-term enterprises
- Bank loan
- Credit card
- Credit from debtor
- Enterprise Allowance Scheme
- Temporary work.

Many young business owners are unlikely to have the assets to provide a guarantee against a loan, as they will not have a lot of their own capital to invest and will not have the track record to be an attractive proposition for funding. At the same time, their business ideas can be quite innovative and as a consequence they are often viewed as risky.

Working capital and reserves

Broadly speaking, the business will need finance to cover the costs of the essential assets required for their activities. Essential assets are the items needed to enable the business to operate, such as premises, shop fittings, equipment and transport. All of these are key items that the organisation must have obtained before it can start its business activity.

Working capital is needed to finance the day-to-day running of the business. Working capital is used to pay for the running costs and raw materials, to fund credit offered to customers and to pay a business's immediate debts. If these debts cannot be paid, a business is considered to be insolvent, or not in a financial position to continue to trade. When considering working capital, the following are taken into account:

- *The value of raw materials in stock* – these are considered part of a business's working capital because they can be turned into finished products and offered to customers.

- *Work in progress* – although they are considered to be part of a business's working capital they may not be of such value to a potential customer.

- *Stocks of finished goods* – these make a contribution to the working capital as they could be turned into cash.

- *Debtors* – all businesses will be owed money by a variety of its debtors. Debt (money owed the business) is regarded as part of a business's working capital.

- *Cash* – in this sense cash is money that the business could reliably obtain, either from within the premises or from the business's bank account.

Identifying appropriate sources of finance

In order to fund the purchase of capital assets, the business will use a number of methods to raise capital, including:

- *Trade credit* This refers to the payment terms agreed between the supplier and the business. It is a way a business can help its cash flow situation, as often it does not have to pay its bills for 30 days.

INDIVIDUAL WORK (9.11) ★★

1 How would the following types of business obtain their working capital?

a) A retail outlet

b) A leisure centre

c) A manufacturer of electrical components.

2 What about their assets? How do they differ from one type of business to another?

Overdraft The size of an organisation's overdraft depends upon its working capital requirements. Generally, the amount is agreed each year with the bank. As the business's customers will want to delay their payments for as long as possible, the business will try to make sure that its working capital is sufficient to make sure they have a positive cash flow.

Factoring This is a cash advance given by a bank or financial service provider. The amount of the cash advance is usually calculated as around 80 per cent of the total of money owed to a business by its customers. The bank would charge a business for this cash advance, which has to be paid back to the bank once the money owed to the business has been paid.

Leasing If an organisation chooses to lease its equipment then it is never the legal owner of that equipment. The equipment remains the property of the leasing company. The equipment is leased in return for a regular schedule of payments. The organisation leasing the equipment cannot count it as an asset and does not benefit from tax allowances on it. There are several forms of leasing agreements, including:
- short period leases, which last for up to five years. The business can buy the equipment at the end of the lease period at a reduced rate.
- long-term leases – although there is a minimum time period that the business has to comply with, the agreements can run for an unspecified period of time.
- reduced payment leases – this type of lease offers the business the advantage of a reduced level of lease repayment during most of the lease period. At the end of this period, the business pays a large final payment to terminate the lease agreement. This is particularly useful for some businesses as the leasing company allows them to find a buyer for the equipment so that it can offset some of this final payment by the cash obtained from the sale of the equipment.

Hire purchase This is different from leasing in that a finance provider buys the equipment and hires it to the business. The business has to agree to make regular payments until the full cost has been repaid. The main advantage to a business of using hire purchase is that it saves the initial outlay of large sums of money.

Loans Loans are often negotiated with a bank or finance provider in order to acquire an agreed sum of money, which may be earmarked for the purchase of a particular piece of equipment. The loan is usually paid back over a fixed period of time, with agreed levels of interest and regular payments. Loans are useful in raising finance to make large purchases but the bank or finance provider will require evidence of the business's income and expenditure so that it can measure the business's ability to meet the loan repayments.

Mortgages A mortgage is a legal agreement between a bank or financial service provider and the business, which gives the lender certain legal rights over the property being purchased via the mortgage. The bank or service provider has the legal right to repossess the buildings or premises if the business is unable to make the required mortgage repayments.

Profit retention This means that the business would put aside a certain portion of any profits they have made to ensure that they have sufficient working capital.

Grants These may be available to a business from central governments, local authorities and the EU. Grants are often linked to social and regional development and the grant provider will offer assistance for projects relating to various business activities. Grants are available from:
- grant aid schemes – assisted area grants, regional development grants and those targeted towards the regeneration of depressed areas
- the Department of Trade and Industry
- local authorities
- Business Link
- EU funds
- business expansion schemes.

GROUP WORK (9.12)
★ ★
If you were partners in a business and only had a limited amount of working capital available to you, which of the available finance options listed here would you consider to be the most beneficial for your business's cash flow if you needed to purchase a piece of equipment? Discuss this as a group and then list the advantages and disadvantages of each option.

INDIVIDUAL WORK (9.13) ★ ★
Visit the following websites:
www.businesslink.gov.uk
www.dti.gov.uk (on the 'Select a DTI site' menu, click 'Regional').
These websites should provide you with information about the many different types of grant available to business in your region.

Using accountants

In choosing an accountant, particularly at the start of the business's operations, the owners will need to make the decision as to whether or not they wish to use the services of a large or small concern. Whilst larger firms of accountants may be unwilling to provide basic bookkeeping services, a small accountancy firm may not be able to offer assistance in raising finance. It is, therefore, a balancing act that needs to be based on the business's particular requirements.

Generally speaking, accountants offer a business the following advice or services:

- Bookkeeping.
- Setting up an accounting system.
- Advice on the use of computerised accounting software.
- Auditing – where the accountant checks the records of the business to make sure they are in order and are a true record of the business's transactions and activities.
- Managing cash flow.
- Raising start-up capital.
- Negotiating additional finance.
- Payment of tax to the Inland Revenue.
- Payment of National Insurance.
- Payment of VAT to Customs and Excise.
- Payment of business tax.
- Production of the financial elements involved in business plans (covered later in this unit).
- Production of budgets and forecasts or predictions.

INDIVIDUAL WORK
(9.14) ★ ★
Accountants that are qualified with particular associations, or examining boards, have letters after their names. Using the internet, find out what the following letters mean:

a) ACA

b) FCA

c) ACCA

d) FCCA.

VAT and income tax

Working out a tax commitment can be a complex issue and it is in the best interests of the individual or small business to have some understanding of how the tax bill is worked out. It is essential to know how the tax system works and what allowances an individual can set against their income. Accounting records need to be kept so that tax calculations can be made. It is often a good idea to use a professional tax adviser, or accountant, to assist in the preparation of accounts.

Self-employed people will normally pay their income tax at the end of January and July every year. The tax is assessed and paid on the previous year's activities. This arrangement is somewhat different to that of employees, who pay their tax on a weekly or monthly basis.

In a partnership, the taxable income is worked out in a very similar way to that of a sole trader. Business expenses can be deducted and tax relief applied for on capital expenditure, National Insurance contributions and losses. The tax burden placed on each partner is in proportion to the profit share of each individual partner.

In the case of a limited company, on the other hand, taxation is not assessed against a particular individual. The limited company will pay capital gains tax and corporation tax.

The VAT (Value Added Tax) system is a method of using businesses to act as tax collectors for the government. VAT is an indirect tax in that it is only paid when a customer buys an article. A business pays VAT on their purchases and also charges VAT on the products or services they sell. If the business has charged more VAT on the products or services it has sold than it has paid on the goods it has purchased, then it will owe the Customs and Excise department the difference between the two amounts.

At the time of writing VAT is charged at 17.5 per cent on most products. It is the individual and not the business that is registered to pay VAT. For VAT purposes, a business is an individual. There is a threshold below which a business does not charge VAT, but they still pay it on the goods they purchase.

INDIVIDUAL WORK
(9.15) ★ ★
Visit the website of Her Majesty's Customs and Excise at www.hmce.gov.uk. Click on the 'Learn about VAT' icon and choose the 'What is vatable' option, then answer the following questions.

1 How many rates of VAT are there?

2 What are the rates?

3 Which products or services have reduced rates of VAT?

4 Thinking about Swan and Fable, does it produce products or services on which it is required by law to charge VAT to customers?

Insurance requirements

Sorting out insurance should be one of the high-priority jobs of any new business. If businesses fail to obtain the correct insurance, they could lose money. Insurance basically fall into two categories:

- Insurance required by law
- Insurance that is desirable in order to cover possible risks or accidents.

Asset insurance attempts to ensure that the business is protected against loss or damage to stock, equipment or processes as a result of various uncontrollable factors. There are four main types of asset insurance:

- *Damage and loss insurance*, which covers the premises and contents of the premises from fire. The term 'fire', used in insurance, also covers floods, lightning, explosions, earthquakes, storms, riots and vandalism.
- *Theft insurance*, which covers the theft of all removable assets, including computers, machinery, office equipment, money and stock. A business must ensure that the insurance provides cover for loss both on and off their premises. Additionally they must be careful to ensure that the insured value is for the replacement value of the items and not the current value. This type of insurance is called 'new for old'.
- *Interruption of business activity insurance*, which may automatically come into operation if the business has suffered damage as a result of a disaster under the fire cover. This insurance also covers the business against loss of business whilst the premises or vital equipment is being replaced or repaired. The cover will also ensure that the business is protected against interruption in production as a result of the loss of power supply.
- *All-risk insurance* Under this type of insurance the business is covered for damage, loss or destruction of items anywhere in the UK. This insurance will compensate the business at full replacement value.

A business will also have to have public liability insurance. This covers them against injury to a member of the public as a direct or indirect result of any occurrence or event related to the business. This insurance will also cover loss or damage to the customer's property. Related to this is the need for the business to obtain employers' liability insurance. It is the responsibility of the employer to compensate an employee who may have been injured or become ill as a result of working for the business. The certificate of insurance for employers' liability should be visible and accessible to all employees.

As an extension of the public liability insurance, a business needs to insure against claims arising from the use of its products or services. If a customer has suffered injury, loss or damage as a result of faulty products or services, the business will be able to refer this claim to its product liability insurance. This insurance also covers the business for any legal costs that may be incurred against claims that are made under consumer protection legislation.

Monitoring financial control, cash flow performance and forecast, profit and loss account

Financial data and forecasts form the basis of a business's ability to raise finance, negotiate the purchase of premises and order raw materials. If a business is inaccurate in their forecasting, then there would be insufficient money available to the business. If a business fails to meet its projected forecasts, it may be difficult or impossible to acquire further finance. A provider of finance will often reject a business that asks for more money because its forecasting has proved inaccurate.

A business starting out for the first time does not want to have to cope with financial problems created as a result of poor or ill-conceived financial forecasts. It must attempt, therefore, to make an estimate of sales, costs and cash balances.

Businesses may choose to detail their financial data and forecasts using different time periods: weekly, monthly or yearly. For cash flow forecasts, it is the monthly time period that is the biggest concern. Totals will have to be calculated for cash received and cash outgoing for each month. It is probable that certain assumptions will have to be made, particularly in the case of forecasts relating to months in the future.

INDIVIDUAL WORK
(9.16) ★ ★

Visit the website of the Norwich Union, which is an insurance company, at www.norwichunion.com. Click on their 'Business' link and then on their 'Self employed insurance' link. Now answer the following questions.

1 What kind of businesses does their small business insurance cover?

2 What do they define as being the insurance needs of a small business?

3 What cover does the self-employed policy provide?

Potential problems regarding cash flow or profitability must be considered at every stage. If there are shareholders, they will demand to know the true state of affairs within the business. It may be necessary for them to make additional share capital available to finance short-term cash flow problems on long-term investments. A financial expert, either within the business or from another firm employed by the business, will attempt to make projections relating to:

- Cash flow forecasts (usually on a month-by-month basis)
- Profit and loss assessments (on a month-by-month basis)
- Balance sheet calculations (on a yearly basis).

All these forecasts are interrelated with one another. In planning terms, it is important that the business compares forecasts with what has happened in the past. The financial projections will be able to provide an indication of:

- The profitability as suggested in the forecasts
- The probable future financial requirements of the business.

This analysis could disclose a number of issues that may require reassessment and the following questions may need to be answered:

- Are there some products that are not performing well and should be dropped so that the resources can be channelled into a new product?
- Are the wage levels too high?
- Do sales per employee indicate that the business is over-staffed?
- How do the discounts and credit levels offered to customers affect profitability?

A profit and loss account is used to calculate the total income derived from invoices received during the month and the costs of any expenses during the same period. This document, produced by an accountant, will give a balance per month, which indicates the profit or loss in that month.

Balance sheets, on the other hand, tend to be drawn up on a yearly basis, working from information derived from actual cash flow and profit and loss. A balance sheet shows what an organisation owes and what it owns at a particular time on a particular day. A projected balance sheet will show an estimate of what the business will owe and own on a particular day in the future.

A cash flow forecast in its simplest form is a record of cash received by the business and an indication as to when cash will be needed for paying bills. Within a business plan, it is usual to make a cash flow forecast that extends for two or three years. Providers of finance may require a business to extend that forecast for up to five years.

A start-up balance sheet can only contain items of income and expenditure of which a business is already aware. It is advisable for a new business to use an accountant to help produce a balance sheet at this stage of their operations. The key headings of a balance sheet include:

- *Fixed assets* – all equipment received, even if this has not yet been paid for.
- *Current assets* – cash, debtors and stock.
- *Capital* – which the owners have put into the business to start it up.
- *Liabilities* – money owed by the business, such as overdrafts, tax or VAT and other businesses they owe money to, such as suppliers.

Keyword

break-even – this means a business has been able to cover its costs by the products or services they have sold, but they have not made a profit

A profit forecast can be made in order to establish the level of profit that the business hopes to produce at the end of a specified period. The projected profit and loss and balance sheet should indicate whether the business will be in a position in the future to either **break-even** or show a small profit.

By constructing a monthly profit and loss account and a monthly balance sheet, an organisation will be able to monitor its adherence to its start-up business plan. This control mechanism should be able to identify any causes for concern and allow the business to react in time. The normal procedure is for a business to create a cash flow forecast, which includes budgeted figures for various items. Then, as the figures become available, the business can compare these with the budgeted figures.

Similarly, the business will be able to compare actual output with production targets and actual sales with projected sales.

Own drawings

Many owners of new businesses and the self-employed choose not to take very much money out of their business in its early stages. Drawings are, effectively, the wages that the small-business owner or the self-employed person pays to themselves. Obviously these individuals do have other financial commitments, mainly to run a home, pay bills and support their family. By minimising the amount of drawings they take from the business in the early stages, they can reinvest the maximum amount of money in the business to ensure its long-term survival and, ultimately, its success.

INDIVIDUAL WORK
(9.17) ★ ★ ★

It is now time to think about the financial considerations for your Swan and Fable product or service.

1 What kind of start-up capital would you need?

2 Where could you go to find appropriate sources of finance?

3 What kind of grants might be available?

4 How would you find an accountant, solicitor or an insurance provider?

5 What contact would you have to make with the Inland Revenue and Customs and Excise?

6 How would you monitor and control your finances?

7 How much would you have to pay yourself each month in order to meet your domestic financial requirements?

DRAFT BUSINESS PLAN

An essential part of this unit's evidence requires you to create a draft business plan. A business plan is a written statement about a business. It is written by the owners or the managers and states what they intend to achieve and how they intend to achieve the objectives.

As we will see, a basic business plan needs to cover:

- The structure of the business.
- The products and services offered.
- The types of customer and how they will be approached to offer the products and services.
- The growth potential of the business.
- How the business intends to finance the operations.

The main purposes of a business plan are to seek sources of finance, gain finance and monitor progress.

As well as stating the business's objectives and identifying its financial requirements, the business plan will also include a section on their marketing plans. This marketing plan will assist the owners of the new business by focusing on:

- The main factors that need to be addressed in order to remain competitive.
- Identifying and examining the business's expansion opportunities.
- Preparing a series of measures to address any future problems.
- Setting identifiable goals and results that it is hoped that will be achieved by them.
- Identifying criteria to be met in the achievement of the business's goals and objectives.
- Setting out a series of measures to allow the monitoring of progress.
- Providing the information required by providers of finance.

Analysis of the market

Researching a market that the business believes to contain profitable opportunities is a vital task. A business will want to find out:

- The size of the market.
- Whether the market is growing.
- Whether the market is supplied by out-of-date or inefficient businesses.
- Whether the market is a niche that has not been considered by the competitors.
- Whether the market is dependent on certain pricing levels, which determine whether or not customers buy.
- Whether the market is already supplied by a competitor's branded products or by products that do not command considerable levels of customer loyalty.
- Whether the market is dominated by lots of competitors or just a few large ones.

It is unlikely that everyone in a particular market is going to want to buy a new business's products or services. Sometimes it is more appropriate for them to consider a segment of the market to focus on. A business has to remember that there are several links in the selling chain before a customer is reached by a business. There may be distributors, agents or dealers through which the product passes before it reaches the retail outlet and then the customer. Knowing how this market structure works will enable the business to establish, or estimate, the potential value of the sales to this market. Direct routes can enable the business to fix a selling price and estimate the number of products they may be able to sell. When there is a network of distributors in the market, the business has to make the selling price low enough to allow each layer of the distribution network to earn their income, but still offer the product to the customer at the right price.

Identification of customer needs, wants and preferences, of competition and market gap

As we discovered earlier in this unit, a business will want to know what products the customers are buying, why they buy them, what they are prepared to pay for them and who they are currently buying them from. A new business will do its utmost to identify their particular target group of customers and meet their needs, wants and preferences. They will also want to make their products or services more appealing to the customers than those of the competition.

Many businesses, before they spend time and resources in developing products and services, look for what is known as a market gap. A market gap is an opportunity for a business to step in and provide a product or services that at present no other business or competitor is providing to customers. A prime example of a market gap being filled is Freeview. Prior to the launch of Freeview, customers could only view what was known as terrestrial television, basically the five main analogue channels, or they could pay a monthly subscription to a satellite or cable provider to receive a much larger range of television stations. With the development of new digital TV stations, it was recognised that this was not significantly increasing the number of people that were paying a subscription and the stations wished to increase their audiences. Freeview came on the scene to provide the solution. For the cost of the purchase of a set-top box and no subscription, customers are now able to access 30 or more digital TV stations.

> **GROUP WORK (9.18)**
> ★ ★
> Think of a product or service that has filled a market gap in the last few years.

Expectations of trading success

All parties involved in the start-up of a business will want to have an optimistic view of what the future holds. They will have high expectations of a successful trading business in the future. The business plan offers the business owners an opportunity to identify a series of objectives with the aim of improving the overall state of the business in the future. For new businesses, this essential objective setting may be not only a basic requirement of any providers of finance, but also of fundamental importance to the eventual success or failure of the enterprise.

GROUP WORK (9.19)

★ ★

You should already know that there are some other common objectives of business from the mandatory units of this book. Write a short explanation on the following four:

a) Achieving sales value

b) Making a profit

c) Breaking even

d) Meeting timescales.

For an organisation entering the market as a new business, their first objective may be to supply their products or services. An analysis of present market conditions and the comparative successfulness of existing businesses operating in related areas will be of prime importance in meeting this objective. The business will also have to look at distribution and see whether it can identify cost-effective methods of bringing products and services to potential customers. A great deal of basic information can be provided in statistical form by the government or agencies working on behalf of the government. A careful analysis of competitors' activities and their published materials, such as company reports, may also prove to be valuable. Trends in customer spending can also be useful data on which to base the criteria needed to establish objectives in relation to the supply of products and services.

Another objective of the organisation may be to achieve particular levels of sales in terms of units sold or to obtain a financial advantage by being able to sell lots of products or services. This level of sales objective could be met by a business supplying their own-label products to wholesalers and retailers. The need to achieve high sales levels is particularly important to a business that produces inexpensive products.

Small business vulnerability

It is generally accepted that the first three years, and in particular the first year, present the greatest risk to a new business. So many things could potentially go wrong. The business may lack sufficient resources, finances or skills and expertise to be able to make it successful. Many small businesses are over-optimistic about how they will perform once they are up and running and they will have made serious financial commitments that they simply cannot cover from the revenues received.

In addition to having to cope with its expected costs, a business may often encounter costs that it could not have reasonably predicted. They may need to seek new suppliers, the premises may need to be refurbished, key members of staff may leave and their financial providers may lose confidence in the business's ability to pay back any loans they may have borrowed.

Whilst the business needs to keep a careful eye on income and expenditure, there are other stronger forces that could influence its success. Established and probably larger competitors will move quickly to try to snuff out new businesses as they emerge. Existing businesses are aware that small businesses are vulnerable in the first year or so of their existence. The small business is still learning and it may make costly mistakes that the competition can exploit. Larger competitors can afford, at least in the short term, to reduce their prices and therefore make the small business follow, in the knowledge that this loss of income will have a greater effect on the new business than it will on the existing one.

Contingency plans for sickness/accident/injury/market failure

Many new small businesses have very few staff. They will rely on the expertise of this handful of people in order to carry out all the tasks and duties related to the smooth operations of the business. The loss of a key individual at the early stages of a small business could be disastrous. A business would find it difficult to run if the sole specialist in a particular area was unavailable due to sickness, accident or injury. This means that at the very beginning of a new business, in order to offset the negative impact of the loss of one of these key members of staff, the others need to be able to step in to fulfil their roles. This can be difficult if the business is that of a sole trader, particularly if they have to have specialist skills or qualifications in order to run the business. It would not be appropriate or desirable, for example, for a sole trader that has been trained to mend computers to be replaced by a sales assistant that has little or no experience in this field.

One possible solution is to encourage multi-skilling between those involved in the business. At the earliest point, the owners or key members of staff need to be trained to do one another's jobs. So, in the event of one of the key individuals being absent for a prolonged period, one of the others could step in and take over their duties.

Preparing for internal disasters may be one thing, but dealing with the collapse of a market is an entirely different matter. Many businesses, when they are in their early stages, focus their attention on single markets. They run the risk of that market failing and the number of customers drying up. If, for example, an electrician carried out most of their work for a handful of local businesses and one or more of these closed, the electrician would be left with a huge hole in their workload and revenue. It is therefore desirable for small businesses very early on to focus on several different markets and spread their risk so that if one market fails they will be able to refocus their attention to providing products and services to other markets they have established.

Developing the resource base and specifying required resources

An essential part of a business plan is to identify the cost and sources of necessary resources, including premises, equipment and material that will be essential to run the business. The business needs to examine a number of different premises to discover which would be the most suitable. Depending on the type of business, the new business may need a constant amount of passing trade, which means being close to where customers shop. Other businesses may need to be close to their business customers in order to make it simple to deliver products and services as required.

Equipment needs differ from business to business, but any providers of finance would need to see carefully considered and costed breakdowns of all equipment needs of the business. They may be able to suggest cheaper or more effective substitutes.

Materials refer to consumable items that may be needed by the business. A retail store, for example, would need carrier bags, a mail order business would need packaging material and a craftsperson would need tools to carry out their work. Again, any advisers or providers of finance would need to see that the business has broken down all of their material needs and costed each of these out precisely.

Presenting information to key audiences

Before we look at the way in which a business plan appears, it is important to understand that various groups or individuals will be interested in ensuring that all of the major areas have been covered. Banks, external investors, grant providers and business advisers will all be interested in how professional the business plan looks and how reliable the information is that is contained within it.

Ideally, a business plan should include the following features:

- *An executive summary* – an overview of the business. This is vital because many lenders and investors will only read this section of the plan.
- *A description of the business opportunity* – what the business plans to sell or offer and why, who the customers are.
- *The business's marketing and sales strategy* – why customers will buy from the business and how the business plans to sell products and services to them.
- *The business's management and key personnel* – the qualifications and experience of all key members, including owners, involved with the business.
- *The business's operations* – including the proposed premises, work facilities, management information systems and IT.
- *Financial forecasts* – which essentially translate all of the previous sections into numbers in terms of income, expenditure and profit.

Above all, the plan should be short. If it is of a manageable length, it is more likely to be read. A well-presented plan will encourage the audience to have a positive impression. The key points are:

- Number the pages.
- Include a contents list.
- Start with the executive summary.
- Use a sensible and large enough font.
- Write the plan so it addresses an external audience.

INDIVIDUAL WORK
(9.20) ★ ★ ★
Your teacher or lecturer will provide you with a blank business plan format. It will have a number of headings that roughly correspond to the areas discussed in the section above.
Complete the business plan, following on from your work in the previous activities in this unit relating to your Swan and Fable product or service.

WANT TO FIND OUT MORE?

Visit the **Business Link** main website at: www.businesslink. gov.uk.
Enter your postcode in the box, which will take you to a link to your local Business Link operator.

WANT TO FIND OUT MORE?

Visit **Barclay's** small business website at: www.barclays.co.uk. Click on 'Business Banking' and 'Turnover less than 500k'.

WANT TO FIND OUT MORE?

Visit the **British Companies** website at: www.british companies.co.uk and click on 'Organisations'. This will show you the huge range of different trade associations which small businesses can join.

- ✎ Edit and re-edit the plan to make sure it makes sense.
- ✎ Show the plan to expert advisers, such as accountants, and ask for feedback.
- ✎ Avoid using jargon.
- ✎ Put all data, such as balance sheets and other tables, at the back of the report as appendices.

Above all, the business plan needs to be realistic. It may need updating at a later point and it is a useful tool to judge the relative successes of the business.

Sources of guidance

There is a huge amount of support and guidance available to those wishing to start a new business. This section focuses on the key areas where potential small businesses could seek assistance. Remember that you will need assistance in a huge number of different areas from different specialists. Not all of the information is necessarily related to financing the business. Some may be able to provide business contacts, relay their own experience of starting a business or provide assistance in marketing.

Business Link partnerships

Business Link is a nationwide service that provides practical advice for businesses and particular expertise in assisting new businesses. Initially the advice provided by Business Link will be free, but additional advice and information can be bought at a discounted price using various grants and schemes offered by local and central government and the EU.

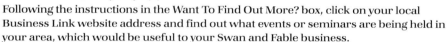

INDIVIDUAL WORK (9.21) ★
Following the instructions in the Want To Find Out More? box, click on your local Business Link website address and find out what events or seminars are being held in your area, which would be useful to your Swan and Fable business.

Small business services provided by banks

Banks are not merely sources of possible finance for a small business, they also provide useful business advice. All of the major high street banks and some online banks offer specific help to small businesses.

INDIVIDUAL WORK (9.22) ★ ★
Find the 'Business banking' section of the Barclay's website. What is included in their start-up package for small businesses? Click on 'Why start up with Barclays?' to find out more information about the kind of services that this bank provides.

Trade associations

There are a huge number of different trade associations related to each particular type of business or the market that business serves. They can provide realistic and practical assistance for small businesses.

Chambers of Commerce

Chambers of Commerce are a nationwide network of organisations that represent 100,000 businesses of various sizes which employ four million people. The Chamber of Commerce claims that it is the voice of UK business and they provide useful information and guidance.

WANT TO FIND OUT MORE?

Visit the main website of the **British Chamber of Commerce** at: www.chamberonline. co.uk.

INDIVIDUAL WORK
(9.23) ★
Follow the instructions on the British Chamber of Commerce website and click on the option 'Contact your local chamber'. This will reveal a map of the UK. Click on the relevant region and find your local Chamber of Commerce.

Friends, family and personal contacts and investors

Anyone that may eventually have a financial interest in the small business may be able to offer useful guidance and assistance. Many members of your family or close friends may have experience of having run a small business, although not necessarily in the area that you wish to develop. They will be able to inform you about many of the pitfalls that they encountered in the early stages of their own business.

Whilst investors may recognise the potential of a new business, they will be keen to ensure that it does not make mistakes and risk their financial commitment. As they may have been involved with other businesses in the past, they too will be able to provide useful guidance and advice.

Government agencies and funding agencies

WANT TO FIND
OUT MORE?

Visit the **DTI**
website at:
www.dti.gov.uk.

The Department of Trade and Industry (DTI) is a good starting point for any investigation into relevant government agencies or funding agencies. The DTI's website contains a huge amount of information related to all forms of support and assistance for businesses of any size.

INDIVIDUAL WORK
(9.24) ★ ★ ★
From the DTI website choose the 'For business' option. There is a section designed for small businesses and new businesses. The page link details loans, grants and consultancy available. Identify anything that would suit your proposed Swan and Fable business.

PERSONAL QUALITIES

This last section investigates the wide-ranging skills and qualities that may be required of an individual or group of individuals that wish to start their own business. Although it may be a daunting list, remember that when more than one person is involved in the business their skills could complement one another.

Uniqueness of selling point or skill base

Most people that start their own business begin with a particular interest or expertise in the area related to the business's operations. An individual that enjoys music, for example, may wish to become a DJ or run a music shop, whilst someone interested in fashion may wish to open a clothes shop. These unique interests form the basis of the skills and knowledge required to run a successful business in any given area.

Conscientiousness, a willingness to work long hours and availability

As we have seen, running a business can be a daunting task that will eat up an individual's time to the exclusion of almost everything else. The individual concerned will have to work long hours, they will need to devote most of their time and attention to their duties and ensure that they are available to step in to deal with any situation as and when it may arise.

For someone starting their own business, a standard working week of 35 or 40 hours is not an option. The new business owner needs to be at the business before anyone else and will leave much later than the last customer or employee. Working weekends is also a distinct possibility as there may be no other time to complete paperwork, research new products and services or reply to correspondence.

Commitment to professional standards of quality and personal development and training

In addition to fulfilling the obligations required of a small business by government agencies, such as the Inland Revenue, customers, suppliers and employees will expect the owners of the business to show the highest standards of professional quality and commitment to the business. There are huge lessons to be learned by simply running the business, but there are also a large number of opportunities available for the owners to develop their own skills or undertake free or subsidised training. Local personal development and training opportunities will regularly be featured and circulated by organisations such as Business Link or the Chamber of Commerce.

Networking ability

Much business success can be put down to contacts. A small business needs to rapidly build up its lists of contacts of suppliers, customers and other businesses that can provide them with services. Chambers of Commerce and other local business meetings provide a useful network forum to meet other local business people and exchange ideas and opinions.

Numeracy and interpersonal communication skills

The owners of the business will be the public face of the business to suppliers and customers. They will need to have developed good interpersonal skills and the ability to talk to people at all levels of society and for a huge variety of different reasons.

The business owners will also have to be able to carry out routine numeracy-related tasks, including working out costings, profit margins and, of course, totalling their income and expenditure.

Decisiveness

Business owners need to make decisions on a daily if not hourly basis. If the business is that of a sole trader, then there will be no one else to assist them in decision-making. Some decisions will have to be made instantly, whilst others will require a more considered approach. Decision-making is all part of the learning process in running one's own business. Poor decisions will be made and the owner can only learn from the experience of making a poor decision not to make a similar mistake in the future.

Willingness to develop or encourage market demand

If a business wishes to succeed in the long term, it needs sustained growth. It can only achieve this by constantly increasing its range of customers and encouraging those customers to recommend the business to others. This is a continuous process of growth and development, which requires the owner to constantly look to the future rather than simply dealing with the present demands.

Efficient administration, honesty and business scruples

Although there are many laws, rules and regulations governing the correct running of a business, a small business should, from the outset, project itself in a positive manner. In addition to maintaining an effective administrative system that does not fail its suppliers or customers, the business must appear to be straightforward and honest with all groups with whom it deals.

The term 'business scruples' refers to ways of doing business that are fair and consistent throughout all the business's dealings. For example, if a customer has overpaid or been overcharged by a small amount then the small-business owner should highlight this fact and refund them. Similarly, if goods have been received from a supplier and not been shown on a statement of account, the business owner would be showing good business scruples to contact the supplier and notify them of this.

Reflecting on and evaluating own achievements, identifying appropriate advice and an awareness of when to seek assistance

A small business will not only learn from its successes, but it will also learn from its failures. Each day will present a new series of challenges that need to be overcome in order for the business to survive and ultimately become a success. The small-business owners will be able to recognise similar sets of circumstances and, on the next occasion they encounter them, remember how they dealt with that situation.

Small-business owners will continually be learning new ways of carrying out old tasks. They will know the pitfalls of dealing with particular suppliers or customers. They will learn to complete paperwork on time.

They will also begin to learn that on occasion situations may be beyond their current knowledge and that it is time to seek the advice of specialists or more experienced advisers. Business Link or the Chamber of Commerce can provide the names and contact details of advisers and specialists such as accountants or solicitors.

It is a skill in itself to know when advice is needed and another to identify the ideal person or organisation that can provide that advice.

INDIVIDUAL WORK (9.25) ★ ★

Using either your local Chamber of Commerce or your local Business Link website, find the name and contact details for each of the following:

a) An accountant

b) A solicitor

c) A marketing specialist

d) An adviser that could help with sales in Europe

e) A computer specialist

f) An employment agency that would provide temporary administrative staff.

Unit Revision Questions

1 What is a niche market?

2 What are the four factors considered in SWOT analysis?

3 What is the difference between primary and secondary market research?

4 State three features of a private limited company.

5 Why might a business need the assistance of a solicitor?

6 What are working capital and reserves?

7 What is meant by the term 'own drawings'?

8 Why might a small business be vulnerable?

9 What is the role of the Chamber of Commerce?

10 Why might it be important for a business to have scruples?

Glossary

acquisition when a business buys another business

aerospace manufacturing industry that produces parts and products for the aircraft industry, including rockets, engines and other equipment

after-sales service a customer service provided by a business after the sale of the product or service has taken place

appraisal this term refers to meetings between employees and their team leaders, line managers or supervisors. During appraisal meetings targets are set and action plans for improvement drawn up

asset an item that has a cash value. In the case of machinery, the asset is used to produce products. Other assets could include land, buildings or patents

auditor an independent individual or accountancy business that checks the accounts of another business

BACS the abbreviation for Bankers Automated Clearing Service – the employees' wages are paid straight into the bank and they can have access to the money immediately

balance of payments the difference between a country's income and expenditure on overseas trade

bank overdraft an agreed amount by which the business can spend more than it has in its account

benefits these include items such as assistance with moving expenses, season ticket loans, company cars or petrol allowances, and a work uniform

break-even this means a business has been able to cover its costs by the products or services they have sold, but they have not made a profit

budget a business's or department's planned income and expenditure

capital the original amount of the loan before any interest charges were added

chain of command the number of levels of management and how information is passed up and down the organisation

charities organisations that exist to provide a service or to support a particular cause, e.g. Help the Aged and Oxfam. All of a charity's income, either from donations or other fundraising, is used to support new activities

consolidation in this context consolidation means maintaining the current market share

constitution the rules made when the business was first started up that state the procedures and policies of the organisation

constructive dismissal when the employee leaves their job due to the employer's behaviour.

consumables items used by a business in the general course of their operations, which are not part of the products or services that they sell

contract of employment a written, legal agreement between the employer and employee that states their rights, responsibilities and duties towards one another

cookie a small text file that is placed on the user's hard drive by a web server. It is a code that is uniquely the users' and can only be read by the server that sent it

cost centre a particular part, perhaps a department, of a business that can have specific costs allocated to it

credit the process by which a supplier provides products or services on the understanding that they will not be paid for immediately, but by an agreed date in the future

credit card a card that allows the user to make purchases on credit, up to a specified limit by the issuing bank, building society or finance provider

creditworthiness the customer's history regarding the paying of money owed to the business. If the customer has missed some payments the business might consider them to be less creditworthy and insist that an order is paid for immediately, rather than on credit

curriculum vitae commonly known as a CV this is a document which is prepared by a prospective employee and is their employment and educational history to date

debit card a modern alternative to a cheque. The funds are immediately taken out of the account of the cardholder after having been checked by the issuing bank

demotivated to lack an enjoyment of work and therefore carry out one's job less effectively

disciplinary procedure a series of warnings or actions that can be taken against an employee

discount a reduction in the price of an order. It would be offered for a variety of reasons, including the payment of cash and if the customer orders regularly from the business

disposable income the money available to an individual or a household after the payment of tax and other deductions and after the payment of all essential bills, such as mortgage, rent, council tax and utilities

domain name a website's address on the internet. It needs to be registered by a business, organisation or service, just like a business name. It allows potential customers to find easily the business's web address and website

domestic consumers household buyers rather than businesses

ethical the way in which a business and its employees should respond to situations if they are to show integrity and social responsibility

exported goods or services that are produced or provided by a UK organisation and sold to an overseas country

exports sales by UK businesses to overseas businesses or countries, earning income for the UK

extranet an extranet site is one that can only be accessed by a user group in the 'outside world', such as customers

gender relates to the sex of the customer; either a male or a female

GPRS General Packet Radio Service, enables networks to offer 'always-on', higher capacity, internet-based content and packet-based data services. This allows internet browsing, email on the move, powerful visual communications, multimedia messages and location-based services

handling costs the costs associated with moving, protecting and storing products

hierarchical a very formal type of organisation with various layers of managers and supervisors

imported goods or services that are produced or provided by an overseas country and brought into the UK

income cash or funding received by an organisation as either payment from customers for goods and services or as a grant of money from another organisation, such as central or local government, to provide those goods and services

incorporation the procedure by which a business registers itself at Companies House and becomes a legal entity. It is also known as registration or formation

inflation a rise in the average price of goods and services in an economy

integrated supply chain a fully working chain of suppliers and customers who work in close contact with one another to reduce the time delays for orders and deliveries

interest this is a charge made for borrowing the money. It is a percentage of the actual amount the bank has loaned the business

intermediaries businesses or individuals that are part of the distribution chain and handle products between the manufacturer and the consumer

investment the money they have put into the business

invoice the document that gives full details of the products or services sold and the prices. This is given to the buyer of the product or service and provides the financial information that will be recorded in the sales daybook

job description a document that explains what the job involves and is useful for matching the right person to that job

market research the gathering of data (information), usually about the buying habits of customers or on the activities of business competitors

media the general term used to describe newspapers, television, radio, magazines and, increasingly, internet news and information services. The media also include marketing, public and community relations

merchandisers individuals who are involved in organising shop displays, laying out the products on the shelves and making the shop as attractive as possible to customers

merger when two or more businesses decide to become one business

minutes a written record of what took place, what was discussed and agreed, including actions to be taken before the next meeting and by whom

mission statement an organisation's vision of what it wants to achieve in the future. A good mission statement needs to be easy to understand, relevant to the organisation, ambitious and useful in motivating staff

MOST Mobile Ordering and Sales Terminal

motivating making employees more willing to work hard and take pride in the work they produce

multinational a business that runs operations in at least two different countries

output the total number of products or services produced or offered by a business in a given period of time

outsourcing using individuals or other businesses to carry out the tasks previously undertaken by employees of the business

overdraft an agreed amount of money that the account holder can spend, even if there is a nil balance in their account

patent a right granted by the government to an inventor to stop others from making, using, offering for sale, or selling the invention

payroll usually a computerised system that informs accounts of the amount of money that needs to be paid to each employee, either weekly or monthly, as their wage or salary

point-of-sale (POS) the physical location in a store where the customer purchases products and services, such as a cash register or payment point

press release a statement by a business outlining a news feature that can be used by the press to help them cover a story

pressure group an organised group that seeks to influence government policy or legislation. They are often referred to as either interest groups, lobby groups or protest groups. There are literally thousands of pressure groups in the UK

productivity the output or efficiency of a particular department or section, or indeed a whole business

profit a business's ability to sell its products and services for more than it costs them to acquire or provide those products and services

public relations using contacts in the media in order to ensure positive stories about the business are featured

regional development agencies set up in England to assist economic development, promote efficiency, investment and competitiveness, as well as attracting employment and the development of skills in their areas. There are nine regional development agencies

revenue the income received by a business in exchange for selling its products and services

screen-saver a moving imagine on the computer screen that appears if the computer is not used for a few minutes

seasonal a term used to describe a part of the year when either products or services are particularly popular, such as fir trees at Christmas or water sports during the summer

shareholder an individual who has purchased a part, or a share, of a limited company and has power over that business in relation to how many shares they own

shift a period of non-standard working hours, such as starting at lunchtime and working through into the evening or beginning earlier in the day and finishing after lunch

span of control the number of employees who are controlled by one manager or a supervisor

staff retention an important aspect for a business, which involves trying to keep experienced and trained members of staff rather than giving them a reason to move to alternative employment

stakeholder an individual or a group of people who have an influence on the organisation or are affected by the decisions made by the organisation

stock control systems that keep track of products held by the business, which alert the business when levels have reached the stage at which they need to be reordered

takeover when one business gains the total ownership of another business

telecommunications the manufacturing and service industries that produce or provide communications equipment

telesales also known as telephone sales, involves calling customers, either at home or at their workplace, and attempting to sell them products and services

undischarged bankrupt an individual who has been declared bankrupt and has not yet paid off their debts

utilities essential services, such as electricity, gas, water and telephone lines

whistle-blowing when a worker raises a concern about dangerous or illegal activity that they are aware of through their work

wholesaler an organisation that takes delivery of large quantities of goods and then sells them on in smaller quantities to other businesses

Index